David Traxel

The Enormous Vogue of Things Mexican

The Enormous Vogue of Things Mexican

Cultural Relations between the
United States and Mexico,
1920–1935

HELEN DELPAR

THE UNIVERSITY OF ALABAMA PRESS

TUSCALOOSA AND LONDON

Copyright © 1992
The University of Alabama Press
Tuscaloosa, Alabama 35487
All rights reserved
Manufactured in the United States of America
Designed by Paula C. Dennis

The photograph on the cover is *The Ames Corn Mural* (1936–1938) by Lowell
Houser, in the main post office, Ames, Iowa. Photograph by Chuck Greiner.
(Courtesy of Mary L. Meixner)

∞

The paper on which this book is printed meets the minimum requirements of
American National Standard for Information Science-Permanence of Paper for
Printed Library Materials, ANSI Z39.48-1984.

Library of Congress Cataloging-in-Publication Data
Delpar, Helen.
The enormous vogue of things Mexican : cultural relations between
the United States and Mexico, 1920–1935 / Helen Delpar.
p.   cm.
Includes bibliographical references (p.   ) and index.
ISBN 0-8173-0582-3 (alk. paper)
1. United States—Relations—Mexico.   2. Mexico—Relations—United
States.   I. Title.
E183.8.M6D45   1992
303.48'273072—dc20   92-6125

British Library Cataloguing-in-Publication Data available

Contents

Preface

In May 1929 New York's Madison Square Garden was transformed into the capital of ancient Mexico as the setting for a benefit pageant called Aztec Gold. Announced as "the most elaborate and resplendent event of the social season," the pageant boasted a cast of one thousand who represented personages ranging from Hernán Cortés and Montezuma to a Hopi Indian chief, who was portrayed by impresario Florenz Ziegfeld. Ted Shawn and one hundred members of his Denishawn company performed Native American harvest dances. The cast also included the Mexican artists Miguel Covarrubias and José Clemente Orozco and two American women, Alma Reed and Frances Flynn Paine, who had dedicated themselves to the promotion of Mexican art in the United States. The Mexican ambassador to the United States was an honorary patron of the event.[1]

In many ways the pageant can be considered a symbol of the flowering of cultural relations between Mexico and the United States that had begun in the early 1920s. By 1929 it was reaching its zenith, prompting occasional remarks that a Mexican "invasion" was under way. The growing popularity of Mexican art in the United States, owing partly to the efforts of Reed and Paine, was bringing recognition to Covarrubias and Orozco, who, like other Mexican artists, spent extended periods in New York. Another participant in the pageant, the American painter George Biddle, had befriended Orozco in New York and had gone to Mexico in 1928, a journey made by many other artists during this period. By helping to organize an exhibition of modern American and French art in Mexico City in 1929, Biddle contributed to the diffusion of American culture in Mexico in the same years. The inclusion of the Mexican ambassador among the honorary patrons testifies to the interest of his government in encouraging a favorable image of Mexico in the United States and, more important, to the easing of the strained diplomatic relations that had existed between the two nations earlier in the decade. The choice of the Aztec theme for the pageant illustrates the interest of contemporary Americans, as well as Mexicans, in the preconquest civilizations of the Western Hemisphere, and the presence of a Hopi chief demonstrates the tendency to link the Native Americans of the United States with those of central Mexico. Finally, the pageant's romanticized depiction of ancient Mexico points up the fact that the development of cultural relations could be replete with distortion and misunderstanding.

My intention in this book is to trace the evolution of cultural relations between the United States and Mexico from 1920 to 1935, identifying the principal individuals, institutions, and themes that made up this fascinating chapter in the history of the two countries. I ordinarily employ the word *culture* in its most traditional sense as designating artistic and intellectual activities: art, literature, music, the performing arts, scholarship, and journalism.[2] Yet it is neither possible nor desirable to divorce these from the modern anthropological or sociological use of *culture* to designate the "whole way of life" of a people or group because the latter was often the subject of the artistic and intellectual products of the era. Moreover, as James Clifford has observed, an aesthetic dimension is embedded in the anthropological concept of culture, which "orders phenomena in ways that privilege the coherent, balanced, and 'authentic' aspects of shared life."[3] American admirers of Mexican culture in the 1920s routinely engaged in such ordering, simultaneously devaluing the contemporary culture of the United States because of its perceived incoherence and lack of authenticity.

I have conceptualized cultural relations as a process of interaction between individuals and private institutions from Mexico and the United States at a time when neither government had as yet formally entered the field. As a result of this interaction, Mexican culture was disseminated in the United States, by both Mexicans and Americans, and Mexicans were exposed to American culture to a greater degree than ever before. I do not attempt to discuss the spread of American values and culture to the Mexican populace as a whole. Such an effort would be beyond the intended scope of this study, requiring treatment of topics not addressed here, such as the export of sports and other leisure activities to Mexico, the spread of American business and educational methods, and the activities of American missionaries in Mexico. The reader will also note that in referring to citizens of the United States, or as an adjective relating to this country, I have used the word *American* rather than *North American*, which Latin Americanists usually prefer. Not only is the latter term overly cumbersome for a study of this kind, but it is not widely employed even in Latin America outside of official documents and academic treatises.

Scholarly literature on the subject of Mexican-American cultural relations is sparse. Only two articles address the subject directly: Henry C. Schmidt's 1977 essay, "The American Intellectual Discovery of Mexico in the 1920's," and a shorter piece by John L. Brown. A 1985 article by Fredrick B. Pike explores what he calls the emergence of a counterculture in the United States in the 1920s and 1930s which looked to Latin America as a whole for moral and spiritual guidance. Many other writers have touched upon the subject in biographies or monographs, among them John A. Britton in his life of Carleton Beals and Laurance P. Hurlburt in his study of the Mexican muralists in the United States.[4] I have mined these works when appropriate and have found them invaluable in guiding my own research. I have also relied heavily on American and Mexican periodicals and on the diaries and letters, both printed and unpublished, of leading participants in cultural exchange.

Cultural relations can flourish only in a fertile environment, and it was not until after 1920 that such an environment existed in the two countries. Therefore, the book begins with a review of the political, economic, and intellectual conditions in Mexico and the United States that created an environment conducive to the development of cultural relations: the return of stability to Mexico after a decade of revolutionary upheaval (1910–20), the global economic ascendancy of the United States after World War I, and the burgeoning of cultural nationalism in both countries. Chapters 1 and 2 focus on general aspects of the evolution of cultural relations. In the early 1920s, when relations between the two governments were strained, "political pilgrims" from the United States who visited Mexico devised an interpretation of Mexican policy and society designed to disarm critics of the revolutionary regime. Even during this period, however, American travelers expressed enthusiasm about Mexico's preconquest heritage and the work of contemporary craftsmen and painters, especially muralists such as Diego Rivera and Orozco. By the late 1920s relations between the two governments had improved, partly because of changes within Mexico and partly because of the astute diplomacy of Ambassador Dwight Morrow, who played an important role in furthering cultural relations during his three-year stay in Mexico City. As tension ebbed, Mexico's art and culture became the principal magnets for American visitors, who in turn introduced Mexicans to cultural trends in their own country. The result of these travels was an outpouring of books, paintings, and other works dealing with Mexico, which by the 1930s was perceived to be enjoying a "vogue" in the United States. So many books on Mexico had been published in the past few years, a critic noted in 1935, that Americans were finding it difficult to escape their "Mexican heritage."[5] Meanwhile, the United States became the destination of cultural migrants from Mexico— painters, composers, actors, and others—whose presence also contributed to the vogue. Paradoxically, many of these cultural migrants achieved great success in the United States even as Americans debated the desirability of Mexican immigration in general and moved to expel thousands of Mexicans during the Great Depression.

The next two chapters are devoted to specific aspects of cultural relations. Chapter 3 examines activities relating to the Mexican Indians, both ancient and modern, who became subjects of study by American archaeologists, anthropologists, and policy makers, frequently in collaboration with Mexican scholars and officials. Chapter 4 discusses the awakening of American enthusiasm for Mexican art in all its manifestations—from preconquest architecture to folk art to modern murals— which was now perceived to be worthy of exhibition in major museums and galleries and of evaluation by serious critics. The last chapter moves to literature and the performing arts, examining the circulation in each country of works produced in the other as well as the images of the two peoples which such works conveyed. The conclusion recapitulates themes developed throughout the text and points out that although cultural relations between Mexico and the United States continued to flourish after the mid-1930s, they did so in an altered context in which the sense of discovery characteristic of the period 1920–35 was absent.

Many persons rendered assistance and encouragement as I conducted the research for this project. The staffs in the various libraries and manuscript repositories I consulted were invariably courteous and helpful. Nancy J. Morris, curator of the Charlot Collection at the University of Hawaii, went out of her way to facilitate the work of a visiting scholar. John Charlot, son of Jean Charlot, directed me to unpublished chapters of his father's book on Mexican muralism which I found very helpful. Jean Beckner, special collections librarian of the Honnold Library of the Claremont Colleges, obtained for me material on the "Friends of the Mexicans."

Several others gave me valuable help as well. I am grateful to Everett Gee Jackson and the late Asael T. Hansen for sharing their memories of Mexico, and to James Oles, George H. Roeder, Jr., and Heidi Zogbaum for giving me access to their unpublished manuscripts. Oles also made several valuable suggestions to me. Helen B. Herring made available material relating to her late husband, Hubert C. Herring, and Carolyn Kennedy Beals, widow of Carleton Beals, granted permission to quote from her late husband's papers. Mary L. Meixner generously shared information about Lowell Houser as well as her photographs of his Corn Mural in Ames, Iowa. Constance Morrow Morgan graciously allowed me to consult the papers of her mother, Elizabeth Cutter Morrow. Encouragement of another kind came from Richard D. Woods and John A. Britton, with whom I had numerous conversations about American expatriates in Mexico. Finally, I wish to acknowledge the assistance of Malcolm MacDonald and staff at The University of Alabama Press and the financial aid I received from various sources: faculty enrichment grants from The University of Alabama and Tulane University and a Travel to Collections grant from the National Endowment for the Humanities.

Introduction

The histories of Mexico and the United States have been intertwined since the beginning of their existence as independent nations. Diplomatic relations were established in 1822 and were maintained despite occasional ruptures and the war of 1846–48. Economic links were also forged early in the nineteenth century and became more important with the passage of time, especially during the regime of Porfirio Díaz (1876–1911), when American capitalists invested millions of dollars in Mexican mining, industry, and transportation. The railroads financed by American capital during the Díaz era brought the cities of the two countries closer together physically than ever before. These investments encouraged the formation of a substantial American community in Mexico, consisting of nearly twenty-one thousand residents in 1910, when the total population of the country was approximately 15 million.[1] In acquiring half of Mexico's territory in 1848, the United States also acquired a sizable Mexican population, which was subsequently augmented by steady and increasing emigration northward across the border. During the violent decade (1910–20) of the Mexican Revolution alone, nearly nine hundred thousand immigrants and "temporary" migrants crossed the border, along with uncounted thousands of refugees.[2] To be sure, the relationship between the two countries was always shaped, and some would say determined, by the relative weakness of Mexico vis-à-vis the economic and military preponderance of the United States, a relationship captured in the wry aphorism attributed to Díaz: "Poor Mexico! So far from God, so close to the United States!"

The start of the Mexican Revolution in 1910 marked the beginning of a distinct if not fundamentally different era in the diplomatic and economic relations between the two governments. This long and violent upheaval, which affected different regions of the country in different ways, has produced an impressive body of scholarship both in Mexico and the United States; the "political pilgrims" discussed in Chapter 1 were among the first to offer a coherent interpretation of the revolution. Many later scholars minimized the significance of the revolution, dismissed as a "great rebellion" by Ramón E. Ruiz, or pointed out continuities between the Porfiriato and postrevolutionary regimes. Two recent interpreters, Alan Knight and John Hart, agree that the revolution had a popular character at its inception, though Knight places greater emphasis than Hart on rural discontent as a cause of the uprising, arguing that "the key to the social revolution lies in the countryside." By contrast, Hart views the revolution as the product of reaction by peasants, urban and industrial workers, the petite bourgeoisie, and provincial elites against foreign economic intrusion during the Porfiriato.[3] Another synthesis suggests that there were two revolutions: "One, which failed, was a radical, and nationalist transformation of Mexican society aimed toward transmuting the changes wrought by the Porfiriato and in eliminating the old order. The other, which succeeded, was a modernizing, capitalistic movement . . . intended to broaden access to, and reduce foreign control over, and to make more productive the modern capitalistic and governmental structures initiated in the late nineteenth century."[4]

The revolution began in 1910 as a movement of political protest directed against the determination of Porfirio Díaz to remain in the presidency for another six-year term. Díaz was overthrown fairly easily by forces under the leadership of Francisco I. Madero, the scion of a wealthy and powerful family from the northern state of Coahuila. Madero became president in 1911 but only fourteen months later was ousted by the reactionary general Victoriano Huerta, whose actions had the blessing of the American ambassador, Henry Lane Wilson. Huerta's usurpation of power and his apparent complicity in the murder of Madero stirred opposition in Mexico and the United States. President Woodrow Wilson refused to recognize the new government and ordered the occupation of the key port of Veracruz by marines in April 1914. By the time Huerta was driven from power in July 1914, the revolution had broadened into a larger and more diffuse movement than it had been under Madero. Its goals were most clearly articulated in the constitution of 1917, which imposed limitations on private property, especially mineral rights (article 27), and committed the state to agrarian reform and the protection of labor. Another feature of the constitution was its strong expressions of nationalism, as in the provision that foreigners who exploited mineral deposits were to have no recourse to their own governments in disputes with Mexico. Also noteworthy were the restrictions imposed on the country's churches, for example, forbidding clerics from publicly or privately criticizing acts of the government.

The constitution was promulgated during the administration of Venustiano Carranza, an elderly civilian who had been the nominal leader of the anti-Huerta forces and later bested his erstwhile revolutionary allies, Francisco Villa, the redoubtable Lion of the North, and Emiliano Zapata, the southern-based champion and symbol of agrarian reform. According to John Hart, Carranza received the support and recognition of the United States government because of the likelihood that he would throttle the social revolution. Certainly his critics on the left complained that he made little effort to introduce measures in behalf of the peasantry and industrial labor, the supposed beneficiaries of the revolution. Yet relations between the staunchly nationalist Carranza and the Wilson administration remained strained, and American investors in Mexico were alarmed by the threat to their property posed by article 27 of the constitution. The two countries came close to war after Villa's raid on Columbus, New Mexico, in March 1916 and President Wilson's dispatch of troops across the border to disperse the Villistas. Even after the withdrawal of the troops in 1917, there were renewed demands for a rupture of diplomatic relations or intervention because of "damages and outrages" against American citizens and property in Mexico.

During the first two decades of the twentieth century, cultural relations between the United States and Mexico were limited. Mexican elites might admire American economic growth and welcome American sports and leisure activities, such as baseball, but they resented past interventions in Mexico and the mistreatment of Mexicans in the United States. Moreover, intellectuals in Mexico as elsewhere in Latin America usually regarded Americans as vulgar materialists who were interested only in amassing wealth and lacked both the desire and the ability to distinguish themselves in artistic creation or appreciation. The corollary, whether stated or not, was that Mexicans, like other Latin Americans and Latin peoples in general, were endowed with superior aesthetic and spiritual sensibilities.[5] Thus a primary school history text used both in the Porfirian and revolutionary eras extolled the enterprise and industry of the Anglo-Saxon peoples but declared Americans to be cold and indifferent to the arts.[6] The novelist and diplomat Federico Gamboa, an admirer of Walt Whitman, was not surprised that this "commercial people" had erected no monument to their great poet.[7] Others derided the artistic pretensions of Americans. In 1920, for example, the composer Manuel M. Ponce ridiculed New York music critics who supposedly reviewed a piece eliminated at the last minute from a concert program.[8]

There were, of course, those who disagreed with such assessments. As early as 1898 the educator Justo Sierra, who had visited the United States three years earlier, expressed admiration for the musical life of New York and asserted that Mexicans were fools if they believed that Americans were boors in artistic matters. He also thought it an "immense error" to believe that Americans were uninterested in pure science or philosophy and, impressed by the universities he had seen, predicted that the United States would become the world's leading center of research in the twentieth century. A younger man than Sierra, the anthropologist Manuel Gamio, also dissented from the prevailing opinion. In a 1916 essay he argued that Mexicans were much more materialistic and money-grubbing than Americans, citing as evidence the disinterested philanthropy of American millionaires.[9]

Ignorance contributed to Mexican contempt for American intellectual life. During the late nineteenth century Mexico's cultural models, especially in literature, were almost entirely French and Spanish, though French influence began to wane after 1900. Little was known of American efforts in the arts and letters. Among poets Henry Wadsworth Longfellow, Edgar Allan Poe, and Whitman were the best known. Poe was particularly admired by poets of the modernist school, who initially became acquainted with his work through their French mentors, such as Charles Pierre Baudelaire, Paul Verlaine, and Stéphane Mallarmé.[10] When Federico Gamboa was assigned to the Mexican legation in Washington in 1903–04, he immediately set about reading the complete works of both Poe and Whitman, a task he completed.[11] Gamboa was able to read these works in English, but others had to depend on occasional translations, such as those of Whitman's "Oh Captain, My Captain" and Poe's "Ulalume," which appeared in the *Revista de Revistas* in 1919.[12] An editorial note accompanying the former called Whitman "a colossus" of American poetry. Harriet Beecher Stowe's *Uncle Tom's Cabin*, Helen Hunt Jackson's *Ramona*, and some of Mark Twain's short stories had been published in Spanish translation in Mexico City, but in general Mexican readers were unfamiliar with American fiction.[13]

American awareness of Mexican culture, art, and literature was even more limited. Americans admired Mexico's natural beauty and its picturesqueness, but since the early nineteenth century their perceptions of its people had been colored by racism, ethnocentrism, and antipathy toward Catholicism. During the Díaz era travelers who wrote accounts of their impressions observed many changes that they considered positive, but they still tended to evaluate the country in terms of its progress toward American standards. Even the most sympathetic were likely to consider Mexicans to be childlike and unsuited to self-government. Charles Flandrau declared in his travel narrative *Viva Mexico!* (1908) that "anyone with the most rudimentary knowledge of Mexico knows that a popular election there is an impossibility and always has been."[14] The conflicts of the revolutionary decade deepened the ordinary citizen's unflattering opinion of Mexico and its people. The singer José Mojica, who later had a successful career in the United States, recalled that during his first foray to New York in 1916 he was advised by managers not to sing Mexican songs or wear national costume because of anti-Mexican feeling.[15] As a *New York Times* editorial explained in 1920: "To the average American the Mexican of today is an insurgent or a bandit or, at any rate, a conspirator against his own Government."[16] Motion pictures reinforced such attitudes by portraying the Mexican as the cowardly and underhanded "greaser," the favorite villain of early American films.[17]

Americans who lived in Mexico might have a more positive opinion of its people. The issue of the *New York Times* cited above carried a letter from a twenty-year resident who argued that most Mexicans "are true blue, kindly, courteous, helpful, desirous of peace and prosperity. They have hearts of gold, are sympathetic, long suffering, altruistic."[18] Before 1920, moreover, a few American residents of Mexico had begun to devote themselves to the study and appreciation of Mexican art and culture. Prominent among them were Frederick W. Davis and Zelia Nuttall.

Davis, a native of Illinois, was a longtime resident of Mexico City noted for his devotion to Mexican art, especially folk art, which he collected for many years. He had come to Mexico as an employee of the Sonora News Company, which purveyed newspapers and other sundries to railroad passengers. When the company opened a showroom for the sale of Mexican curios and art, Davis was put in charge. During the 1920s the showroom attracted many visitors, including archaeologist Sylvanus G. Morley, who admired the "treasures" Davis had accumulated: "old furniture, rugs, church things, and a large collection of modern Mexican artists."[19]

Another Mexico City showplace was the Casa de Alvarado, the home of Zelia Nuttall, who was prominent as an archaeologist as well as a collector of Mexican art. Born in San Francisco to a Mexican mother and an Irish father, she married a French archaeologist in 1880; after the dissolution of the marriage, she settled in Mexico and purchased the Casa de Alvarado in 1902. She filled the house with furniture, porcelains, and other objets d'art from the colonial period and created a garden that visitors found unforgettable. Portrayed as Mrs. Norris in D. H. Lawrence's novel *The Plumed Serpent* (1926), she is described as an archaeologist who "had studied the Aztec remains so long, that now some of the black-grey look of the lava rock, and some of the experience of the Aztec idols, with sharp nose and slightly prominent eyes and an expression of tomb-like mockery, had passed into her face." To Jean Charlot, a young Frenchman of part-Mexican ancestry who moved to Mexico in 1921, she seemed an incongruous figure in that revolutionary era. Years later he recalled his "astonishment close to repulsion" at the sight of white-gloved Indians serving tea in her drawing room.[20]

Until 1920 people living in the United States had few opportunities for exposure to Mexican art or culture unless they were members of the Hispanic community. A 1919 article pointed out that if Americans were unfamiliar with Latin American art, the fault was only partly theirs. Latin Americans were willing to send their poets and artists to Paris or Madrid but not to the United States, noting that "in literature and art there seems to be a distrust, even a disdain of Anglo-Saxon appreciation."[21] That was undoubtedly true, but American indifference was also great. Except for a few works of poetry, Mexican literature remained untranslated, and the visit of poet Amado Nervo to New York in 1918 passed virtually unnoticed. When Manuel Ponce gave a recital of his music in New York's Aeolian Hall in 1916, it was dismissed in a brief review in the *New York Times*, whose critic declared: "Neither as pianist nor composer does Mr. Ponce demand extended consideration."[22]

Despite frequent tension and mutual disdain between the United States and Mexico, forces were at work in both countries after 1900 that would produce a flowering of cultural relations in the 1920s. This development must be seen in the context of the larger international role of the United States after 1900 and the expansion of its hemispheric consciousness. The United States had emerged as a major economic and military power by 1900, and its position was strengthened as a result of World War I and the subsequent revolutionary upheavals, which left Europe prostrate. American economic ascendancy was accompanied by the export of American values. Emily S. Rosenberg coined the term *liberal developmentalism* to describe the prevailing ideology, which embraced faith in private free enterprise, support for the free flow of goods, information, and culture, and the belief that the American model of development could be replicated elsewhere. According to Frank Costigliola, war-weary Europeans willingly accepted American cultural leadership, which seemed an inevitable consequence of the economic and technological superiority of the United States. "Since the machine civilization was most advanced and apparently most successful in the United States, many European artists, businessmen, and politicians alike looked westward for models."[23]

The expanded international role of the United States also brought increased attention to the cultures of other peoples. To some scholars, this new interest exhibited the racism and conviction of Anglo-Saxon superiority that characterized American thinking in the early twentieth century. Burton Benedict and Robert Rydell, for example, found that exhibits involving Native Americans and other "backward" peoples at international expositions were designed to emphasize their differences from the dominant groups. Richard H. Collin, by contrast, maintains that American imperialism stimulated a disinterested cosmopolitanism and appreciation of art, symbolized by the Asian collection of Charles Freer, which he donated to the nation.[24] After 1900 American efforts to promote intercultural knowledge and understanding were institutionalized with the establishment of privately funded organizations such as the Carnegie Corporation and the Institute of International Education.[25]

An important aspect of the increase in international awareness was a growth of interest in Latin America after 1900. In part, this was a by-product of the war with Spain in 1898 and the subsequent hegemony of the United States in the Caribbean area, coupled with the expansion of American investment throughout the region. World War I, by weakening European political and economic influence, intensified a trend already under way.

The new interest in Latin America can be seen in the explosive growth of enrollment in Spanish-language courses in secondary schools. In 1910, about 5,000 students had been enrolled in such courses. This figure had risen to 35,000 by 1915 and soared to over 260,000 by 1922, partly as a result of plummeting enrollments in German during the war. The development of Spanish-language studies was accompanied by the expansion of instruction at the college and university level. This trend was reflected in the establishment in December 1917 of the American Association of Teachers of Spanish, which had an initial membership of more than four hundred. Meanwhile, the University of Missouri had become the first college in the United States to offer a course in Spanish-American literature (1916).[26]

This period also saw the establishment of a major historical journal devoted to Latin America, the *Hispanic American Historical Review*, the first number of which appeared in February 1918. In that issue J. Franklin Jameson, managing editor of the *American Historical Review*, called the new journal a product of growing American acceptance of the field, which now had able practitioners to devote themselves to it. He also believed that by creating the journal Americans were filling the breach that the ravages of war had created in European historical scholarship.[27]

Scholars of Latin America could find a rich store of research material in the United States. In 1921 the University of Texas laid the foundation of its Latin American collection by purchasing the private library of Mexican historian Genaro García, which consisted of 25,000 printed items and 300,000 pages of manuscripts. The Library of Congress, which had exhibited a strong commitment to the Hispanic world since the Spanish-American War, when bibliographies on Cuba and Puerto Rico were compiled, acquired several important collections in subsequent years, and in 1927 Archer M. Huntington donated approximately $112,000 for the purchase of books on Hispanic and Portuguese art, literature, and history. By 1930 the library held an estimated 250,000 volumes on the region.[28]

Among the rising historians of Latin America in this period was Herbert E. Bolton of the University of California, who became known for his belief that the nations of the Western Hemisphere share a common history. In 1920 he attracted nearly eight hundred students to his first course on "Greater America."[29] In 1932 he expounded his views as president of the American Historical Association in a celebrated address titled "The Epic of Greater America." Here he argued that the broad phases of national history were common to most of the Western Hemisphere, the "essential unity" of which had been revealed by the war. Bolton's thesis was controversial, but in emphasizing the elements of uniformity among Western Hemisphere nations he was reasserting an old theme that enjoyed great currency in intellectual circles after 1920. American intervention in Haiti and other countries continued, but that did not prevent politicians from employing the concept too. When President Warren G. Harding unveiled a statue of Simón Bolívar in New York's Central Park in 1921, he linked George Washington with the South American liberator, spoke of a common desire for freedom among the peoples of the Western Hemisphere, and declared: "The great war has brought to us of the Americas a new conception of our place in the world and a larger appreciation of the opportunity which is ours."[30]

Assertions of a commonality of experience and identity among Western Hemisphere nations had always implied a separation from Europe, which was now frequently depicted as enervated by the effects of the war. Americans who thus distinguished the Western Hemisphere from Europe were voicing a sense of cultural nationalism, another important theme of the 1920s. Some of its adherents devoted themselves to identifying and recovering the components of the American past. Others hoped to create and promote a distinctively American art, literature, and music that would be organically related to the life of the people.

Cultural nationalism was evident in the United States before World War I, associated with the painter and teacher Robert Henri and with the magazine *Seven Arts* (1916–17), and survived into the following decades. Interest in the American past was reflected in the growing appreciation of folk art and the art of the American Indian during the 1920s. The American Wing of the Metropolitan Museum of Art, which was inaugurated in 1924, was significant not only as a repository of national antiques but also because it displayed them alongside the masterpieces of the Old World. Meanwhile, composers such as Aaron Copland and artists such as Thomas Hart Benton sought to draw upon native sources in their creative endeavors. Charles C. Alexander argues that "the vision of a genuinely native, nationally representative artistic expression was the single most significant feature of American cultural commentary in the years after 1900 and up to the Second World War."[31]

Some elements of cultural nationalism, such as exaltation of the Native American, meshed with another theme of the prewar period that lingered into the 1920s: what has been called antimodernism or romantic primitivism.[32] Although many American artists and intellectuals were excited by the aesthetic and social promise of the machine, others decried the dehumanization and materialism that had overtaken modern American society. Cultural critics of this orientation often found an inspiriting contrast to the evils of machine civilization in the ways of simple but more authentic communities, such as might be found in less technologically advanced nations or among backward groups in developed nations. Alternatively, those offended by the economic exploitation of capitalism and the reduction of labor to a commodity could look to societies experiencing revolutionary change that would uplift and ennoble the worker materially, mentally, and spiritually.

The cultural and political life of Mexico after 1920 exhibited many qualities bound to enhance its appeal to American artists and intellectuals. Not only was it the Latin American nation closest to the United States, but its ancient monuments and artifacts offered eloquent testimony to the grandeur of the aboriginal civilizations of the hemisphere, which could be claimed as part of the heritage of the United States. Moreover, those in search of premodern communities still relatively unscathed by the industrial revolution might find them throughout rural Mexico. Because Mexico was already in the incipient stages of industrialization, it could also be viewed as a battleground between man and the machine. When Charlot arrived in 1921, he was struck by the clash between what he considered two incompatible forces: the spirituality of the Indian and the machine-driven culture of Europe and the United States.[33] The ascendancy of the latter was probably inevitable, but under enlightened leadership Mexico might avoid the evils that afflicted the United States and other industrial societies.

The restoration of relative peace to Mexico in 1920 created an environment conducive to the development of cultural relations. Carranza's insistence on naming his own successor produced a successful revolution in 1920, which ended with the president's murder after he fled the capital. An interim government headed by Adolfo de la Huerta was installed, but it soon gave way to the administration (1920–24) of Alvaro Obregón, the genial, one-armed leader of the anti-Carranza forces. As president, Obregón sought to reestablish stability after a decade of violent upheaval, to curb the power of the military, and to consolidate revolutionary gains made to date. Some of his supporters looked to him to launch a thoroughgoing program of land distribution, to improve the condition of industrial labor, and in general to help the country's poverty-stricken masses, especially the Indians.

The Obregón administration distributed four million hectares of land in selected areas, far more than the amount distributed under Carranza. Industrial workers also made modest gains under the leadership of the dominant labor organization, the Confederación Regional Obrera Mexicana (CROM). Relations between Obregón and the CROM later cooled, but it would consolidate its favored position during the administration of Plutarco Elías Calles (1924–28), when its head, Luis N. Morones, was named secretary of industry, commerce, and labor. Under the Obregón and Calles administrations imaginative if limited educational programs were introduced in an effort to reduce adult illiteracy, which had been more than 70 percent in 1910, and to integrate non-Spanish-speaking Indians into the national society. Accordingly, emphasis was placed on rural education and on building schools that would also be community centers offering instruction to both parents and children in hygiene, agriculture, and arts and crafts as well as the conventional subjects. During these years local officials also embarked on programs of social and economic reform in Yucatán, Veracruz, and other states.

The apparent commitment of Obregón and his supporters to agrarian reform and other elements of the revolutionary creed alarmed conservatives everywhere, especially in the United States, where political figures and businessmen continued to inveigh against Mexican threats to property rights and feared the establishment of a Bolshevik regime in the Western Hemisphere. American liberals and leftists, however, found much to praise in the Obregón agenda. In reality, Obregón was a compromiser who protected private property and foreign investment under the aegis of a newly strengthened state. Therefore, although historians such as Hart and Knight conclude that the Mexican Revolution brought greater geographic and social mobility as well as a stronger, more nationalistic state, there is also ample reason to see continuity with the

Díaz era. But neither Obregón nor any other major revolutionary leader ever promised a drastic reordering of society, as was then occurring in Bolshevik Russia, and their essential moderation and pragmatism came to be gradually understood by well-informed contemporaries. Thus the early hopes of some were dissipated and the fears of others assuaged.

Many American observers were deeply impressed by the cultural renaissance that began during Obregón's administration. This renaissance was strongly nationalistic in orientation and was based on the exaltation of Mexico's indigenous and popular traditions in the arts. Historian Daniel Cosío Villegas later recalled that what was "truly marvelous" about the early 1920s was the "nationalist explosion" that occurred throughout the country.[34] National songs and dances became fashionable overnight, and every home had examples of popular crafts, a gourd from Olinalá or a pot from Oaxaca. This nationally rooted renaissance entailed a repudiation, explicit or implicit, of the aesthetic values attributed to the Díaz era, whose elites were accused of despising national arts while slavishly admiring all that was foreign.

The episode that was most frequently cited as exemplifying the elitist and antinational spirit of the Díaz regime was the celebration that took place in Mexico City in 1910 to commemorate the centenary of the beginning of Mexico's independence movement. In reality, the festivities included several events with a national and popular emphasis, such as a parade featuring representations of prominent figures in Mexican history and a great fiesta with fireworks in Chapultepec Park. The centennial was also an occasion for the development of cultural relations between Mexico and other countries, including the United States. American universities were invited to send representatives to the reopening of the National University, which took place during the celebration, and psychologist James M. Baldwin was the first lecturer when the Escuela de Altos Estudios, a graduate school devoted to the liberal arts, was inaugurated at the same time.[35] Americans were also prominent among those who attended the Seventeenth Congress of Americanists, which met in conjunction with the centennial. A highlight of the meeting was an excursion to the ruins at Teotihuacán, where the government opened a new museum and hosted a banquet near the Pyramid of the Sun.

Despite such affirmations of the national heritage, critics of the centennial complained that many indoor ceremonies were open only by invitation. Others were indignant over the construction at government expense of a building in which to exhibit modern Spanish art. Angry young Mexican artists countered with an exhibition of national art at the Academy of San Carlos.[36]

By contrast, in 1921 the Obregón administration celebrated the centenary of the attainment of independence with a month-long series of events that had a consciously national and popular character, among them a major exhibition of folk art, a demonstration of *charro* cowboy skills, and the distribution of toys and candy to ten thousand needy children. The celebration culminated with a Mexican Night in Chapultepec Park attended by thousands and enlivened by fireworks and folk dances and music.[37]

Another example of officially sponsored cultural nationalism took place during the 1930 Christmas season when the preconquest deity Quetzalcoatl was introduced into holiday celebrations, supposedly because of the desire of Acting Secretary of Education Carlos Trejo Lerdo de Tejada to displace Santa Claus and the Three Kings. On December 23 the god appeared at the National Stadium in Mexico City in a holiday pageant featuring Indian music and popular dances. President Pascual Ortiz Rubio was in attendance with his wife, who distributed presents to poor children. The event produced some controversy, leading the Mexico City newspaper *Excelsior* to point out that Quetzalcoatl was as alien as Santa Claus and the Three Kings.[38]

The official most closely associated with the promotion of cultural nationalism during the Obregón administration was the philosopher and man of letters José Vasconcelos, who became secretary of public education in 1921. Vasconcelos himself did little directly to advance cultural nationalism, but he did allow Diego Rivera and other artists to use the walls of public buildings to create murals depicting national themes and events in Mexican history. The murals in the National Preparatory School and the Secretariat of Education were at first controversial among many Mexicans, but they soon won the praise of foreign critics precisely because they seemed so strongly rooted in national themes and techniques. Another example of the encouragement of cultural nationalism by Vasconcelos was his commissioning of a ballet based on Aztec musical themes by composer Carlos Chávez.

Vasconcelos left the cabinet in 1924 to pursue an ill-fated political career, but his successors during the 1920s continued to express a commitment to nationalism in the arts. In her study of Mexican education

Mary Kay Vaughan faults the cultural nationalist movement of the 1920s for its lack of revolutionary content and for serving as a mechanism of social control of the masses.[39] In the United States, however, revolutionary sympathizers as well as apolitical observers hailed the nationalist orientation of Mexico's cultural programs.

The nationalism of leading artists and intellectuals in Mexico during the 1920s was not xenophobic and did not exclude continuing interest in cultural trends elsewhere. In his influential *Perfil del hombre y la cultura en México* (1934), the philosopher Samuel Ramos asserted: "To believe that we can develop an original culture unrelated to the rest of the world constitutes a total misunderstanding of what culture is." In particular, the novels and poetry of the decade exhibited a vanguardism and concern for renovation that often reflected foreign influences.[40]

The emergence of the United States as a cultural center after 1920, coupled with its economic power and propinquity to Mexico, meant that the latter would be exposed to American cultural models as never before, especially in urban areas. The philosopher Antonio Caso deplored Mexico's "fascination" with the United States, but American popular culture exerted a pervasive influence during the 1920s as Henry C. Schmidt has observed: "Rapid change was evident as traditional Mexican life was being modernized, mostly through American influence. The bob was replacing the classic braid of the Mexican woman. Jazz and chewing gum became popular, as did English-language phrases, expensive cars, weekends, the beach, and women's sports. In the salons, a product of Porfirian Mexico, waltzes and mazurkas gave way to the saxophone playing the hit parade."[41]

Moreover, there were Mexican artists and writers who, though not renouncing the ideal of a nationally based culture, were intrigued by the very machines and cities that many of their American contemporaries despised. In a famous manifesto issued in Barcelona in 1921, the painter David Alfaro Siqueiros declared: "We must live our marvelous dynamic age! love the modern machine . . . our cities in the process of construction, the sober and practical engineering of our modern buildings."[42] Mexican votaries of modernity, like their counterparts in Europe, were likely to be fascinated by the United States, which they considered the leading postwar representative of industrialization and urbanization. After 1920 cultural influence did not flow exclusively from Mexico to the United States but extended southward across the border as well.

CHAPTER 1

Political Pilgrims in the "New Mexico"
Cultural Relations, 1920–1927

From 1920 to 1927 cultural relations between the United States and Mexico unfolded against a backdrop of apparently revolutionary change in Mexico and frequent periods of tension between the two governments. During these years American intellectuals, journalists, and artists, most of them of a leftist persuasion, were drawn to Mexico because of their interest in the revolution's impact on society and the arts and their desire to defend Mexico from attack in the United States. Nearly all of them can be classified as political pilgrims, the term used by sociologist Paul Hollander to characterize intellectuals who visited the Soviet Union and other revolutionary societies in the twentieth century.[1] Similarly, American political pilgrims to Mexico were often alienated from their own society and therefore disposed to be attracted to alternatives elsewhere. The seemingly leftist inclinations of the Mexican government in the early 1920s made that country even more appealing to those political pilgrims who saw socialism as the means of escaping the materialism, inequality, and conflict they associated with capitalism. They also feared that the government of the United States, acting at the behest of American business interests, might again intervene in Mexico or in some way move to check its revolutionary progress.

The political pilgrims who traveled to Mexico in the early 1920s found an American community that had been reduced by more than half by the turmoil of the previous decade. According to the census of

1921, there were only 11,090 individuals with American citizenship residing in Mexico.[2] Moreover, although transportation to Mexico and accommodations in the major cities were good and relatively inexpensive, tourism from the United States remained low. In 1923, Mexico accounted for only 4.6 percent of American expenditures for foreign travel. By contrast, Europe and the Mediterranean accounted for 45.4 percent and Canada for 36.9 percent.[3] In the early 1920s Mexico's reputation as a land of violence, banditry, and radicalism still deterred visitors.

At the same time the economic prosperity and cultural dynamism of the United States exerted its own attraction upon Mexican performers, composers, and artists who moved northward to pursue careers in New York and Hollywood. This exodus was part of a larger outflow of Mexicans to the United States during the 1920s. In that decade the Mexican population in the United States nearly doubled, growing from 729,992 in 1920 to 1,422,533 in 1930.[4]

Emigrants were driven from Mexico mainly by economic pressures and the continuing political and religious turbulence of the 1920s. Although there was a demand for workers in the United States because of the booming economy and a decline in European immigration, organized labor and those who considered Mexicans unassimilable and inferior urged greater restrictions on their entry. In 1928, for example, the novelist Kenneth L. Roberts published a series of articles in the *Saturday Evening Post* attacking immigration from Mexico.[5] According to Roberts, the "constantly increasing flow of chocolate-colored Mexican peons" into the United States might benefit employers, but their ignorance, filthy habits, and high fertility made them a burden on taxpayers.

The Friends of the Mexicans represented another response to Mexican immigration. Organized in 1922, the group held an annual conference at Pomona College that attracted teachers, social workers, and scholars as well as speakers from Mexico. Although conference participants tended to see the Mexican presence in California as a "problem," they also expressed concern about the educational and housing needs of migrants and tried to inform themselves about Mexican society and culture.[6]

Despite warnings such as Roberts's, no new legislation was enacted, and it was not until 1929 that efforts were made to limit the entry of Mexican workers. The concentration of the Mexican population in the still politically and economically marginal western states meant that their presence was not fully registered in the country as a whole. According to Ricardo Romo, "Americans knew more about Mexicans in Mexico than Mexicans in the United States."[7] To the extent that this statement was true, it was so in part because of the labors of American political pilgrims who visited Mexico and the activities of Mexican cultural émigrés, which in most cases were centered on the East Coast.

From the perspective of eight decades it is clear that Alvaro Obregón and Plutarco Elías Calles were at most bourgeois reformers, not radicals bent on establishing a Bolshevik regime in Mexico. Nevertheless, many contemporary American diplomats and businessmen were deeply alarmed by the course of events in Mexico. They feared that efforts to implement article 27 of the constitution would result in confiscation of American-owned mining and agricultural properties in Mexico; some were also distressed by the virulent anticlericalism of the Calles administration, which led Roman Catholic priests to leave their churches in 1926 for a three-year period. For these reasons diplomatic relations between the two governments were strained during these years. Initially, the United States refused to recognize the Obregón administration; it was not until 1923 that the so-called Bucareli agreement was negotiated whereby Mexico offered guarantees regarding American property, and the United States reciprocated by reestablishing diplomatic ties. Even then relations failed to improve sigificantly, in part because of the hostility to Mexico of the American ambassador (1924–27), James Rockwell Sheffield, a New York Republican with no previous diplomatic experience. He was convinced of the radicalism of the Mexican government and repelled by its corruption and inefficiency and by "the futility of attempting to treat with a Latin-Indian mind, filled with hatred of the United States and thirsting for vengeance."[8] Mexico's recognition of the Soviet Union in 1924 fanned fears that the Calles government was bent on establishing Bolshevism in Mexico and spreading it throughout Central America. These fears found confirmation in Mexican support in 1926–27 for Nicaraguan Liberals who were in revolt against the American-backed government of Conservative Adolfo Díaz. Sheffield and others who were alarmed by the threat of Bolshevism in Mexico were unaware of the tension that existed between the Calles administration and the first Soviet ambassador, S. S. Pestkovsky. It seemed to the Mexicans that Pestkovsky behaved like the emissary of the Communist

International rather than the representative of his government. He in turn regarded the Calles regime as "a petit-bourgeois militaristic dictatorship,"[9] and his successor, Alexandra Kollantai, had a similarly negative opinion.

The American government never seriously contemplated drastic action against Mexico such as withdrawal of recognition, aid to anti-government rebels, or armed intervention. The American public in general remained unmoved by the controversy over Mexico. Even Americans with business interests there did not agree on what policy to recommend. At the same time, congressional leaders and members of the executive branch as well as private groups often assumed such a hostile tone toward Mexico that intervention seemed a definite possibility.

For their part, both the Obregón and Calles administrations tried to disarm criticism of their policies in the United States and to cultivate relations with sympathetic Americans. Journalists, businessmen, and other influential persons were welcomed to Mexico, to the chagrin of government critics. In 1921, for example, W. F. Buckley, head of the American Association of Mexico and a foe of recognition of the Obregón government, complained of recent visits to Mexico by American businessmen, which he said were arranged for political rather than commercial reasons: "Mexican officials from the President on down are acutely cognizant of the value of influencing public opinion in the United States." In 1923 the American consul-general in Mexico City, Claude I. Dawson, remarked that the Obregón administration had been trying to sway American public opinion in favor of recognition, "and the efforts and treasure expended have been more than justified."[10]

An important cultural vehicle for increasing American understanding of the revolutionary process was the Summer School for Foreigners at the National University. Established in 1921 under the direction of the Dominican man of letters Pedro Henríquez Ureña and modeled after a similar institution in Spain, the Summer School offered courses in Spanish language and literature as well as Mexican history, folklore, archaeology, economic development, and other subjects. The cost of tuition was low—$30 for a full course load of twenty to twenty-five hours per week during a six-week term in 1926—and students could receive discounts on rail and steamship fare and on the cost of hotel accommodations.[11] In addition to the courses, students were offered excursions to nearby sites of interest such as Teotihuacán and Cuernavaca, as well as social gatherings in their honor.

Among the instructors were Mexican intellectuals, including Daniel Cosío Villegas and archaeologist Alfonso Caso. In addition, distinguished foreigners were invited to offer courses on a variety of topics. Art critic and painter Walter Pach, who had become acquainted with Henríquez Ureña at the University of California, was a lecturer in 1922. In 1926 John Dewey offered courses on educational problems and contemporary philosophic thought. Thus the Summer School attracted to Mexico not only American students but also well-known intellectuals who might otherwise not have come.

By 1927 an estimated sixteen hundred American students had attended the Summer School, most of them teachers of Spanish in colleges and secondary schools in Texas, California, and other southwestern states. Meanwhile, starting in 1922 Mexican teachers were afforded the opportunity to take professional courses in educational psychology, school administration, and other subjects while the Summer School was in session to encourage development of "the fraternal relations that should exist among educators of all nations."[12]

Laudatory appraisals of the Summer School often appeared in American newspapers and magazines. In a letter to the *New York Times* in 1924, Walter Pach praised it for introducing Americans to "the new Mexico that is growing up today." He especially admired the regime's concern for "the cultural values of music and art, for which the Mexicans, one of the few peoples possessing a genuinely popular art today, show the greatest aptitude." In both countries the Summer School was portrayed as a means of improving mutual understanding. In answering the question "why not Mexico this summer?" social worker Helen Bowyer stated: "It is largely to the teachers and students of Spanish in the United States that Mexico looks for that growth of sympathy between the two nations which more and more is to be a factor in the happiness of both."[13]

Those like Consul-General Dawson, however, who were critical of the Mexican government, had an unfavorable opinion of the school. In May 1923 he reported that he had begun to receive inquiries about the Summer School, which he believed to be under the direct supervision of

American radicals in the Secretariat of Education. He declared: "This matter is linked with the intensified propaganda being carried on openly by the Mexican regime; and I cannot conceive it to be my duty to encourage Americans to come to Mexico to be the victims and tools of a regime which is using every disagreeable means within its power to embarrass the government of the United States, even to the extent of setting the American people themselves against their own government."[14]

If Ambassador Sheffield and like-minded compatriots considered Mexico to be a hotbed of radicalism under Obregón and Calles, other Americans were attracted to Mexico for that very reason, following the example of American leftists who had been viewing events in that country with sympathy if not always with unanimity or comprehension since 1910. From the start of the revolution in 1910, periodicals such as the *Appeal to Reason*, the *Masses*, and *Mother Earth* carried reports of events in Mexico, supported the revolt of the dispossessed, and expressed opposition to intervention by the American government. Leftist organs also protested the persecution of Mexican radicals in the United States by American authorities. Authors of these articles might be Mexicans with ties to one or another of the revolutionary factions or prominent American journalists such as John Kenneth Turner, John Reed, and Lincoln Steffens. Reed, who spent several months with Francisco Villa early in 1914, depicted the Mexican general as an untutored but intuitive military genius and reformer. Turner, best known for his exposé of the Díaz regime in *Barbarous Mexico* (1910), was initially a supporter of the anarchist Ricardo Flores Magón and his Liberal party; he later became a partisan of Carranza, as did Steffens.[15]

Other American leftists found their way to Mexico along with the thousands of draft evaders who crossed the border after the United States declared war against Germany in 1917. Some, such as Linn Able Eaton Gale, dabbled in Mexican politics and reported on developments there for American periodicals. Gale, an idiosyncratic socialist, founded his own organ, *Gale's Magazine*, and tried unsuccessfully to launch a Communist party in Mexico, all the while receiving a stipend from the Carranza government.[16] Other radicals who surfaced in Mexico during World War I were Michael Gold, who "in those days was fluctuating between literature and Marxianism, Bohemia and the class-struggle," and Charles Phillips, who edited the English-language section of *El Heraldo de México*, a Mexico City daily published by Salvador Alvarado, the reformist governor of Yucatán from 1915 to 1918.[17] In 1920 Phillips attended the Second Congress of the Comintern as the delegate of the newly created and "official" Partido Comunista de México.

A leftist who made Yucatán his base was Robert Haberman, a lawyer and naturalized American citizen of Romanian birth. An activist in socialist and labor circles in New York City, Haberman went to Yucatán in 1917 at the invitation of Modesto Rolland, a New York propagandist for the Alvarado administration. Haberman became a close friend and adviser of Felipe Carrillo Puerto, president of the state Socialist party and future governor, and for a time headed a system of cooperative stores in Yucatán. In 1918 the American consul in the port of Progreso described Haberman as "poor, sincere, and honest but disposed to place the principles of socialism above the principles of any established government, including his own, the United States."[18]

That American leftists were not always agreed on the nature of Mexico's revolutionary regimes can be seen in an exchange between John Kenneth Turner and Michael Gold in the *Liberator*, successor to the *Masses*. A defense of the Carranza administration by Turner in the June 1919 issue brought a rebuttal from Gold, who said that he had gone to Mexico bemused by the tales of Reed, Steffens, and Turner himself, only to experience "the most painful disillusionment." Gold likened the Mexican Revolution to P. N. Miliukov's in Russia: it was the work of businessmen and landowners whose ambitions had been blocked by the Díaz regime. When Turner reiterated his position and said that Gold's article was full of "remarkable inaccuracies," the latter replied that Turner was ignorant of recent events in Mexico and accused him of abetting "the bloody and sinister gang under the bourgeois Carranza who are wrecking the labor movement of Mexico." The baffled editor of the *Liberator*, Max Eastman, could only promise to send "a hard-headed historian" to Mexico to get at the truth.[19]

By this time, however, Carranza had been overthrown and a seemingly more revolutionary regime installed. Although it was not immediately clear in 1920 where Mexico was headed under the leadership of Obregón, there seemed no reason to believe that Mexico's revolutionary momentum had been halted. On the contrary, labor and agrarian support for the new government augured a revitalized commitment to significant change, if not a drastic restructuring of society. Moreover, Mexico's continuing conflict with the American government and the ever-present threat of covert or overt intervention served to fix the attention of American liberals and radicals on Mexico.

Many American leftists were also intrigued by what journalist Gregory Mason called "a communistic state in old Mexico"—namely, Yucatán, whose communist experiment he dated from the governorship of Salvador Alvarado.[20] The Alvarado administration is currently considered to have been one of bourgeois reform, but such policies as his support of organized labor and feminism and his assertion of state control over the marketing of henequen, Yucatán's leading export, seemed radical and innovative at the time and were publicized in the United States through the efforts of such propagandists as Rolland and Haberman. Even greater attention was directed at Carrillo Puerto, who became governor in 1922. He not only continued many of Alvarado's policies but, in contrast to his predecessor, he moved toward agrarian reform. Yucatán under Carrillo Puerto also gained notoriety because of a liberal divorce law enacted in 1923 that allowed foreigners to obtain a divorce after a residence of only thirty days and required the presence of only one of the spouses. The shocked American consul in Progreso conjectured that the legislation represented an effort by the Yucatecan government, abetted by Russian interests, "to demoralize American civilization as a part of a greater program of political dissolution."[21] For American liberals and radicals, then, in the early 1920s Mexico, or at least Yucatán, offered a revolution older than Russia's, at least as interesting, and certainly more accessible.

Of course, the evolving policies of the Obregón and Calles administrations affected leftist attitudes toward revolutionary Mexico, as did developments within the radical parties and labor unions. Obregón showed the limits of his toleration of foreign radicals in April and May 1921, when he ordered the deportation of Linn Gale and Charles Phillips under article 33 of the constitution, which allows the president to expel any foreigner without hindrance. The administration promised similar treatment to all foreigners who propagated Bolshevik ideas in Mexico.[22] Soon after his expulsion, Phillips assured readers of the *Liberator* that Mexico had a capitalist government and that he had been deported "as part of a general clean-up drive on the whole labor movement, a drive that did not stop until every foreigner who was identified even remotely with the labor movement had been kicked out of the country."[23]

Robert Haberman, by contrast, became a person of considerable influence in the Mexican government in the early 1920s, acting as a liaison between the CROM and the American Federation of Labor (AFL) and the Socialist Party of America. For a time he headed the Department of Foreign Languages in the Federal District for the Secretariat of Education. In this capacity he was in a position to befriend other Americans in Mexico. One of Haberman's associates in the secretariat was Frederic W. Leighton, a conscientious objector who had been imprisoned during World War I. Leighton also served as manager of the Mexican office of the Chicago-based Federated Press.[24]

Haberman attended the Socialists' 1923 convention, at which the delegates urged recognition of the Obregón administration and asserted that "the Mexican people for the first time in their history have established a government which is primarily interested in the economic welfare of the working classes."[25] He also represented the CROM at a 1923 meeting in El Paso attended by Samuel Gompers, head of the AFL. It was decided there that the AFL would hold its 1924 convention in El Paso while the CROM met across the border in Ciudad Juárez. On the last day of the AFL convention, Haberman invited the delegates to Mexico City as guests of the government to attend the inauguration of "Brother and Comrade" Calles on December 1.[26]

Those on the far left continued to question Obregón's commitment to revolutionary change. An editorial in the *Liberator* in October 1923 stated flatly that the recent recognition of Obregón by the United States represented a surrender to Wall Street by the Mexican president. The same article called Haberman "a fawning professional anti-bolshevik job hunter."[27] Despite their criticism of Obregón, the far left along with moderates condemned a revolt led by Adolfo de la Huerta in 1923–24 as blatantly reactionary. There was also consensus among leftists that Mexico should be supported when attacked by American businessmen or politicians.

During the years 1920–27 the political and economic dimensions of Mexico's ongoing revolutionary process thus remained a source of interest and curiosity to Americans of the left. At the same time the limited scope of Mexico's revolutionary regimes made it difficult for political pilgrims to regard Mexico as the Soviet Union was regarded by sympathetic travelers in the late 1920s: a laboratory "where the world's most gigantic social experiment" was taking place.[28] Moreover, although the Obregón and Calles administrations sought to create favorable impressions of Mexico among influential visitors and to encourage the dissemination of official Mexican viewpoints in the United States, the Mexican government lacked the Soviet Union's ability and the inclination to control the experiences of travelers.[29]

For American leftists attracted by the Mexican Revolution, the revolutionary process entailed more than changes in political, economic, and social structures. Their concept of revolution envisioned psychological and aesthetic transformation as well, a transformation that would alter the consciousness and values of both masses and elites. As Hollander has observed about the political pilgrims he studied, their alienation from capitalist society often derived not only from their revulsion at the inequality between rich and poor but also from the conviction that capitalism offered no values or goals except for material gain. In short, they might well share the disdain for contemporary American society expressed by the apolitical Harold E. Stearns in his classic 1922 formulation: "the most moving and pathetic fact in the social life of America today is emotional and aesthetic starvation. . . . We have no heritages or traditions to which to cling except those that have already withered in our hands and turned to dust." Political pilgrims expected that revolutionary governments would instill a new sense of purpose, based on the group rather than the individual. Michael Gold articulated such a vision in 1920, when he wrote that a social revolution should do more than give land to farmers or put workers in charge of factories: "I conceive of the revolution as an attack on all that we have named western civilization—its great, nervous cities, the gray commercialism and shallow, eager competitiveness that marks its every feature—even its art and science and so-called culture."[30]

Another conviction shared by contemporary leftists was that revolution would make the best in art, music, and literature available to the masses instead of its being restricted to economic elites. They were also convinced that the masses would spurn the meretricious and commercialized diversions they were now offered and embrace art of the highest quality. John Dewey, who visited the Soviet Union in 1928 and was impressed by the crowds who thronged the Hermitage and other museums, expressed this outlook when he speculated: "Perhaps the most significant thing in Russia, after all, is not the effort at economic transformation, but the will to use an economic change as the means of developing a popular cultivation, especially an esthetic one, such as the world has never known."[31]

In Mexico these concerns found a twofold outlet. First, political pilgrims interested in the aesthetic dimension of revolution could admire the artistic renaissance encouraged by Secretary of Education Vasconcelos in the early 1920s. Not only were the muralists reinterpreting Mexican history in accordance with revolutionary principles, but the style of the murals and their location in public buildings made them accessible, both figuratively and literally, to the most humble and unlettered of Mexicans. The formation by the muralists of a short-lived union of painters and sculptors further suggested that Mexico's revolutionary artists were abandoning elitism by identifying themselves with workers and artisans. Second, those for whom psychological transformation was implicit in revolutionary change were enthusiastic about the cult of the Indian that flourished during the 1920s. They could only applaud the revolution's promise to the Indian not only of improved material conditions but also rightful restoration to the center of the nation's consciousness. The harmony and communal orientation they associated with Indian culture seemed especially appealing in contrast to the selfish individualism of capitalist society and indeed of Europeanized Mexico and would, they believed, temper the inevitable onslaught of industrialization.

The many political pilgrims drawn to Mexico from 1920 to 1927 represented a wide range of leftist views, from liberalism to communism. They varied also in the length of their visits and the degree of their commitment to Mexico. For some Mexico was but an interlude in careers spent mainly elsewhere. Others spent extended periods in Mexico or returned again and again. They longed, as Frederic Leighton put it in a 1924 letter, to be in the thick of history and in a sunny climate and to experience "the indefinable joy of being among the Mexican people."[32] In their writings they presented a generally positive view of the revolution, defended Mexico from what they perceived to be the malign intentions of American investors and diplomats, and defined the nature of the revolution for a generation of sympathetic readers. Their writings appeared in a variety of publications, ranging from such pillars of the liberal left as the *Nation* and the *New Republic*, to more radical organs, such as the *Liberator* and the *New Masses* as well as more specialized journals such as the *Christian Century*. Less frequently, their views found an outlet in the *Century* and other general magazines with large circulations.

Of the political pilgrims who visited Mexico in the early 1920s, the most prominent was Ernest Gruening, a physician turned journalist who had become managing editor of the *Nation* in May 1920. Concerned about what he considered the biased and inaccurate stories about Mexico appearing in most American newspapers, Gruening arranged to write articles based on firsthand reporting for *Collier's*, which had a circulation much larger than that of the *Nation*, and sailed for Mexico in December 1922 with his wife and two small sons.[33]

Upon arriving in Mexico, he found everywhere "the rising hum of revolutionary fervor, of a people reborn, of hopes rekindled," a mood symbolized for him by the figure of Diego Rivera at work in the Preparatory School.[34] During his six-month stay Gruening met frequently with President Obregón, who cracked jokes and came to his house just before his departure with an autographed copy of his book, *Ocho mil kilómetros en campaña*. At Obregón's suggestion Gruening visited Yucatán in the company of Charles W. Ervin, former editor of the *New York Call*. There he met Felipe Carrillo Puerto, of whom he became a warm admirer, and Sylvanus Morley, who had been a Harvard classmate, though they did not know each other at the time. Gruening and Morley shared several meals in Mexico, though the conservative archaeologist was not enthusiastic about Gruening's connection with the *Nation*. "Ugh," he wrote in his diary. "If he only wrote for something else." At lunch with the future labor leader Vicente Lombardo Toledano, Gruening and Morley argued over whether the United States was a "heartless" aggressor in Latin America; Gruening was a staunch adherent of nonintervention.[35]

After his return to the United States, Gruening decided to write a book describing the revolution and its origins in the Mexican past. The book appeared in 1928 as *Mexico and Its Heritage*, but before its completion he made four additional trips to Mexico. In 1924 he met President-elect Calles, who invited him to attend the upcoming inauguration as his guest. He sailed to Tampico on the same ship as Calles and rode to Mexico City on the presidential train, though he insisted on paying for his hotel accommodations in the capital.[36]

As a result of his visits to Mexico, Gruening published articles in *Collier's*, the *Nation*, the *Century*, and other magazines in which he traced the course of the revolution from a liberal perspective; he was sympathetic yet aware of Mexico's massive problems and of the essential moderation of the Obregón and Calles regimes. In 1923 he praised Obregón in *Collier's* for his lack of affectation and "gorgeous sense of humor" and for restoring order while reducing the size of the armed forces. By 1925, however, though still extolling the "good-natured tolerance" of Obregón's presidency, he was critical of the indiscipline of some labor groups and of widespread corruption in both military and civilian circles. Gruening devoted a second *Collier's* article to the work of Vasconcelos in the Secretariat of Education, but a 1925 piece in the *Nation* pointed out that despite recent achievements "the net country-wide progress in education has been infinitesimal." He bestowed his most lavish encomiums on Carrillo Puerto of Yucatán. After the latter's execution in 1924 by adherents of de la Huerta, he eulogized the Yucatecan chief as "the most enlightened, the most courageous, the most lovable man in Mexico." Carrillo had been a victim of the hatred of Yucatán's landowners and of his own "kindliness" and "trust in his fellow-beings."[37]

When Frank Tannenbaum made his first trip to Mexico in 1922, he too was a well-known figure in leftist circles in the United States. Born in Poland in 1893, he had earned notoriety in 1914 by leading an "army of the unemployed" into several New York churches and demanding food and lodging. When he was arrested and sentenced to a year in jail for participating in an unlawful assemblage, his case became a cause célèbre among radicals. After his release in 1915 and military service during World War I, he combined journalism with attendance at Columbia University, from which he graduated in 1921.[38]

Tannenbaum made his first trip to Mexico in 1922 with credentials from the *Survey*. A letter of introduction from José F. Gutiérrez, secretary-general of the CROM, stated that "Comrade" Tannenbaum planned to study labor organization and tactics. This initial glimpse left Tannenbaum enthusiastic: "[Mexico] is the country of the future. There is no wonderful spot on the face of the globe than can compare to this."[39] He returned to Mexico the following year, having been commissioned by the *Survey* to gather and edit articles that would appear in an issue of the magazine devoted exclusively to Mexico.

The result of Tannenbaum's efforts was a richly illustrated, multifaceted view of contemporary Mexico, published May 1, 1924, with contributions by several Americans as well as Mexicans, such as Calles, Vasconcelos, Rivera, and "the martyred Maya leader," Felipe Carrillo Puerto. To the editors the work of Mexico's writers and artists suggested comparison with Renaissance Italy: "In Mexico, a similar group of young enthusiasts . . . have caught up ideals which have enflamed a people. They are finding expression in art, literature, education, politics, in an emphatic statement of the importance of the individual, and of his goal in the common welfare."[40]

Tannenbaum returned to Mexico late in 1924 with the AFL delegation that attended Calles's inauguration, and soon afterward he decided to devote himself to Mexico. Having been admitted to the Robert S. Brookings Graduate School, he chose the Mexican agricultural system as his dissertation topic and spent fifteen months in Mexico in 1925–26 doing the required research.

During these early stays in Mexico he renewed an old friendship with Robert Haberman, whom he had known since 1916, and who contributed an article to the Mexican number of the *Survey*. Tannenbaum also formed many new friendships in Mexico City and told his wife in 1925 that he was part of "a regular little family," which included Mexicans such as Rivera and the composer "Tata Nacho" (Ignacio Fernández Esperón) and Americans such as Gruening. A fascinating new friend was Joseph Retinger, whom he described as "one of the most interesting

Frank Tannenbaum with Indian *principales* in Mexico. This photograph may have been taken during the 1926 scientific expedition. (Frank Tannenbaum Collection, Rare Book and Manuscript Library, Columbia University)

and baffling and yet simple people I have ever met." It seemed to Tannenbaum that the Polish-born Retinger, who spoke fourteen languages and had been jailed in five countries, had the "absolute confidence" of Luis Morones, the powerful labor leader and cabinet member under Calles.[41]

Tannenbaum's friendship with Haberman and Retinger probably facilitated his access to Morones during his 1925–26 sojourn. On November 30, 1925, Tannenbaum confided to his wife that he had had a long talk with Morones that day on Mexico's foreign property law and agrarian policy. "He told me that I must consider myself as one of the group and that my judgement to them was of the outmost [sic] importance. . . . I am really making a friend of Morones and developing an influence with him." But when Morones asked him to become a publicist on behalf of the government, he refused.[42]

Tannenbaum's access to Morones and other Mexican officials allowed him to try his hand at diplomacy on two occasions in 1926. In February he arranged a secret luncheon attended by Morones, Secretary of Agriculture Luis León, Secretary of Education José Manuel Puig Casauranc, and Ambassador Sheffield, who Tannenbaum believed was "almost painfully isolated from contact with the Mexican government." He was obviously pleased with his feat in bringing Morones and Sheffield together. "I am confident," he told his wife, "that Morones would have gone at the invitation of no other American in Mexico at this time—that Sheffield would perhaps would not have gone with any one else who could also have had the confidence of Morones." Tannenbaum was even more excited when he arranged a meeting on March 24 between Morones and the newly arrived apostolic delegate, Archbishop George Caruana. "In some ways," he wrote, "that is the most important meeting that took place in Mexico in twenty years."[43] The meeting bore little fruit, however, for Caruana was expelled on May 12, and Mexico's religious crisis deepened in the following months.

Tannenbaum acted as an intermediary between citizens and groups in both countries in a variety of ways. He helped arrange for the invitation to John Dewey, one of his Columbia mentors, to lecture at the 1926 session of the Summer School. He took an active interest in a "miracle" school in a tough Mexico City slum, which was the subject of his first article on Mexico, and organized the Friends of Mexico Committee to raise money for the school. Members of the committee, whose motto was "seeking better acquaintance between the peoples of Mexico and the United States," included Dewey, Gruening, Samuel Gompers, and other prominent Americans. Through the committee Tannenbaum also collected three thousand English-language books which were installed in the Lincoln Library at the Centro Escolar Benito Juárez in Mexico City. At the inauguration of the library in December 1927, Esperanza Velázquez Bringas, head of the Department of Libraries of the Secretariat of Education, paid tribute to Tannenbaum's "indefatigable labor" on behalf of the project.[44]

In his early writings on Mexico, Tannenbaum viewed the revolution in a positive light and, like Gruening, praised the work of the Obregón administration in restoring peace and promoting education. Although he had modified his earlier radicalism, he still saw great promise in the labor movement (that is, the new organizations of industrial and agricultural workers), which he considered a vehicle of mass mobilization that had been conspicuously absent in the past. The result had been the ascendancy of the army: "Mexico was ruled and ruined by a military caste because there was no means of control, no method of resistance, no source of stability." The stabilizing force of the labor movement had been shown when it rallied behind Obregón during the de la Huerta revolt, which he called "the latest stand of the reactionaries."[45]

That Tannenbaum was aware of the revolution's limitations can be seen in his observations when he was invited to join a scientific expedition to southern Mexico in 1926. He was especially distressed by the poverty of the Indians in Chiapas and by the heavy loads carried by coffee workers. "It is hard to get excited about the burden the Indians carry here," he wrote in his journal. "But to see a woman with a load like that after twelve years of revolution [tugged] at the heart strings—especially when one thinks of Mexico City and its cabaries [*sic*] and its revolutionary generals spending thousands of pesos in high living."[46]

Carleton Beals, whom Tannenbaum met frequently in Mexico City in 1925–26, had made his first trip to Mexico in 1918. A native of Kansas and a graduate of the University of California and Columbia University, Beals had been a conscientious objector during World War I. He described his initial journey southward as an act of rebellion against his life as an employee of the Standard Oil Company. "Ever since college the great American duty of work and success—clock-punching, column-adding, push, and bluff—had held me in its iron claws, but had never commanded my reverence."[47] Accompanied for a time by his younger brother, Ralph (the future anthropologist), Beals eventually made his way to Mexico City, where he became acquainted with Haberman. He earned his living as a teacher of English, but free of the bourgeois restrictions he had known in California, he also began to write; when he finished a book on Mexico and had four articles accepted for publication, he concluded that he could survive as a free-lance writer. After losing his job at the American School in 1920, he left for Spain and Italy but returned to Mexico in 1923, convinced that Europe "was weary, weary to death, *rigor mortis* already in its veins."[48]

Beals spent the next few years in Mexico, except for occasional trips to the United States and a daring foray to Nicaragua for an interview with Augusto C. Sandino in 1928. He explained to H. L. Mencken in 1923: "Mexico is the country of my choice; . . . when once the southland countries have spilled their magic into one's being—well, the dye is indellible [*sic*] and the pattern too richly satisfying ever to be erased. I have come to love Mexico and the Mexicans, and I only wish that my own people could understand them."[49]

Like Gruening and Tannenbaum, Beals appraised the Obregón administration favorably, though with more overt qualifications than either of the other two. In the first of two articles written in collaboration with Haberman and published in 1920 in the *Liberator*, he hailed the recent revolution that had ousted Carranza and said that it was supported by "every man of decency and vision—such as it is—that has appeared in Mexico in recent years." Moreover, he justified the probable moderation of any regime headed by Obregón: "Should he institute a real social revolution such as we have witnessed in Russia—and that is impossible because the people are not organized for it—[American] intervention would come with the suddenness of one of their own tropical storms." In an article for the Mexican number of the *Survey*, he acknowledged the persistence of serious financial problems but expressed an opinion similar to Tannenbaum's by stressing "the clear-cut emergence of popular social control" and "the strengthening of the historical racial regionalism" as the most significant achievements of the Obregón administration. "Both tendencies will ultimately revolutionize Mexican political practices; both will ultimately make possible stabilized social liberation."[50]

Early in 1927 Beals praised Calles, calling him "a continental figure with a moral courage unparalleled since the death of Sun Yat-sen."[51] Beals admired Calles in part because of the Mexican president's stance toward the Catholic church, of which Beals was consistently critical at this point in his career. In his 1923 volume, *Mexico: An Interpretation*, he flayed the church for its failure to elevate the Mexican people morally or materially, and in a 1926 article he observed that it had "opposed every necessary reform of the past fifteen years."[52] By mid-1927, however, he was privately expressing reservations about the Calles regime, especially its treatment of the church, but he was reluctant to state them publicly lest he provide ammunition for critics of the government, which he believed should be preserved. He thus found himself in a dilemma, one that presumably confronted other revolutionary sympathizers: "To portray conditions here brighter than they are jeopardizes one's reputation for veracity; to criticize them, even in a generous spirit, plays into the hands of . . . the 'Chicago Tribune' and 'Liberty.'"[53]

During his visits to the United States, Beals spoke in public on Mexican issues. A talk at New York's Civic Club in 1925 prompted Haberman to write: "We are all quite happy over your interest in Mexico, and have been thinking out how to make it possible for you to go from one end of the country to the other lecturing on the subject." No such tour took place, but late the following year Carrie Chapman Catt invited Beals to speak on Mexican-American relations at a conference on the cause and cure of war. In his talk Beals implicated former ambassador Henry Lane Wilson in the overthrow and death of Francisco Madero. His comments evoked angry protests from several persons, including Wilson, who called the charges libelous and untrue, and Beals was persuaded to omit them from the published version of his talk.[54]

If Gruening can be considered a liberal and Tannenbaum and Beals moderate leftists, Bertram D. Wolfe was a radical upon his arrival in Mexico in 1923. A 1917 graduate of the City College of New York, Wolfe was drawn into politics by his opposition to World War I and later became active in the fractious communist organizations of the postwar era. In 1922 he attended a clandestine communist conclave in Michigan, which hastily adjourned just before federal authorities appeared on the scene. Wolfe fled to Boston, but on a visit to New York he met Robert Haberman, who offered him and his wife employment in Mexico as teachers of English.[55]

The Wolfes appeared at the Secretariat of Education on February 1,

1923, and were each assigned two English classes daily at a girls' high school. A few weeks later, Haberman, who had quarreled with Beals, asked Wolfe to collaborate on articles dealing with Mexico. Wolfe refused because he disagreed with Haberman and Beals's depiction of Mexico as a socialist paradise. As a result, he and his wife were nearly dismissed from their teaching positions but were kept on the payroll after the intervention of the director of the high school.

In Mexico City Wolfe and his wife avoided the American colony, developed friendships with many Mexicans, and studied literature at the National University. Plunging into left-wing politics, Wolfe joined the Communist party, became a member of its central committee, and made his first trip to the Soviet Union in 1924 as its delegate to the Fifth Congress of the Comintern. In addition, he gave lectures on the class struggle through the ages and wrote furiously for periodicals in Mexico and the United States, among them the communist organ *El Machete*.

According to Wolfe, he fought the intention of Communist party leader Rafael Carrillo to ally the party with the forces of Adolfo de la Huerta before the latter's revolt. This was a reactionary movement, Wolfe informed readers of the *Liberator*. "Obregón has the bulk of the army, the mass of workers and peasants, the vacillating middle class that dislikes resolute action, and the timid elements even among the reaction." He conjectured that with the defeat of the revolt Obregón and Calles might move to the left, but he conceded that the latter was unlikely to chart a radical course. Indeed, even before Calles took office, Wolfe attacked Luis Morones as an instrument of Samuel Gompers, whom he denounced as an "agent of Yankee imperialism."[56] On June 29, 1925, Wolfe was deported from Mexico because of his communist activities and his participation in a projected strike of railroad workers.[57]

During his stay in Mexico, Wolfe began his long association with Diego Rivera, whose biography he would later write. He was also one of the first writers to identify for American readers the aesthetic dimensions of the Mexican Revolution. In a 1924 article in the *Nation*, he described the revolution as a "patchy and unsystematic affair" but added that the work of artists and poets had given it system and unity. "The new content and form of art and poetry . . . seem to be the most complete, the most logical, the most 'revolutionary' of the by-products of the Mexican Revolution."[58]

The conjunction of art and revolution in 1920s Mexico made it an attractive destination for other Americans besides those such as Tannenbaum or Gruening, whose interests were primarily political. The contingent of political pilgrims also included Americans who sympathized with the revolution yet whose concerns were more broadly cultural and aesthetic than those of Tannenbaum or Beals. Through their writings and other activities these visitors also helped to disseminate favorable views of Mexico in the United States at a time of diplomatic strains.

One of the earliest visitors was Katherine Anne Porter, who was to spend only a few years in Mexico but gathered enough material there for a lifetime of writing. Although Porter described a childhood visit to Mexico in conversations with Enrique Hank López, her most recent biographer, Joan Givner, makes it clear that her first trip to that country occurred in 1920.[59] Both López and Givner indicate that Porter's interest in Mexico was whetted by her contacts with Mexicans living in New York City, among them "Tata Nacho" and the artist Adolfo Best Maugard. She herself wrote that as a Texan, she considered Mexico her "familiar country" and that she had gone there "to study the renascence of Mexican art—a veritable rebirth, very conscious, very powerful, of a deeply racial and personal art."[60] She arrived in time to witness the inauguration of Obregón on December 1, 1920. Porter's life in Mexico has been recounted in detail by herself and her biographers: her introduction to marijuana at a party in Cuernavaca, her first bullfight, and her rowboat ride with Felipe Carrillo Puerto on the lake in Chapultepec Park. She returned to the United States in 1921 but was back in Mexico the following year. At this time she wrote the catalog for an exhibit of Mexican folk art that was shown in Los Angeles in 1922.[61]

During these early visits Porter also wove her Mexican experiences into articles and stories that soon won her recognition as a major literary figure. In her nonfiction pieces, she deftly sketched the uncertainties of the early days of the Obregón administration and the obstacles, both foreign and domestic, to significant change. She also skewered the foreign visitors who became Mexican specialists overnight. "We have had a constant procession of these strange people: they come dashing in, gather endless notes and dash out again and three weeks later their expert, definitive opinions are published."[62]

A young visitor who forged an even closer bond with Mexico was Alma Reed, who is remembered as a journalist, as a promoter of Mexican art in the United States, and as a romantic legend because of her relationship with Felipe Carrillo Puerto. Born in San Francisco in 1894, she studied archaeology at the University of California and became a journalist in her native city. She attracted attention in Mexico when she was credited with encouraging passage of a 1921 California law that prohibited capital punishment for persons under age eighteen; among those saved by the law was a seventeen-year-old Mexican, Simón Ruiz, who had been sentenced to death for killing a man in San Bernardino County. Therefore, when she first visited Mexico City in September 1922, she was honored by the Secretariat of Foreign Relations and feted by *El Universal* and *Excelsior*, which described her as a "charming little American with blue eyes and an angelic face" who could be taken for a movie star. She in turn declared that "Mexico should be the Mecca of all the world's artists: here every object and every scene is an occasion for art and beauty."[63]

Reed returned to Mexico as a correspondent for the *New York Times* in the company of a party of American archaeologists and journalists who toured Yucatán in February 1923. In Mérida, the state capital, she was singled out for attention: the state journalists' association gave a reception in her honor and the feminists' league tendered an evening of poetry and music.[64] One result of her visit was a series of articles in the *Times* discussing Maya civilization, "more interesting in some ways than the Egyptian," and past and future archaeological work in Yucatán. Of a piece on March 18 about the Maya "ghosts" who awaited archaeologists, Sylvanus Morley commented: "It was a splendid article, splendidly written, indeed it was almost the best popular article from a scientific point of view which I have ever read."[65]

Less than two weeks after Reed's arrival, Morley referred in his diary to rumors that Carrillo Puerto was "very much enamored" of her, and a few days after that he described a conversation with the governor, who told him that he was deeply in love. Morley observed: "I could see she would be the type to attract him, for she has a really good head, and down here would be considered beautiful. Above all else she was stylish and wore her clothes well."[66] The affair was complicated because the forty-eight-year-old governor had a wife to whom he had been married for more than twenty years as well as a mistress.

Reed returned to Yucatán the following July but did not leave the ship that brought her to Progreso. While the ship was docked, poet Luis Rosado Vega and composer Ricardo Palmerín came aboard, and the latter sang for her "La Peregrina," a song they had written in her honor.[67] She went on to Mexico City, followed by Carrillo Puerto. After his return to Yucatán, he again confided in Morley. "Silvano, I am in the greatest difficulty of my life," he is supposed to have said. "This morning I am going down to Progreso to meet my wife and children. Behind in Mérida is that poor girl [his Mexican mistress] for whom I have only the kindliest feelings but whom I no longer love, and in Mexico waits Alma till I send her the telegram which will tell her to come. The only woman I love madly!"[68]

To Morley, it seemed like an impossible situation and, indeed, the plans of Carrillo and Reed never reached fruition. He was divorced in November 1923 but was killed the following January. Reed later covered archaeology in North Africa and Italy for the *Times* but renewed her Mexican ties in 1927 by taking up the cause of José Clemente Orozco in New York.

Another "ardent propagandist" on behalf of Mexican culture was Frances Toor, a graduate of the University of California, who came to Mexico in 1922 to attend the Summer School of the National University. She knew little of Mexico at the time but was overwhelmed by an exhibit of folk art sponsored by the Secretariat of Industry, Commerce, and Labor: "The beauty of it was one of the motivating factors in my remaining. I wanted to know more of the country in which humble people could make such beautiful things."[69] She stayed on in Mexico, teaching English in government schools, taking courses at the National University, and traveling to rural areas during her vacations.

In 1925 she conceived the idea of a periodical devoted to Mexican folklore. "Because of my own joy in the discovery of an art and civilization different from any that I had previously known, I thought it would interest others as well."[70] The first number of the bilingual magazine, which she called *Mexican Folkways*, was dated June–July 1925. In that first issue she acknowledged the encouragement of Manuel Gamio, who had recently held the position of undersecretary in the Education Department and had offered a monthly subsidy. By the time the first issue appeared, he had lost his post, but by the end of the year Secretary Puig Casauranc agreed to finance the magazine, which survived until 1933.

An exemplar of the American of leftist political views who was drawn to Mexico as much for cultural as political reasons was the novelist John Dos Passos, who arrived in 1926, exhausted by his labors on behalf of

Sacco and Vanzetti and the New Playwrights' Theatre. Years before he had read and admired John Reed's *Insurgent Mexico*, and now he found himself exhilarated by his early experiences in Mexico. "Mexico City is a darn sight more interesting than I expected," he wrote soon after his arrival. "Everything, people, air, food, drink, tobacco is of the first water—And everything is exciting and comical and full of drunkenness and fornication."[71]

In Mexico City Dos Passos looked up an old friend, Susan Smith, who was living in the same apartment building as Carleton Beals, with whom he was also acquainted because both were associated with the recently founded *New Masses*. Dos Passos became friendly with the painter Xavier Guerrero, with whom he went on a walking tour of the mountains behind Toluca, and was impressed by his dedication to communism. "I sat looking and sketching while Xavier, who ought to have been doing the drawing, spread the gospel of Lenin and Marx among the villagers."[72] Dos Passos also struck up an acquaintance with a onetime labor radical, Gladwin Bland, who was now a small business-man in Mexico City and became the model for Fenian McCreary in *The 42nd Parallel* (1930).

Dos Passos left Mexico in March 1927 "with as many stories in my head as a dog has fleas." He soon contributed three articles on Mexico to the *New Masses*, one of which contrasted Rivera's murals with other con-temporary painting: "little fruity still lifes, little modern designs of a stovepipe and a bisected violin . . . stuff a man's afraid to be seen look-ing at." He considered the murals a means of explaining the revolution to an illiterate population. "Even if the paintings were rotten, it would have been worthwhile to prove that in our day a popular graphic art is possible. Maybe it's not possible anywhere but in Mexico." In another article he emphasized the continuing importance of the agrarian issue and predicted that Mexican politics would remain unstable until the issue was resolved.[73]

In the early 1920s even those Americans who remained largely aloof from Mexico's political ferment were likely to endorse the general goals of the revolution and to condemn American policies toward Mexico. This was true, for example, of Witter Bynner and Willard (Spud) Johnson, who accompanied D. H. Lawrence and his wife on their Mexi-can travels in 1923. Bynner, a well-established poet, and Johnson, his secretary and editor of the satirical magazine *Laughing Horse*, were the models for Owen Rhys and Bud Villiers in *The Plumed Serpent*, which drew heavily on their 1923 experiences.

In Mexico City the party became acquainted with Haberman and Frederic Leighton, who proved an "agreeable guide," and were introduced to several Mexican writers as well as Luis Morones.[74] They were scheduled to have lunch with Vasconcelos, an occasion to which Bynner looked forward, but the lunch was canceled and the enraged Lawrence lashed out at Leighton. A few days later, on May 1, 1923, Bynner and Johnson "accompanied the proletariat" to the tower of Mexico City's cathedral and "tolled the Christian bells with street-cleaners in honor of Bolshevism and the Chicago martyrs for an eight-hour day."[75]

The party then set out for Chapala. While en route, Bynner renewed his friendship with Idella Purnell, who had been a student of his in a poetry class at the University of California and was living in Guadalajara with her dentist father. Employed as a secretary at the American consulate, Purnell had recently launched a magazine of verse, *Palms*, with the blessing and collaboration of Bynner.[76] The poet continued to give his support to the magazine, which was published in Guadalajara until 1927.

Chapala reminded Bynner of China, which he had twice visited: "Not so systematized as the United States, but fresher and freer. I feel that Mexico may be a barrier against the blighting southward progress of Anglo-Saxondom."[77] In 1925 Bynner returned alone to Chapala, where he found some changes: "Too much elegancia now, constant shrill clatter, no calzones, not so many guaraches [*sic*], no plaza-market." Even so, he could not help writing "Chinesey" verses that he was gathering for a collection of Chapala poems.[78] He also found several other American writers in Chapala as well as the painter Lowell Houser, making up "a real little colony." Bynner remained sympathetic but relatively indifferent to Mexico's political upheaval. In an article published in 1927, he acknowledged that Mexican officials might be corrupt, yet he held that the government was more helpful to laborers and peasants than the government of the United States was to its citizens.[79]

Perhaps no prominent American visitor to Mexico in the early 1920s was as indifferent to politics and the revolution as the photographer Edward Weston. Weston went to Mexico in 1923 to escape an unhappy marriage and to find new aesthetic directions. He chose Mexico because of the friendship he and his Italian-born lover, photographer Tina

Modotti, had formed in Los Angeles with poet Ricardo Gómez Robelo, who returned to Mexico after Carranza's ouster and took up a post in the Secretariat of Education under Vasconcelos.[80] Convinced that Mexico offered an exciting artistic environment, Weston, Modotti, and Weston's son Chandler sailed from California on July 29, 1923, arriving in Mazatlán a week later. Weston remained in Mexico until December 1924; after a visit to California he returned in August 1925 for a stay of more than a year. Modotti never again took up permanent residence in the United States; after Weston's departure, she stayed in Mexico perfecting her photographic art.

During his months in Mexico, Weston found appreciative viewers for his photographs. After the closing of an exhibit in Mexico City on November 3, 1923, he exulted: "I have made quite a definite break into the consciousness of the Mexican public—especially among the painters and poets and lovers of the arts—many of whom returned again and again, and many of whom would have bought but for their purses." As it was, he had sold eight prints. Weston's second exhibit, in October 1924, was also successful. "I have had—as last year—applause; real homage—yes, even more than last year."[81] Exhibitions of Weston's photographs were held in Guadalajara in 1924 and 1925, and his photographs were reproduced in *Mexican Folkways*, to which Rivera contributed an enthusiastic assessment of his work.[82]

In 1926 Weston had the opportunity to travel extensively outside of Mexico City after signing a contract to take photographs for a projected volume on Mexican decorative arts. The assignment took Weston and Modotti to Puebla, Oaxaca, Michoacán, Jalisco, Guanajuato, and Querétaro, where despite hardships caused by torrential downpours and poor transportation, he took four thousand photographs, among them some of his most celebrated, such as "Hands of Amado Galván" and "Janitzio, Lake Pátzcuaro."

There is no evidence in Weston's published journals that he was affected by the social and political ferment of the day. He was, rather, overwhelmed by the picturesqueness of Mexico and entranced by its folk art. He frequently derided contemporary American life, contrasting it with the sights and sounds of Mexico. For example, he compared Mazatlán with Glendale, California, where he had recently lived. "Exploring the [Mazatlán] streets at night, we found life both gay and sad—. . . vital, intense, black and white, never grey. Glendale, on the contrary, is drab, spiritless, a uniform grey." Although he was critical of some aspects of Mexican life, such as the ubiquity of firearms, he concluded before leaving in 1926 that Mexico had had a positive effect on his life and thought: "Not so much the contact with my artist friends as the less direct proximity of a primitive race. Before Mexico I had been surrounded by the usual mass of American burgess—sprinkled by a few sophisticated friends. Of simple peasant people I knew nothing. And I have been refreshed by their elemental expression,—I have felt the soil."[83]

Regardless of their specific political or aesthetic concerns, the American intellectuals, artists, and journalists who visited Mexico in the early 1920s and sympathized with the revolution were likely to know each other. Thus the apolitical Weston was acquainted with Bertram and Ella Wolfe, and Carleton Beals was friendly with Frances Toor and Tina Modotti, who photographed the brooding young journalist. Beals also knew Katherine Anne Porter, who probably used the breakup of his marriage in 1924 as the inspiration for her story "That Tree." These expatriates formed a somewhat Bohemian community that included friendly Mexicans such as Diego Rivera, who readily welcomed visitors and disciples. Many years later Emily Edwards, an artist who went to Mexico in 1925, remembered her first meeting with Rivera, then painting in the Secretariat of Education: "He was just like the sun, shining with the pleasure of his work, the world, and with meeting people."[84] But the Bohemian expatriates disliked most longtime American residents, whom they criticized for their attitude toward Mexico and its people. Of these Americans, Beals wrote: "Class-pride, race-hatred, and provincial backwardness mark their narrow minds. They despise the Mexican and his ways of living."[85]

A young woman who played an important role as a link among the various Americans and their Mexican friends was Anita Brenner. She was born in Aguascalientes in 1905, the daughter of a European immigrant, but the family was forced to leave Mexico for the United States during the revolution. After attending Our Lady of the Lake College in San Antonio and the University of Texas, she returned to Mexico in 1923 to continue her studies at the National University. During these years she assisted Gruening in gathering material for his book on Mexico, and it was she who engaged Weston to take photographs for a projected volume on decorative art. She was also one of the first to inform readers in the United States of the artistic renaissance generated by the Mexican Revolution and of its inspiration in indigenous sources.[86] Visitors to Mexico in these years invariably found her to be helpful and kindly, as did Lowell Houser, who called her "a real person and human." Houser's fellow painter and quondam companion in Mexico, Everett Gee Jackson, also admired her. "She was a brilliant, sensitive person, with a mind capable of entertaining anything as possible."[87]

At the same time that American political pilgrims and others who sympathized with the revolution crossed the border in the early 1920s, a wave of Mexican artists, performers, and intellectuals began moving north. These cultural emigrants were attracted to the United States in part because of the greater economic rewards to be found there, but their selection of the United States as their destination also reflected its growing importance as a cultural center. Although Mexico's cultural emigrants often labored for years in poverty and obscurity, the intellectual and aesthetic climate that sent Americans to Mexico increased the likelihood that their contributions would eventually be noticed and rewarded. Moreover, the way had been prepared by the reports of American visitors to Mexico and, in the case of painters, by exhibitions of their work preceding their arrival in person. After spending six years in New York, the composer "Tata Nacho" declared in 1925: "A welcome exists for Mexican artists [in the United States]. There is a sincere and noble sympathy of which we should take advantage in order to tighten the bonds of friendship between the two peoples and to make our art known."[88] In 1926 José Vasconcelos was quoted in the *Revista de Revistas* as saying that the United States was a young and vigorous nation that was inclined to help everyone and that "we [Mexicans] need only know how to use this disposition for our benefit."[89]

Among the earliest cultural emigrants was the poet José Juan Tablada, who remained an ardent nationalist despite his residence in New York from 1920 to 1936. A biographer wrote: "It is doubtful if any Mexican ever lived so intensely the life of a Mexican away from home. . . . The poet's home was a minor museum of Indian and Mexican art and to his North American friends in New York and Washington he talked and lived Mexico."[90] It was this intense national feeling that led Tablada to launch what he called a "holy crusade" on behalf of Mexican culture in the United States. Long interested in the visual arts, he published numerous articles designed to acquaint American readers with the work of contemporary Mexican painters. He also took credit for an exhibition of Mexican art at the Whitney Studio Club in March 1924. On exhibit were caricatures by Miguel Covarrubias, wax sculptures by Luis Hidalgo, and paintings by José Clemente Orozco. With some exaggeration he reported that those who had attended the vernissage had been "stupefied" by the talent of the three artists. He had laid the groundwork for the showing of Orozco's work by an article in *International Studio* in which he dubbed the painter the Mexican Goya.[91] By this time Tablada was already being described in *Current Opinion* as the "kindly patron" of a small group of Mexican artists who had peacefully invaded New York and who were refuting by their talent those who regarded Mexico only as a country of cactus and revolutionaries. The author of the article remarked: "That there is a real revival of interest in Mexico's quickening is evidenced by the number of articles on this subject in the press."[92]

Among the "little band of pioneers" described by the writer cited above was Miguel Covarrubias, who was the first Mexican artist to achieve success in the United States. According to Covarrubias, Tablada played an important role in furthering his career. On seeing the youthful artist's caricatures exhibited in a Mexico City restaurant, Tablada persuaded the Secretariat of Foreign Relations to provide him with a sinecure and funds for a three-month stay in New York in 1923. When Covarrubias's money ran out, Tablada offered him hospitality and promoted his work, arranging his introduction to journalist Sherrill Schell. Schell in turn introduced Covarrubias to the novelist Carl Van Vechten and the publisher Alfred A. Knopf. Van Vechten was enthusiastic about Covarrubias's work, which he brought to the attention of Frank Crowninshield, the influential publisher of *Vanity Fair*.[93] Covarrubias's caricatures soon began to appear in *Vanity Fair* as well as in the *New Yorker*, and Knopf published two collections of portraits: *The Prince of Wales and Other Famous Americans* (1925) and *Negro Drawings* (1927). The first of these firmly established Covarrubias's reputation in New York.

Schell also introduced Covarrubias to the Theatre Guild, which gave him the opportunity to design the set for a segment called "Rancho Mexicano" in the 1925 revue *Garrick Gaieties*. Covarrubias's work on "Rancho Mexicano" led the Theatre Guild to engage him to design the sets and costumes for its production of George Bernard Shaw's *Androcles and the Lion*, which opened on November 23, 1925. The sets drew considerable comment from critics. Percy Hammond described the scenery as "bizarre but unfortunate" in the *New York Herald Tribune*, Alexander Woollcott found it "gay" and "facetious," and a reviewer in the *New York Times* singled out the "extravagant comic settings" in praising the entire production.[94]

Leading composers of art music also spent long periods in the United States during the 1920s. Silvestre Revueltas labored in obscurity, first as a student at the Chicago Musical College and later as a violinist and conductor in theaters in San Antonio and Mobile.[95] Two others, Julián Carrillo and Carlos Chávez, established ties with important members of the American musical community and earned a measure of fame for their compositions and theories.

Born in 1875, Carrillo lived in New York during World War I. He organized the short-lived American Symphony Orchestra in 1915 and became an exponent of the need for a New World music to counter European dominance. He later returned to Mexico, where he served as head of the National Conservatory and devised a microtonal system called Sonido Trece, or the Thirteenth Sound, which divided musical tones into quarters, eighths, and sixteenths. New York was first exposed to the Thirteenth Sound at a concert of new music on March 13, 1926, offered by the League of Composers. Carrillo himself conducted his *Sonata casi-fantasía*, which struck critics as significant mainly as an illustration of his microtonal system.[96]

Perhaps the most important result of this concert for Carrillo was that it led to his long association with Leopold Stokowski, director of the Philadelphia Orchestra and a champion of contemporary music. On March 4, 1927, the Philadelphia Orchestra gave the world premiere performance of Carillo's *Concertino*, at which the composer himself was present. Stokowski wrote a message explaining the microtonal system, which was enclosed with the program. Even so, according to critic H. T. Craven, "the audience was pardonably dazed by the experiment." When the Philadelphia Orchestra repeated the concert in New York, the reaction was different. "Hearty applause attested the cordiality of the audience . . . and Mr. Carrillo beamed his acknowledgement when summoned forth to face the audience." Stokowski's approval of Carrillo's work brought lengthy and respectful comment from critics, who again seemed more taken with the possibilities of Sonido Trece than with Carrillo's composition. After the New York performance, Lawrence

Gilman remarked in the *Herald Tribune* that "we heard enough, and enjoyed enough, of what was offered to our ears to realize that there is potentially wonderful music imprisoned in this infinitely subtle and iridescent web of tones."[97]

Younger by a generation than Carrillo, Carlos Chávez found the musical life of New York more congenial than that of Mexico or Europe. He was self-taught and completed his first symphony in 1918 before he was out of his teens. Although most of his early music bore the imprint of European models, in 1921 he was commissioned by José Vasconcelos to compose a ballet based on preconquest themes. The resulting work, *El fuego nuevo*, was suggested by an Aztec rite. After an unsatisfactory excursion to Europe in 1922–23, he left for New York in December 1923. During this initial visit, Chávez was favorably impressed by the quality of American orchestras, the advanced technology for the diffusion of music, and the dynamism of jazz. He returned for a longer stay in December 1926, accompanied by the painter Rufino Tamayo, with whom he shared an apartment on Fourteenth Street. Chávez now emerged as a composer of note among contemporary musicians who admired his merging of modern technique and national allusions.[98]

Meanwhile, a young Mexican tenor named José Mojica was beginning to make his mark on the opera stage. A native of Jalisco, he received some vocal training in Mexico City. After singing in several operas there, he was offered a contract by the Chicago Civic Opera and made his debut in 1919 as Bucklaw in *Lucia de Lammermoor*. In 1921 he portrayed the melancholy prince in the premier performance of *The Love of Three Oranges*, which was directed by the composer, S. S. Prokofiev. Mojica remained an "indispensable" member of the company for the rest of the decade and also gave recitals throughout the country. A highlight of his operatic career was his performance as Pelleas in 1925, which moved the *Musical Courier* to remark that "he brought to the role not only the youth and ardor that are indispensable for its effective portrayal, but also notable artistic restraint and beauty of voice."[99]

Despite the success attained by Covarrubias, Mojica, and others, the most celebrated of Mexico's cultural emigrants during the 1920s were several actors who became motion picture stars. During the decade Mexicans were featured more prominently in American motion pictures than ever before or since. That Mexicans should be tempted to try their fortunes in Hollywood is not surprising given the decadence of the motion picture industry in Mexico and the global dominance of American films after World War I. Although many found their hopes frustrated, two—Ramón Novarro and Dolores del Río—reached stardom in the mid-1920s.

Novarro, a native of Durango, left for Los Angeles in 1916 determined to break into show business. His rise began in 1922, when he played the role of Rupert of Hentzau in *The Prisoner of Zenda*, directed by Rex Ingram, who shaped the career of another "Latin lover," Rudolph Valentino. Novarro quickly became a top Hollywood star, especially after his performances in *Scaramouche* (1923) and in the title role in *Ben Hur* (1925).[100]

Dolores del Río was also born in Durango. A young matron of upper-class background, she was described as "stunning" and "a real beauty" by Edward Weston when he met her in 1924. The following year she was lured to Hollywood by director Edwin Carewe, to whom she was introduced by painter Adolfo Best Maugard. At a time when "exotic" types such as Pola Negri and Theda Bara were in fashion, she too enjoyed a rapid rise and played starring roles in *What Price Glory?* (1926) and *Resurrection* (1927). Of her portrayal of the self-sacrificing Katusha in the latter, the reviewer of the *New York Times* said: "Few actresses have ever given so fine a performance in a role as difficult."[101]

Neither of these stars was given an opportunity to play Mexicans in their motion picture roles during the early and mid-1920s in part because the American motion picture industry avoided producing films with recognizably Mexican characters and settings to forestall complaints from the Mexican government (see Chapter 5). Even though Novarro and Del Río were not cast as Mexicans, their compatriots followed their careers with interest, and their success was seen as a vindication of Mexican national honor. In 1923 Rafael de Zayas Enríquez hailed Novarro's performance in *Scaramouche* and added: "Mexico is now being represented with dignity in the theatres of the United States, showing that we produce something besides bandits, revolutionaries, and ragamuffins."[102] Three years later another writer applauded Del Río—"our Dolores"—not only for proclaiming her nationality but also for demonstrating the charm of the Mexican woman.[103]

If creative artists sought to establish reputations in the United States during the 1920s, other Mexicans crossed the border for broadly political reasons. Some were persons in forced or voluntary exile who interacted mainly with their compatriots in the United States, but others sought to explain Mexican policies to influential Americans and thereby mold public opinion. In June 1924, for example, Secretary of Education Vasconcelos headed a delegation of Mexican officials that made a ten-day tour of Texas cities. The delegation was well received. In Austin the party was honored at a luncheon attended by some three hundred persons, including the acting governor and his wife. About seventy-five members of the University of Texas faculty turned out to greet the visitors at a lawn smoker at the home of historian Charles W. Hackett. Vasconcelos in turn lauded the university for its role in initiating educational exchange with Mexico.[104] Later that year President-elect Calles visited the United States. He met with leaders of the American Federation of Labor and with President Calvin Coolidge and tried to assuage the fears of American investors in Mexico.[105]

A more frequent visitor was Moisés Sáenz, who had close ties with the United States. A native of Mezquital, Nuevo León, and a Protestant, he received a bachelor's degree in 1912 from Washington and Jefferson College and a master's degree in 1921 from Columbia University Teachers College, where he was exposed to John Dewey's educational philosophy. Returning to Mexico, he served as director of the Summer School in 1923–24 and as undersecretary of public education from 1925 to 1930.[106] In the latter position his efforts to use rural schools to integrate the Indians into national life attracted much attention in the United States.

Sáenz often traveled to the United States during the 1920s. In 1924 he was a member of the party that accompanied Vasconcelos to Texas. In 1925 Sáenz addressed the Friends of the Mexicans conference in California, and in 1926 he and Vasconcelos, who was no longer part of the government, gave lectures at the University of Chicago which were subsequently published in book form.[107] In the summer of 1927 Sáenz again spoke in several locations in the United States, including the Institute of Politics in Williamstown, Massachusetts. His remarks at Williamstown were criticized by Vicente Lombardo Toledano and others, who accused Sáenz of recommending the introduction of Protestantism to the public schools of Mexico. Sáenz publicly refuted the charges, but this was not the last time his American associations would produce controversy.[108]

Despite criticism in Mexico, the efforts of Sáenz as well as those of American journalists such as Beals to defend Mexico, seemed all the more necessary as its relations with the United States deteriorated in 1926–27. The issues that had produced tension since the start of the revolution had become aggravated by differences over Nicaragua and by American criticism of the government's anticlerical policies, which to many constituted an unwarranted assault on freedom of conscience. Another source of conflict was the enactment late in 1925 of legislation affecting rights to subsoil petroleum deposits and landownership by foreigners. The laws were intended to implement article 27 of the constitution and were not to go into effect until 1927, but the State Department feared that they might be applied retroactively and threaten property and mineral rights acquired by Americans before 1917. This tense period brought visits to Mexico by a new type of American political pilgrim: clergymen, educators, and journalists who traveled in groups and systematically dedicated themselves to developing an understanding of the Mexican situation and explaining the Mexican point of view to American audiences.

In view of the controversy over the church-state issue, it is not surprising that American missions to Mexico in the mid-1920s often included Protestant clergymen, who rarely commiserated with the beleaguered Catholics to the south. In the summer of 1926 Alva W. Taylor, an editor of the *Christian Century* and head of the National Service Commission of the Church of the Disciples, led a "goodwill" mission consisting of thirty-two members, many of whom were clergymen. While in Mexico, they adopted a resolution endorsing Calles's "great program of social reform," which merited the support of all who were interested in the welfare of Mexico. The group met with Bishop Pascual Díaz of Tabasco, secretary of the episcopal committee, but Taylor at least remained convinced that the Catholic hierarchy exploited Mexico. "Sensitive as they are to questions of religious conscience," he wrote in the *Christian Century*, "the American people will not fail to differentiate between liberty of conscience and the claims of a moribund and medieval ecclesiastical hierarchy in a land written all over with the story of their failure to contribute to social progress."[109]

Another 1926 mission led by a clergyman had more lasting consequences, for it was the first of a long series of seminars, as they came to be known. The founder of the seminars was Hubert C. Herring, a graduate of Union Theological Seminary and executive secretary of the Social Relations Department of the Congregational church. In 1924, while attending the AFL convention, he took advantage of the Mexican government's invitation to attend President Calles's inauguration. Writing in the *Congregationalist* about this, his first visit to Mexico, he described the scene in the stadium, crowded with fifty thousand people—"Spanish types, and fifty-seven brands of Indian types"—as Calles took the oath of office. He concluded: "We can add our voice right lustily to the voices of Mexico, and can add our *Viva México! Viva Calles!* to the rest. We can help to make real their dreams."[110]

The first seminar group, which consisted of twenty-two clergymen and laypersons, including former governor William E. Sweet of Colorado, spent ten days in Mexico City in April 1926. They met with President Calles, cabinet officials, religious leaders, educators, artists, and intellectuals but, according to Herring, did not delude themselves as to what they could learn about a new country in such a short time. The group concluded that the Mexican government had "espoused the cause of the poor, the unprivileged and the disinterested" and was reconstructing national life through agrarian reform, popular education, and more democratic forms of government. "We believe that the government and the people of the United States should seek to understand the conditions that lie behind the government going on in Mexico today, and should exercise forbearance as well as justice toward a neighboring nation striving to secure for all its people a share in the good things of life."[111] Herring and other members of the first seminar used the pages of the *Congregationalist* and the *Christian Century* to report on their trip to Mexico. Herbert A. Jump, a Congregationalist minister from Ann Arbor, Michigan, stated that he had given twenty talks on conditions in Mexico but was alarmed by the American press's "skilful barrage of silence" against positive portrayals of Mexico.[112] Herring was convinced that the Mexican people, with their courtesy and their love of music and art, had much to teach the United States: "It will be a happy day when America is cured of its delusions of superior virtue, and is ready to learn the art of living from these Indians of Mexico. It can only come as we move back and forth across the line of the Rio Grande, seeking neither financial advantage nor political power, seeking rather to enter into the cultural and spiritual wealth which these sons of the soil have so hardly won."[113]

Only a few months after the first seminar, Herring organized a second one. Its sole purpose, he said upon arriving in Mexico City on December

29, 1926, was to increase the members' understanding of Mexico so that they might interpret that nation to the American people. "We believe that each country has much to offer through the interchange of cultures and ideas."[114] This second contingent numbered thirty-eight, including Herbert Croly of the *New Republic*, Paul Hutchinson of the *Christian Century*, Rabbi Isaac Landman of the *American Hebrew*, and Margaret Jenkins of the Women's International League for Peace.

While in Mexico City, the members of the seminar had an interview with Calles which made headlines in the United States, for the Mexican president indicated that a diplomatic rupture between the two countries was likely and offered to submit disputes over new land and petroleum laws to the Hague arbitration tribunal to avert more serious difficulties with the United States. The next day the seminar met with Bishop Díaz and other Mexican prelates. Bishop Díaz was banished from Mexico soon afterward and attributed his expulsion to Calles's annoyance over his statements about the religious crisis to the Herring seminar.[115]

Back in the United States, Herring reported that he had given eighteen lectures about his Mexican trip in Chicago alone. He urged President Coolidge to display American chivalry toward "the best government which Mexico has ever known." Croly warned that if American progressives failed to defend Mexico from predatory foreign investors, their own interests would eventually suffer: "they will themselves in the long run have to submit to treatment as rough and as unfair as that to which the State Department and the oil interests are now subjecting the Mexican government."[116]

Some Americans, however, were critical of the seminar. A Roman Catholic who considered it "an elaborate frame-up" publicly rebuked Rabbi Landman for minimizing the persecution of the Catholic church in Mexico.[117] Another rabbi who had taken part in the seminar agreed that it was designed mainly as a "political maneuver." He noted that nearly all the information the members had received had come from partisans of the goverment who had entertained them. "A group, just like an individual, is indisposed to assume a searching and scrutinizing attitude while partaking of hospitality. It is bad taste, if not undiplomatic, for a guest to be critical of his host." The rabbi's reservations coincided with those of Ambassador Sheffield, who reported that only five members of the seminar had visited the embassy while in Mexico City and that their guides had been selected by the Mexican government.[118]

Representative John B. Sosnowski of Michigan, who was alarmed about communist influences in Mexico, also found fault with the seminar: "So far as I am able to learn, not one of the members of this unofficial gang of meddlers had the slightest fundamental knowledge to equip him to make any kind of an investigation. . . . They, knowingly or unknowingly, are agents for the world revolutionary movement."[119]

Ambasssador Sheffield's reservations about the seminar reflected the concern often voiced by American diplomats in Mexico, journalists, and members of Congress regarding "propaganda" efforts by the Obregón and Calles administrations. Critics were unhappy over the propaganda because they thought that it blinded Americans to Mexico's violations of the rights of foreign investors and to the government's efforts to advance the cause of Bolshevism in the hemisphere. The critics were even more unhappy that American citizens seemed to be active in the dissemination of Mexican propaganda and were convinced that some of them were being paid for their services by the Mexican government.

Among those accused of being Mexican agents were several Americans mentioned in this chapter. Robert Haberman was often depicted as the chief propagandist of the Mexican government. A *Chicago Tribune* article in 1923 went further to say that his true role was that of "the leading representative in the western hemisphere for the world revolutionists of Moscow and Berlin." From his post in the Secretariat of Education Haberman was said to head a network of American draft dodgers and radicals who worked on behalf of the Mexican government. These included Frederic Leighton, Frank Tannenbaum, and Ernest Gruening. According to Consul General Dawson, they had also been charged with preparing the courses for the 1923 session of the National University's Summer School, which was to be used "to spread radical doctrines."[120] Representative James A. Gallivan of Massachusetts aired similar accusations in a speech on March 3, 1927, in which he inveighed against the "malignant propaganda" directed by Mexico against the United States and called Haberman and Tannenbaum "hirelings" of Calles who were ready to slander their compatriots for a price.[121]

Ambassador Sheffield was also convinced that disloyal American radicals on the Calles payroll were undermining the policies of their own government. He considered Haberman "a communist in thorough sympathy with Moscow" and questioned his right to claim American citizenship. He also thought it probable that Carleton Beals had received money from the Mexican government and was in the employ of the Soviet Union to boot. Frances Toor was described as a Mexican agent as well as a Soviet sympathizer and a friend of Alexandra Kollantai, the Soviet ambassador to Mexico.[122]

Ernest Gruening was another target of Sheffield's suspicions. In 1926 the ambassador accused Gruening of acting as an intermediary between the Calles administration and Senator Robert LaFollette of Wisconsin. Gruening had supposedly forwarded to Mexico a letter from the senator pledging to prevent a rupture between the United States and Mexico. "It is understood," wrote Sheffield, "that when Gruening's work is completed he will receive handsome remuneration from the Mexican government."[123] Although LaFollette denounced the letter as a forgery, a position with which the State Department concurred, Sheffield continued to insist that the senator had been in communication with the Mexican government.

Similar allegations about Gruening, as well as other Americans sympathetic to Mexico, arose as a result of Mexican documents published in the Hearst press in late 1927. The documents purported to show that Gruening, Herring, Oswald Garrison Villard, editor of the *Nation*, and others had received large sums for services on behalf of the Mexican government. Gruening promptly filed a libel suit against the *New York American*, which was eventually settled for $75,000. Meanwhile, the U.S. Senate established a special committee to investigate the documents, especially a letter authorizing payments by Mexico of $1.2 million to four senators: LaFollette, William H. Borah of Idaho, George Norris of Nebraska, and Thomas Heflin of Alabama. In its report on January 11, 1928, the committee concluded that all the documents were "fraudulent and spurious" and that no senator had ever accepted or been offered money by the Mexican government. The Hearst organization had received the forged documents from John Page, an American journalist in Mexico, and Miguel Avila, a Mexican-American who was at one time an employee of the Secret Service of the Mexican presidency. These men had also been the source of Sheffield's allegations against Beals and Gruening.[124]

Sheffield was also exercised about the activities of clergymen and other "uplifters" who visited Mexico and returned to the United States as advocates of the "wretched Calles administration." The ambassador suspected that some clergymen endorsed Mexico's anti-Catholic policies in the hope of safeguarding Protestant missions there, but he was concerned about the impact these clerics had in the United States. "They write articles for the religious magazines and papers which, by reason of the positions they hold, are extensively read and believed by thousands of readers who could not think that men of their standing would misstate the facts."[125]

There is no evidence that any of Sheffield's bêtes noires—Gruening, Beals, or Tannenbaum—were secretly in the pay of the Mexican government. Frances Toor declared in response to charges leveled against her in 1927 that her only income from the government was a modest subsidy for *Mexican Folkways* and her salary for teaching English in local schools; she wished that she received more.[126] The English classes taught by Toor and others did provide an official stipend for friendly Americans in the early and mid-1920s, and the courtesies extended to other travelers such as Tannenbaum and the members of Herring's seminars undoubtedly reinforced their already positive sentiments toward Mexico. Yet the recipients of these favors can hardly be considered agents of the Mexican government.

In light of his annoyance over American propagandists for Mexico, it is not surprising that the ambassador rejoiced over the appearance early in 1927 of a series of articles in the *Saturday Evening Post* by Isaac F. Marcossen that were critical of revolutionary Mexico and its government. Sheffield was convinced that Marcossen would "paint an unprejudiced and truthful picture" and that the articles would "carry the truth to an immense reading public."[127] Sheffield's enthusiasm about the Marcossen articles and his diatribes against pro-Mexican propaganda by Americans testify to his belief in the efficacy of such efforts.

In this period of strained relations between the governments of Mexico and the United States, political pilgrims provided an interpretation of Mexico that represented an alternative to the critical view espoused by many American diplomats, members of Congress, businessmen, and religious leaders. Not only did their political writings help defuse attacks on Mexico, but the contemporary belief in the capacity of revolution to effect psychological and aesthetic change led them to emphasize trends in Mexico that suggested realization of that belief. These trends, especially glorification of indigenous ways and popular culture and the mural renaissance, also evoked a favorable response from those who were apolitical, such as Edward Weston. The simultaneous travel to the

United States by Mexican artists and intellectuals meant that even Americans who stayed at home would receive a greater exposure to Mexican culture than ever before. Thus by 1927, political and cultural travelers had laid the groundwork for a new appreciation of Mexican art, history, and culture that would flourish in subsequent years.

CHAPTER 2

The Mexican Vogue at Its Peak
Cultural Relations, 1927–1935

Cultural interchange between Mexico and the United States reached its apogee in the years after 1927. Contemporaries frequently expressed the belief that Mexico was arousing unusual interest among Americans, an impression confirmed by the entries in the *Book Review Digest* for the years 1920–35. A count of the nonfiction titles listed in the index under the category "Mexico" showed that thirty-five such books were reviewed between 1920 and 1927. In the years 1928–35 the number increased to sixty-five (see Table 1). In 1933 the *New York Times* noted the phenomenon in a reference to "the present enormous vogue of things Mexican," adding: "It came into being at the height of our prosperity when people gave signs of being fed up with material comforts and turned, for a respite from the Machine Age, to primitive cultures. Mexico lay close at hand."[1] This explanation is accurate but incomplete. Despite its origins in an era of economic prosperity, the Mexican vogue attained its greatest strength in the Depression years of the early 1930s. It was rooted in cultural issues, but it would not have flowered without the marked improvement in diplomatic relations between the two countries that occurred in the late 1920s. In part, the more cordial relationship resulted from the skillful diplomacy of Dwight W. Morrow, who succeeded James R. Sheffield as ambassador in October 1927. In part, it reflected the waning of revolutionary momentum in Mexico during the same period. Mexico was no longer a destination for political pilgrims but became a mecca for cultural pilgrims who wished

Table 1.   Nonfiction Books on Mexico, 1920–1935

1920: 2	1928: 8
1921: 3	1929: 7
1922: 5	1930: 1
1923: 3	1931: 8
1924: 4	1932: 9
1925: 5	1933: 6
1926: 3	1934: 11
1927: 10	1935: 15
Total: 35	Total: 65

Source: Cumulative indexes, *Book Review Digest,* 1920–35. A count was made of books under the category Mexico and the subcategories Antiquities, Description and Travel, Foreign Relations, History, Politics and Government, Social Life and Customs, and under the category Mexico City. The years are those in which reviews appeared, not necessarily those in which the books were published.

to peer at ancient monuments and the works of contemporary muralists and to imbibe the atmosphere of authenticity and harmony that pervaded Mexico's Indian communities. During this same period Mexican artists, performers, and other cultural emigrants found a warmer welcome than ever before in the United States. These Mexicans encountered a friendly reception even though the border was closed to most of their compatriots and many of those within the United States were encouraged to leave during the Great Depression.

By the late 1920s it seemed less likely than ever that Mexico's revolutionary regime was bent on radical change. In 1928 the constitution was amended to allow Alvaro Obregón to seek a second presidential term. He was elected but was assassinated just sixteen days later, on July 17, 1928. President Calles, who was due to step down in November, moved quickly to fill the political vacuum created by the death of Obregón. Emilio Portes Gil was installed as president to succeed Calles, but the latter remained a powerful influence. In 1929 Calles brought together the supporters of the revolution in a new political party, the Partido Nacional Revolucionario, which supported Pascual Ortiz Rubio for a term beginning February 5, 1930. Ortiz Rubio won the election by a landslide, defeating José Vasconcelos, the former secretary of education,

who complained bitterly that official violence and fraud had deprived
him of victory. Ortiz Rubio soon clashed with Calles, however, and resigned in 1932. He was succeeded by Abelardo Rodríguez, who served
out the remainder of the presidential term.

The governments of these years did not disavow the revolutionary
initiatives of the past or spurn the constitution of 1917, but by 1930
there was little interest in implementing the redistributive features of
that document. Portes Gil stepped up land distribution during his year in
office, but doubts about the results to date, together with unsettled conditions at the start of the Depression, nearly halted agrarian reform in
1930. On the day of his inauguration, Ortiz Rubio, who had just survived an assassination attempt by a young Vasconcelista, suggested that
the revolution was over, telling American reporters that the "Mexican
social movement is a consummated fact. It remains only to develop
Mexico as a modern state to enable Mexico to take her proper place
among the civilized countries of the world."[2]

Diplomatic relations between the United States and Mexico improved, and the always remote threat of armed intervention on behalf of
American investors had apparently disappeared. An indication of the
new concord was the arrival in Mexico City of twenty-five hundred
American businessmen and political leaders to attend the inauguration
of Ortiz Rubio in 1930. *Excelsior* declared that "the influx of American
visitors to attend the inauguration . . . reached proportions . . . surpass-
ing any similar invasion of visitors from north of the Río Grande in
recent years and equaling the large number of excursionists who used to
be a common sight on the streets of Mexico City during the pre-1910
period."[3]

The presence of so many American visitors at the inauguration reflected not only improved relations between the two governments but
also an ongoing Mexican campaign to revive the tourist industry. Starting in 1928, American tourists were no longer required to present pass-
ports to enter Mexico but were allowed entry with tourist cards valid for
six months. Customs officials were instructed to expedite examination
of tourists' luggage. The growing importance of this sector is shown by
the convening of Mexico's first national congress of tourism in April
1930 and by the creation of the National Commission of Tourism the
same year.[4]

These efforts bore fruit in the arrival of increasing numbers of visitors, both individual travelers and "excursionists" such as the railway men who descended on Mexico City in two large trains for the 1929 convention of the American Association of Railroad Superintendents and the 150 Rotarians who arrived the next day.[5] Such excursions became so numerous that one observer was moved to remark the same year: "As a result of them more Mexicans have had the privilege of viewing Anglo-Saxons in herd formation than at any time since General Winfield Scott's lamented invasion. . . . The Mexican highways and byways now know the Americano in his glory almost as well as a county seat that has entertained an Elks' State convention."[6]

Mexico was promoted in the United States as a safe yet unspoiled destination for travelers who would enjoy its quaintness, natural beauty, and artistic treasures. In a 1932 article Katharine Dos Passos, wife of the novelist, pointed out: "A trip to Mexico is more exciting than a trip to Europe, because the country is not standardized or touristed, and even the most inexperienced traveler makes his own discoveries."[7] The relatively low cost of travel to Mexico probably contributed to increased tourism during the early years of the Depression. In 1930 expenditures by American travelers to Mexico totaled $38 million, more than three times the amount spent in 1923; this sum represented 8.2 percent of all American expenditures on foreign travel, or nearly twice the 1923 figure. By 1933 the amount spent on Mexican travel had fallen to $33 million, but this figure represented 16.7 percent of the sum spent on foreign travel.[8]

If American Rotarians found a welcome in Mexico during these years, radicals, both foreign and domestic, received less gentle treatment from the government. Communist belligerence toward Portes Gil in accordance with Comintern opposition to bourgeois regimes led to a crackdown beginning in December 1929; party headquarters were raided, a dozen foreign communists were deported, and several Mexican communists were jailed. When communists in Washington, Buenos Aires, and Rio de Janeiro protested these actions by picketing Mexican embassies in the three cities, Mexico reacted by severing diplomatic relations with the Soviet Union on January 23, 1930, on the grounds that it had been responsible for the demonstrations. Another roundup of communists occurred after the assassination attempt against Ortiz Rubio. Tina Modotti, who had formed close ties with the Mexican left, was jailed for ten days and deported on February 22, 1930.[9]

Carleton Beals also fell afoul of the federal authorities. On February

14, 1930, he was arrested and held for several hours before being released into the custody of the American military attaché. Ortiz Rubio later conveyed his apologies to Beals, who attributed his arrest to General Eulogio Ortiz, federal commander in Mexico City, about whom Beals had made disparaging remarks in a recent *New Republic* article. Beals had also criticized the Mexican government in private letters which had been intercepted by the authorities.[10]

In view of these trends it is not surprising that a contributor to the *New Masses* labeled Ortiz Rubio "a conservative of the most pronounced type" during the presidential campaign of 1929 and declared that "Reaction" was "in full swing" in Mexico. Beals echoed the latter sentiment in a 1931 article for the *New Republic*. He concluded that Mexico had washed its hands of the revolution after 1926: "However altered the social structure of Mexico may be, it is an undeniable fact that the country is repudiating Indianism, communal landholding and proletarian doctrine in favor of the old economic doctrines of Europe and Díaz."[11]

Ernest Gruening, who also remained interested in Mexican affairs, was less pessimistic than Beals, though he too criticized many aspects of contemporary society in *Mexico and Its Heritage*, which was favorably received upon its publication in 1928. The historian H. I. Priestley, for example, called it "the most important and comprehensive study of Mexico that has been given to the English-speaking public for many years." In his encyclopedic survey Gruening had harsh words for the record of the Catholic church and was concerned about the persistence of personalism, corruption, and militarism, but he felt that the Calles administration had several accomplishments to its credit: "it has turned the corner in agrarian reform and laid the basis for the economic emancipation of 'the twelve million who live on the fringe of civilization,' as Calles expressed it."[12]

Beals thought that Gruening's discussion of state and local politics was outstanding. "The result is a terrific indictment of Mexican state political practices: a sordid picture of corruption, imposition, brutal injustice, military arrogance." Beals also praised the sections dealing with the church, but Frank Tannenbaum felt that they revealed an anti-Catholic bias. The sections on the church also drew the ire of the Mexican writer Carlos Pereyra, who accused Gruening of ignorance and willful distortion.[13]

In subsequent writings about Mexico Gruening continued to condemn militarism and in 1929 suggested that the army be abolished or drastically reduced. By September 1929 he too believed that the revolution was over, but in contrast to Beals, he stressed positive developments: the destruction of the feudal land system, rapprochement with the United States, the end of the church-state conflict, and Calles's apparent surrender of power after Obregón's death. Thus he thought that "a new era of peace, progress, and prosperity" was at hand.[14]

Like Beals and Gruening, Frank Tannenbaum continued his association with Mexico during this period, visiting the country in 1931 and 1933. On the latter occasion he was lionized by Mexican officials and was granted an hour-long interview with former president Calles.[15] Tannenbaum's new celebrity in Mexico was occasioned by publication of two major studies, The Mexican Agrarian Revolution (1929) and Peace by Revolution: An Interpretation (1933). The former, his doctoral dissertation for the Brookings Institution, was a detailed analysis of land tenure in Mexico and the impact of the constitution and subsequent legislation on landholding patterns. The latter was a broader survey which viewed the revolution as a positive development for Mexico but acknowledged its limited achievements in such areas as agrarian reform: "The Mexican Revolution . . . has not to date recognized the rights of the Mexican peon, Indian, or landless peasant to land except under certain specified limitations." He also admitted that "for the moment the labor movement in Mexico and even the leadership has declined, as so often everything seems to decline in Mexico, sacrificed to political ends and personal fortune."[16] Most reviewers were enthusiastic about the volume, and historian J. Fred Rippy called it "a brilliant attempt at synthesis."[17] Beals, however, was critical of some aspects of the book; he considered "inexcusable" Tannenbaum's failure to emphasize the fact that the revolution had reached its maximum expression in 1926 and that since then the leadership had betrayed popular aspirations.[18]

Ironically, during these years Beals was the subject of attacks by José Vasconcelos, who accused the American journalist of publishing an account of the 1929 presidential election that deliberately ignored the fraud and violence directed against his followers. In 1931 an unsigned article in a periodical published by Vasconcelos asserted that it was because of writers like Beals that Calles had enjoyed high esteem abroad. Now Beals was expressing the same view that Vasconcelistas had espoused all along: that Calles had betrayed the revolution. Beals was unimpressed by the attacks of Vasconcelos, who he said had an "inflated ego" and overestimated his popularity in Mexico.[19]

The diminution of revolutionary fervor and the improvement of relations with the United States lessened Mexico's appeal to political pilgrims. Veteran political observers such as Beals and Tannenbaum retained and deepened their Mexican ties, but culture now became the primary magnet for artists and intellectuals who visited Mexico. Mexico had always attracted some cultural pilgrims, and several of them remained devoted to Mexico, encouraging the interest of others by their example.

Katherine Anne Porter returned to Mexico for a long stay in 1930 during which she hoped to finish a novel, but she found herself unable to accomplish all that she had planned. At first she stayed with Dorothy Day, the future Catholic radical, who was living with her small daughter in a rented house in Xochimilco. Later she met Eugene Dove Pressly, whom she would eventually marry, and set up housekeeping with him and Mary Louis Doherty, a longtime American resident, in a large house in the suburb of Mixcoac. Here she could indulge her fondness for cooking and gardening as well as tend a brood of animals that included dogs, cats, and an assortment of fowl. These distractions, coupled with her natural conviviality, impeded progress on the novel, but she did produce several shorter pieces, such as the essay "Leaving the Petate," a perceptive analysis of cultural change, which was published in 1931, and an early version of the story "Hacienda," which appeared in the *Virginia Quarterly Review* in 1932. The latter was the result of a visit to the Hacienda Tetlapayac, about sixty-five miles southwest of Mexico City, where Sergei Eisenstein was filming a segment of his controversial motion picture *Que Viva México!* [20]

Witter Bynner also retained his interest in Mexico. In 1929 he published a collection of poems, *Indian Earth*, which contained numerous short poems inspired by his visits to Mexico in 1923 and 1925. He made his third trip late in 1931 with his friend Robert Hunt. They spent some time in newly fashionable Taxco, but Bynner preferred Chapala. Even though it was only two hours by car from Guadalajara, Bynner wrote, "Chapala survives without a single foreigner living there and, despite its hotels and shabby mansions, continues to be primitive and feel remote." He, too, had several opportunities to observe Eisenstein at work. Willard (Spud) Johnson, Bynner's companion of 1923, also returned to Mexico, traveling in 1932 with Mabel Dodge Luhan and her husband, Tony. While Johnson was visiting Oaxaca, he ran into several friends from New Mexico. "Such a tiny globe," he mused.[21]

Frances Toor continued to publish *Mexican Folkways*, having expanded the magazine on the advice of Herbert Croly and secured additional funding from Dorothy Straight Elmhirst. After being forced to suspend publication in 1931, Toor revived the magazine in 1932–33 with the hope of renewed financial support from the Mexican government and private sources in the United States, but it proved to be short-lived. In 1930 she toured California, giving lectures on Mexican art and culture in Berkeley, Oakland, and other cities.[22]

Anita Brenner divided her time between Mexico and the United States. In 1928 she took charge of a new department on Latin American life and culture for the *Nation*, and in 1929 she published *Idols behind Altars*, a study of Mexican art and culture with elements of autobiography and photographs by Edward Weston. The writer Waldo Frank called the book "a remarkable synthesis, in personal form" that would be enjoyed most by those like himself who had firsthand experience of Mexico's arts and crafts. Eisenstein used the book as a "spiritual scenario" while filming *Que Viva México*! Brenner had also enrolled as a graduate student in anthropology at Columbia University and received her doctorate in 1930. Her dissertation, written under the direction of Franz Boas, was an analysis of the pottery of ancient Culhuacán.[23]

The writings of Brenner, Toor, and other veteran admirers of Mexican culture helped to disseminate information about Mexico in the United States and contributed to the Mexican "vogue" and the influx of cultural pilgrims. But other forces specific to the years 1927–35 were also at work. Prominent among these were the cultural diplomacy of Ambassador Morrow and his wife, Elizabeth Cutter Morrow; the impact of the Great Depression in sharpening the image of Mexico as a society primitive in many ways yet more authentic and soul-satisfying than the highly industrialized United States; and the establishment in the United States of formal programs to develop cultural relations with Mexico.

The emergence of Mexico as a destination for cultural pilgrims from the United States owed much to the efforts of Ambassador Morrow and his wife. An Amherst classmate of President Coolidge and a partner in J. P. Morgan and Company at the time of his appointment, Morrow proved to be more conciliatory and more respectful of Mexican sovereignty than Sheffield. Accordingly, during his three years as ambassador, long-standing disputes over petroleum and land were settled amicably, and Morrow helped bring about a resolution of the bitter church-state conflict in 1929. Whatever the ultimate verdict on his still controversial mission to Mexico, Morrow evinced a strong interest in Mexican history and culture, which he effectively promoted in the United States. In part Morrow's cultural diplomacy can be seen as furthering his objective of maintaining amicable diplomatic and economic relations between the two countries, but there is no reason to doubt the sincerity of his interest. Even before his departure for Mexico, he was described as being "deeply interested in the problems of education and cultural cooperation between the United States and other countries."[24] Morrow's interest in Mexico was also reflected in his acquisition of books and documents on Mexican history, including Gruening's *Mexico and Its Heritage*. He wrote to Gruening in 1929, praising the volume as well as a recent article by Gruening in the *Nation*. Gruening in turn hailed Morrow's achievements in effecting an entente cordiale between the United States and Mexico.[25] Morrow also reached out to another of Sheffield's bêtes noires, Carleton Beals, who was invited to tea at the embassy.[26]

Soon after arriving in Mexico in 1927, Morrow accepted President Calles's invitation to accompany him on a rail tour of northern Mexico. Morrow's acceptance was criticized because the trip took place just after the execution of a Jesuit priest, Father Miguel Pro Juárez, and three associates for alleged complicity in an assassination attempt against Obregón on November 13. The trip was well publicized in the United States because of the presence of humorist Will Rogers, who arrived in Mexico on December 1 and immediately transferred to the presidential train. Rogers described his Mexican adventures in a series of articles in the *Saturday Evening Post* which were a marked contrast to the Marcossen articles of the previous year. Rogers informed readers that he had not come to Mexico with an open mind. He had come with "No mind at all" and wished to "enjoy the people and the Country and get some Real Chili con Carne and Tamales, see the Mexican Ropers—the best in the World—see the Señoritas dance, and mebbe, if fortunate, see 'em shoot a Presidential Candidate." Despite his occasional barbs, Rogers found much to praise in Mexico. He called Calles "a regular big two-fisted He Man" with "a corking sense of humor" and defended Mexico's right to regulate foreign investment.[27] "They got to passing laws, what they could do with their own lands and their own Natural resources, and here they wasent asking us anything about em," he observed ironically. "Can you imagine the nerve of some little upstart Nation telling an

American Oil Millionaire that he could dig Oil only fifty years more before taking out another lease."[28]

After the week-long junket with Calles, Rogers remained in Mexico City as the guest of Ambassador Morrow and was on hand to greet another celebrated visitor, Charles A. Lindbergh. Morrow had known Lindbergh in the United States and had proposed that he make a Latin American flight before leaving for Mexico. According to *Excelsior*, the Mexican capital was "electrified" in anticipation of Lindbergh's flight, and more than one hundred thousand persons, including President Calles, awaited his arrival at Balbuena Field. The *Spirit of St. Louis* arrived on December 14, about three hours later than expected, to a delirious reception.[29]

Lindbergh spent a busy two weeks in Mexico. He introduced Calles and Obregón to flying, taking each one up in a Fairchild monoplane. He attended a bullfight, disappointing animal lovers in both countries. He formally inaugurated the Lincoln Library, the repository for the three thousand English-language volumes collected by Frank Tannenbaum and the Friends of Mexico Committee. He also met his future wife, Anne Spencer Morrow, the ambassador's daughter, whom he married in 1929.[30]

Reporting on his experiences in a series of newspaper articles, Lindbergh repeatedly spoke of the beautiful and interesting sights of Mexico and of the expressions of goodwill toward the United States he had heard. "My stay has been one of my pleasantest experiences, and I hope that the flight has been of some value in bringing about a better feeling between the people of Mexico and my own country," he wrote upon departing for Guatemala on December 28 on the first leg of a tour of Central America and the Caribbean. Calles in turn proclaimed the visit to be evidence of the goodwill of the American people toward Mexico.[31]

Morrow was on hand in Washington the following June to greet Emilio Carranza, a young Mexican aviator who flew to the United States in a gesture of reciprocity after Lindbergh's flight. Carranza, who had previously flown from San Diego to Mexico City in a record 18.5 hours, was forced on this occasion to land in North Carolina but was warmly received in New York and Washington, where President Coolidge hosted a luncheon in his honor. Shortly after he took off from Long Island's Mitchell Field on his return journey, a bolt of lightning destroyed his plane, sending the pilot to his death.[32]

Ambassador Morrow's wife, Elizabeth Cutter Morrow, played an equally important role in encouraging cultural relations between the two countries. Although she had accompanied her husband to Mexico with "prejudice & condescension" in her heart, "prepared to be the noble self-sacrificing wife of the movies," she was quickly captivated by the beauty and charm of Mexico City and immediately began to learn Spanish.[33] During her three years in Mexico she developed contacts with a wide range of artists and intellectuals and acquired a collection of folk art as well as works by contemporary painters. She also wrote verse and magazine articles on Mexican subjects for American readers and in 1930 published a book for children called *The Painted Pig*, which dealt with a Mexican toymaker.

Shortly after arriving in Mexico, Elizabeth Morrow visited Cuernavaca and was much taken with the narrow cobbled streets, red roofs, and old churches of the city. In 1928 the Morrows purchased a property there from Frederick W. Davis and converted it into a weekend retreat called Casa Mañana. Davis supervised the plans for the adobe house, which was furnished exclusively with Mexican objects. The Morrows also created a secret garden on the property; at one end was a covered loggia on which was painted a panoramic fresco of Cuernavaca which Mrs. Morrow pronounced "perfectly enchanting."[34]

In Cuernavaca the Morrows entertained numerous American and Mexican visitors. Among the latter was Diego Rivera, who drank innumerable cups of tea while Mrs. Morrow tried to converse, half in English, half in Spanish. She found him "an interesting man, looking fat, good-natured, simple, sympathetic."[35] In December 1929 the Morrows commissioned Rivera to do a series of frescoes on the rear wall of the Cortés Palace in Cuernavaca, for which the artist received $12,000. It took nearly a year to complete the murals, during which time Rivera and his new wife, the painter Frida Kahlo, stayed in the Morrows' house while they were away.[36] After Mrs. Morrow returned to Cuernavaca the following September, she watched Rivera at work on the murals, which she declared to be "very fine," and was happy that they were to be finished before her final departure from Mexico. Although the ambassador had hoped that his sponsorship of the murals would remain confidential, the secret was soon out. Communists criticized Rivera, who had recently been expelled from the party, for accepting a commission from a symbol of American capitalism while others were outraged by the artist's unflattering portrayal of the Spanish conquerors and the Catholic church.[37]

The artist who painted the fresco in Casa Mañana was another recent arrival to Mexico, René d'Harnoncourt, who became a good friend of the Morrows and would play an important role in advancing the cause of Mexican art in the United States. Born in Vienna in 1901, Harnoncourt was trained as a chemist but showed an interest in art even as a youngster. He left Vienna after his family suffered financial reverses and arrived in Mexico in January 1926 nearly penniless and knowing neither Spanish nor English.[38]

Harnoncourt's artistic talents enabled him to survive in Mexico by painting lampshades and watercolors of bullfights for tourists and collecting antiques on behalf of a wealthy American. He was employed in a similar capacity by Fred Davis when the latter decided to devote his shop entirely to Mexican silver, textiles, and folk art. Harnoncourt thus had an opportunity to travel around the country, where his six-foot six inch stature made him conspicuous. Edward Weston, who was with him in Pátzcuaro, described the reaction: "The small-statured Indians looked up, stretching their necks as though René might be a New York skyscraper,—first amazed, then convulsed."[39]

Harnoncourt's travels in Mexico also gave him inspiration for his own art. He published two collections of drawings portraying scenes of daily life and culture in Mexico. In the introduction to *Mexicana: A Book of Pictures* (1931), he stated: "The pictures . . . in this book are records of things seen and heard in market places and along the highways. Unimportant as such small incidents may seem in themselves, they are significant as the truest and most spontaneous expression of the people."[40] Harnoncourt also did a series of brightly colored drawings to illustrate Elizabeth Morrow's text for *The Painted Pig*. A reviewer in the *New York Times* remarked: "Only a lover of Mexico and a lover of toys could have drawn these pictures and so filled them with the atmosphere of the country and the spirit of play."[41]

Another friend of the Morrows who made an even greater commitment to Mexican art and culture than Harnoncourt was William Spratling. Born in New York in 1900, the son of an Alabamian, he studied architecture at Auburn University, where he was also an instructor from 1919 to 1921. He then accepted an appointment at Tulane University, becoming acquainted with William Faulkner and other writers in New

Orleans as well as with Frans Blom, head of the Middle American Research Department at Tulane.

Spratling credited Blom for making possible his first trip to Mexico, which took place in the summer of 1926 and resulted in two articles published in the *Architectural Forum* in 1927. During this visit he met Harnoncourt, Frances Toor, Diego Rivera, and other Mexican artists. After returning to Mexico in the summers of 1927 and 1928, Spratling decided to leave Tulane and to settle in Mexico temporarily. He had received a $200 advance from the firm of Cape & Smith for a book on Mexico, *Little Mexico* (1932), and could count on additional income from newspaper and magazine articles.[42]

Soon after arriving in Mexico for what turned out to be a permanent stay, Spratling became acquainted with the Morrows. They visited him in Taxco, where he had acquired "a tiny house set in a triangular garden, shielded from the street by coffee plants and plumbago vines," and a deer, a green parrot, and a duck to keep him company.[43] They commissioned him to purchase pottery on their behalf and bought drawings he made of their Cuernavaca house. In addition, Spratling was engaged to design and illustrate a privately printed volume on the house, which appeared in 1932 with the title *Casa Mañana*. For Spratling the sums paid to him by the Morrows were an important source of income, as he acknowledged in thanking Mrs. Morrow profusely for an advance payment for his work on the Cuernavaca volume. The payment, he said, "came at a time when I simply couldnt see daylight financially in any direction."[44]

In his autobiography Spratling said that the ambassador had suggested to him the revival of silver craftsmanship in Taxco, a successful project that would occupy him for the rest of his life. Spratling's house became a magnet for American visitors to Mexico, such as writer Susan Smith, the friend of Beals and Dos Passos. Spratling also designed a Taxco house for Moisés Sáenz and became a member of the Asociación de Amigos de Taxco, which was founded to encourage tourism and to preserve the city's historical and artistic monuments.

Beals also visited Spratling on occasion, recalling that when the latter first settled in Taxco he had been virtually the only American there, but within a few years "the picturesque place became the haunt of Bohemian American artists and literati." In 1931 Witter Bynner found Taxco to be "beautiful beyond description, with cobblestoned lanes leading always up and up into a hundred little heavens, all at strange angles, and the huge ornate church standing in the center like the giant parent of eight other smaller churches." But the fastidious poet was put off by the American households in Taxco, "all semi-crazy and completely drunken." He reported to Idella Purnell that he felt no inclination to do any work in Taxco, where everything, even bathing, was put off. Elizabeth Prall Anderson, the former wife of writer Sherwood Anderson, who settled in Taxco in 1931, recalled by contrast that the artists and writers she knew there were all hardworking: "Taxco was no sleepy little town in the sun; an air of vitality and purpose permeated everything."[45]

Appreciation of Mexico's peasant culture, which was often equated with its indigenous heritage, had always existed to some extent among American artists and intellectuals who visited the country in the early 1920s. Partly because of the influence of the Morrows and their circle, it became even more prominent in the latter part of the decade as Mexico's political appeal receded. This heightened appreciation can also be attributed to Mexico's Indianist programs and to reports of archaeological marvels being unveiled there as well as to revival of interest in indigenous civilizations of the United States (see Chapter 3). Mexico's peasant culture seemed even more appealing as the Great Depression confirmed the suspicion of American intellectuals that life in the United States was not only barren spiritually and aesthetically but rested on a shaky economic base as well. One result of this state of mind, according to Richard H. Pells, was a burgeoning interest in peasant communities, such as those in Mexico, which seemed to embody an integrity and authenticity that no longer existed in the United States.[46] Pells cites Waldo Frank and Stuart Chase as exponents of this point of view.

Frank traveled to Mexico for the first time in June 1929 to lecture at the Summer School of the National University. He had already attracted attention in Mexico because of his books *Our America* (1919) and *Virgin Spain* (1926), and José Juan Tablada had expressed gratitude for his praise of Mexican culture as early as 1921. While in Spain in 1924, Frank became acquainted with Alfonso Reyes, Mexico's ambassador in Madrid; Reyes took with him to Mexico a message from Frank to Mexican writers in which he called for an intellectual union among writers of the Americas to fight "materialism, imperialism [and] the sterile pragmatism of the modern world" and to create a new "spiritual culture."

Later Frank began a correspondence with Mariano Azuela, for whose novel *Los de abajo* he had "profound admiration."[47]

In his memoirs Frank recalled some misadventures during his month-long stay in Mexico—an attack of illness following a meal at a famous restaurant with Rivera and an apparent insult from Moisés Sáenz—but his lectures were very well received. More than two hundred persons filled the hall in which he gave his first lecture at the university, and about one thousand listened to him via loudspeakers in the courtyard outside. When he spoke about the materialism and competitiveness of life in the United States and the aggressiveness of American women, he confirmed the beliefs of many Mexicans. "What is tragic," the chronicler Alfonso Taracena observed, "is that we too are being contaminated because of proximity to those people."[48] To Americans attending a seminar organized by Hubert C. Herring, Frank spoke on the problem of the relations between the two Americas, suggesting that Mexico and all of Spanish America were in a state of chaos out of which new life might emerge. He also expressed concern that the "dominating, expanding economic organization" of the United States was interfering with the region's spiritual and cultural development.[49]

Because of Mexico's "merger" of Indian and Spaniard, Frank believed that it had achieved "that connection with both self and soil without which man must perish" yet which the Protestant culture of the United States denied.[50] As he moved toward communism, he saw in the Indo-Hispanic tradition of Mexico and Latin America a basis for societies in which each person would be fully integrated yet develop his or her personality: "The Spaniard has a sense of the whole which needs only to be transported from its false Christian symbols to prepare for a true communism. . . . And the great Indian cultures have always had communistic roots; have always preserved that sense of the individual as a *social integer*, which we must achieve in North America, before we can think of overcoming the false individualism that is the essence of our capitalistic order."[51]

If Frank became the darling of Latin American intellectuals because of his strictures against American capitalism, Stuart Chase had a greater impact in the United States because of his *Mexico: A Study of Two Americas* (1931), which was a selection of the Literary Guild and a best-seller for six months. Chase, a well-known economist, spent five months in Mexico in 1930, having made the journey at the instigation of painter

George Biddle. He was a guest in William Spratling's house in Taxco and married his second wife, Marion, there.

Chase's book, which Diego Rivera illustrated, is a lively survey of Mexico, which the author found to be "more remote and strange" than any other country he had visited. The governing concept of the book is a comparison between the "machine-made" civilization of the United States, as exemplified by Middletown, the city analyzed in the recent sociological treatise by Robert and Helen Lynd, and Indian Mexico as exemplified by Tepoztlán, a village in Morelos. Chase found life in villages like Tepoztlán to be more attractive than in Middletown in several respects. Mexican villagers, who were self-sufficient and "wantless," had greater economic security than their American counterparts, who had to worry about mortgages and installment payments. Chase also believed that Mexican villagers had more fun than Middletown residents. "They take their fun as they take their food, part and parcel of their organic life."[52] Chase recognized that Tepoztlán was no rustic utopia and that it would benefit from some of the products of industrial civilization, such as scientific agriculture, electricity, and a telegraph line, but many readers in Depression-racked America probably ignored his reservations, as did the advertising copywriter who described Tepoztlán as a place where "the whole population plays one day in three the year round" and "there is no unemployment, no dole, no breadlines."[53]

A reviewer in the *New Masses*, of which Chase had once been an editor, predictably dismissed the book as "a Liberal bourgeois hodge-podge of journalistic bunk."[54] In general, however, it received favorable reviews from Beals, Gruening, and others, though Elizabeth Cutter Morrow was dubious about the pleasures of life without machines, especially for women. She remembered the incessant labor of Indian women in Mexico: grinding corn, washing clothes in stony streams, carrying babies, wood, or water.[55] Several critics wondered whether Tepoztlán could accept the good parts of urban civilization while rejecting the bad. In the *Spectator* of London, Aldous Huxley asserted that the introduction of these amenities would cause Mexico's Indian communities to lose what was most attractive about their way of life. Accepting Chase's implicit message, he advised industrial societies to emulate the "wholeness" of the "primitive" man, who is "trained in all the skills of the community [and] is able to fend for himself in all circumstances."[56]

Beals's *Mexican Maze*, which appeared shortly before Chase's book and was also illustrated by Rivera, attracted less attention, though it was the June 1931 selection of the Book League of America. It was broader in scope than the Chase volume and informed by the author's long Mexican experience, yet it addressed similar questions. Beals depicted the poverty-stricken inhabitant of Milpa Alta as far happier than the New York clerk who followed his eight hours at the office with evenings of pleasure unrelated to his daily work. "The American lives in compartments of uncorrelated action," Beals wrote. "The Mexican peasant's life is one texture. Work is pleasure; and pleasure is work. The day, for him, is woven into a unity, satisfying in its completeness." Beals predicted that industrialism would spread across the border from the United States, but he suggested that Mexican culture was strong enough to survive this new conquest. "The patience of the Mexican Indian is eternal. His very lack of aggressiveness will save him. The humble will conquer the earth—for only the strong can be humble."[57]

Mary Austin, who visited Mexico in 1930, was one of many who echoed the views of Frank, Chase, and Beals in her own writing. In a 1931 article she claimed that the mestizo population of both Old and New Mexico evinced traits stemming from a legacy of collectivism and communism dating to preconquest cultures. Thus, "the children of communism have wantlessness for their inheritance." In her autobiography, published the following year, she recalled that she had wept when she saw Rivera's murals at the Secretariat of Education, for in them she found "the things I had so long missed from American life; the thing every woman misses from American life; tenderness, the strength of tenderness, compassion, surrender."[58]

The writings of Chase, Beals, and others therefore helped to create the "vogue of things Mexican" by shaping their readers' conception of Mexico and encouraging travel to that country. Before going to Mexico in 1932, the painter Marsden Hartley was "thoroughly converted to Mexico by reading a remarkably fine & beautiful book called 'Mexico Maze' [sic] by Carleton Beals."[59] Another Mexican traveler, historian Lesley Byrd Simpson, later recalled the "shoals" of American refugees from the Depression who headed for Mexico, "the New Land of Promise," under the influence of Chase's book. "Painters, writers, and scholars swarmed in to breathe in the invigorating air."[60] Even a character in a short story by Edna Ferber, in defending her knowledge of Mexico, told her husband: "I know more about it than you do. I've been reading Gruening and Stuart Chase and Beals and all of them." In California Edward Weston also read the books by Beals and Chase and wondered whether he might earn some cash by publishing his Mexican journal. Not only was he in the limelight as a photographer, but "Mexico is on everyone's lips,—Mexico and her artists."[61]

To be sure, there were occasional expressions of dissent from the prevailing image of Mexico, especially from those on the far left. Joseph Freeman, a young communist who spent six months in Mexico in 1929, considered the writings of Chase and the others to be well-intentioned but harmful distortions of the brutal reality of contemporary Mexico. Moreover, by romanticizing the poverty, ignorance, and superstitions of the Mexican masses, these "bourgeois" writers were playing into the hands of the imperialists who exploited Mexico. They could, however, be sure of financial success: "If like Stuart Chase, William Spratling, Anita Brenner and a dozen others you will sing lyrical paeans of praise about the skies and the golden sunlight and the magic mountain and the fiestas and the pulque and the paintings and keep your mouth shut about the white terror, the brutal exploitation of the 'noble and happy' Indians, the systematic slaughter of the peasants robbed of their land, the predatory role of American capital which owns and runs Mexico— then yours is the world and everything that's in it, and what is more you'll be a successful writer my son."[62]

Both Marsden Hartley and Lesley Byrd Simpson traveled to Mexico as fellows of the Guggenheim Foundation, their journeys made possible by a special program to promote cultural relations between the United States and Latin America. By the early 1930s several institutions, in both Mexico and the United States, were working toward this end. In Mexico City the Summer School of the National University continued to draw teachers of Spanish from the United States. Over two hundred students, mainly women, attended the 1928 session and heard a variety of Mexican, European, and American lecturers, including sociologist Edward A. Ross of the University of Wisconsin and author of *The Social Revolution in Mexico* (1923), an ambivalent assessment based on an earlier visit. In 1930, when approximately 250 students were in attendance, the director of the Summer School, Julio Jiménez Rueda, declared that university diplomacy had become much more important than traditional diplomacy. "Professors and students from different countries who discuss together the problems that affect their peoples collaborate more effectively in the maintenance of peace than all the pacts that governments may conclude."[63] In 1932 a summer school was established at the University of Guadalajara, with Idella Purnell as director.[64]

In the United States the Friends of the Mexicans continued to hold their annual conference at Pomona College, drawing five hundred registrants in 1928. By that time Pomona was sending students to the Summer School in Mexico City, and Mexicans were attending the summer school of the California college. Pomona and the Claremont Colleges also sponsored the Inter-America Institute "for the development of mutually intelligent relations between American peoples." The institute held a three-day conference on Mexico in February 1928 at which economist Ramón Beteta and educator Andrés Osuna were among the speakers, and Frank Tannenbaum gave a series of lectures under its auspices the following December.[65]

The seminars organized by Hubert Herring were also prominent in the effort to promote cultural understanding between Mexico and the United States. In July 1928 Herring led his third group of Americans to Mexico; the eighty-two participants in this seminar spent three weeks addressing such issues as the agrarian situation, labor, and the church. In October of the same year Herring moved to establish the seminars on a permanent footing by organizing the Committee on Cultural Relations with Latin America, which had three general goals: "to assist in the spread of accurate information concerning the Latin-American peoples; to increase appreciation of the cultures of Latin America; and to provide means for bringing representative citizens of the United States into sympathetic contact with the life of Central and South America."[66] Among the initial members, besides Herring, were several who had had personal experience in Mexico, such as Frank Tannenbaum, Herbert Croly, and John Dewey, who became honorary chairman.

As its first step the committee assumed responsibility for the Mexican seminars, which were to be held every summer. More than 90 persons participated in the 1929 seminar, which met from July 14 to August 2 and featured excursions to Teotihuacán, Cuernavaca, and Puebla as well as talks by Mexican and American intellectuals. The participants also had an opportunity to take part in roundtable discussions in various fields. The following year 189 persons took part in the seminar.[67]

The "root idea and purpose" of the seminar, Herring wrote, was "to speed along that interchange of cultures which enriches all. We believe that the United States and Mexico will each be enriched through larger understanding of each other's literature and religion and art and racial genius." Herring's emphasis on the expansion of cultural relations underscores the lessening of revolutionary momentum in Mexico and of diplomatic conflict with the United States. He realized that seminar participants could gain only a superficial knowledge of Mexico in a few weeks and that they might be "liberally loaded with all sorts of propaganda," as had occurred with the first seminar in 1926. Nevertheless, he was convinced of the value of the seminars as a vehicle for introducing Americans to Mexican society and culture and for stimulating in them a desire to expand their knowledge in the future. He especially sought as seminar participants those who were in a position to influence others through speaking and writing.[68]

In addition to conducting the Mexican seminars, the committee launched a Caribbean seminar in 1931. By 1932 the committee had expanded its activities in other ways: it had purchased a house in Taxco, brought Moisés Sáenz to the United States for a fifteen-city speaking tour, organized local chapters of former seminar participants, and published *The Genius of Mexico* (1931), a collection of lectures delivered at the 1930 seminar. According to Herring, the cost of the committee's program for 1931 totaled approximately $38,000. Of this sum, $32,000 came from members and $6,500 from contributors, with Dorothy Straight Elmhirst providing the largest amount.[69] Although the onset of the Depression brought financial difficulties, the Mexican seminars continued to be held until 1941.

Cultural relations with Latin America were also advanced by the John Simon Guggenheim Memorial Foundation, which financed the Mexican sojourns of Marsden Hartley, Lesley Byrd Simpson, and other Americans. In 1929 the foundation announced the establishment of Latin American Exchange Fellowships, to be open to citizens of the United States, Mexico, and six South American republics. The fellowships were to be financed by a $1 million addition to the endowment of the foundation by Simon Guggenheim. In his letter establishing the fellowships, Guggenheim observed that though he and his brothers had long been engaged in commerce with Latin America and knew that its economic relations with the United States were close, "a similar commerce of things of the mind, of spiritual values, is yet to be accomplished." He hoped that cultural relations would be furthered by assistance to worthy scholars and artists so that they might devote themselves to research and creative work in the freest possible condition. Guggenheim denied any nationalistic or propagandistic intent in establishing the fellowships: "we desire only that scholars and artists from the American republics should meet and learn and teach what to them is Truth. For better understanding among the citizens of the American republics nothing is needed but more knowledge—a knowledge of the other's culture that yields nothing in zeal for one's own."[70] Like other Guggenheim fellows, recipients of the Latin American awards were to receive twelve-month stipends of $2,500 each and travel expenses.

The first fellowships under the program were awarded in 1930. Whereas only six fellowships had been awarded for Latin American projects between 1925, when the foundation was established, and 1929, four Americans received fellowships for work in Mexico in 1930, and two Mexican scientists were awarded fellowships for study in American universities. In all, in the three years 1930–32, ten of the twenty-nine fellowships awarded to Latin Americans went to Mexicans, nearly all of them scientists. One of the exceptions was Moisés Sáenz, who received an award in 1932 to study the educational problems of Indians in the American Southwest. During the same three years, twenty-four fellowships were awarded to Americans for projects to be carried out in Latin America; of these, nineteen intended to do all or part of their work in Mexico. The Guggenheim awards, therefore, provided a new opportunity for artists and intellectuals from the United States to enjoy extended stays in Mexico. Another beneficiary of the Guggenheim program was Eyler N. Simpson, a sociologist, who was the foundation's Mexican secretary as well as the representative in Mexico of the Institute of Current World Affairs. Simpson remained in Mexico from 1928 to 1935, becoming known as an expert on Mexican issues, though Anita Brenner disliked his "pontifical manner."[71] He also gathered material for his study *The Ejido: Mexico's Way Out* (1937).

After 1932 the Guggenheim Foundation stopped setting aside special fellowships to be used by Americans in Latin America, and the number of fellows who traveled to Mexico diminished drastically. In the years 1933–36 only one fellow offered a project requiring a visit to Mexico, the novelist Harvey Fergusson, a 1935 fellow, who wished to gather material for a book on the folklore and history of the American Southwest. During these years some fellowships continued to be reserved for Mexicans and other Latin Americans.

Six of the nineteen American fellows who went to Mexico between 1930 and 1932 were artists: Emil Bistram, Marsden Hartley, Ione Robinson, and Doris Rosenthal, all awarded fellowships in 1931, and Howard Cook and Andrew Dasburg, in 1932. Three were writers: Hart Crane, 1931, and H. L. Davis and J. Frank Dobie, 1932. Most of the others were scholars, such as Ruth Bunzel, an anthropologist from Barnard College (1930), and historian Lesley Byrd Simpson from the University of California (1931). Another recipient was Martha Graham, the first dancer to be awarded a Guggenheim. She spent the summer of 1932 in Yucatán and Mexico City, visiting archaeological ruins and studying indigenous dances. When the award was announced, John Martin of the *New York Times* remarked: "It is hardly a surprise that she has elected to go to Mexico and Yucatan rather than to Europe. For the last two years she has been turning more and more to the actual soil of the Western world for inspiration."[72]

One can only speculate about applicants who were interested in pursuing Mexican projects yet did not receive awards. Idella Purnell, for example, applied unsuccessfully in 1932. Her project was a study of life near Lake Chapala that would combine fiction and anthropology and result in a novel to be called *Canoa*. She hoped that the book would "convey to the reader the idyllic atmosphere of the Mexican countryside."[73] Two others who at least considered applying for fellowships were Frances Toor and the chronicler Alfonso Taracena, who asked Carleton Beals to write him a letter of recommendation.

Experience in Mexico was obviously no bar to receiving a fellowship because several successful applicants were already well acquainted with Mexico. Anita Brenner was a recipient in 1930. She planned to delineate the geographic area of Aztec art, concentrating on masks. Carleton Beals was appointed in 1931 to write a biography of Porfirio Díaz. He explained to a Mexican interviewer that understanding of the Porfiriato was necessary if Americans, who found themselves stirred by contemporary Mexico, were to understand the country. The interviewer observed that it was fitting for the Guggenheims, who had taken so much money out of Mexico, to return some of it through the fellowships.[74]

Another Guggenheim fellow who had had experience in Mexico before receiving the award was Ione Robinson, a young painter. She had first traveled to Mexico in June 1929, armed with a letter of introduction to Rivera from George Biddle. She remained until the following October, working as an assistant to Rivera and becoming acquainted with Tina Modotti, Frida Kahlo, and other Mexican painters. At a party for David Alfaro Siqueiros at Modotti's she met Joseph Freeman, who was the Mexico correspondent for Tass. She soon fell in love with Freeman and, though she was sometimes bewildered by the quarrels and demands of the communists she met, she felt that her four-month stay in Mexico had been productive. "I have learned to paint on a wall," she wrote to her mother, "I am engaged to be married, and I have done enough pictures for an exhibition."[75]

Robinson married Freeman, who also returned to New York, but the marriage was not happy. She continued her artistic career and, after being awarded the Guggenheim fellowship, left for Mexico in March 1931. In Coyoacán she rented a house where she was joined by Zohmah Day, a young art student who met her future husband, Jean Charlot, at a party she hosted with Robinson.[76] Robinson renewed her friendship with Mexican artists and worked for a time on the frescoes in the National Palace until, according to her account, a jealous Frida Kahlo, now married to Rivera, drove her away. She also painted a series of pictures on tin during a sojourn in Uruapan, worked at the Academy of San Carlos in Mexico City doing sculpture and lithography, and spent two weeks at the Hacienda Tetlapayac with Eisenstein and his colleagues. She returned to the United States in the spring of 1932 convinced that Mexico had had "a tremendous influence" on her "as a human being and as an artist."[77]

The Mexican misadventures of Hart Crane, another Guggenheim fellow for 1931, have often been described. Malcolm Cowley, who had spent a month in Mexico in 1930, suggested that Crane use his award money for a stay in Mexico instead of going to France as he originally intended. Cowley recalled: "I spoke with enthusiasm about [Mexico's] somber landscapes, its baroque churches, and its mixture of Spanish and Indian cultures. Life there was even cheaper than in Europe. One heard of sexual customs not unlike those of the Arabs." Crane warmed to the idea, mentioning a projected poem about the conquest of Mexico. Another friend, Waldo Frank, also encouraged him to go to Mexico, though warning him against drinking anything stronger than beer at that altitude, and gave him letters of introduction to Mexican writers.[78]

Crane, who arrived in April 1931, was grateful for the letters, but he ignored Frank's advice about alcohol and was soon proclaiming tequila to be his favorite drink. His early impressions of Mexico were mixed, he informed Frank: "But humanity is so unmechanized here still, so immediate and really dignified (I'm speaking of the Indians, peons, country people—not the average mestizo) that it is giving me an entirely fresh perspective. And whether immediately creative or not, more profound than Europe gave me. . . . This is truly 'another world.'" To an interviewer from *Excelsior* who inquired why he had not gone to Europe, Crane replied: "I have already been in France, and I learned then that the hour of creative poetry is in America."[79]

Crane soon became acquainted with several Mexican poets and intellectuals but found their manners "baffling" when they planned social engagements for him that never happened. He was most enthusiastic about Moisés Sáenz, who invited him to his house in Taxco, and David Alfaro Siqueiros, whom he considered to be the greatest of Mexico's contemporary painters. Crane purchased a watercolor of the head of an Indian boy from Siqueiros, who also painted a portrait of the poet. Crane later destroyed the life-sized likeness in a drunken fit of despondency and rage.[80]

Like other American visitors, Crane was charmed by Taxco. "Taxco is so extremely beautiful—and the townsfolk still so affable—that whatever one has to say about the Yankee occupation (and that ultimately seals its doom) it's still one of the pleasantest places to be." There he met William Spratling, whose collection of folk art he admired.[81]

Crane explored another facet of Mexican culture when he observed the quadricentennial celebration of the apparition of the Virgin of Guadalupe on December 12, 1931. He was most interested in the dances he saw and was impressed by their somberness and by the devotion to tradition that they represented. The previous September he had had an even more exhilarating experience when he spent five days in Tepoztlán in the company of a young archaeologist from Wisconsin. Their visit coincided with a festival in honor of Tepoztecatl, the god of pulque, and Crane and his companion had an opportunity to watch the night-long ritual. The high point came before dawn when Crane was allowed to beat a tattoo on an ancient drum atop the cathedral. "It seemed too good to be true, really, that I, who had expected to be thrown off the roof when I entered the evening before, should now be invited to actually participate."[82]

Upon his arrival in Mexico City, Crane stayed for a time with his "old and wonderful friend" Katherine Anne Porter in Mixcoac and later rented a large house of his own around the corner. But Crane's drunkenness, his homosexual escapades, and his fits of truculence eventually resulted in a permanent rupture of their relationship. Porter and Eugene Pressly relayed news of Crane's activities which reached the Guggenheim Foundation and produced a letter of censure. Samuel Loveman, who saw Crane when the latter visited the United States briefly after his father's death, asserted later that Porter had caused him "incalculable misery." She "was the transmitter of all the gossip to New York—so much so that Hart dreaded to go back to Mexico the second time."[83]

Crane had more harmonious relations with other Guggenheim fellows in Mexico, such as Lesley Byrd Simpson and Marsden Hartley, whose company found to be delightful.[84] While Crane was in the United States, Peggy Baird, the wife of Malcolm Cowley, arrived in Mexico to get a divorce. She and Crane renewed their friendship upon his return and became lovers when she moved into his house in Mixcoac. They were returning to New York together in April 1932 on the *Orizaba* when Crane committed suicide by jumping overboard near Havana.

Hartley, still in Mexico, lamented Crane's death, though acknowledging that he demanded a great deal of those he admired. He singled out Mary Doherty, then employed by the Guggenheim Foundation, as "a devoted friend" of Crane's who had saved him from an earlier suicide attempt.[85] Another woman identified as a loyal friend of Crane's during his troubled stay in Mexico was Anita Brenner, "who understood Hart perfectly, even in his tantrums."[86]

Crane did not write his projected poem about Cortés and Montezuma, but his months in Mexico did yield "The Broken Tower." To the end he remained bemused by Mexico: "Mexico with its volcanoes, endless ranges, countless flowers, dances, villages, lovely brown-skinned Indians with simple courtesies, and constant sunlight—it enthralls me more than any other spot I've ever known. It *is* and isn't an easy place to live. Altogether more strange to us than even the orient. . . . There is never an end to dancing, singing, rockets and the rather lurking and suave dangers that give the same edge to life here that the mountains give to the horizon."[87]

Hartley was awarded a Guggenheim fellowship in 1931 but did not leave for Mexico until 1932. He had previously spent two years in New Mexico and was now attracted to Mexico by its artists and by the contemporary mural movement, "the only one that shows any signs of spiritual re-birth." As he made plans for the journey, he expressed trepidation about Mexican food and hygiene but looked foward to the experience. "Thank God some new sensation to encounter—something less sterile than the U.S. robotization."[88]

Once in Mexico, Hartley studied Spanish and made contact with other Americans besides Crane, such as Andrew Dasburg, also a Guggenheim fellow, and John Evans, the son of Mabel Dodge Luhan. His exploration of preconquest ritual stimulated his spiritualist interests, which underlay a dramatic change in his style evident in the paintings he did in Mexico. But though Hartley was at first "wildly enthusiastic" about Mexico and produced important paintings while there, he eventually developed a profound dislike for the country. This dislike appears to have been compounded by a fear of Mexican food and water, an aesthetic distaste for the Mexican landscape and population, and a conviction that the Mexican milieu was enervating. By mid-March 1933 he was not sorry that he had come and still admired the volcanoes and the "wondrous pyramids & temples out of Aztec times," but he was "tired of looking at black & dark green people" and concluded that though Mexico was picturesque, "all picturesqueness wears on the eyes & leaves the senses dulled."[89]

H. L. Davis, a Guggenheim fellow in 1932, also expressed reservations about Mexico. His lack of enthusiasm is understandable because he had hoped to go to Spain but was persuaded by the foundation to choose Mexico instead to reduce travel costs. It was not until he had reached Mexico that he learned that he was a Latin American exchange fellow who was supposed not only to write poetry but also to foster international understanding.[90]

Davis found little in Mexico to excite his imagination. "Mexicans don't interest me much; that is, as literary timber," he wrote in a journal. "They're too much costumed cut-outs from the Ladies' Home Journal. . . . No paradoxes, no contradictions that define characters in the

North. Unless one counts as a contradiction (the upper-class Mexicans do) the fact that their pelados should possess any reasoning power at all." Nor was Davis impressed by American writing about Mexico, much of which he said was "boloney." He so labeled Chase's work, and he dismissed Beals as a propagandist for the government, which consisted of "crooks, numskulls [sic], bullshit-peddlers and ex-pelado generals."[91] Despite his apparent distaste for Mexico, Davis remained there until 1935, writing his first novel, *Honey in the Horn*, which won the Pulitzer Prize in 1936.

The "vogue of things Mexican" of the late 1920s and early 1930s ensured a better reception than before for the efforts of Mexican performers and artists in the United States. Those such as Miguel Covarrubias and Dolores del Río, who had achieved recognition before 1927, continued their careers, but they were now joined by a rising stream of cultural emigrants. Howard Phillips, editor of *Mexican Life*, saw them as part of the emigrant flood that was reconquering the American Southwest for Mexico: "The sizable group of Mexican painters, sculptors, caricaturists, dramatic artists, composers, opera and concert singers residing and enjoying fame and laurels in the United States, is probably the greatest cultural mission that has ever gone forth out of a country as small in population as Mexico. This group is an aesthetic vanguard that is building up respect and admiration for Mexico in the outside world."[92]

When Phillips wrote these words in 1927, Mexican emigrants were still pouring into the United States. Within a few years, however, although some cultural emigrants prospered, overall immigration from Mexico to the United States had been curbed because the Hoover administration responded to critics of Mexican immigration not by supporting the passage of new restrictions but by strictly enforcing existing legislation such as the literacy requirement of the Immigration Act of 1917. With the start of the Great Depression, complaints arose that Mexican aliens in the United States were holding jobs and receiving welfare benefits that should have gone to native Americans. Accordingly, federal, state, and local authorities, often abetted by chambers of commerce and other private groups, moved to encourage repatriation or deportation of Mexicans. The repatriation drive reached a peak in 1931, when more than 138,000 Mexicans returned to their homeland; by 1937, nearly 500,000 had left the United States.[93]

During the Depression a few prominent Mexicans in the United States rendered assistance to their less fortunate compatriots. Ramón Novarro and other Mexican celebrities as well as Will Rogers, who was introduced as Guillermo Rodríguez, appeared at a 1931 benefit in Los Angeles to raise funds for needy Mexicans.[94] During his 1932–33 stay in Detroit to do a mural at the Art Institute, Diego Rivera became a founder and officer of the Liga de Obreros y Campesinos, which sought to help Mexican immigrants who wanted to stay in the United States and to assist those who wished to return to Mexico. For the latter the Liga sponsored several small agricultural colonies in Mexico, none of which proved successful.[95]

During these years Hollywood continued to beckon to some who were undoubtedly dazzled by the careers of Del Río and Novarro. Both of them survived the transition to sound but were still cast in "exotic" roles such as the Russian aviator played by Novarro in *Mata Hari* (1929) and the title character in *Evangeline* (1929) played by Del Río. At the world premiere of the latter in New Orleans, the Mexican consul-general asserted that Mexico was "glowing with pride over the artistic accomplishments of her most beautiful daughter"[96] Del Río finally portrayed a Mexican woman in *Girl of the Río* (1932), which co-starred a Mexican-American, Leo Carrillo, as the villain, but the film drew heavy criticism in Mexico.

José Mojica continued to sing on the concert stage, but in 1930 he too embarked on a motion picture career when American production companies began shooting films in both Spanish and English versions so as to retain Latin American audiences after the advent of "talkies." Starting with *One Mad Kiss* (1930), the "singing Valentino" (as he was called in studio publicity) made films in both languages throughout the 1930s.[97]

These stars were joined by several others in the late 1920s. Gilbert Roland, a native of Chihuahua who had moved to the United States as a child, was playing starring roles by 1927. Even greater success was attained by Lupe Vélez, later to be dubbed the "Mexican Spitfire," who became a motion picture star and also performed on Broadway. Other actresses who attained a measure of fame in Hollywood were Conchita Montenegro, Lupita Tovar, and Raquel Torres, who played featured roles in *The Bridge of San Luis Rey* (1929) and *Duck Soup* (1933). In another example of cultural exchange, some of these performers also played a role in the Mexican motion picture industry, which experienced a resurgence in the 1930s. One of Mexico's most successful films, *Santa* (1931), starred Lupita Tovar as the title character and was directed by Antonio Moreno, the Spanish-born actor who had been a major Hollywood star in the 1920s.[98]

Beginning in the late 1920s, Mexican painters traveled to the United States in connection with exhibits of their work or for more extended stays. By this time, reports in the American media of the exciting developments in Mexican art made it likely that these painters would eventually attract attention, especially in New York. They also received assistance from other Mexicans resident in the United States as well as from American admirers of Mexican culture. When Rufino Tamayo arrived in New York in 1926, he looked up Walter Pach, whom he had met in Mexico and who helped arrange an exhibition of the painter's work at the Weyhe Gallery. In 1927 José Clemente Orozco joined Miguel Covarrubias and Rufino Tamayo in New York, having found conditions in Mexico uncongenial. His travel costs and initial expenses were defrayed by a stipend from the secretary of foreign relations, Genaro Estrada, but he hoped to support himself and his family, which remained in Mexico, by producing small works such as drawings, lithographs, and engravings. These were respectable as art yet might be sold fairly easily.[99]

At first, Orozco felt isolated and lonely in New York, but he was befriended by several persons who had recently been in Mexico and above all by Anita Brenner. When she had come to New York the previous August, she had brought with her most of the drawings in his series *Mexico in Revolution* in the hope of arranging for their exhibition. She had been unsuccessful in achieving this goal, but she had published an essay on Orozco for the *Arts* (October 1927), in which she likened the artist to the revolution itself, depicting both as forces that combined destruction with creativity.[100]

Brenner also introduced Orozco to Alma Reed. Within a short time Reed had assumed the role of "mother, sister, agent and 'bootlegger'" to Orozco, this last an allusion to the bottles of ouzo she occasionally gave him.[101] Reed had access to ouzo because when she met Orozco in August 1928 she was sharing a Fifth Avenue apartment with Eva Sikelianos, a wealthy American woman who was married to the Greek poet

Angelo Sikelianos and had dedicated her life to the revival of classical culture in Greece. Orozco became a habitué of the apartment, and it was there in September 1928 that his first one-man show in the United States was held. Drawings of the series *Mexico in Revolution* were hung on the walls of the apartment, along with a recent oil painting, *The Factory*, and photographs of his murals in the National Preparatory School were circulated among the guests. Sixty persons attended the private showing. Orozco was soon at work on a portrait of Eva Sikelianos, "something new, with a complicated palette and treated as a mural," and she took a selection of his drawings with her to Europe. According to Orozco, she had "very good connections in Europe, the best magazines in Paris and so on."[102]

Two decades later, Brenner stated that she had brought Orozco and Reed together in the hope that Eva Sikelianos and her "Greek salon of mystics" might take an interest in the painter. "It worked," she said. Despite her efforts on his behalf, however, relations between Brenner and the prickly painter were often strained, and as early as February 1928 he was calling her "hypocritical and false."[103] The artist voiced unfavorable opinions about other American women whom he encountered in New York, such as Frances Toor and Frances Flynn Paine. The latter, a native of Laredo, Texas, had spent her childhood years in Mexico as the daughter of an American businessman with extensive interests there. Now she devoted her considerable energies to advancing the cause of Mexican culture, especially the visual arts, in the United States. Orozco described her in February 1928 as "a kind of Dr. Atl in skirts, involved in a thousand different schemes, all half baked and very different from one another."[104]

Orozco's animus against Paine may have contained an element of misogyny, but more fundamentally it stemmed from two other closely related causes. He was unhappy over the contents and arrangement of a group show at the New York Art Center in which he and other Mexican artists had been represented; he was also indignant because the show seemed to be but a prelude for an exhibit of folk art, organized by Paine, which had followed the paintings at the Art Center. Orozco complained to his friend the painter Manuel Rodríguez Lozano that "our works have merely served as propaganda placards for a commercial private business of foreigners!"[105] Orozco erred in ascribing mercenary motives to Paine, but even if he had known the full story of the folk art exhibit, he probably would not have altered his judgment of her. In the eyes of Orozco, Paine, along with Brenner and Toor, was guilty of another offense. He saw all three as partisans of Diego Rivera, whom Orozco disdained as a "Mexicanist 'con man.'" Thus he was annoyed when Frances Toor, who had seen the exhibit of his work in the Sikelianos apartment, suggested that she give a talk on Rivera there, and he was pleased that Reed turned down the proposal. The event was held instead at a students' club, "which Frances [Toor] filled with *ollitas*, *cazuelas*, and *petates* and then [she] spoke about the Great Folkloric Leader to her heart's content."[106]

If Orozco was angry over the attention given Rivera in the United States, he in turn provoked resentment for similar reasons in Antonieta Rivas Mercado, who arrived in New York in the fall of 1929. A wealthy patron of the arts and ardent supporter of José Vasconcelos's 1929 presidential bid, she came to New York to promote his campaign and plunged into the city's cultural life, among what she called the *mexicanada*. She scoffed at José Juan Tablada's claim to be the dean of Spanish-American culture in New York and was outraged when Hubert Herring and others asserted that all was well in Mexico.[107] But, above all, Rivas Mercado, who was separated from her husband and in love with Manuel Rodríguez Lozano, was annoyed that Orozco and Rivera seemed to be monopolizing the field of Mexican art in New York to the exclusion of Rodríguez Lozano and other artists, whom she considered to be of equal or superior merit. She therefore resented the promotional activities of Alma Reed, who she said was full of goodwill but lacked brains, a common failing among Americans, and of Anita Brenner, whose *Idols behind Altars* she denounced as a travesty written in bad faith.[108]

Rivas Mercado had a more favorable impression of Frances Flynn Paine, who put her in touch with the Theatre Guild, which she hoped would mount an English-language dramatization of *Los de abajo*. She was also in contact with Waldo Frank, whose novel *Rahab* (1922) she wished to translate into Spanish. In the event, few of Rivas Mercado's plans were realized; tormented by emotional and economic difficulties, she committed suicide in Paris in 1931.[109]

Soon after his arrival, Orozco also came into contact with Walter Pach, whose lectures in Mexico City he had attended six years earlier. Although Pach also came under censure for his enthusiasm about Rivera,

Orozco was appreciative of the critic's praise for his work in *Ananias* (1928) and accepted an invitation to his summer residence. Early in 1928 Orozco became acquainted with George Biddle, whom he described as "a very nice fellow." Biddle was partly responsible for a major exhibition of Orozco's work at the Little Gallery of the New Students' League of Philadelphia in February 1929 and introduced him at a large reception to mark the opening of the show. At this time George's brother Francis, the future attorney general of the United States, purchased a small oil painting by Orozco, *Coney Island—Side Show*. From this point on, Orozco's career in the United States took on a new momentum, and by the fall of 1930 *Time* was reporting that he had become "almost as essential to smart dinner conversation as backgammon."[110] Moreover, other Mexican artists began to arrive in the United States, notably the Mexicanist con man himself, Diego Rivera, who traveled to San Francisco in November 1930 to paint a mural in the city's new Stock Exchange. The presence of Orozco, Rivera, and other artists in the United States, coupled with the promotional efforts of their supporters, contributed to an explosion of interest in Mexican art in the early 1930s (see Chapter 4).

Another creative artist who enhanced his reputation in the United States in the late 1920s and early 1930s was Carlos Chávez. The composer returned to New York in 1926, traveling in the company of Rufino Tamayo, with whom he shared a loft in lower Manhattan. Despite financial straits that forced him to take a job as an organist in a motion picture theater, Chávez quickly became part of the musical avant-garde in the city and formed friendships with Aaron Copland and Edgard Varèse, whose portrait Tamayo painted.[111] Soon after Chávez's arrival, "The Dance of Men and Machines," part of his as yet unfinished ballet *H.P.*, was performed at a concert sponsored by the International Composers' Guild, which Varèse had founded in 1921.[112] This concert marked the first time Chávez's orchestra music had been performed outside of Mexico. On April 22, 1928, Chávez himself played his *Sonata for Piano* at the first of the Copland-Sessions concerts of contemporary music, during which his *Three Sonatinas* were also performed. Earlier that month Chávez had been named one of four vice-presidents of a newly formed Pan American Association of Composers, of which Varèse was president. Its purpose was to encourage performance of works by North, Central, and South American composers throughout the region to "promote wider mutual appreciation of the music of the different republics of America, and . . . stimulate composers to make still greater effort toward creating a distinctive music of the western hemisphere."[113] Chávez also won the admiration of Frances Flynn Paine. After he left New York in 1928, she urged Elizabeth Cutter Morrow to become a patron of the composer. "There is absolutely no doubt as to his genius," she said, "and that he can hold his own with the greatest of modern musicians. . . . He deserves whatever recognition and encouragement we can extend to him."[114]

Although Orozco, Chávez, and other Mexicans who lived in New York for periods of varying length won a measure of success and celebrity, they often experienced considerable hardship as well. They had fewer financial resources than the Americans who traveled to Mexico during the same period and were likely to feel greater alienation, partly because New York was much larger in population than Mexico City. In addition, the extremes of climate and especially the snow and frigid temperatures of winter were a shock, though Orozco was amused by the sight of children so bundled up against the cold that only part of their faces was visible. But above all Mexican cultural émigrés in New York were impressed by the frenetic pace of life in the metropolis, which reminded the poet Jaime Torres Bodet of an express train. The city's skyscrapers added to the strangeness. In 1931 José Vasconcelos called them ugly boxes that would not last and described the Empire State Building as the plaything of a child who lacked the talent to conceive a cupola. To the poet Xavier Villaurrutia, who visited the city in 1935, the skyscrapers suggested a petrified jungle. Many probably shared the reaction of Villaurrutia's friend Salvador Novo during his first brief visit in 1933: he likened New York to a fragile machine and could not imagine how so many people could spend their lives subjected to it. In short, as Orozco told his wife in September 1930: "This country is very difficult, not only for the foreigner but also for the native." He had, however, begun to dominate it artistically.[115]

The career of Carlos Chávez exemplified the cultural exchange that developed between Mexican and American artists and intellectuals during the 1920s. The inclusion of his work on the program of the 1928 Copland-Sessions concert was the result of his growing friendship with Aaron Copland, whom he had met in 1926. Of Chávez, Copland declared that "he is one of the few American composers about whom we can say that he is more than a reflection of Europe."[116] When Chávez returned to Mexico in July 1928 to become director of the new symphony orchestra, he invited Copland to perform his new *Piano Concerto* there. Although Copland was unable to go to Mexico until 1932, Chávez did welcome another important musical figure to Mexico City: Leopold Stokowski, director of the Philadelphia Symphony, who arrived on January 19, 1931, after spending a week inspecting archaeological sites in Yucatán. During Stokowski's stay in Mexico City, Julián Carrillo served as interpreter.

Stokowski was well received in Mexico City and was the guest of honor at a banquet offered by Secretary of Education Puig Casauranc and his wife at their home. Stokowski also met Chávez for the first time and on January 24, 1931, joined him in conducting the Symphonic Orchestra of Mexico in a benefit concert for the victims of a recent earthquake in Oaxaca. A second benefit concert with the Symphonic Orchestra was held on February 1 at Chapultepec Park. Stokowski also conducted the Sonido Trece Symphony during his two-week stay in Mexico City.[117]

Stokowski returned to Mexico the following January. With Chávez he visited Oaxaca and Michoacán, studying Indian dances and musical instruments. He also conferred with Chávez about plans for the world premiere performance of the latter's ballet-symphony, *H.P. (Caballos de Vapor)*, which Stokowski was to conduct in Philadelphia, donating his services "as an expression of his admiration for Mexican culture." The premiere on March 31, 1932, was a major event, attended by musical and social luminaries from New York as well as Philadelphia.[118]

In 1931 Chávez had become accquainted with the photographer Paul Strand, who expressed an interest in working in Mexico. In 1932, armed with an official invitation from Chávez, Strand and two companions set out from Taos, New Mexico, in an old Model A Ford. "I started working in Mexico the minute I crossed the border," he recalled later, for he had already begun to question the conventional notion that a photographer had to know a place well if he was to avoid superficiality in his work.[119]

Once in Mexico City, Strand showed some still photographs of New Mexico to Chávez. The composer proposed that they be exhibited and introduced him to the secretary of education, Narciso Bassols, who offered Strand space on the ground floor of a building belonging to the secretariat. Marsden Hartley, who was still in Mexico, helped Strand hang the prints, and the painter Gabriel Fernández Ledesma designed a poster to advertise the show, which opened in February 1933. Although it lasted for only two weeks, Strand considered it one of the most rewarding exhibitions he had ever had. "All sorts of people came: policemen, soldiers, Indian women with their babies, and so on. I've never had such an audience anywhere else."[120]

In March 1933 Chávez took on the added responsibility of serving as head of the Fine Arts Department of the Education Secretariat. He now offered Strand an opportunity to join his nephew Agustín Velásquez Chávez in making a survey of art education in Michoacán. During their tour of the state, Strand used an extension with a fine optical prism on his five-by-seven Graflex to photograph unsuspecting subjects. In a 1974 *New Yorker* profile Calvin Tompkins wrote: "The portraits that Strand took in Morelia, Pátzcuaro and other towns in western Mexico with this device were extraordinarily successful. The subjects were usually shown full-face, looking gravely at the camera that they do not suspect is focussed on them. There is a beauty and a gentle dignity about each face—even the faces of the children—that suggest Strand's feelings about them. More than ever, his portraits were acts of love."[121]

Chávez involved Strand in another project of his, the creation of a series of films for Mexican audiences about the production of wealth in their country. Strand was reluctant to abandon his still photography, and he had little experience in cinematography, but he agreed to participate in the project, which was to show the Mexican people their own lives without condescending to them. Only one of the planned films was made. This was *Redes* (1934), produced and photographed by Strand and directed by Fred Zinnemann, then an unknown. Silvestre Revueltas created the score for the sixty-five minute film, which relates the story of fishermen in Pátzcuaro. With English subtitles by John Dos Passos, it opened in New York in 1937 as *The Wave* to mixed notices: critics praised the cinematography but uniformly found the pace of the film too slow.[122]

Aaron Copland accepted Chávez's invitation to visit Mexico in the late summer of 1932. With his pupil and companion Victor Kraft, Copland drove to Laredo, then took the train to Mexico City, arriving on September 2. That evening Chávez offered an all-Copland concert, the first to be given anywhere, at the National Conservatory. Before the concert *Excelsior* declared Copland's work to be of special interest to Mexicans because of his efforts to provide the New World with a music of its own.[123]

Copland remained in Mexico for four months. He spent a great deal of time with Chávez and heard his own music played on several other occasions, to varying reactions from audiences and critics. He spent two months in the town of Tlalpam and a few days in Acapulco before leaving at the end of the year. After returning to the United States, he began work on a piece of music which he called *El Salón México* after the name of a raffish dance hall he had visited with Chávez. In it he combined folk tunes he found in a collection by Frances Toor, *Cancionero mexicano* (1931), and a scholarly work by Rubén M. Campos, *El folklore y la música mexicana* (1928). The first performance of the work was given by the Symphony Orchestra of Mexico, with Chávez conducting, in Mexico City on August 27, 1937.[124]

Copland summed up his Mexican experience in a letter to a friend on January 13, 1933: "Mexico was a rich time. Outwardly nothing happened and inwardly all was calm. Yet I'm left with the impression of having had an enriching experience. It comes, no doubt, from the nature of the country and the people. Europe now seems conventional to me by comparison. Mexico offers something fresh and pure and wholesome—a quality which is deeply unconventionalized. The source of it is the Indian blood which is so prevalent. I sensed the influence of the Indian background everywhere—even in the landscape."[125]

In this passage Copland touched upon the various aspects of Mexico and its people that proved so attractive to Americans in the years from 1927 to 1935. In contrast to the early 1920s, when the revolution was a powerful lure, in the later period Americans were drawn above all by the seemingly timeless elements of the native culture, especially those bearing the stamp of the Indian. That this culture was distinctively American strengthened its appeal as the political and cultural hegemony of Europe was diminishing. At a time of economic crisis that threw into question the benefits of capitalism, the apparent "wantlessness" of the Mexican peasant and the coherence of village life, despite its material poverty, exerted an even greater appeal than before 1929. As American artists and intellectuals traveled to Mexico, and their Mexican counterparts traveled to the United States, they received unprecedented exposure to the art, music, and popular culture of each other's country. Thus the bases for a new and mutual appreciation were being laid.

CHAPTER 3

Native Americans in the Spotlight

I n both Mexico and the United States the Native American—the Indian—became a focal point of interest during the 1920s. Embracing the philosophy of *indigenismo*, Mexico's revolutionary elites asserted their commitment to the moral and economic elevation of the Indian, who they claimed was central to the national experience. In a talk to participants in Herring's 1930 seminar, the economist Ramón Beteta named the Indian population as the most important social force in Mexico. Their influence was evident in Mexican diet, dress, housing, and medicine and in the national character, which reflected their endurance and resignation.[1] Governments of the period thus promised preferential attention in education and agrarian reform to rural Mexicans, who in many places could be equated with Indians, if not in language at least in ancestry and many elements of their culture. In 1921 Indians still represented a substantial proportion of the population. The Mexican census of that year classified as Indians 4,179,449 persons, or 29.16 percent of the total population. The same census indicated that 1,802,844 Mexicans above the age of five spoke an indigenous tongue as their first language.[2]

In addition, the cultural nationalism encouraged by the Mexican Revolution emphasized the importance of indigenous themes and forms in music, literature, and art and accordingly exalted the Indians both as a subject of art and as a major creative force in their own right. Archaeology was invested with a new significance for the light it might shed on the origins of Mexican culture, both past and present. It might also serve as a guide to those who were seeking the economic and social betterment of the descendants of Mexico's preconquest peoples. This concern informed Manuel Gamio's landmark study in applied anthropology in the Valley of Teotihuacán, which examined the life of the region in preconquest and colonial times as well as the present. Although Gamio, Moisés Sáenz, and other reformers admired indigenous culture and favored preservation of some of its features, their goal was to incorporate the Indians into a Mexican nation that would be culturally homogeneous, modern, and Spanish-speaking.

In the United States the Native American was also the object of heightened attention, partly in response to the cultural nationalism evident there in the postwar era. According to Robert F. Schrader, "In the aftermath of world war, many Americans awakened to a new interest in Americana and found that the Indians were at the core of America's national experience. Their private convictions, publicly expressed by the more articulate leaders, now lacked the sense of racial superiority that previously had tainted attitudes toward Indian life."[3] To those who sought to foster the development of authentically American arts, the Indian—both north and south of the border—was of significance both as a creator and as a source of aesthetic inspiration to others. At the same time, neoromantics who rejected industrialism and urbanism could look at the Indian in New Mexico and other parts of the United States as well as in Old Mexico as an example of a more primitive yet more satisfying civilization, one based on the community rather than the individual. In 1922 John Collier, the future commissioner of Indian affairs, rhapsodized about the Pueblo communities of Taos, which he described as "so indolently industrious, so ecstatic while yet so laughing, so great with color, flooded with body-rhythm and song, so communal yet so individually reckless, so human and so mystic." In these communities the men were tough and untamed, yet quarrels were unknown and children were never scolded or whipped.[4]

As the previous chapters have suggested, the American artists and intellectuals who visited Mexico after 1920 were likely to share the belief of their Mexican counterparts that its Indian population was central to both the past and future of the country. Ernest Gruening indicated as much in the title of his 1928 volume and asserted in the text that "one cannot escape in Mexico's everyday life the all-pervading manifestations of the persistent native culture."[5] Many also shared the conviction of Mexican revolutionary leaders that programs to benefit the Indians indicated overdue if limited acknowledgment of centuries of exploitation and denigration. Some viewed *indigenismo* in a global context. Socialist veteran Frank Bohn saw the "return of the native" in Mexico as part of a regeneration of colored races then under way throughout the world.[6]

Other Americans were most deeply impressed by the harmony and authenticity which they discerned among Mexico's Indians. Witter Bynner, who as a resident of New Mexico was familiar with the conditions of Native Americans in the United States, wrote eloquently about the qualities he found in Mexican Indians: "a proportioned sense of the values of life, a power to work when work is necessary, a power to endure where endurance is necessary, a power to oppose when opposition is necessary, to smile and live and fight at happy intervals and to loaf magnificently when the earth commands."[7] The writings of Gruening, Bynner, Stuart Chase, and others helped to acquaint American readers with the culture of Mexico's Indians as did Frances Toor's *Mexican Folkways*, which she called an outgrowth of her "great enthusiasm and delight" in traveling among Mexican Indians and studying their customs.[8] During this period more scholarly data were gathered by American anthropologists who emulated Gamio by undertaking their own studies of Mexican communities.

In the United States the decade of the 1920s also saw the mobilization of pro-Indian activists such as Collier and Bynner against the Bursum Pueblo Land Bill of 1922, which threatened spoliation of Pueblo landholdings. The campaign against the abortive legislation soon broadened into a movement strongly critical of all federal policies affecting the Indian.[9] To many activists, it seemed that the Mexican program of Indian rehabilitation might well be a model for the United States. In short, the entire range of issues related to the Native American—from archaeology to anthropology to government policy—afforded many opportunities for interaction between Mexicans and Americans, though they were occasionally jeopardized by the nationalism of the former and the bumptiousness of the latter.

The archaeology of Mesoamerica was a field in which Americans had long been active. Indeed, a Mexican historian coined the phrase *archaeological Monroism* to describe what he saw as the tendency of John Lloyd

Stephens (1805–52) and his contemporaries to appropriate Mesoamerican antiquities for the United States, excluding both Europeans and Latin Americans.[10] In reality, the late nineteenth century brought investigators of various nationalities to the field of Mexican antiquities—the Briton A. P. Maudslay, the Mexican Francisco del Paso, the German Eduard Seler, the American William Holmes, for example—some of whom worked as individuals while others had institutional support. In the United States Harvard University and the Peabody Museum of Archaeology and Ethnology played a leading role in Maya studies under F. W. Putnam and Alfred M. Tozzer. After joining the Harvard faculty in 1905, Tozzer trained numerous scholars in his celebrated Maya seminar.[11] Meanwhile, the Mexican government had acted to protect its interest in the antiquities on its soil by creating the position of *inspector y conservador de monumentos arqueológicos* in 1875 and by enacting legislation in 1897 that declared all archaeological monuments to be the property of the nation and forbade the export of movable objects without official permission.[12]

Most of the early scholars in the Mexican field focused on the study of objects and eschewed large-scale theorizing, leaving to others the elaboration of general hypotheses about the nature of Mexico's preconquest civilizations. The most influential interpretation in the United States was developed by Lewis Morgan and his disciple Adolph Bandelier. In "Montezuma's Dinner" (1876) and other writings Morgan rejected the picture of an advanced and complex Aztec civilization set forth by the Spanish chroniclers and their nineteenth-century followers, such as William H. Prescott and Hubert Howe Bancroft. Denying that any Native Americans had reached the stage of civilization, he argued instead that the Aztecs, though more advanced than North American Indians, were still in a state of barbarism and that Montezuma was not an emperor but rather a war chief who headed a confederacy of three tribes. The Morgan-Bandelier thesis gained no acceptance in Mexico, where scholars were familiar with evidence that contradicted it.[13] It had come under challenge in the United States by 1900, and Paul Radin presented a systematic refutation in "The Sources and Authenticity of the History of the Ancient Mexicans" (1920).[14]

More fanciful than the Morgan-Bandelier thesis was the theory of Charles Etienne Brasseur de Bourbourg (1814–73), who held that the inhabitants of preconquest Mesoamerica were the descendants of the survivors of the lost continent of Atlantis.[15] An adherent of this theory was Charles G. Dawes, vice-president of the United States under Coolidge and later ambassador to England. In 1929 he engaged classical scholar Charles Upson Clark to conduct research in European libraries in the hope of finding links between the Maya and the lost continent.[16] Augustus Le Plongeon (1826–1908) also believed that such a link existed, but he is best known for his conviction that the Maya were the source of all human civilization, which they had spread to Egypt and other parts of the world.[17]

As the twentieth century began, Mexican archaeology still remained largely in the hands of gifted and self-taught individuals who received only sporadic institutional backing. Prominent among the American citizens in the field were Edward H. Thompson, William Niven, and Zelia Nuttall, all of whom remained professionally active after 1920, though such independent, self-taught scholars were being displaced by academically trained, institutionally funded investigators. Thompson's interest in Mexico was sparked by reading a book by Brasseur de Bourbourg which inspired him to write an article, "Atlantis Not a Myth," published in *Popular Science Monthly* in 1879. This in turn led to a proposition from Stephen Salisbury, Jr., vice-president of the American Antiquarian Society, that Thompson go to Yucatán as consul and devote his spare time to research on behalf of the society and the Peabody Museum. Arriving in Mérida with his wife and daughter in 1885, Thompson investigated the ruins at Labná and Chacmultún, but he will always be associated with Chichén Itzá, where he purchased the hacienda house in the mid-1890s with financial help from Allison V. Armour, also a researcher in archaeology. Thompson now devoted himself to exploring Chichén Itzá, and resigned the consulship in 1909. He was especially interested in the sacred well, or cenote, which he believed might contain objects thrown into it in preconquest times. With funds provided by American benefactors, Thompson began to dredge the cenote in 1904 and in 1909 dived into the well. His efforts were rewarded when human bones and a large number of gold and jade objects were brought out of the mud. Thompson's dredging of the cenote, which continued until 1911, though not kept secret at the time, would later involve him in difficulties with the Mexican government.[18]

The Scottish-born Niven was a mineralogist who had discovered new minerals in Texas and in the Mexican state of Guanajuato, but when he found the remains of an ancient city in Guerrero in 1891, he decided to devote himself to archaeology.[19] In the early 1920s he ran a museum and shop in Mexico City and conducted excavations at nearby Atzcapotzalco on Sundays. Visiting the shop in 1923, Sylvanus Morley was bemused by the number of archaeological specimens Niven had accumulated and speculated that some might be fake. He was certain that Niven was honest, but he might have been fooled by the laborers at Atzapotzcalco. A few days later, Morley visited Niven's excavation and was impressed when a carved andesite figure, similar to those whose authenticity he had doubted, was dug up. "It was a knockout," Morley observed, "a perfect vindication of the old man." Edward Weston also visited Niven's collection and was much taken by the old Scot. "Niven is so willing, anxious to talk, to explain," he remarked. "He is 74 years old, but vigorous and enthusiastic." Still another visitor was Katherine Anne Porter, who used him as the model of the archaeologist in her sketch "The Charmed Life," whose only interest in life was digging up ancient Indian cities. "He was the only person I ever saw," she wrote, "who really seemed as independent and carefree as a bird on a bough."[20] In 1924 Niven moved to Tampico, where he continued his archaeological work.

During her first visit to Mexico in the mid-1880s, Zelia Nuttall made a collection of small terra-cotta heads from San Juan Teotihuacán which became the subject of her first paper (1886). In the following decade she made her most significant contributions by discovering the Codex Magliabechiano in Florence (1890) and tracking down in England the Mixtec pictorial codex that bears her name (1898). When she settled in Mexico City in 1902, she continued her research, studying archaeological remains on the Island of Sacrificios near Veracruz. She was well received by other scholars in Mexico but feuded with Leopoldo Batres, inspector of monuments, whom she accused of incompetence and illegally trafficking in antiquities.[21]

During this period Nuttall became a patron of the young Manuel Gamio, whose excavations at Chalchihuites, Zacatecas, stirred her interest. As a result of her efforts, he received a fellowship in 1909 to study at Columbia University under Franz Boas. It was Nuttall's hope that the twenty-six-year-old Gamio, who was a temporary professor of history at the National Museum in Mexico City, would one day become director of the archaeological section of the museum and replace Batres as inspector of monuments. In New York Gamio became a protégé of

Boas, who made it possible for him to do fieldwork in Ecuador for six months in 1910.[22] The following year Gamio received a master's degree from Columbia.

Gamio's studies at Columbia coincided with a period of enthusiasm for Mexican archaeology and anthropology on the part of Boas. Several factors, including his belief in the unity of indigenous New World cultures and dissatisfaction with the empiricism of the School of American Archaeology in Santa Fe, New Mexico, which was planning fieldwork in Mexico, aroused Boas's interest in launching an international institute for anthropological research in Mexico. Although initially support for the project in the United States and Europe was lukewarm, the Mexican government was more receptive because the proposal meshed with plans to reopen and rejuvenate the National University.[23]

The Seventeenth Congress of Americanists, which met in Mexico City in 1910, furnished the occasion for the formal establishment of the school, which boasted an international roster of sponsors: the governments of Mexico, France, and Prussia, the Hispanic Society of America, and Harvard, Columbia, and Pennsylvania universities.[24] The patrons agreed to send salaried directors to the school each year on a rotating basis and to fund fellowships for advanced students in archaeology, folktales, myths, and Mexican languages.

The International School of American Archaeology and Ethnology was inaugurated on January 20, 1911, with Eduard Seler as the first director. During its approximately four years of existence, its principal contribution was the application of stratigraphic methods to excavations in the Valley of Mexico as a means of establishing the chronology of preconquest civilizations there. In 1911–12, for example, Gamio conducted an investigation at San Miguel Amantla near Atzcapotzalco, which resulted in the still accepted tripartite division of cultural sequences for central Mexico.[25] Fellows of the school also studied the structure and distribution of Mexican languages.

Although Boas gamely assured readers of the *New York Times* in May 1912 that travel in Mexico was safe, the activities of the school were disrupted by the revolution, and the world war inflicted another blow. In a larger sense, the winds of nationalism, which swept over Mexico and so much of the world at this time and which Boas deplored, contributed to the demise of the school.[26]

Boas had not been especially sensitive to the political currents in Mex-

ico after the start of the revolution, but by 1919 he was disturbed by
efforts in the United States to damage relations between the two countries. To Gamio he wrote: "I fear that your wish for hearty cooperation
between Mexico and the United States will be very slow of realization,
because our public press is driving all the time toward misunderstand-
ings. . . . There is a powerful party which . . . want to clean up Mexico,
forgetting entirely that we have enough to do to clean up in our own
country." He was also outraged to learn that several American archaeologists, displaying credentials from scholarly institutions, had conducted investigations in Mexico and Central America on behalf of
American naval intelligence during the war. This prompted his controversial 1919 letter to the *Nation*, entitled "Scientists as Spies," in
which he condemned such activities, pointing out that as a result "every
nation will look with distrust upon the visiting foreign investigator who
wants to do honest work, suspecting sinister designs."[27]

As late as 1928 Boas still hoped that the International School might
be revived, but Zelia Nuttall assured him that it was "absolutely out of
the question" because of "the changed conditions in Mexico and the
decided anti-foreign animus."[28] The changed conditions included a
greater emphasis on applied anthropology than on archaeology and a
more direct government role in anthropological and archaeological investigation. These changes can be seen in the career of Gamio, who
received his doctorate from Columbia in 1921. In 1917 he was appointed head of what became the Dirección de Antropología, which was
housed in the Department of Agriculture. In this capacity he began
large-scale excavations and restorations at Teotihuacán, but the project
expanded to become a massive, multidisciplinary study of an area
Gamio considered representative in one of the ten rural regions into
which Mexico might be divided. Gamio hoped that the study would
help official and private entities by stimulating the economic and social
development of the region and thereby promote the goal of creating a
truly integrated nation.[29]

The decade of the 1920s, then, began with a tradition of cooperation
between Mexico and the investigators and scientific institutions of other
countries. This tradition was strengthened after 1920, though the Mexican government was more determined than before to oversee archaeological activities and to protect its archaeological treasures from looting
or destruction at the hands of foreigners. In the immediate postwar

period, however, only institutions from the United States were in a position to undertake major projects in Mexico.

The postwar era was also characterized by a strong popular interest in archaeology, which was bolstered by the massive publicity given to the discovery of the tomb of Tutankhamon in Egypt in 1922. To cultural nationalists such as Gregory Mason, who bemoaned America's "hemispheric inferiority complex," archaeological remains in Yucatán and other parts of Mexico were impressive evidence that great, if mysterious, civilizations had flourished in the New World as well as the Old.[30] In Mexico, ancient remains served not only as reminders of its great preconquest heritage but also to attract tourists, both foreign and domestic. Accordingly, the government of Felipe Carrillo Puerto in Yucatán set about improving access to Maya sites. In July 1923 more than five thousand persons attended the inauguration of a twenty-kilometer road linking the town of Dzitas with Chichén Itzá.[31] Tourists might now ride the train from Mérida to Dzitas and travel by car to the ruins.

The earliest and most important example of postwar Mexican-American archaeological collaboration was the contract signed in 1923 for the excavation, repair, and restoration of the ruins at Chichén Itzá by the Carnegie Institution of Washington. The discussions that preceded the signing of the contract were fraught with pitfalls, and their successful outcome can be attributed to the energy and tact of the principal negotiators, Sylvanus G. Morley and Manuel Gamio. Morley proved extremely skillful in cultivating amicable relations with archaeologists and public officials in Yucatán and Mexico City. He was also an admirer of Gamio, whose work at Teotihuacán he praised in an interview in *Excelsior*. He was fond of Gamio personally as well and observed in his diary at one point in the negotiations: "What a joy to work with a Mexican who moves like an American, as Gamio always does."[32]

Morley had first visited Chichén Itzá in 1907 while studying archaeology at Harvard under Alfred Tozzer.[33] He spent approximately three weeks there, taking measurements of various buildings and drawing bas-reliefs, facades, and murals. Even before he joined the staff of the Carnegie Institution of Washington (CIW) in 1914, he had formulated the desire to launch a major research project at Chichén Itzá. His plans were interrupted by World War I, during which he served in naval intelligence and was one of the "scientific spies" denounced by Boas in 1919. All the while, Thompson had continued to live at the site, though he was not unaffected by the turbulence of the revolution. In 1921, while he was in Mérida, the main hacienda house was sacked and badly burned; Thompson's furniture as well as what he called the "museum" were destroyed.[34]

By February 1923 plans had advanced sufficiently for John C. Merriam, president of the CIW, to visit Chichén Itzá in person, in the company of Morley and William Barclay Parsons of the recently established Archaeological Institute of America. Merriam and Parsons, along with Alma Reed and Morley's sister Elinor, formed part of a group of nineteen visitors who were welcomed to Yucatán as the advance guard of future tourists.[35] The visitors were taken to the caves of Loltún and to Uxmal, which Morley found more interesting in some ways than Chichén Itzá. "The buildings are more massive and purer Maya, but Chichén has a wider scientific interest and somehow a more human appeal." Morley spent three days at Chichén with Merriam and Parsons, both of whom were "tremendously impressed" with the cenote. "Dr. Merriam said he never recollected having been anywhere so impressive, where the solemnity of what once was, was so vividly brought home."[36] The portly Parsons was briefly stuck in the spiral passage of the Caracol, but otherwise there were no mishaps. Most important, Merriam had become committed to Morley's project and before leaving Yucatán instructed him to initiate exploratory discussions with the Mexican government.

Morley was encouraged by a conversation with the Mexican inspector of monuments, José Reygadas Vertiz, who was also in Yucatán at this time. Reygadas considered it likely that the government would award a long-term concession to the CIW, though it would insist on the presence of a permanent inspector at the site. Reygadas expected opposition from the anti-American press, but the Carnegie's position would be strengthened because it did not plan to retain any specimens but to turn over everything to the Mexican government.[37]

The travels of the archaeologists and other visitors were recorded in a series of articles in the *New York Times*, some unsigned, others under the byline of Alma Reed. The articles were calculated to whet popular interest in Mexican archaeology and stressed that, although little was known about Maya civilization, its remains were at least as interesting and impressive as those of Egypt. "Yucatan," Reed asserted, "is being hailed as the 'Egypt' of America."[38] Several articles had another result, for they set off a presumably unexpected controversy by publicly revealing not only Thompson's dredging of the cenote at Chichén but also his removal of objects found therein in defiance of Mexican law.

The first of these articles appeared on March 2, 1923, and described an account by Thompson of "what is conceded to be the most important find of archæological objects ever made in America." The objects in question were those that Thompson had found years before in the cenote, which had been removed to the Peabody Museum. Reed wrote a more detailed story about Thompson's activities at the cenote, touching upon the "virgins of flawless loveliness" who had supposedly been sacrificed at the site.[39] By making it clear that the objects from the cenote had been taken to the museum in violation of Mexican law, the articles placed Thompson in a vulnerable position. Morley expressed concern over the effect that the publicity about Thompson might have on his negotiations with the Mexican government, but he was not unduly alarmed because the CIW did not plan to take any objects out of the country.[40] Nevertheless, in an interview that appeared in *El Universal*, he took pains to explain that the CIW was not a museum and was not interested in taking artifacts out of Mexico.

For the moment, the Mexican government took no action against Thompson, and Morley traveled to Mexico City to begin discussions with the government representatives, Gamio and Reygadas. By early June negotiations were sufficiently advanced to warrant a second trip to Mexico by Merriam. On June 3 Merriam, along with Morley and Reygadas, went to Teotihuacán, where they lunched with Gamio. Afterward Merriam spent more than three hours presenting the CIW's case to Gamio. Back in Mexico City they met with the undersecretary of agriculture, Ramón de Negri, who gave his support. The following day they had a twenty-minute interview with President Obregón, who also indicated his approval of the project. When Merriam returned to the United States, Morley was pleased with the progress to date. "No one has ever come to Mexico City, seen such big people (including the President), despatched their business satisfactorily and got away in such a minimum of time. . . . Of course, it could not have been done without Gamio's hearty cooperation and assistance at every point."[41]

Despite the promising auguries, numerous difficulties had to be resolved before an agreement could be reached. These included differences over the length of the concession to be granted the CIW and its desire to borrow specimens, which Gamio and Reygadas pointed out would violate Mexican law. In addition, critics sniped at the proposed contract. Morley was accused of vandalizing the ruins at Tulum, which he had visited in 1922. He denied the charges but admitted that his companion, Samuel Lothrop, had removed three stone idols from the site without his knowledge. By June 14, however, a final draft of the contract was ready. Merriam's reservations about the draft were quickly dispelled, but Morley's relief soon turned to pessimism when the Mexican government raised minor objections of its own. Zelia Nuttall speculated that the Obregón administration was holding the contract hostage to the outcome of negotiations over American recognition of the government, but Gamio and Reygadas deprecated such fears.[42]

At last, on July 6, Morley received a call from Gamio, who asked: "Hello, Morley, have you got a bottle of champagne?" The dream that Morley had pursued for more than fifteen years had become a reality, for the contract had been signed the day before. The final version granted the CIW the right to explore, excavate, and preserve the ruins at Chichén Itzá for ten years under the supervision of the Department of Agriculture.[43] The CIW was to spend at least $20,000 per year on the project while the department was to spend $8,000 for the repair of buildings at the site. All objects found during exploration of Chichén were to be the property of the Mexican government. During the life of the contract and for three years thereafter the CIW was to have the exclusive right to publish the results of its labors, but the Mexican government might publish Spanish translations of these works. A story in the *New York Times* greeted the signing of the contract with the assertion that it would result in the development of "historic ruins of a magnitude as great if not greater than those of Egypt."[44]

After the negotiations in Mexico City, Morley returned to Yucatán in the company of Gamio, Reygadas, and Thomas Gann, a British physician and archaeologist. Because their ship was late in sailing, they just missed the ceremonies on July 15 opening the road from Dzitas to Chichén Itzá. Morley was delighted with the new road when he and his companions traveled on it en route to the ruins a few days later. His attention was now drawn to the negotiation of an agreement with Edward H. Thompson for the use of the hacienda house and adjacent buildings as well as a hundred-acre tract of woodland. In desperate need of funds, Thompson pestered Morley for an advance on the money he was to receive from the CIW Morley was alternately annoyed with and sympathetic toward the old man: "One cannot help but keep feeling dreadfully sorry for him, the whole place is so run down at the heel, including himself, and so extensively overrun by his left hand progeny and their even more numerous descendants, that one feels a wave of pity for him. And yet amidst all the squalor and filth . . . he carries it off with the greatest aplomb." Matters were complicated by a legal judgment that had been entered against Thompson because of his failure to repay funds he had borrowed after the attack in 1921. Thompson was fearful that the authorities might order the auction of his property to satisfy the judgment. Governor Carrillo Puerto was willing to arrange for a postponement of the sale until Thompson concluded his negotiations with the CIW, which agreed to rent the property for $100 per month with an option to buy. Another complication emerged the following year when Thompson revealed that he owed approximately $450 in taxes on the property; this problem was resolved when the CIW agreed to pay the back taxes.[45]

The CIW's first formal season of excavation at Chichén Itzá got under way in 1924 under the leadership of Morley and a team of archaeologists, including Earl H. Morris, James O. Kilmartin, and Monroe Amsden. While work continued on the construction and repair of buildings for the CIW staff, excavation began at the Temple of the Warriors under the supervision of Morris.[46] Meanwhile, the archaeologist Miguel Angel Fernández represented the Mexican government at the site and continued work on the Ball Court group which he had begun the previous year.

Excavation continued until 1933, when it was suspended by the CIW. Over the years additional archaeologists joined the staff, among them Karl Ruppert, Oliver Ricketson, Jr., J. Eric S. Thompson, and George C. Vaillant, who undertook a study of Maya pottery in 1926. Jean Charlot, who had previously been employed as a muralist in Mexico City, spent three seasons at Chichén Itzá as a staff artist, making drawings and writing analyses of the aesthetic aspects of stelae and other artifacts. "It was an enlightening experience," he wrote later, "thus to dig at the roots of Mexican art that I had helped to some of its newest buds."[47] A second artist engaged by Morley was Lowell Houser, who had lived in Mexico since 1923. At the same time the Mexican government continued excavation and repair of the Castillo–Ball Court group under Eduardo

Martínez Cantón and J. M. Erosa Peniche. Chichén was also the head-quarters for other CIW projects in Middle America, such as expeditions to Cobá in eastern Yucatán in 1926. By the end of the decade, however, Morley's emphasis on archaeological excavation as the primary means of learning about the prehistoric Maya had come to seem narrow and restrictive to those who believed that a multidisciplinary approach would yield greater knowledge. The CIW then broadened the scope of its Middle American program to encompass the natural sciences, history, and anthropology under the direction of Alfred V. Kidder, who became head of the Division of Historical Research, established in 1929. Kidder believed that to reconstruct the history of the ancient Maya, archaeology had to be complemented by other disciplines. Therefore, the CIW became committed to a "panscientific attack" on the problem.[48]

During these years the work of the CIW at Chichén was well publicized in both the United States and Mexico. The CIW held two conferences in Washington in 1924, one dealing with the Chichén project, the second with the work of Manuel Gamio. Gamio himself addressed those attending the conferences, and an exhibition was held illustrating the arts and crafts revival he had initiated at San Juan Teotihuacán, a village near the archaeological site. In addition to scholarly reports on the progress of the work at Chichén, CIW staff members published two popular volumes on the subject, both in 1931; Earl H. Morris wrote *The Temple of the Warriors*, and his wife, Ann Axtell Morris, wrote *Digging in Yucatan*. Morley proved particularly effective in stimulating enthusiasm for the Maya in the United States. Many years later J. Eric S. Thompson recalled: "In his lectures delivered from one end of the country to the other he could take some rather dull piece of excavation, and with his magic personality lead his hearers to feel themselves participants in a glorious and momentous undertaking." Morley was also assiduous in presenting the results of CIW efforts before Mexican audiences and, despite his execrable Spanish, often spoke in Mexico City under the auspices of the Secretariat of Education. In 1926 several of his talks were broadcast on the radio from Mexico City.[49] Morley's flair for public relations helps explain why he and the CIW were generally successful in avoiding Mexican criticism of their work.

"In developing the Chichén Itzá Project," Morley wrote in 1925, "the policy has been from the beginning to consult frequently the Mexican officials concerned, in order that there should be entire agreement at all times as to the work done, and the best interests of the research thus secured."[50] Accordingly, he regularly conferred with officials in Mexico City and with the government's representatives at the site. In March 1928 a formal ceremony was held to mark the end of the CIW's work on the Temple of the Warriors, which was turned over to the Mexican government for maintenance. John C. Merriam attended the ceremony, as did the governor of Yucatán, Alvaro Torre Díaz, who paid tribute to the CIW's contribution in furthering mutual understanding between Mexico and the United States. In 1934, after the expiration of the 1923 concession, the Mexican government granted a new contract to the CIW, allowing it to do research at Chichén and other sites for five additional years, with the option of renewal for another five.[51]

The generally harmonious relations between the Mexican government and the CIW can also be attributed to the institution's apparently scrupulous observance of Mexican laws forbidding the removal of antiquities from the country. Morley knew that the law was often violated by foreign archaeologists. In August 1923 he returned from Mexico to the United States by train with Thomas Gann. As soon as they had crossed the border, Gann revealed to Morley a "magnificent" piece of Maya jade which he had concealed on his body. He had purchased it in Mexico City from a dealer in antiquities for $250. Morley was pleased that Gann had acquired the object, but Merriam heard about the incident and refused to engage Gann as physician at Chichén because he had broken the law.[52] The following year Morley himself turned over to Reygadas, who was visiting Chichén, two golden objects from the cenote—a small bell with a bird on top and an anthropomorphic pendant—which he had purchased fifteen years earlier. A turquoise mosaic found in 1928 in a sealed stone urn buried in the Temple of the Chac Mool was turned over to the Mexican government a few months later.[53]

In view of the sensitivity of this issue, it is not surprising that in 1926 the Mexican government began legal action against Edward H. Thompson because of his removal of ancient objects from the cenote at Chichén. Three years had elapsed since the first public disclosure of Thompson's activities, and the government apparently acted at this time because it believed that he was about to sell his property at Chichén to the CIW. A second motive was the recent publication of *The City of the Sacred Well* by Theodore A. Willard, head of the Willard Storage Battery Company and a Maya enthusiast. A patron and admirer of Thompson,

Willard gave a detailed account of the dredging of the cenote and of the objects found therein. Since not all of the objects mentioned were in the Peabody Museum, it was surmised that Thompson had sold some of them to Willard.

The case against Thompson began in July 1926, when Secretary of Education Puig Casauranc requested an investigation of Thompson's activities. In September Thompson was formally charged with the illegal removal of artistic treasures from Mexico. The value of the objects was set at 1,036,410 pesos, and all of Thompson's property was attached as a guarantee of civil responsibility.[54]

To buttress its case, the government released documents showing that Thompson had asked for permission to dredge the cenote in 1911, years after he had begun his operations there, and that his request had been denied unless he agreed to accept government supervision of his activities. Also released was a vitriolic attack on Thompson written about 1909 by the German archaeologist Teobert Maler, who had settled in Yucatán in 1884. Maler denounced Thompson as "a greedy treasure-hunter come from Yanquilandia," who not only removed many objects from Chichén Itzá but also wantonly destroyed works of art there and even allowed his cattle to graze upon the ruins, damaging the steps of the pyramids.[55] The government's action against Thompson earned the praise of *Excelsior*, which saw him as one of the many foreigners who had despoiled Mexico of its artistic treasures. The newspaper was also critical of the Díaz government for neglecting its responsibilities in the matter. Thompson argued as justification that he had acted in the interest of science and not for personal profit. In his autobiography he minimized the monetary value of the objects recovered from the cenote and, though not mentioning their removal from Mexico, claimed that he had felt obliged to ensure their permanent safety.[56] The activities of the CIW were not affected by the suit against Thompson, which had not been resolved at the time of his death in 1935. A settlement was finally reached in which Thompson's heirs were allowed to keep the hacienda buildings and the government retained the rest of the property.[57]

Mexico's Maya zone had been the preferred field of American archaeologists from John Lloyd Stephens to the CIW. The establishment of what might be called an American archaeological sphere of influence was furthered by the work of the Department of Middle American Research of Tulane University, which was established in 1924 through the largesse of Samuel Zemurray, president of the Cuyamel Fruit Company. The first head of the new organization was William Gates, an unconventional Maya scholar, who engaged Frans Blom as staff archaeologist. Blom, a native of Denmark, had moved to Mexico by 1919.[58] While in the employ of the Eagle Oil Company, he visited Palenque in 1922 and decided to devote himself to archaeology. Over the next three years he studied at Harvard and did fieldwork for the Dirección de Antropología and the CIW.

In 1925 Blom went to Mexico on behalf of the Middle American Research Department to carry out a reconnaissance of preconquest sites in several southern states. Accompanying him in the capacity of ethnologist was Oliver LaFarge, son of architect Christopher Grant LaFarge and a graduate student in anthropology at Harvard, who already had considerable experience with Indians of the American Southwest.[59] In Tampico they visited "the famous old pot hunter" William Niven and examined a collection of primitive clay figurines he had unearthed at a nearby railroad station.

Blom and LaFarge spent more than five months in Mexico, exploring sites in Veracruz, Tabasco, and Chiapas before crossing the border into Guatemala and ending the expedition there. In his diary Blom described the expedition as "five months in Hell" and frequently found fault with LaFarge, who seemed absent-minded and lazy. Blom often expressed satisfaction with his surroundings, however, as, for example, the village of Ocosingo, Chiapas: "What a quiet and pretty place this is, horses grazing on the streets, sounds of church bells, and during the afternoon the girls . . . walk around the plaza, some of them quite good looking."[60] In the published account of the expedition, Blom provided data on more than forty sites in the three states containing monuments or preconquest artifacts. The sites visited included La Venta, Veracruz, where they found several interesting objects, including stelae and a colossal stone head that resembled one that had been uncovered at Hueyapan over sixty years before. Blom was so concerned about finding possible Maya influences that he failed to realize that he and LaFarge had unwittingly discovered the most important site of the civilization Hermann Beyer called Olmec in a 1927 review of their book.[61]

In the book LaFarge described the dwellings, dress, and household objects of the Indians they encountered during their journey. He also compiled word lists of the Indians' languages. Their joint account, like

Blom's diary, suggests that they found an appealing tranquillity in the regions they traversed, especially Chiapas. They spent some time among the Tzeltal-speaking natives of this state, who "came to take us for granted, and allowed us to see unfolding the harmonious, dignified family life, with its feeling of unvoiced yet real affection that is so typical of the American Indian where European contact has been slight."[62]

LaFarge, who remained on the staff of the Department of Middle American Research until 1928, became a nationally known literary figure with the publication of his novel about Navajo life, *Laughing Boy*, in 1929. According to his biographer, the 1925 expedition had a strong influence on LaFarge's life: "From his previous association with Indians in the Southwest, he had accepted the notion then current that the Indian people and their way of life were destined to assimilate to the white world and to disappear. But in southern Mexico and Guatemala, he saw tribes large and small that had experienced profound change yet remained staunchly Indian."[63]

At the conclusion of their book on the 1925 expedition, Blom and LaFarge asserted that preconquest culture played a "stupendous role" in the daily life of modern Americans and expressed the hope that the volume would draw attention to New World archaeology. "The old saying that charity should begin at home can well be applied to American Archaeology. Vast sums are spent by American Institutions in distant fields, while only a few of them conduct explorations on American soil."[64] Over the next few years Blom, who supplanted Gates as head of the Department of Middle American Research in 1926, attempted both to publicize Maya achievements and to raise funds to support his ambitious plans for the department.

Blom had only limited success in reaching the latter goal. He was able to finance the John Giddings Gray Memorial Expedition of 1928 to Chiapas, Yucatán, and Guatemala with funds donated by Gray's children but was unable to publish an official account of the sometimes dangerous six-month journey.[65] Although Blom made appeals to foundations and appointed honorary associates such as Theodore A. Willard to his staff, he was unable to raise more than small sums.

Blom also worked vigorously to promote Maya studies at Tulane University and in New Orleans. He regularly kept local newspapers apprised of the activities of the department. Before setting out on the Gray Memorial Expedition, he tried to stimulate interest in the project by displaying its equipment in the department. He was especially energetic in developing the collections of the department's museum.

The combination of scholarship and popularization that characterized American Maya studies during the 1920s can best be seen in the career of Gregory Mason, a one-time editor of the *Outlook* who had been sent to Yucatán in 1914 to assess the impact of the revolution there. A visit to Uxmal awakened his interest in the ancient Maya. In subsequent years he contributed several articles to popular magazines in which he lauded the archaeological wonders to be found in "our own Egypt."[66]

In 1926 Mason had an opportunity to lead an expedition of his own, in association with Herbert J. Spinden of the Peabody Museum, noted for his pioneering study of Maya art (1913) and his work on Maya chronology. The *New York Times* financed the expedition, which began with an exploration of the eastern coast of Yucatán by schooner.[67] Mason and Spinden then traveled by mule from Lake Bacalar to Peto, becoming the first archaeologists to make the journey. During the expedition they found seven unknown Maya cities, the most important of which was Muyil, located near Ascension Bay. Mason described the expedition in a lengthy series of articles for the *Times*, which did not fail to mention the perils of the journey and the mysteries of the ancient Maya.

Two years later Mason headed another expedition to Yucatán and British Honduras, this time a primarily ethnological venture on behalf of the Museum of the American Indian (Heye Foundation) and the *New York Herald Tribune*.[68] Another sponsor of the expedition was Thomas A. Blodgett, president of the American Chicle Company, who had caught the "Maya bug" but at the last moment had to cancel plans to take part himself. The principal accomplishment of the expedition was the discovery of two caves in British Honduras containing many preconquest artifacts and of the ruins of Ixil in northern Yucatán near an elevated road ten feet high and forty feet wide. "I wish," Mason wrote in an article for the *Herald Tribune*, "that American millionaires who are spending millions on excavations in Greece and Egypt would give half a million to restore this causeway, a real wonder of the ancient world, to attract thousands of modern tourists."[69]

Scholarship and popularization, this time coupled with the most modern technology, can also be seen in Charles Lindbergh's well-publicized aerial reconnaissance of the Maya zone in 1929. In Spinden's opinion, parts of this region—southern Yucatán, the Usumacinta Valley, and northeastern Guatemala—were well suited for archaeological exploration by air because they were so heavily forested that travel by land was extremely difficult.[70]

Lindbergh's flight was sponsored by the CIW, which earlier that year had received photographs he had taken while flying over Indian ruins in New Mexico in what was described as the first successful application of aerial photography for archaeological purposes. Accompanied by his wife and A. V. Kidder of the CIW, Lindbergh flew a giant Sikorsky plane for four successive days over Guatemala and the Yucatán peninsula. During their twenty-five hours aloft the party sighted several previously unknown Maya ruins and took more than one hundred photographs, which were turned over to the CIW.

Kidder claimed that the Lindbergh reconnaissance had accomplished in twenty-five hours what it would have taken a ground party five years to achieve, but Blom was skeptical about the usefulness of aerial reconnaissance. "Frankly, I cannot see the scientific value of the Lindbergh exploit," he wrote to a friend, "but it is great for publicity for the Mayas and will undoubtedly help us." Mason also had doubts, claiming that the mule was the best "ship of the bush," but this did not deter him from undertaking a similar venture, sponsored by the University of Pennsylvania, the following year. The party, which included archaeologist J. Alden Mason, covered more than twenty-five hundred square miles of the Maya region in a twin Wasp-motored Sikorsky amphibian. Reversing his earlier opinion to some extent, Gregory Mason wrote: "A great deal more is seen from an air plane than is seen from the back of a mule, but it is not seen nearly so well."[71]

While American archaeological efforts were focused on the Maya zone, archaeology in central Mexico continued to be dominated by Mexicans. Zelia Nuttall, a pioneer in the field, was in poor health and straitened finances by the late 1920s and reduced her professional activities. During these years she devoted much of her remaining energy to a campaign to have Mexico establish as a national holiday the first of the two days each year when the sun casts no shadow. She maintained that this phenomenon, caused by the sun's being at its zenith, was the new year's day of the Aztecs, marking the start of the rainy season. On the day in question, usually May 17, she would give a demonstration of the phenomenon at the Casa Alvarado, where guests could see the shadow of an upright stick disappear when the zenith was reached. On May 17,

1928, the occasion was celebrated at the Mexico City Normal School and at the Lincoln Library in ceremonies attended by Nuttall and Mrs. Morrow. At the Normal School, students dressed in white and wearing garlands of roses in their hair danced around maypoles and sang an invocation to the sun.[72]

Only a handful of Americans conducted excavations in the central region, and these took place under the direction of Mexican authorities. From 1922 to 1925 Byron Cummings of the University of Arizona excavated a mound surrounded by the lava flow known as the Pedregal at Cuicuilco in the Federal District. Cummings's investigation, which was sponsored by the Mexican government, the University of Arizona, and the National Geographic Society, revealed the mound to be a temple dating back to what was then called the Archaic period; it was the oldest building known up to that time.[73] In 1924, at the suggestion of Gamio, Alfred L. Kroeber of the University of California also excavated at several sites in the Valley of Mexico. His study of pottery shards collected at these sites led him to conclude that the Archaic period should be subdivided into four periods rather than the two then accepted.[74]

The most important work performed in central Mexico by an American archaeologist was the series of stratigraphic studies carried on from 1928 to 1934 by George C. Vaillant, assistant and later associate curator of Mexican archaeology at the American Museum of Natural History in New York, who "changed the course of Mexican archaeology and placed it on a new and professional footing." Encouraged by Clarence L. Hay, a trustee of the museum, who had worked in Mexico himself, Vaillant sought to test the "Archaic Hypothesis" of Herbert Spinden that the origins of sedentary life in the Western Hemisphere were to be found in the early ceramic culture underlying the remains of Teotihuacán civilization. The Secretariat of Public Education authorized the project, which was to be carried out under the supervision of the secretariat's Archaeological Department, and Vaillant was to turn over to the National Museum any objects the department found interesting. At the end of the first season's work, the director of the American Museum, George H. Sherwood, thanked Mexican officials for their courtesy and advice. "This relationship of amical [sic] cooperation between the Ministry of Public Education and the American Museum of Natural History is a shining example of international research forwarded by the brotherhood among scholars," he wrote. Relations between Vaillant and Mexican scholars remained cordial. In 1931, for example, he reported to Sherwood: "The [Mexican] officials have been more than kind not only letting us work anywhere we want at Teotihuacán but also providing us with a beautiful room rent free at the government house at the foot of the pyramid."[75]

Vaillant's excavations at Zacatenco, Ticoman, El Arbolillo, and other sites in the Valley of Mexico and his analysis of the material recovered led him to substitute a "Middle" period for the "Archaic," thereby postulating a cultural phase or phases in the valley earlier than the latter. He not only produced scholarly monographs but also shared his findings with readers of the museum's popular magazine, *Natural History*. Later, while serving as a cultural affairs officer in Lima, he recalled "the great progress in social and intellectual understanding between Mexicans and North Americans" that he had witnessed as an archaeologist even though political and economic relations between the two countries were strained at the time.[76] In particular, Vaillant developed a close association with Alfonso Caso, whose work at Monte Albán, Oaxaca, coincided with his own.

Caso began fieldwork at Monte Albán in December 1930. His findings attracted little interest outside professional circles in the United States until his discovery in January 1932 of Tomb 7 and its treasures of gold, silver, jade, and turquoise. News of the find was featured prominently in the American press amid predictable comparisons to the tomb of Tutankhamon. An article in *Popular Mechanics* described the "breathtaking" sight that greeted Caso and his associates as they entered the tomb: "On the floor lay the mummies of ten warriors. . . . Over the mummies was strewn a glittering pile; they were literally buried in gold, silver, costly gems and semi-precious stones. Ten heavy, solid-gold crowns of exquisite workmanship testified to the station of the long-dead men. Pearls, as large as pigeons' eggs, attested their wealth in a vanished civilization." Caso himself asserted in the *National Geographic* that Tomb 7 had yielded "works of art comparable, and in many respects superior, to the finest productions of the ancient Egyptians, Greeks, and Chinese." From the beginning, Caso affirmed that the objects were of Mixtec origin though the tomb had originally been used by the Zapotecs. Zelia Nuttall, however, ignited a minor controversy by suggesting that the tomb was that of the Aztec leader Cuauhtémoc.[77]

The contents of the tomb aroused so much excitement that they were removed to Mexico City and shown at the National Museum. Residents of the United States had an opportunity to view the treasure of Monte Albán in 1933, when the objects were exhibited at the Century of Progress exposition in Chicago and in other cities. In New York they were on display for nearly a month in Pennsylvania Station, earning the admiration of art critics, who praised their form and proportions. The exhibition then traveled to Washington, where it attracted ten thousand visitors in a week.[78]

In addition to exhibiting the treasure of Monte Albán, planners of the Chicago fair commissioned the construction of a Maya building and allocated $100,000 for the project. In keeping with the practice of including Native Americans among the exhibits at fairs, planners of the Chicago exposition designed an anthropological section featuring a Sioux encampment and Navajo hogan with the Maya building rising in the background. The commission was entrusted to the Department of Middle American Research at Tulane and Frans Blom, who planned a reproduction of the Nunnery at Uxmal. Early in 1930 he took a team of engineers, architects, sculptors, and photographers to Uxmal, where they carefully studied the structure. As it turned out, however, fair officials concluded that it would be too expensive to recreate the entire Nunnery and built only a portion of the north wall. Inside the wooden structure a few Maya artifacts were displayed, along with a reproduction of the murals from the Temple of the Warriors at Chichén Itzá. Neither Blom nor Morley was happy with the exhibit, but it was reported that ten thousand persons were passing through the building each day.[79]

If the decade of the 1920s was characterized by collaboration between American and Mexican archaeologists and by popularization of their findings on preconquest civilizations in the United States, it also marked the beginning of interest in the culture of Mexico's contemporary Indian communities by anthropologists and other students of Native Americans. Robert Redfield initiated the study of folk communities with his pioneering book on Tepoztlán and went on to examine social change in Yucatán. John Collier found inspiration in Mexican policy for his efforts to reform federal programs for the Indians of the United States. In their relations with these scholars and officials, Manuel Gamio and Moisés Sáenz played major roles as cultural mediators between Mexico and the United States.

In 1920 anthropology was a relatively new discipline. Between 1892 (when the first Ph.D. in anthropology was awarded) and 1920, only forty-one persons received doctorates in the field from universities in the United States. Fieldwork took place mainly among Native Americans, and few anthropologists studied other peoples of the United States or groups in other countries. During the 1920s, however, several developments occurred within the United States which contributed to the beginning of Mexican community studies: the rise of professional interest in cultural dynamics; the establishment of organizations such as the Social Science Research Council (1924), which directed research into nontraditional channels; and the growth of private philanthropic foundations, which provided funding for such research. In addition, anthropologists often shared the dissatisfaction with industrial society expressed by cultural critics in the United States. In an essay titled "Culture, Genuine and Spurious," for example, Edward Sapir described the Indian's salmon spearing as "a culturally higher type of activity" than that performed by the industrial worker because "there is normally no sense of spiritual frustration during its prosecution . . . because it works in naturally with all of the rest of the Indian's activities instead of standing out as a desert patch of merely economic effort in the whole of life."[80] In such a context, the Mexican rural community beckoned as a promising yet practical site for the study of cultural change.

Manuel Gamio had laid the basis for Mexican community studies with his work at Teotihuacán, but he had subsequently been enmeshed in adminstrative duties as head of the Dirección de Antropología. In December 1924 he resigned this position, which was abolished, and became undersecretary of education in the Calles administration. Only a few months later, however, he became embroiled in a dispute over corruption in the department and the unwillingness of Secretary Puig Casauranc to allow a full investigation. As a result, Gamio was dismissed on June 8, 1925, and was succeeded by Moisés Sáenz.[81]

Upon his dismissal, Gamio left for the United States. In 1926 he received funding from the Social Science Research Council for a major study of Mexican immigration to the United States. For several months the Mexican government contributed $500 per month to the project; when this funding was halted in June 1928, Dwight Morrow donated $3,500 to the study. Gamio's wide-ranging analysis of the immigrants' culture and the effects of their residence in the United States was published in 1930. It was well received by American reviewers at a time when the growth of the Mexican population was attracting increasing attention. In Mexico, however, there was resistance to his contention that short-term emigration was beneficial to that country for several reasons: it offered a safety valve for the unemployed and exposed emigrants to machinery and the discipline of modern life while the remittances they sent back were also helpful. As a result, Gamio's work was not published in Mexico until long after his death.[82]

Concern about Mexican emigration to the United States also helped Robert Redfield obtain financing from the Social Science Research Council for his study of Tepoztlán. "It is apparent," he wrote in his fellowship application, "that a description of the life of . . . Mexicans in their home communities would facilitate an intensive study of the problems arising out of the growing Mexican immigration to the United States." Redfield, originally trained as a lawyer, had begun graduate work in sociology and anthropology at the University of Chicago in 1924. His interest in Mexico had been stirred by a visit in 1923 at the invitation of Elena Landázuri, a Mexican feminist whom he had met in Chicago. During this trip Redfield became acquainted with Gamio and with Frances Toor and was deeply impressed by the artistic and humanitarian aspects of the Indianist movement.[83]

The village of Tepoztlán, which Stuart Chase was to describe in *Mexico: A Study of Two Americas* (1931), was chosen as the site of the study at the suggestion of Gamio. Redfield arrived in Tepoztlán in November 1926, accompanied by his wife, Margaret Park Redfield, their two small children, and his mother-in-law, who remained for four weeks. They settled down in a one-room house with "an extraordinarily beautiful" view of a subtropical valley. As work got under way, Redfield's wife gathered data on culinary practices and on birth customs and postnatal care. The younger child, an infant, attracted much attention in the village and served as a means of collecting local lore on child care.[84] The Redfields' idyllic existence in Tepoztlán was cut short after three months by the growing insecurity of the region. After a band of rebels invaded the village and engaged in a battle with the townspeople, Redfield sent his wife and children to Mexico City while he continued his fieldwork alone, remaining until July.

When Redfield's *Tepoztlán, a Mexican Village: A Study of Folk Life* was published in 1930, it was immediately recognized as a landmark comparable only to Gamio's work on Teotihuacán and reminiscent of *Middle-*

town by Robert and Helen Lynd. Although Redfield discussed the elements of material culture in keeping with traditional ethnology, his emphasis on urbanization and on social change as an ongoing process was innovative. Alfred L. Kroeber remarked on Redfield's neglect of Tepoztlán's historical development,[85] but neither he nor other contemporary reviewers questioned the essential accuracy of his structural-functionalist analysis, which focused on the cooperative aspects of life in this simple village, where land was adequate, festivals dotted the calendar, and no one watched the clock. That study would be left to a later generation of scholars, notably Oscar Lewis, who found many divergences from Redfield's depiction when he restudied Tepoztlán in the 1940s.

In a review of Redfield's volume for the *New Republic* Chase adumbrated the themes that he would stress in his own book, declaring that he would rather live in Tepoztlán than in Middletown because he would have more fun and economic security.[86] Interestingly, Redfield, in his review of Chase's book the following year, wondered whether the villagers of Tepoztlán were as contented as Chase believed. He observed that at the fiestas Chase admired so much the women did little more than prepare food. "More important, the villagers are often underfed, and underslept; some villagers are sodden with drink."[87]

Redfield's work at Tepoztlán paved the way for his involvement in a more ambitious project: a study of the folk-urban continuum in Yucatán. Begun in 1930, the Yucatán project was sponsored by the CIW as part of Kidder's "panscientific" approach to the region. The project eventually involved the study of several communities—tribal villages in Quintana Roo, Chan Kom, Dzitas, and Mérida—selected to illustrate the dynamics of the diffusion of modern urban culture from Mérida and the corresponding reduction of folk culture in the other communities.

Redfield spent several seasons in Yucatán in the early 1930s, along with his associate, Asael T. Hansen, who had recently received a doctorate in sociology from the University of Wisconsin and was assigned responsibility for research in Mérida. Hansen and his wife, Greta, a trained ethnologist, arrived in Yucatán in August 1931. Gradually and with difficulty, he learned Spanish and became acquainted with Mérida. "Most of the first year, I dreaded defeat," he recalled later. "During the second year it slowly apppeared to me that I was beginning to cope with my task. By the end of the third year, I knew a great deal about Mérida—big and diversified as it was."[88]

Another important member of the research team was Alfonso Villa Rojas, a native of Mérida who had been put in charge of Chan Kom's school in 1927. Because of the proximity of Chan Kom to Chichén Itzá, he became friendly with Morley, who lent him books on Maya history and archaeology and introduced him to Redfield in 1930. Villa proved to be the CIW's principal Mexican collaborator. Perfecting his knowledge of Maya, he conducted fieldwork in the absence of Redfield and kept a detailed diary of life in Chan Kom. He also did research in Quintana Roo, site of the least acculturated villages in Redfield's folk-urban continuum. In 1933 he began graduate work in anthropology at the University of Chicago, which afforded him an opportunity to study Native Americans in the United States. According to Hansen, the only other Mexican scholar to emerge from the Yucatán project was the historian José Ignacio Rubio Mañé, who did archival research for the CIW.[89]

The Yucatán project yielded numerous publications, including a summary volume by Redfield, *The Folk Culture of Yucatán* (1941), as well as three detailed studies of individual communities, which appeared at varying intervals: *Chan Kom: A Maya Village* (1934) by Redfield and Villa Rojas, *The Maya of East Central Quintana Roo* (1945) by Villa Rojas, *A Village That Chose Progress: Chan Kom Revisited* (1950) by Redfield, and *Mérida: Su transformación de capital colonial a naciente metrópoli* (1984) by Hansen and Juan R. Bastarrachea M. Redfield's work in Yucatán, like his Tepoztlán study, was important for several reasons. Not only was the folk-urban model a novel concept, but it also implied rejection of the orthodox diffusionist view of the passive acceptance of "modern" traits by non-Western cultures. As Milton Singer put it: "He demonstrated the importance and feasibility of looking at the process of modernization from the point of view of the traditional societies, their own values and world view, their changing moods and biographies. The traditional societies could no longer be regarded as passive obstacles on the road to progress which must be removed or converted into carbon copies of the 'progressive' societies of the West."[90]

Redfield himself in his 1950 volume and other scholars later raised questions about the validity of the folk-urban model. By the 1960s his failure to address the effect of historical phenomena such as the Caste

War and the spread of henequen monoculture on the communities was perceived as a major weakness of the CIW's studies. These studies, however, along with the monumental works on Maya ethnohistory and the Spanish colonial period prepared for the CIW by historians Ralph L. Roys and France V. Scholes, laid the basis for all subsequent research on the lowland Maya by historians and anthropologists. Indeed, the period of the Yucatán project has been called "a golden age" in Maya studies.[91]

During the early 1930s other American scholars followed Redfield's lead in studying Mexican peoples and communities. Contemporary American preoccupation with Mexican immigration was reflected in the work of Paul S. Taylor, who was awarded a Guggenheim fellowship in 1930 to study emigration from the perspective of a Mexican community. Taylor, an economist who had studied Mexican labor in the United States on behalf of the Social Science Research Council, selected as the site of his fieldwork the municipality of Arandas in the state of Jalisco, from which many Mexicans had emigrated since the late nineteenth century. It differed from other Mexican communities chosen for anthropological fieldwork in being composed mainly of people of Spanish ancestry. In addition, Taylor's primary concern was the process of immigration and its impact on those who remained and those who returned.[92]

Another scholar who produced a study of a Mexican community was Elsie Clews Parsons. Trained as a sociologist at Columbia University, she was in her mid-thirties when a trip to the Southwest in 1910 led her to ethnology and a series of studies on the Pueblo Indians. These in turn led her to Mexico, where she could study a living culture and attempt to determine which cultural traits were Spanish and which were Indian. The community she chose was the Zapotec town of Mitla in the state of Oaxaca, which she had previously visited in 1913.[93]

Parsons made three visits to Mitla from 1929 to 1933, narrowly escaping death when the earthquake of January 14, 1931, caught her as she was writing in bed in a hotel there.[94] The principal result of her research was *Mitla: Town of the Souls* (1936), a personalized, rather discursive work, which addressed the question of cultural change along with the origins of discrete traits. She concluded that "the aspects of culture more clearly associated with women—'remedies,' weaving, cookery, and feasting—have outlasted the cultural activities of men—hunting, war, the ritual arts, and ceremonial and political organization, all of which have either disappeared or been largely hispanized." At the same time, she believed that the adoption of European traits, whether voluntary or the result of force, was always affected by indigenous habits and attitudes. Unlike other students of contemporary Mexican rural communities, she did not find the Mitleños to be unmaterialistic, but rather the reverse. "Money cost enters into the evaluation of things and experience to a degree I have never found equaled in any other society, including the most plutocratic circles."[95] Although Redfield had reservations about her methodology, especially her ability to evaluate processes of acculturation that had occurred long before her arrival at Mitla, he offered to publish the book in a series he edited at the University of Chicago.[96]

During the early 1930s Parsons traveled extensively throughout Mexico, at times in the company of Ralph Beals, younger brother of Carleton and a fledgling anthropologist. Ralph, who had shared Carleton's first arduous trek to Mexico, received his doctorate from the University of California in 1930 with a dissertation on the ethnology of northern Mexico before 1750, a topic dictated in part by his lack of money for fieldwork. His first research trip to Mexico, made possible ·by a grant from the National Research Council, was a study of acculturation among the Yaqui-Mayo Indians of Sonora.[97]

Unable to find employment upon the expiration of his grant in 1932, Beals was rescued by a fellowship from Parsons. At the beginning of the year, they did research among the Yaqui-Mayo in Sonora, traveling as aunt and nephew so as not to offend the sensibilities of the local people. In November they set out again, spending several weeks in Tepic, Nayarit, interviewing Cora and Huichol Indians. She found Tepic to be a "charming" town and was delighted with her informants. She wrote to Franz Boas: "At last, *real* Indians, in psychology and culture! And they link up with the Pueblo in most interesting ways."[98] They then traveled to Mexico City and Mitla, after which Beals searched for indigenous survivals among the Mixe of Oaxaca, where he found the culture even more vital than among the Yaqui and Mayo.

Beals hoped to convert his experiences among the latter into a volume for general readers, discussing the evolution of the Indians' culture and the impact of new influences from the United States. "Studies of acculturation and cultural dynamics are the coming thing in Anthropology," he told his brother, "and this book will be in a sense an advance guard and the first attempt to make palatable for general consumption one of the more significant movements in social studies." As it turned out, Beals was unable to produce the book he envisioned, but in 1940 he began work on a collaborative study of the Tarascan Indians of Michoacán with Daniel Rubín de la Borbolla of the National Polytechnic Institute and other scholars. Modeled on the Yucatán project, the Tarascan study combined a multidisciplinary approach with applied anthropology.[99]

By 1940, then, thanks to the work of Redfield and his colleagues, the study of Mexican peasant or indigenous communities had been established as a means of exploring the process of social change and acculturation. After Ruth Bunzel was awarded a Guggenheim fellowship in 1930, she was advised to alter her plans to do fieldwork in Mexico and to go instead to Guatemala, still virtually untouched by American anthropologists. In 1932 she did visit Chamula, Chiapas, but, ironically, found little of the serenity that Redfield had described for Tepoztlán. Chamula was no isolated, primitive community, she wrote Boas, but part of a country in revolution: "I am seeing the class struggle a little closer than I had expected. The agrarian committees are busy taking land away from the *fincas* and giving it back to the Indians. The Indians come to the meetings armed with rifles and the *finqueros* employ other Indians to attack school teachers."[100]

At a time of ferment in the United States over federal policy toward American Indians, Mexico attracted the attention of reformers because of the seemingly innovative programs being created for its Indian population, especially in the realms of education and agrarian reform. As reformers gained ascendancy in the federal Indian bureaucracy in the early 1930s, they were in a position to suggest emulation of the Mexican model. For information and guidance on Mexico's Indian policies, Americans often looked to Moisés Sáenz, who served as undersecretary of education from 1926 to 1930.

American interest in Mexican educational programs for Indians is illustrated by the February 1932 number of *Progressive Education*, which was devoted to Indian education. An introductory article coauthored by W. Carson Ryan, Jr., director of Indian education for the Bureau of Indian Affairs from 1930 to 1935, pointed to Mexico as an example of a country that was successfully working to integrate its Indian population into the larger society. An article by Sáenz identified as the goal of Mexican education "to weave a civilization out of the various cultural strands that comprise our Mexico." Whereas education in the past had emphasized rote learning from books, the new Mexican schools offered functional learning that was related to the daily lives of those they served, adults as well as children. Thus the schools undertook such projects as improving local water supplies, teaching the Spanish language, and preserving artistic traditions.

In the same issue, Oliver La Farge proposed that experimental schools based on the Mexican model be set up for the Navaho. These schools would instill pride in the Indian heritage as well as offer instruction in farming, nutrition, sanitation, and other basic fields.[101] Ryan had a first-hand look at Mexico's rural education programs during a visit in 1933, when he toured Oaxaca, Morelos, and Tlaxcala in the company of Mexican education officials. He was especially impressed by Mexican work in adult education and indicated that the United States had no comparable programs.[102]

Mexican policies toward Indians had earlier made a profound impression on John Collier, a leading proponent of reform in the United States. Born in Atlanta in 1884, Collier had been engaged in social work and adult education projects in New York and California. By 1919 he had become disillusioned with the "occidental ethos and genius" and lamented the demise of the sense of community in industrial society. During a visit in 1920 to Taos, New Mexico, however, he found among the Pueblo Indians a vital, communally centered culture. Many years later he recalled: "The discovery that came to me there . . . was of personality-forming institutions . . . which had survived repeated and immense historical shocks, and which were going right on in the production of states of mind, attitudes of mind, earth-loyalties and human loyalties, amid a context of beauty which suffused all the life of the group. What I observed and experienced was a power of art—of the life-making art—greater in kind than anything I had known in my own world before." Collier's experiences in New Mexico profoundly altered his life. He now devoted himself to the cause of the American Indian and in 1923 was named executive secretary of the American Indian Defense Association. In this capacity, Collier sought to encourage preservation of Indian religion, arts and crafts, and cultural traditions in general. He also opposed the Dawes Act of 1887, which authorized the allotment of land to individual Indians.[103]

Collier first visited Mexico in 1930, when he set out with his wife and three sons on a rugged journey in a five-year-old Pierce-Arrow. During this visit, he avoided officials but had many friendly encounters with Indians, who often helped to push the automobile along in places where there were no roads.[104] He returned to Mexico the following summer, and this time he became acquainted with Moisés Sáenz and other officials and with Mexican programs for the Indian. Upon his return to the United States, Collier helped to arrange a visit by Sáenz, whom he called "one of the most evolved, experienced and educated humans I have ever met."[105]

Collier was also enthusiastic about Mexico's current approach to its Indians. He approved of its community-oriented schools and of the fact that it treated Indians as citizens, in contrast to the "tyrannical arbitrary" guardianship the United States exercised over its Native American population. Collier spelled out his views in an article for the Indian education number of *Progressive Education* in 1932. He began by stating that "Mexico has lessons to teach the United States in the matter of schools and Indian administration, lessons which are revolutionary and which may be epoch-making." In the United States boarding schools for Indian children produced "split souls, unequipped minds, and homeless social natures," and the Indian Service perpetuated dependency on the federal government. In Mexico, by contrast, the rural school was "a property of the community, a flowering, an incandescence of the community, and a communal tool for improving life and its rural conditions."[106] Collier also expressed approval of Mexican programs in agrarian reform and other fields that capitalized on the Indians' communal inclinations.

Collier had additional opportunities to adapt Mexican practices to the American environment after being appointed commissioner of Indian affairs in 1933, a position he held until 1945. In this position he continued to cite the Mexican example as he pressed for changes in federal laws that would abandon the assimilationist policy of the nineteenth century and seek to restore or preserve communal aspects of Native American culture. Thus, in calling for an end to allotment and the return of land to tribes, he was quoted as saying: "Mexico . . . recognizes its moral obligation to restore to all Indians enough land for a healthy living. And this restoration is being carried out in Mexico as a matter of duty by the government, nor does any Indian pay a dollar for the acreage restored to him. . . . Our duty of land-restoration affects perhaps only 200,000 Indians, while Mexico, a very poor country, has assumed as a moral obligation the restoration of land to more than 2,000,000

Indians!"[107] Similarly, in urging passage of the Wheeler-Howard Act of 1934, he pointed out that both Mexico and Canada had given their Indian populations educational opportunities and the right to live as they chose. "The result has been that the Indians of both countries have retained, by choice, their tribal institutions, remolding them to meet modern conditions as they saw fit, and that they have increased and prospered in reasonable proportion to their white neighbors."[108] Besides backing the Wheeler-Howard Act, Collier supported establishment of an Indian Crafts Board in 1935; René d'Harnoncourt, to whom he as introduced by Sáenz, was named assistant to the general manager of the board in 1936 and general manager in 1938.[109] In the end, however, Collier found that his visionary pursuit of authentic, communally based Indian cultures was not shared by all Native Americans in the United States, many of whom favored assimilation and individual landownership.[110]

As Indian commissioner, Collier remained interested in Mexico and returned for a brief visit in 1936. He continued to maintain friendly relations with Sáenz, who was present at a conference of Indian-oriented groups early in 1934. Collier wrote at the time: "Dr. Sáenz's visit has stirred us up as few contacts have ever done." Collier became an admirer of Lázaro Cárdenas and his agrarian reform program, especially his effort to promote the communally owned holding known as the *ejido*. Mexico, he wrote in 1938, was engaged in a struggle "to achieve a new and better life at the agrarian level, as over against industrial Fascism on the one hand and industrial syndicalism on the other."[111]

Collier's continuing ties with Mexico were also related to a project that increasingly occupied his attention during the 1930s: the development of inter-American cooperation in Indian affairs. This project had its origin in a discussion in Sáenz's Taxco home in 1931. Collier, Sáenz, and other Mexicans present agreed to work for the establishment of an internationally oriented clearinghouse for data about Indians. An early result of their efforts was the formation of an inter-American group to present evidence on the growth of Indian populations before the Third International Eugenics Congress in 1932. Collier and his colleagues prepared a graphic display of the population record of the native races of America to demonstrate that the Indians were not dying off, as many believed, but were actually increasing in number.[112]

Collier's initiatives eventually led to the convening of the First Inter-American Conference on Indian Life at Pátzcuaro, Mexico, in April

1940, attended by representatives from nineteen Western Hemisphere republics, social scientists, and Indians representing tribes from Panama, Mexico, and the United States. The ten-day conference produced an ambitious set of recommendations, not all of which were realized, and it resulted in the establishment of the Inter-American Institute of the Indian in Mexico City in 1941. Sáenz was named its first director, and after his death the following year he was succeeded by Gamio.[113]

In 1943 Collier sent Oscar Lewis to Mexico as the American representative to the Inter-American Indian Institute. With the help of his wife and collaborator, Ruth, a trained psychologist, Lewis was to conduct a personality study corresponding to several then under way in the United States. Tepoztlán was selected as the site on the advice of Gamio and anthropologist Julio de la Fuente. The project was halted in 1944 because of lack of funds, but it was the genesis of Lewis's *Life in a Mexican Village: Tepoztlán Restudied* (1951), which he dedicated to Redfield yet which differed markedly from the latter's 1930 volume. Lewis questioned Redfield's division of village society into two classes: the *tontos*, or representatives of folk culture, and the *correctos*, or representatives of urban culture. Lewis found that *tontos* and *correctos* did not exist as Redfield described them and that therefore much of Redfield's analysis of Tepoztlán was "oversimplified, schematic, and unreal." Also misleading, Lewis believed, was Redfield's casual treatment of land tenure and the implication that the Tepoztecans were a landed peasantry. In addition, Redfield had overlooked some of the "negative and disruptive aspects of village life, such as the fairly high incidence of stealing, quarrels, and physical violence."[114]

In a 1948 letter Lewis told Redfield that the belief that folk cultures produced fewer frustrations and better human relationships than non-folk cultures was "sheer Rousseauan romanticism."[115] Lewis thereby dismissed one of the most widely held and cherished notions among those who had studied Mexican Indians in the 1920s and 1930s. Although new paradigms arose after World War II to replace the "Rousseauan romanticism" of the interwar years, the Mexican community, both ancient and contemporary, remained a legitimate field of scholarly inquiry. Because of the efforts of Gamio, Sáenz, Morley, Collier, and others, the tradition of collaboration between Mexican and American investigators also remained firmly in place.

CHAPTER 4

The Mexican Art Invasion

After 1920 cultural relations between the United States and Mexico blossomed most fully in the field of art, which epitomized all that American intellectuals and artists found most attractive about postrevolutionary Mexico and its people. Indeed, contemporary writers fostered the belief that Mexicans had a unique, innate aesthetic sensibility, in effect equating Mexico with its art. In *Idols Behind Altars*, for example, Anita Brenner asserted that "nowhere as in Mexico has art been so organically a part of life, at one with the national ends and the national longings, fully the possession of each human unit, always the prime channel for the nation and the unit."[1] Accordingly, all forms of Mexican artistic production—from preconquest architecture to contemporary folk art—were widely exhibited and garnered respectful and generally favorable attention from curators, critics, and collectors. But it was the murals and canvases of José Clemente Orozco, Diego Rivera, and other living painters that generated the greatest enthusiasm in the United States. Not only were their works masterful technically, but they were also rooted in the history and popular culture of Mexico. In short, the Mexicans seemed to have created what many members of the American art world were seeking: an authentically national mode of art.

During these years, Mexican artists were welcomed to the United States and their American counterparts traveled south to contemplate at first hand works deemed to be masterpieces and to absorb the aesthetic and social atmosphere that had nurtured them. For the art critic, one observer remarked in 1930, a trip to Mexico City "of late years has become almost the Way of Santiago de Compostela . . . or the Grand Tour marking the completion of his period of study and preparation."[2] Not even the leftist, anticapitalist orientation of Rivera and other artists deterred members of the financial and artistic establishment from extending their patronage, though the celebrated "battle of Rockefeller Center" showed the limits of their support.

The "Mexican art invasion" began in the mid-1920s and reached its peak in the early 1930s, when Orozco and Rivera executed their controversial murals in the United States. Although these artists soon returned to Mexico, their influence continued to be felt throughout the decade in the work of American muralists who had been inspired by their example.

Before 1920 American exposure to contemporary Mexican art was limited and sporadic. Paintings by Rivera were exhibited in New York in 1916 and 1918, but these were modernist works of his European years, lacking the nationalistic and didactic elements of his later murals. A one-man show in 1916 included, for example, the pointillist *Landscape (Monserrat)* of 1911 and the cubist *Portrait of Marievna*, which a reviewer for *Art News* found incomprehensible.[3]

This exhibit was held at the Modern Gallery, which had been founded in 1915 by a Mexican, Marius de Zayas, to show contemporary works "of the most advanced character." Son of the writer Rafael de Zayas Enríquez, he had left Mexico in 1907 and found employment in New York as a caricaturist for the *World*. His biting caricatures came to the attention of Alfred Stieglitz, who showed twenty-five of them at his gallery, 291, in 1909. Zayas became a close friend and collaborator of Stieglitz as well as one of the earliest and most articulate exponents of modernism in the United States.[4]

In 1919 New Yorkers had two opportunities to view exhibits with a definite Mexican flavor; ironically, both of the artists in question were of foreign extraction. In April the Dudensing Galleries exhibited more than one hundred watercolors by the Anglo-Irish artist Cecil Crawford O'Gorman, who had lived in Mexico since 1895. The watercolors, depicting native subjects such as colonial buildings and flower markets, reminded critic Peyton Boswell that "Mexico is a place of something else besides revolution, outlawry, and hazardous occupation."[5] In December

Adolfo Best Maugard, who was of partly French origin, exhibited paintings in tempera in which the Mexican influence could be discerned not only in the subject matter, as in *Ranchera*, but also in the artist's "rhythmic lines, glowing color, and great beauty of design."[6]

Mexico's relative political stability after 1920 and the patronage of government officials created conditions conducive to the production of a variety of art works. Although art remained a financially precarious endeavor there, postwar cultural trends in the United States made it likely that Mexican artists would seek recognition and sales across the border. During the 1920s the American art world experienced considerable expansion. Sixty art museums were founded between 1921 and 1930, and the number of artists, sculptors, and teachers of art rose from 35,402 in 1920 to 57,265 in 1930, far outpacing population growth. Similarly, enrollments at leading art schools increased by 50 percent between 1920–21 and 1930.[7] In 1930 José Juan Tablada observed that Mexican artists painted without regard to local demand and were fortunate that their work was admired in the United States: "A result of the economic pressure felt in Mexico and of the spontaneous appreciation accorded her artists in the United States has been the migration of many of these painters over the border and the creation of their exotic art upon [American] soil."[8]

The artistic environment in the United States was receptive to Mexican artists for several reasons. According to Francis O'Connor, the Mexicans "filled a cultural and ideological vacuum" at a time when there were few recognized artists of stature on the scene.[9] Modernism appeared to be winning increasing acceptance, but many artists rejected abstraction. To those who retained a belief in the power of art to alter society, modernism was disappointing because it seemed to touch the public at large only superficially, if at all. As George H. Roeder observed in his study of the American reaction to modern art: "Most writers of the time who tried to gauge the general public reaction to modern art concluded that this reaction was largely negative or uncomprehending."[10] Others found modernism unacceptable because of its European origins and cosmopolitanism; they sought instead to create an American art that would depict native subjects with native styles and techniques.

To artists and critics who shared such concerns, contemporary Mexico offered the example of a national art that drew upon indigenous sources of inspiration both for themes and for forms yet was untainted by academism and was indisputably "modern." American leftists found exhilarating the idea that Mexico's new art was a direct outgrowth of the revolution: aesthetic upheaval had accompanied political and social upheaval, or, as Anita Brenner explained, "the reversal of values found its contemporary plastic expression."[11] Some who were indifferent or hostile to the revolution admired the murals of Orozco, Rivera, and others because of their public and didactic quality. The closing years of the nineteenth century had seen increasing support for murals in the United States, partly as a means of demonstrating the cultural vitality of the nation and of bringing art to the masses, goals triumphantly achieved by Mexico's postrevolutionary muralists.[12] These aspects of Mexican muralism seemed all the more enticing to those who had misgivings about the elitism and narrow concerns of modernism. Years later Thomas Hart Benton recalled his interest in the Mexican muralists during the 1920s: "I saw in the Mexican effort a profound and much-needed redirection of art towards its ancient humanistic functions. The Mexican concern with publicly significant meanings and with the pageant of Mexican national life corresponded perfectly with what I had in mind for art in the United States. I also looked with envy on the opportunities given Mexican painters for public mural work."[13]

Contemporary Mexican art's links—both thematic and stylistic—with preconquest and folk art enhanced its appeal in the United States, where there had been interest in what was then called "primitive art" since the early years of the twentieth century. American and European artists, especially those associated with the modernist movement, became convinced that "primitive" peoples—whether ancient Etruscans or contemporary Africans—were more instinctively creative than the inhabitants of more "civilized" societies, who would benefit if they could bring a similar spontaneity to the production and enjoyment of art.[14] In New York Marius de Zayas became a leading student of primitive art, which he considered to be akin to modern art in that both attempted to appeal directly to the viewer's emotions. In 1914, at the suggestion of Zayas, Stieglitz held the first important American exhibition of African sculpture at 291. Zayas featured African art at the Modern Gallery and in 1916 published a study of its influence on modernism. Zayas saw African art as the product of a "savage race" capable of apprehending the natural world only with raw emotion. Thus exposure to African art served as a stimulus to the overintellectualized sensibility of modern times.[15]

If Zayas and others detected affinities between African art and modernism, the artistic gifts of a "primitive" people closer to home also stirred interest in the early decades of the twentieth century. White patrons in the Southwest such as Edgar L. Hewett of the School of American Archaeology in Santa Fe, New Mexico, encouraged Native Americans to create new paintings and crafts and defended the aesthetic value and authenticity of these contemporary productions. White artists who settled in Santa Fe and Taos not only supported the revival of Indian arts and crafts but also used Native Americans as well as the New Mexico landscape in their own work. These whites considered the American Indians, especially those of the Southwest, a deeply creative and spiritual people. Hewett found that the Indians, in comparison with other races, were distinguished by "the scope, the purity, the integrity, and the universality of their arts." In the opinion of the painter John Sloan, a resident of Santa Fe, the "Indian seems to be naturally gifted in the fine arts."[16] Sloan, a leading proponent of Indian art, arranged for the inclusion of New Mexican native works in the 1920 Independents' show in New York. In 1931 he organized a major exhibition of Indian art, which filled seven rooms of New York's Grand Central Palace Gallery.

In this era of admiration for primitive art, including that of southwestern Indians, the art of the preconquest civilizations of Mexico gained greater recognition for its aesthetic qualities. Walter Pach regarded the sculpture and architecture of preconquest Mexico as "the greatest art which has yet been produced in the Western Hemisphere" and was certain that it did not belong in museums of ethnography and anthropology "among the productions of savages."[17] Increased appreciation for the artistic value of preconquest art was also to be expected when archaeological excavation was bringing wondrous artifacts to light every day.

Marius de Zayas was also a pioneer in the exhibition of preconquest art in the United States. In December 1914, at his urging, ancient Mexican pottery and stone carvings were exhibited at 291 while other rooms held works by Picasso and Braque. "Thus," the New York Times critic observed, "one has in close juxtaposition primitive art that has kept its appeal through many centuries and art of the fullest sophistication."[18]

The 1916 exhibition of Rivera's modernist paintings at the Modern Gallery also included ten examples of preconquest Mexican art.[19]

On the West Coast, Francisco Cornejo, a native of Baja, California, was another champion of the aesthetic value of ancient Mexican art. In his Aztec Studio in San Francisco he displayed numerous examples, both originals and reproductions, of Maya and Aztec textiles, pottery, and other artifacts. One room, which he called the Temple of the Sun, contained a reproduction of the Aztec calendar stone in its original colors. In 1921 an exhibit of objects from his collection was presented at Stanford University and at the San Francisco School of Art, along with modern adaptations by the sculptor Manuel Centurión. The Mexican Building at the Pacific Southwest Exposition in Long Beach in 1928 contained a large number of his oil paintings in addition to reproductions he had made of Maya and Aztec designs and stone carvings.[20]

But Cornejo was more than a devotee of preconquest art. He also believed that it could serve as an inspiration and model for contemporary artists. In 1921 he declared: "We talk about having an American art, but our architects, our sculptors, our painters, our craftsmen look for inspiration to Egypt, Greece and the Orient. Sad to say, they neglect what we possess on our own continent. If we are to be influenced by any form of art, why not make use of the wealth of ornamentation and decoration from our primitive sources? Maya and Aztec art bears no real resemblance to that of any other ancient nation and is our heritage." Cornejo's enthusiasm infected dancer Ted Shawn, who turned to preconquest myth in creating the first dance performed by Martha Graham. This was "Xochitl," which told of the discovery of pulque. Cornejo designed the sets and costumes for the dance, which was first performed in June 1920 and was later taken on the Pantages vaudeville circuit.[21]

In his advocacy of preconquest art as a model for contemporary American artists, Cornejo contributed to the spread of the Mayan Revival style, which flourished after World War I. According to Marjorie Ingle's engaging study, the style originated about 1910 and gained popularity, especially in its southern California "heartland," as "a partial answer to the American quest for a new, indigenous design inspiration." The Mayan Revival style was evident in the buildings of numerous architects working in California. Frank Lloyd Wright borrowed from Maya architecture in building his Hollyhock House (1917–20) in Los Angeles. Built of poured concrete with a frieze of stylized hollyhocks, the house is clearly reminiscent of structures in Uxmal or Chichén Itzá. Wright also adapted the Maya use of carved and studded stones for four residences he designed in the Los Angeles area in 1923–24—the Millard, Freeman, Storer, and Ennis houses—which were made of textured concrete blocks reinforced with steel rods. Wright's son Lloyd, also an architect, supervised much of the construction of his father's five Los Angeles houses and made use of the Maya style in his own designs, most notably in the Sowden House (1926), which contained an interior court with Maya stelae and pyramid entrances. The Los Angeles City Hall (1926–28), designed by John C. Austin, is topped by a pyramid that recalls Chichén Itzá's Castillo.[22]

The most articulate California booster of the Mayan Revival style was Robert B. Stacy-Judd, who credited the writings of John Lloyd Stephens with stirring his interest in the ancient Maya and visited Yucatán himself in 1930. Like Cornejo, Stacy-Judd believed that the Maya style was a more appropriate model for American architecture than styles derived from Europe and tirelessly propounded his views to garden clubs, magazine editors, and all who would listen. His best-known structure in the Maya style was the incorrectly named Aztec Hotel (1926) located in Monrovia.[23]

The Mayan Revival style was considered especially appropriate for theaters, such as the Mayan Theater (1927) in Los Angeles, constructed, despite its name, with both Aztec and Mayan elements. Francisco Cornejo designed the exuberant decorations, which cover nearly every inch of the theater's facade and interior. Sylvanus Morley acted as consultant during the construction of Detroit's Fisher Theater (1928), which borrows from Maya sculpture, tilework, and murals at Chichén Itzá and other sites. Other Mayan-style theaters were constructed in Denver (1930) and in Queens, New York (1930).[24]

Some architects believed that Maya pyramids offered solutions to the problems posed by the setback skyscraper. The English-born architect Alfred C. Bossom found parallels between the pyramids and modern skyscrapers, such as the use of ornamented silhouettes in both, and adapted Maya details in at least one of his buildings, the Magnolia Petroleum Building in Dallas. Commenting on the work of the Tulane University expedition of 1925, he declared that ancient Maya buildings might well serve as the basis of a distinctively American architecture. "Mayan architecture shows a complete understanding of great masses of material, and at the same time it employed carving with reserve and simplicity. It can be made a basis for our new types."²⁵ Another New York–based architect, Herman Lee Meader, told the *Diario de Yucatán* that adaptation of Maya architecture and design for modern buildings would lead to "an Indo-American" style capable of generating structures rivaling those of the Middle Ages and the Renaissance.²⁶ George Oakley Totten assisted those inspired to attempt a Maya building by publishing *Maya Architecture* (1926), which offered an illustrated inventory of Maya design elements.

Maya styles were also adopted for interior decoration. As early as 1915, a faience panel called *Sun God* exhibited at the Architectural League was said to be inspired by Maya art. In the 1920s the Batchelder-Wilson Company, which was based in Los Angeles, produced tiles with Maya motifs that decorated the interiors of many buildings, among them the Santa Fe Railroad Station in Pasadena. Cornejo created wall sculptures and reproductions of Maya murals for the Rosarita Beach Club in Santa Monica, California, and Bossom used a combination of Mesoamerican styles for his New York apartment. One enthusiast went so far as to suggest that each home should have at least one room—a library, music room, or study—in the Maya style.²⁷

During the 1920s Adolfo Best Maugard gained an audience in the United States by applying his knowledge of preconquest design to another form of primitive art popular in the early twentieth century: children's art. Commissioned by Franz Boas to make some two thousand drawings of ancient pottery from the Valley of Mexico in 1911, Best Maugard began to formulate the theory that all preconquest design was based on seven primary motifs. Moreover, he believed that all primitive peoples expressed themselves with similar, though not necessarily identical, signs. These insights formed the basis of a system of creative design, which he had developed by the early 1920s and which was adopted by the public schools of the Federal District in 1922 under the name of *dibujo mexicano*, or Mexican drawing. The following year Best Maugard set forth his principles in a volume called *Método de dibujo: Tradición, resurgimiento y evolución del arte mexicano*. In 1923 the Mexican exhibit at the Independents' show in New York included drawings by Mexican schoolchildren taught in accordance with Best Maugard's system, leading critic Thomas Craven to assert that the children's contribution "was much better both in drawing and design than the canvases of some rather prominent New Yorkers." When Best Maugard presented his theories to audiences in California in 1922, he made a deep impression, according to Alma Reed: his "lectures and demonstrations not only provided fascinating information on the art of Mexico, they proved to be a genuine stimulus north of the Rio Grande among groups then consciously seeking light on their own cultural origins and groping for the road to an authentic American continental art." In 1926 Alfred A. Knopf published a revised and expanded version of Best Maugard's 1923 volume in English with the title *A Method for Creative Design*. The American architect Claude Bragdon hailed the book as "a breath of fresh air in a cellar, the cellar being that condition of impotence and apelike imitation into which the arts of design have fallen." In 1932, however, Diego Rivera told American readers that while Best Maugard's method had been valuable in sparking appreciation for Mexico's decorative tradition, it hampered the development of children's imagination.[28]

While preconquest Mexican art excited the imaginations of some American artists and architects during the 1920s, many others were enchanted by Mexican folk art, which was considered in part a product of the crafts tradition of the Maya, Aztecs, and other ancient peoples. During the decade, the status of folk art—sometimes called applied art as well as primitive art by Americans—was elevated in both the United States and Mexico as artists and intellectuals probed for their cultural origins.

In the United States, modern artists, aware of contemporary European attention to primitive art, began to be attracted to folk art about 1910. Interest was stimulated by the first public exhibition of American folk art, which took place at the Whitney Studio Club in 1924 under the direction of the painter Henry E. Schnakenberg. Other showings followed, notably an exhibit of 175 objects at the Museum of Modern Art in 1932. In the catalog Holger Cahill defined folk art as "the work of people with little book learning in art techniques, and no academic training." He also rejected the belief that Americans were not inclined toward artistic expression because of their Puritan heritage; the Puritans' way of life may have been simple and austere, but these qualities had never been a barrier to art anywhere.[29] Meanwhile, collectors such as Abby Aldrich Rockefeller, wife of John D. Rockefeller, Jr., began to acquire folk art for aesthetic rather than antiquarian reasons.

Events in Mexico followed a similar pattern. Here, too, artists such as Dr. Atl, Jorge Enciso, and Roberto Montenegro led the way in creating appreciation for folk, or popular, art. In 1921 the three organized an exhibition of folk art that was held in conjunction with the celebration of the centenary of Mexican independence, and Dr. Atl published a monograph aimed at furthering the study of this form of art, which he considered to be quintessentially Mexican.[30] As the decade progressed, American residents joined Mexicans in collecting folk art. Among the former were the Morrows and William Spratling, as well as Frederick Davis, who was a pioneer collector of Mexican folk art. Davis, along with René d'Harnoncourt, also promoted a revival of a long-abandoned process of lacquering in Olinalá, Guerrero. American travelers to Mexico found themselves acquiring handicrafts, too, as did Hart Crane. "I haven't been able to resist buying . . . things like serapes, giant hats, embroideries, lacquer trays and Guadalajara pottery," he wrote in November 1931. "You've never seen such beautiful arts and crafts as the Indian element here has perpetuated."[31]

Folk art was often discussed in writings about Mexico and its art that appeared in the United States. These writings, regardless of the nationality of the author, repeatedly conveyed the idea that Mexicans— and especially rural Mexicans of Indian ancestry—had a profound and innate sense of beauty that permeated all aspects of their daily life, including the manufacture of objects for their own use or for sale in the marketplace. In short, as Frances Toor put it, "every Indian is either a creative or a potential artist." This belief underlay *Made in Mexico* (1930) by Susan Smith, who had published a book on American craftsmen the previous year. "In Mexico," she wrote, "art isn't something that is kept in museums and spoken of only by critics. It is a part of everyday life, and Mexicans make beautiful things as a matter of course. They don't know how to make anything ugly." She found the Mexicans' natural artistry reflected in their love of flowers and even in the arrangement of vegetables in a salad in a modest restaurant. Stuart Chase had a similar reaction: "It is impossible for Mexicans to produce the humblest thing without form and design. A donkey wears a load of palm leaves arranged on either flank in green sunbursts. Merchants hang candles by their wicks to make patterns in both line and colour. . . . To the traveller from the north, used to the treatment of cold, dead produce as cold, dead produce, this is a matter of perpetual wonder and delight."[32]

Although folk art was still being produced in Mexico, in the industrialized world such objects had to be sought out in museums. Yet there was widespread agreement that the handicraft tradition was on the verge of drastic alteration as Mexico became more highly industrialized or at least more fully exposed to the machine-made products of its northern neighbor. Carleton Beals predicted that "Americanization" would destroy the best of Mexican folk art. Five-gallon oil cans were already replacing native jars, and "Kewpie dolls will probably crowd out the delightful terra cotta figurines and straw-woven horsemen." A related concern was the effect of increased tourism from the United States on Mexican arts and crafts. "Clouds of Buicks, swarms of Dodges, shoals of Chevrolets—mark my words, they will come," Chase warned. "They will demand souvenirs to take back. . . . The Mexicans will have to preserve their craft integrity against that southward-moving cloud of dust."[33]

After 1920 Americans had several opportunities to see Mexican folk art in a museum or gallery setting. The first major exhibition took place in Los Angeles in November 1922. Sponsored by the Ministry of Industry, Commerce, and Labor, the exhibit consisted of approximately five thousand items that had been shown during the centennial celebration the previous year. It attracted considerable attention: average daily attendance was reported to be three to four thousand during its two-week run. In a pattern that would be repeated elsewhere, the folk art show was paired with an exhibition of modern Mexican art consisting of watercolors and drawings by Best Maugard and Xavier Guerrero and by Mexico City schoolchildren.

Katherine Anne Porter wrote a guide to the exhibit, tracing the history of Mexican arts and crafts from preconquest to the present.[34] She, too, wondered how contact with modernity would affect the Indians' artistic traditions, but she had confidence in the strength and permanence of Indian culture. To critic Antony Anderson of the *Los Angeles Times* the exhibit "represented the last remnant of native handicraft on the continent." He did not think, moreover, that these objects could be compared with the crafts of the North American Indian, for "the native Mexican has retained much of the culture of the Aztecs which lacks a good deal of the crudeness of that of the more northerly tribes." Machinery was fast killing Mexican handicrafts, however: "Another generation and it will be gone."[35]

Like many other exhibits of Mexican art held in the United States after 1920, the Los Angeles show was presented and perceived as a means of improving Mexican-American relations, even though a duty of $10,000 had been paid on the artifacts. Mayor George E. Cryer and officials of the Chamber of Commerce formally inaugurated the show on November 10 amid Mexican music and dancing. At the public opening the following day, Guerrero, who had accompanied the exhibit as artistic director, said: "We wished to show Los Angeles people these beautiful displays first, as there is a particular bond of sympathy between the residents of this city and our Mexican population." Guerrero spoke again at a luncheon of the Commercial Board and stressed the desire of Mexicans to create a completely American art. Another speaker was the Mexican consul, Leandro Garza Leal, who said that it was time to emphasize the qualities that Mexico and the United States shared: "The ideals of the Pilgrims were the same in basis as those of the Mexican Revolutionists, first against the Spanish in 1810, against the French in 1863, against Díaz in 1910, and against Huerta in 1913. Like your ancestors, the Mexicans were fighting for life, liberty and the pursuit of happiness as they understood it."[36]

A second large exhibition of Mexican folk art in 1928 had more far-reaching consequences. The exhibition was the brainchild of Frances Flynn Paine, who enlisted the support of Alon Bement, director of the Art Center in New York. Exhibitions of both fine and applied arts were envisioned. The Mexican government offered to finance both exhibits, but Bement appealed to the General Education Board, a Rockefeller philanthropic organization, for a grant to cover the cost of the folk art exhibit because he wished to emphasize American recognition of the achievements of Mexico's craftsmen. In applying for funds to the General Education Board, Bement also expressed the belief that such an exhibition might influence art in the United States: "The preconquest arts of Central America [sic] are the artistic heritage of the Western Continent and therefore a natural, as well as a vigorous source, from which we as Americans may draw inspiration for our native creative design. An established familiarity with these art forms would soon find expression and reflection in our contemporary arts. Demand for it is already felt, owing to the strong Mayan influence expressed in some of our modern urban architecture." Bement had ambitious plans for publicizing the exhibit, including presentation of an Aztec ballet with music by Carlos Chávez at the newly opened Roxy Theater. He hoped that the exhibit would mark "the beginning of a more friendly and intimate interest between the people of Mexico and the United States and result in an active exchange of ideas and the utilization of artistic material which will be of mutual benefit."[37]

The Aztec ballet was never performed at the Roxy, but the other hopes expressed by Bement came closer to realization. With the help of $5,000 from the General Education Board, Paine visited thirty towns and cities in Mexico to gather material for the exhibit: more than thirty-two hundred objects, nearly all of them purchased. Because her stay in Mexico was prolonged as a result of a revolutionary outbreak, the folk art did not go on display at the Art Center until mid-March 1928, several weeks after the government-sponsored exhibit of fine art had closed. The objects shown included pottery, textiles, hand-made glass, and lacquered trays, and all were for sale to visitors.[38]

Abby Aldrich Rockefeller visited the show four times, as did Robert De Forest, president of the Metropolitan Museum of Art, who had been collecting Mexican pottery since 1903. Starting in August 1928, selected pieces from the show were circulated among museums and other institutions in a dozen American cities and Canada, Denmark, and Sweden. In 1933 seventy pieces of pottery that had escaped breakage were donated to the Teachers' College of Columbia University, the Pratt Institute, and the Newark Public School of Fine and Industrial Art.[39]

During the exhibition several observers commented on the suitability of borrowing Mexican motifs for American designs or using Mexican crafts in American homes. Paine shared this belief. "The exhibition has proven," she wrote to the head of the General Education Board, "that the material appeals to the people of the United States and that they will purchase it. The Indians will, if encouraged, produce it and can become economically independent through their work." She now attempted to act on her convictions by proposing the formation of a cooperative craft guild in Mexico that would make advances of raw material or money to members and market their wares in the United States. Such a guild would help preserve Mexican craft traditions, increase American appreciation of Mexican folk art, and generally improve relations between the two countries. Although Latin American antagonism against the United States had increased "alarmingly" in the past few years, she believed that "the Arts, fine and applied, offer possibilities of lessening the feeling of antipathy Mexicans feel for us."[40]

Paine's appeal for funds was rewarded by an offer of support from John D. Rockefeller, Jr., in the amount of $25,000 through 1931. The only condition was a requirement that she form a corporation because Rockefeller did not make donations to individuals. Armed with this promise of funding, she formed the Paine Arts Corporation, rented a gallery in the Art Center, and purchased part of the original folk art exhibit. She arranged additional purchases of pottery and other items for Abby Aldrich Rockefeller and De Forest and ordered objects to be sold in New York stores. She also hoped to commission a ceramic expert to make recommendations that would lessen breakage. All the while, she continued to argue that Mexican folk art might not only be used in the American home but could also inspire American designers. In an edition of the magazine *Design* devoted to Mexico she wrote: "We of America are blind if we refuse to see our good fortune in being in close proximity to a group who can create such exquisite utilitarian things suited to our modern needs—articles every bit as lovely as anything created by the ancients; we are foolish if we ignore our opportunities to tap this rich source of creative art inspiration." José Clemente Orozco was contemptuous of Paine's projects, observing that what he called the "Folklore business" could prove very lucrative.[41]

The profit-making aspect of Paine's enterprise led to a reorganization of her corporation in 1930. The reorganization seems to have been inspired in part by the Morrows, who were supportive of her projects but turned down an invitation to serve on an advisory board of the Paine Mexican Arts Corporation. Plans were soon under way to establish a new, nonprofit organization, to be called the Mexican Arts Association, whose principal object would be "to create closer cultural contact between the [two] countries and to give the people of Mexico a market and outlet for their arts and to give the people of this country for practical use the motifs and designs used by the Mexicans in their Applied and Fine Arts."[42] The Morrows agreed to serve on an advisory committee on condition that the proposed association be nonprofit. It was also to be free to deal with any dealer or promoter of Mexican art and not merely be an adjunct to the art business of any individual or corporation.[43]

By the time the Mexican Arts Association was incorporated on June 16, 1930, Paine's corporation was defunct, though she was to receive an annual salary from the association. The purposes of the association had also been expanded:

> To promote friendship between the people of Mexico and the United States of America by encouraging cultural relations and the interchange of fine and applied arts,
> To maintain a permanent exhibition of Mexican applied arts and to

sponsor special exhibitions of the fine and applied arts of Mexico and the United States of America. . . .

To encourage craftsmen of Mexico to maintain the best traditions of their arts and stimulate certain arts which are in danger of becoming lost. . . .

To sponsor and encourage the introduction of music, drama, literature and motion pictures, and the giving of lectures on the arts of the two countries.[44]

Directors of the association included Paine, Elizabeth Cutter Morrow, and Abby Aldrich Rockefeller. The president was Winthrop W. Aldrich, Mrs. Rockefeller's brother, and publisher Frank Crowninshield was secretary.

Despite the association of so many prominent personages with the Mexican Arts Association, it appears to have carried out only a small part of its ambitious agenda. Financial constraints stemming from the Depression, delays caused by the reorganization of the corporation, the preoccupation of the officers with other matters, and doubts about Paine's reliability kept the association from moving energetically. Paine, however, remained active in the promotion of Mexican art, with the blessing of the association. In 1931 she organized three exhibits at the John Levy Galleries under the title "A Cycle of Mexican Painters," and she assembled a large number of drawings, models, and photographs from Mexico which were shown at the annual exhibition of the Architectural League of New York. She also oversaw a major exhibition by Diego Rivera at the Museum of Modern Art. In 1933 she accompanied Nelson Rockefeller on his first trip to Mexico, during which he made the initial purchases of what became a major collection of Mexican folk art.[45]

When the Mexican Arts Association was founded in 1930, American interest in modern Mexican art was reaching its peak. Since the early 1920s that interest had been whetted by exhibitions in the United States, by the presence in New York of Mexican artists such as Covarrubias and Orozco, and by the reports of travelers to Mexico. These reports announced an explosion of modern art, of which the mural movement was the center and which was closely related to the recent revolution. It was, as Rivera asserted, "an art that went hand in hand with revolution, more powerful than war, and more lasting than religion."[46]

The most frequently articulated idea about Mexico's modern art was that its aesthetic and social importance was enhanced by its grounding in the popular culture and artistic traditions of Mexico. Thus, explicitly or implicitly, it was contrasted with Mexican art of the nineteenth century and especially of the Porfirian period, during which imitation of Europe had produced "progressive decadence." In this context the revival of muralism was explained as a return to a preconquest and colonial art form that had survived in popular art. Anita Brenner explained in *Idols behind Altars* that "murals in public buildings would return to art the social meaning and function that it possessed in its great periods in Mexico and elsewhere, and modern murals with a new social ideology would dovetail into the Mexican tradition—would follow up, or complete, the pre-Hispanic temple walls, the colonial church frescoes, and the *pulquerías* [popular drinking shops]. It was a most obviously legitimate form of great native art."[47]

Although Best Maugard, Roberto Montenegro, and many other artists had used Mexican themes before 1920, the early years of the decade witnessed an outpouring of self-consciously nationalist and revolutionary art, most dramatically visible in the murals painted in the National Preparatory School and the Secretariat of Education between 1922 and 1928. Jean Charlot was the first to employ fresco in his *Massacre in the Templo Mayor* (1922–23) in the Preparatory School, but he was soon followed by others, notably Rivera, José Clemente Orozco, and David Alfaro Siqueiros. Rivera, who returned to Mexico in 1921 after fifteen years in Europe, painted an Italianate allegory, *Creation*, in encaustic in the auditorium of the Preparatory School, but his subsequent frescoes in the education building celebrated Mexican labor and festivals. Although Orozco's initial murals in the Preparatory School also emphasized universal themes, those he did there after 1926 were stark commentaries on the suffering and upheaval caused by the revolution.[48]

According to Charlot, Walter Pach played an important role in validating modern Mexican art both in Mexico and in the United States.[49] Pach came to Mexico City in July 1922 to lecture on modern art on behalf of the Summer School of the National University, illustrating his remarks with slides and an exhibition of graphic works by Picasso, Matisse, and others at the Academy of San Carlos. The first foreigner to evaluate Mexico's contemporary art, he praised its national roots in an article in *México Moderno* in October 1922.

At the National Preparatory School, ca. 1922. Among the artists and intellectuals pictured are Jean Charlot, first row, fifth from left; José Clemente Orozco, last row, directly behind Charlot; David Alfaro Siqueiros, second row, second from right, wearing dark glasses; Carlos Mérida, on Siqueiros's left; and Ernest Gruening and his wife, last row, extreme right. (Jean Charlot Collection, University of Hawaii Library)

Before his departure, Pach invited Mexican painters to take part in the 1923 Independents' show in New York. In addition to watercolors by schoolchildren using Best Maugard's system, thirteen works were included, among them a gouache of a Yucatecan mother and child by Rivera, watercolors of prostitutes by Orozco, and an oil, *Women of Metepec*, by Carlos Mérida, a Guatemalan who had settled in Mexico in 1920. The Mexican representation evoked a mixed response from the critics. The reviewer for *Art News* found little evidence of native influence in their work, "it being a dispiriting reflection of recent art movements in Paris." By contrast, Thomas Craven believed the Mexican contribution to be the best in the show. "Not that it was great art, but it offered a tonic relief in a desert of horrors. The critic must keep an eye on the Mexicans: they are close to actualities, and if they can be saved from the vitiating formulas of Paris cafés, they will undoubtedly arrive at high achievement."[50]

Charlot suspected that the tepid notices for the Mexican exhibit, coupled with Vasconcelos's declining political fortunes, encouraged attacks on the murals of Orozco and Siqueiros and the dismissal of the two painters in July 1924. Mutilation of the murals by students brought a protest by Charlot, Beals, Toor, Edward Weston, Bertram and Ella Wolfe, and other foreigners living in Mexico. In a letter sent to newspapers, they denounced the students as barbarians who were undermining the efforts of the signers to win support for Mexico abroad. The arts of a country, though derived from national culture, belonged to the world, they declared. "Damaging the paintings of the Escuela Nacional Preparatoria injures our cultural assets as well as your own." To the surprise of many, Vasconcelos's successor, José Manuel Puig Casauranc, recalled Orozco to the Preparatory School in 1926 and retained Rivera, another target of the students, in the Education building.[51]

Meanwhile, Mexican painters continued to exhibit their work in the United States. They received considerable recognition at the First Pan American Exhibition, which attracted huge crowds to the Los Angeles Museum of Fine Arts in 1925–26. The United States and Canada sent 239 paintings while Latin America was represented by 136, of which 30 were Mexican. Rivera's *Flower Day* (*Día de flores*) was awarded the $1,500 first prize offered by the museum. Mexican painters (Manuel Varela, María Ramírez Bonfiglio, and Luis Martínez) also won three of the four prizes specifically assigned to the Latin American section.[52]

By the mid-1920s, moreover, Mexican artists were beginning to present their work in one-man shows in New York. Carlos Mérida exhibited oils and watercolors at Valentine Dudensing in the spring of 1926. He was also the subject of articles by Anita Brenner and Carleton Beals in *International Studio* and *Arts & Decoration*, respectively. Mérida was grateful to Beals for writing the article, which he believed would be "great publicity" for him.[53] Rufino Tamayo exhibited his paintings at the Weyhe Gallery in the fall of 1926, but critical notices of the show were brief, stressing the purely Mexican sources of his work. A second show of watercolors and oils at the Art Center a year later drew a similar reaction, but Tamayo sold some woodcuts which he had done at the suggestion of Carl Zigrosser, director of the Weyhe Gallery, and received $500 for designing the abortive Aztec ballet planned for the Roxy.[54]

Despite these modest successes, it was not until the later years of the decade that group exhibitions and an increasing number of one-man shows, combined with the continuing stream of reports on the mural movement in Mexico and the presence of Orozco and other artists in the United States, produced an upsurge of enthusiasm for Mexican art that lasted throughout the 1930s. It was during these years that American artists began traveling to Mexico for work and inspiration even as Mexican artists received mural commissions in the United States.

The most important group show to date was the Art Center exhibition that preceded Frances Flynn Paine's folk exhibit early in 1928. Sponsored by the Mexican government, the show included works by Orozco, Rivera, Tamayo, Covarrubias, Roberto Montenegro, and others. The exhibition received extensive if somewhat ambivalent notice from the press. After a "preliminary glimpse," Elisabeth L. Cary concluded: "The work as a whole, with all its inequalities and range from academic to feverish rebellion, makes a deep mark upon the consciousness." The *Art Digest* found some of the artists "so vividly expressive as to take away the breath of the average beholder of their work." This critic considered Orozco's *Father God* to be the outstanding piece in the collection, but the reviewer for the *Herald Tribune* thought that the tone of his and Rivera's work was "deplorably heavy."[55]

The 1928 Art Center exhibits of fine art and folk art were dwarfed by a much larger show two years later, which opened at the Metropolitan Museum of Art and toured throughout the country. Dwight Morrow is credited with conceiving the idea of a major show to acquaint the American public with the various manifestations of Mexican art and with enlisting the support of the Carnegie Corporation of New York, which became the sponsor. Homer Saint-Gaudens, director of the Department of Fine Arts of the Carnegie Institute of Pittsburgh, then spent a month in Mexico surveying the field. At the suggestion of Morrow, René d'Harnoncourt was chosen to collect and organize the items to be displayed. In asking the cooperation of Ezequiel Padilla, the secretary of public education, Harnoncourt pointed out that the exhibition would benefit both Mexico and the United States: "The series of exhibitions which are planned will present Mexico's artistic treasures, as well as the lofty elements which make up its culture, to critics and all the American people. This cannot help but contribute to a greater appreciation of this country [Mexico] by the people of the United States. The United States will also derive advantages from this project, for it will be able to admire . . . some of the artistic works which have given Mexico just renown abroad."[56] Harnoncourt later recalled that Edward Robinson, director of the Metropolitan and an authority on classical art, disliked Mexican art and was very reluctant to accept the exhibition but succumbed to pressure from Morrow, the Carnegie Corporation, and De Forest, the museum's president.[57]

Over three hundred objects were selected to illustrate the applied arts, which the catalog called "the truest form of self-expression of the Mexican people." The objects exhibited dated from the colonial period to the present and included featherwork, lacquered bowls and boxes, pottery, straw work, embroideries, masks, basketry, and toys. Among the fine arts on display were colonial portraits and *retablos*, or votive pictures. Also included were contemporary paintings, which were described in the catalog as being an outgrowth of the country's heritage: "The roots of the modern painter go deep into the simple life of the Mexican people, and the tradition of his work is genuinely Mexican, dating from the picture writing and frescoes of the pre-Conquest Indian, through the primitives, the *retablos*, and the native secular paintings, down to the turbulent present."[58] Twenty-four painters were represented, among them Orozco, Rivera, Mérida, Charlot, Tamayo, Covarrubias, Manuel Rodríguez Lozano, Joaquín Clausell, and Fermín Revueltas. Upon seeing the paintings exhibited in Mexico City before they were sent to New York, a Mexican journalist praised Harnoncourt not only for his judicious selection but also for his "astute diplomacy" in bringing together works by artists who usually avoided group shows. "Thus, it was curious and gratifying indeed to see upon this occasion the canvasses of Diego Rivera amiably surrounded by the works of such traditional non-conformists as Tamayo, Mérida, and Manuel Rodríguez Lozano."[59] Other sections of the comprehensive exhibition featured modern sculpture; contemporary woodcuts, etchings, and engravings; books and periodicals; and children's paintings and drawings. In conjunction with the show, the museum also exhibited a selection of Mexican prints, mainly from its own collection, thereby offering "the first public collective showing of prints of the Mexican school."[60]

Unveiled on October 13, 1930, at a reception attended by government officials, socialites, and members of the art world, the exhibition proved to be a great success. Harnoncourt later described the reaction of the public and the press as "phenomenal." More than 25,000 persons saw the show during its four weeks at the Metropolitan Museum. From New York, the exhibit traveled to thirteen other cities, twice as many as origi-

Mexican folk art exhibited at the Metropolitan Museum of Art in 1930. (The Metropolitan Museum of Art. All rights reserved.)

nally intended, including Boston, Pittsburgh, Washington, Louisville, and San Antonio. At the Witte Museum in San Antonio an attendance record was set on August 16, 1931, when there were more than 6,000 visitors, most of whom crowded onto the second floor where the Mexican exhibit was being shown.[61] It was estimated that all together more than 450,000 persons saw the exhibition in the United States.

Although critical notices of the exhibit as a whole were generally favorable, the most enthusiastic praise was directed at the applied art. The reviewer of the *Sun* asserted: "There seems no question . . . that it is in the applied arts that the Mexican genius is most fully realized—particularly in textiles and potteries." Virgil Barker was disappointed by the paintings, most of which were "too heavy-handed and purposely limited in scope to afford permanent satisfaction," but he was pleased by the joy and vigor expressed by the crafts. In the *Herald Tribune* Royal Cortissoz found that the folk art and the modern paintings were linked by a primitive power: "even Rivera, so just in line, so sure in touch, so clearly the accomplished craftsman, holds us chiefly by his alliance with that native well-spring of energy which we have identified in the anonymous potters." Albert Franz Cochrane, who saw the exhibition both in New York and in Boston, was not impressed by any of the contents: "When first I saw the exhibition at the Metropolitan Museum it interested me very little—the gallery in which it was displayed resembled nothing more nor less than a huge toy shop thronged with visitors. When the exhibition was being installed here [Boston] I thought it better suited to a natural history museum than to one of fine arts—a view which even a subsequent visit has not entirely altered."[62]

As the sponsors had hoped, comments elicited by the exhibition also suggested that it raised doubts about stereotypes of Mexico and provided new insight into the country. A librarian in El Paso wrote that the show had been a revelation to the people in that border town, for whom rural Mexico was an unknown land. According to the director of the department of fine arts at the University of New Mexico, the exhibition had thrown new light on Mexico; instead of being a backward country full of bandits as many imagined, it was now seen as a nation of culture. In addition, the exhibition had given new life to the movement to preserve and encourage native arts in New Mexico. An editorial in the *New York Times*, after taking note of the conflict and misunderstanding between the United States and Mexico that had occurred since 1910, observed: "Mexico seems so alien, so remote. Yet when we are privileged, as now, to seek her national point of view, in terms of art that has been so wisely and comprehensively chosen, barriers tend to go down and there grows a neighborly impulse toward reciprocity."[63]

Interest in the exhibition was undoubtedly heightened by the simultaneous triumphs of Orozco and Rivera in the United States. After spending more than a year in obscurity in New York, Orozco began to gain serious and sustained notice in 1929. Following his successful Philadelphia show in February, he exhibited recent paintings at the Downtown Gallery in New York in March, and the following month a comprehensive showing of his work—113 items in all—took place at the Art Students' League. The latter exhibition, held at the suggestion of Thomas Hart Benton, was widely and favorably reviewed. The drawings of *Mexico in Revolution* evoked the greatest admiration, being described as "instinct with life" in the *Sun*, while another critic commented in *Inter-*

national Studio: "It is doubtful whether his drawings and lithographs . . . are surpassed in power and beauty by any living artist." Carlyle Burrows in the *Herald Tribune* summarized the situation: "Few artists have been received more cordially this year than the Mexican mural painter, José Clemente Orozco."[64]

Meanwhile, Alma Reed was making plans to open a gallery in which the work of Orozco and other contemporary Mexican and American painters might be exhibited. In February 1930 the gallery, which was called the Delphic Studios, mounted an exhibition of recent oil paintings and gouaches by Orozco. Both Edward Alden Jewell of the *New York Times* and Lloyd Goodrich of the *Arts* had reservations about some of these canvases, which seemed to be overly abstract and to lack a Mexican flavor. Jewell did find two so-called pulquería paintings—*Echate la otra* and *El gran amor*—"a joy." Margaret Breuning of the *Evening Post*, however, was enthusiastic about every aspect of the "fascinating" exhibition. "Lithographs, murals, gay signs for drinking shops, figure paintings, abstractions all seem to receive the same concentrated energy and white heat of creation." In sum, despite a few reservations, the general opinion was that expressed in *Parnassus*: "Every showing of José Clemente Orozco's works reveals more clearly his importance and power." The critical encomiums encouraged sales, which exceeded the expectations of Reed in the aftermath of the Wall Street crash. Orozco, however, soon became dissatisfied with his financial relationship with Reed, who he felt was not giving him an adequate share of the proceeds from the sale of his works. His wife, Margarita Valladares, later expressed the opinion that his dealings with Reed had brought him to financial ruin.[65] Despite his grievances, Reed continued to represent Orozco in the United States, and in 1932 she published a volume devoted to his work for which she wrote the introduction.

Two months after the Delphic Studios show, Orozco began work on his first mural commission in the United States, the *Prometheus* fresco in Frary Hall at Pomona College. According to Laurance Hurlburt's recent study of the American murals of Orozco, Rivera, and Siqueiros, the commission resulted from the efforts of Jorge Juan Crespo de la Serna, a Mexican artist working in Los Angeles, and José Pijoan, a Spanish art historian at the college. Orozco's depiction of Prometheus's act of bringing fire to humanity generated strong feelings. The president of Pomona considered the mural an "abomination," but Arthur Millier, art critic of the *Los Angeles Times*, wrote: "Orozco . . . energized that wall with his sublime conception of Prometheus bearing fire to cold, longing humanity, until it lives as probably no wall in the United States today."[66]

Orozco returned from California in time for the opening of the Metropolitan show, in which he was represented by seven oil paintings, including the monumental *Zapata* and *Echate la otra*, and four drawings. He was pleased by the design of the exhibition, which afforded the first opportunity for his work to be evaluated in a museum alongside that of other Mexican painters. "Above all," Alma Reed wrote later, "he welcomed the prospect of finally confronting Diego Rivera on an equal footing—in an environment where, as he said, 'works, not words,' and 'painting' not 'circus tricks' must decide their relative merits." Orozco still resented the seemingly favored position which Rivera had attained in the United States and which he attributed less to the latter's artistic gifts than to his inveterate self-promotion and his ability to enjoy the patronage of the Mexican government and American capitalists while proclaiming himself a communist. After a meeting with Orozco and Reed in New York soon after the Metropolitan opening, Ione Robinson commented: "Mrs. Reed has a rare quality. No matter what cause she is devoted to, she makes the most of every moment in order to arrive at some climax. She is determined that Orozco will paint a fresco in New York, that his genius will be recognized, and that with his recognition Diego Rivera will fall into oblivion."[67]

The first of Reed's goals was soon realized. In 1931 Orozco painted a set of murals in the new building of the New School for Social Research in New York. He received only a derisory sum for the work but accepted the commission because he and Reed thought that it would showcase his skills as a muralist and lead to additional commissions. According to Hurlburt, Reed inspired the uncharacteristically optimistic theme of the murals, which depict twentieth-century revolutionary struggles and leaders, including Felipe Carrillo Puerto. This commission was followed by a series of fresco panels called *Epic of Civilization on the American Continent* for the Baker Library at Dartmouth College, which were completed in 1934.[68] Both works, especially the latter, brought recognition and controversy. Edward Alden Jewell's criticism that the New School murals lacked a sustained rhythm or pattern drew an indignant rejoinder from the artist's sole assistant on the project, Lois Wilcox, who declared:

"Even conventional souls for whom Orozco's work is too strong a food were impressed with the beautifully balanced masses and varied rhythms."[69] After viewing the Baker Library frescoes, Harvey M. Watts expressed astonishment that a foreigner should have been permitted to perpetrate what he considered an attack on the American system of higher education. Equally ludicrous, in Watts's estimation, was the notion that Dartmouth students should be expected to revere the Toltec-Aztec deities whom Orozco had painted on several panels.[70] Orozco, however, had numerous defenders, including Lewis Mumford, who argued that the panels embodied the best traditions of New England culture, which had always been receptive to external influences. Jewell also praised the Dartmouth murals and suggested that they constituted "the finest mural accomplishment to date, from any hand, in the United States."[71]

If Orozco attained recognition in the United States for his murals, Rivera by no means fell into oblivion. Long before he arrived in the United States in November 1930, his murals at the National Preparatory School and at the Secretariat of Education had been the subject of numerous articles in art periodicals, starting with an appraisal in 1923 in the *Arts* by Tablada, who stressed the Mexican roots of Rivera's mature work, as did Frederic Leighton in *International Studio* the following year. Of the frescoes in the Secretariat of Education, Leighton stated: "Every picture is a bead on a rosary of the life of native Mexico."[72]

Rivera's murals were not only based on Mexican sources, these early commentators noted, but they also glorified the culture and history of the Indian. "Rivera's prime purpose has been to reveal the soul of the despised Indian to both himself and to the world."[73] The murals in the education building which depicted industrial and agricultural labor also inspired optimistic comments about the present and future impact of machinery on Mexican life. In a 1926 article Ernestine Evans wrote: "Nowhere have I seen paintings of machinery where the possible reconciliation of the spirit of man and the machine . . . is even suggested. I have known painters who worshiped machinery, painters who hated machinery. In these walls of Diego's, the multiple loom, the smelter's caldron, the sugar refinery, appear simply as the tools of man, as simple as the hoe or flail."[74]

These published descriptions of Rivera's murals were supplemented by the reports of visitors to Mexico, such as Lee Simonson, stage designer for the Theatre Guild. After a trip to Mexico in 1927, he wrote an article on Rivera for *Creative Art,* of which he was editor and which Orozco called an "organ of Dieguist propaganda."[75] The reports of San Francisco artists who had visited Mexico also stimulated the interest of art patron Albert Bender, who began to acquire oils and drawings by Rivera.[76] By 1929 the artist was sufficiently recognized in the United States to be honored by the American Institute of Architects, which awarded him its Fine Arts Medal. He was only the second foreign artist to be so honored. The institute's Committee on Allied Arts had recommended the award because Rivera's work was an integral part of the wall on which it was painted and because it simply and powerfully represented the Mexican national character. "No other American artist is today expressing the spirit of his time and place so vitally as Rivera is expressing modern Mexico."[77]

Inclusion of the artist's easel paintings and drawings in numerous exhibitions also served to stimulate American awareness of his work. At the 1930 Metropolitan exhibition he was represented by nine items, including part of a mural decoration that had been lent by Dwight Morrow. Earlier that year San Franciscans had seen a sampling of his work at the Galerie Beaux Arts, which exhibited an oil painting and sketches made by Rivera during his recent trip to the Soviet Union.[78]

After arriving in San Francisco in November 1930, Rivera painted two major murals there: an allegory of California in the Luncheon Club of the Stock Exchange and a larger mural at the California School of Fine Art depicting artistic and manual labor.[79] Rivera's presence in San Francisco also served as a stimulus to exhibitions of Mexican art in that city. In November 1930, for example, a major show of his watercolors, drawings, and oils, some of them from the collection of Albert Bender, filled three galleries of the California Palace of the Legion of Honor. The following February, the art gallery of the City of Paris department store presented an exhibition that included sketches by Rivera and lithographs by Orozco as well as folk art from the 1928 Art Center show.[80]

While Rivera was at work on his California murals, his Mexican frescoes were again attracting attention in New York. The Mexican section assembled by Frances Flynn Paine for the 1931 exhibition of the Architectural League of New York included large eye-catching photographs of Rivera's murals in Cuernavaca. According to critic Henry McBride, "Rivera has by this time become the hero of the entire western world."[81] Rivera in turn predicted upon his return to Mexico that the United States would eventually become the artistic capital of the world. "I was able on my visit to the United States to see the error of the popular belief that there are no great painters in the United States," he said. "There is much talent, especially among the young, and there are some real masters; but they all must struggle against European schools which dominate the public."[82]

Rivera returned to Mexico in the summer of 1931 to continue his work on murals in the National Palace. There he was visited by Frances Flynn Paine, who was making arrangements for a one-man show of his work at the Museum of Modern Art in New York. According to her own account, she conducted her business with Rivera while sharing his scaffold in the National Palace. "I have a tiny little American soap box upon which I sit very carefully, and another in front of me as a desk." To avoid the fierce mosquitoes, she tucked her feet into the box, and periodically she and Rivera sprayed each other with insect repellent. On behalf of Abby Aldrich Rockefeller she paid $2,500 for forty-five watercolors which Rivera had painted in the Soviet Union. She also purchased for Mrs. Rockefeller an antique table and a pair of candelabra, but the Mexican government would not permit export of the table.[83]

Rivera was only the second living artist after Matisse to be accorded the honor of a one-man show at the Museum of Modern Art. The exhibition, which opened on December 23, 1931, for a five-week run, consisted of more than 140 works, including oils, encaustic, and watercolors. The highlight of the show was eight large movable panels which Rivera painted especially for the occasion, applying the plaster to a base of steel netting supported on a steel framework. Five of the frescoes were redoings of details from his Mexican murals, including one of Zapata from the Cortés Palace in Cuernavaca; three showed scenes of New York. The exhibit proved to be a great popular success; attendance totaled 56,575, many more than had seen the Matisse show.[84] The exhibition was also a success with the critics. Edward Alden Jewell was especially moved by the Zapata fresco, which he pronounced "as powerful a composition as you will find anywhere in the realm of fresco painting."[85] Margaret Breuning also welcomed the movable frescoes, for they gave those who had not been to Mexico an opportunity, however imperfect, to evaluate Rivera's skill as a muralist. She concluded that Rivera had been successful in conveying the epic sweep of Mexican history.

"The artist has found the exact means to carry his tremendous theme over to us in his work." Like Jewell, she praised the Zapata panel, pointing out its "power of design" and "beauty of tonality."[86] One dissenter was Harrison Kerr, who found Rivera, "pressagented from Mexico to Montparnasse and back," to be derivative: "We need only to glance about the gallery to see Gauguin, Matisse, Picasso, Derain, Rousseau, and even the trivial Spaniards that were popular ten years ago looming out of three-fourths of his canvases. This hospitality to every style is the more disquieting in that it confines itself to no one period in his development. In fact one questions whether he has developed at all." Kerr also objected to the didacticism of Rivera's work. "Posing as a prophet of righteous wrath and piteous indignation is a dangerous pastime for an artist."[87]

Kerr might criticize Rivera's didacticism, but by 1930 the painter's radical political views were ignored or minimized in the United States. The sincerity and strength of his convictions might well be doubted, given his expulsion from the Communist party in 1929 and his continued service to a government that suppressed communists and had severed diplomatic relations with the Soviet Union. A writer in *Commonweal*, who detected a diminution of Rivera's anticlericalism in the Cuernavaca murals, considered this "an aesthetic symptom of the sea-change which has swept over the Mexican nation" now that priests could say mass unhindered and former Zapatistas had become conservative landowners. Frances Flynn Paine believed that Rivera and other "red" artists in Mexico would become less committed once they received recognition. Now that Rivera had been expelled from the party and had accepted Morrow's Cuernavaca commission, she assured Mrs. Rockefeller in 1930, "he still is, sincerely and intensely for 'the people' but one can now reason with him and from that viewpoint, much can be hoped." In an essay for the catalog of Rivera's exhibition at the Museum of Modern Art, she again deemphasized his political allegiances: "Diego's very spinal column is painting, not politics. Every inclination of his life has led to painting. The political movement interested him because it was to him a vital part of contemporary life."[88] None of Rivera's work in the United States to date could be construed as conveying a radical political message. The one possible exception was *Frozen Assets*, one of the movable frescoes created for the Museum of Modern Art exhibit, which showed contrasts in New York during the Depression.

Indeed, at this time criticism of Rivera's political orientation came from supporters of the Communist party who condemned his association with the Mexican government and with American capitalists. The John Reed Club of New York, having invited Rivera to speak at a meeting on January 1, 1932, jeered him into silence and returned a $100 contribution made by the artist. It denounced him as an opportunist and renegade whose art had grown "increasingly sterile." Joseph Freeman, using the pseudonym John Evans, issued a more detailed condemnation in the *New Masses*. Despite the Mexican government's persecution of the Communist party and other reactionary policies, Rivera had accepted an appointment as head of the National School of Fine Arts. He had also accepted commissions from Dwight Morrow and other American millionaires and painted the wives of the latter, ignoring his earlier strictures against "bourgeois" easel painting. Since his expulsion from the party "which leads the Mexican workers and peasants," he was cut off from the sources of his best work and thus faced "corruption as a man and bankruptcy as an artist."[89]

After 1932, however, aesthetic and political controversy dogged Rivera's steps in the United States. He was given an opportunity to work in the nation's industrial center when he was commissioned to paint a series of murals in the garden court of the Detroit Institute of Arts. Unveiled in 1933, the twenty-seven frescoes were a sensuous exploration of science and technology. A panel on vaccination drew criticism because religious groups found its allusion to the Holy Family blasphemous; others complained that the murals were inappropriate for their setting or objected because the commission had gone to a foreigner. But officials of the institute stoutly resisted suggestions that the murals be whitewashed, and the controversy aroused public interest in Rivera's murals. The museum set a monthly attendance record of 86,522 in March 1933, mainly after the start of the furor over the murals.[90]

Even greater controversy erupted during the celebrated "battle of Rockefeller Center" (1933–34). Late in 1932 Rivera was commissioned by Todd-Robertson-Todd Engineering Corporation, the project manager, to paint a mural in the lobby of the RCA building. Perhaps smarting from Communist party criticism of him, Rivera included not only scenes that demonstrated his leftist sympathies but also a labor leader whose visage gradually but unmistakably became that of Lenin. Rivera's refusal to remove the head of Lenin eventually led to the destruction of the entire mural on February 11, 1934. Throughout the furor over the mural, many artists and intellectuals protested vehemently in behalf of the painter while others deplored the propagandist aspects of the work or argued that Lenin was an unsuitable figure for an American mural. As a result of this episode, Rivera lost a commission to paint a large mural in the General Motors building at the Century of Progress exposition in Chicago. With part of his Rockefeller Center fee, he next painted a Marxist interpretation of American history on twenty-one movable panels at the New Workers' School, which was affiliated with an anti-Stalinist communist faction. According to Bertram Wolfe, a founder of the school, the murals traced class conflict in the United States, showing both negative and progressive forces.[91]

By 1933 the granting of mural commissions to Mexicans was causing increased criticism on purely economic and nationalistic grounds, for it meant that native artists were being deprived of walls. After the completion of Rivera's Detroit murals, an official of the American Artists Professional League acknowledged their power but declared that his style was "alien and . . . hard to assimilate" and that controversy over the murals would have been averted had an American artist been engaged. Thomas Craven, reviewing Rivera's American career after his dismissal from the Rockefeller Center project, took a similar position, praising his Mexican work but arguing that his murals in the United States demonstrated merely "prodigious competence" because of his unfamiliarity with the American environment.[92] In 1933 the newly formed National Commission to Advance American Art applauded Rivera's dismissal from Rockefeller Center and observed that the incident proved the folly of bringing foreign artists to the United States when native artists were just as good. The selection of Orozco to paint the Dartmouth murals was another "hard blow" to American artists in the opinion of the association, which urged that future commissions be awarded on a competitive basis. Even Ione Robinson, the former student of Rivera, stated in *California Arts and Architecture* that American artists had to learn to create from the life around them and needed the chance to work: "in order to develop a national art, painters need the support of our political and educational leaders to see to it that they have opportunities for commissions, and thus avoid the importing of foreign artists."[93] To such assertions, John Sloan retorted that Rivera and Orozco were "the most purely and truly American artists (with the exception of our own Indians) who are now working on this continent."[94]

The accolades and occasional notoriety achieved by Orozco and Rivera should not obscure the fact that they were by no means the only Mexican artists whose work earned plaudits in the United States in the early 1930s. Among these was Luis Hidalgo, whose wax figures had been included in the 1924 Whitney Studio Club exhibition organized by Tablada. Hidalgo came to New York in 1926 and in 1929 and 1931 successfully exhibited his tiny but mordant representations of real persons such as Tablada and Al Smith as well as American types such as the flapper and the Bowery bum. In 1929 Frank Crowninshield called Hidalgo and Miguel Covarrubias the two greatest caricaturists in America.[95] As for Covarrubias, his career took a new direction when he received a Guggenheim fellowship in 1930 and went to Bali with his wife for a nine-month stay.

In 1930 and 1931 several easel painters exhibited their canvases at New York galleries. The Delphic Studios showed oils and watercolors by Carlos Mérida in the spring of 1930 after his return from a two-year stay in Europe. Edward Alden Jewell preferred the watercolors to the oils, describing the former as being "alive with universal significance." *Art News* lauded his "stubborn adherence" to native tradition and the absence in his work of the "studied naivete" and tragic overtones seen in that of Orozco and Rivera. "Here are cows and peasants, hills and water seen with evident enjoyment of line, rhythm, and color."[96]

In 1931 Rufino Tamayo again exhibited his paintings in New York, along with landscapes by Joaquín Clausell, this time at the John Levy Galleries. This show, in contrast to Tamayo's exhibitions in 1926 and 1927, was widely and favorably reviewed. One critic singled out Tamayo's still life *Guitars,* which he said suggested "the economy and discreet decorative allure" of Braque. Jewell also praised Tamayo for not allowing his Mexican roots to overpower his personal identity.[97]

The Tamayo-Clausell exhibition was the second in a series "A Cycle of Mexican Painters" organized by Frances Flynn Paine. That the series was held at the John Levy Galleries drew comment because the gallery had previously been identified with old or near-old masters. The series opened on April 1, 1931, with an exhibition of work by Jean Charlot, which the critic of *Parnassus* called one of the most exciting of the season. Although she acknowledged that Charlot's work was uneven, she found some of his pieces, such as *Bathers*, "literally dazzling."[98] Only Henry E. Schnakenberg was unenthusiastic; he considered the fullness of Charlot's forms to be empty and suggested that the artist was attempting to achieve in paint what might better be accomplished in sculpture.[99]

Charlot had the distinction of holding two one-man shows in a single season, for on May 8, 1931, another exhibition of his work, mainly watercolors and drawings, opened at the John Becker Gallery. These, too, garnered praise from the critics, such as the reviewer from *International Studio*, who pronounced *Torso of a Woman* to be "particularly beautiful" and "drawn with consummate skill." In a wide-ranging and positive assessment of Charlot's work published in *Creative Art*, Lincoln Kirstein called his mural *Massacre in the Templo Mayor* one of the "noblest and most dramatic of the murals in Mexico."[100]

During these years many lesser-known Mexican artists also exhibited their work in the United States. In 1930, while the Mexican show was at the Metropolitan Museum of Art, an exhibit of artists associated with an open-air school of painting in Coyoacán opened at the Wolfson Gallery in New York. A show at the Delphic Studios in December 1930 called "Mexican Artists and Artists of Mexican School" included works by Mérida, Best Maugard, Jorge Juan Crespo de la Serna, Cordelia Urueta, and Tamiji Kitagawa. Other promising artists whose work was exhibited at the Delphic Studios were Agustín Jiménez and Roberto del Río; the photographs of the former and the fresco projects of the latter were shown in 1931.[101]

California also attracted Mexican artists, such as Alfredo Ramos Martínez, a former director of the Academy of San Carlos, who exhibited his paintings in San Diego and San Francisco in 1932 and 1933.[102] David Alfaro Siqueiros spent six months in Los Angeles in 1932, having been invited to give a course on murals at the Chouinard School of Art. During this period he completed three murals: *Workers' Meeting* in the Chouinard School of Art, which showed a red-shirted orator addressing workers; *Tropical America* on a wall in Olvera Street, which showed an eagle perched atop a cross on which an Indian was hanging; and *Portrait of Present-Day Mexico*, painted in the home of film director Dudley Murphy. Siqueiros was deported in November 1932 but was able to travel to New York in 1934. In March of that year he exhibited ten paintings and photographs of his murals at the Delphic Studios.[103]

As Mexican artists traveled to the United States during the 1920s and the early 1930s, many of their American counterparts ventured southward, especially after 1925. Like Marsden Hartley, they were attracted by Mexico's artistic renaissance and by accounts of the strength and coherence of the native culture. The artists who visited Mexico were a heterogeneous group, varied in age, artistic style, and reputation and in the ways in which they responded aesthetically to their Mexican experiences.

Older artists appear to have been influenced least. An example was George "Pop" Hart, who made six trips to Mexico from 1923 to 1929. Born in Illinois in 1868 and largely self-taught, Hart earned his living as a painter of signs and movie sets until he won recognition for his watercolors and lithographs during the 1920s. He was an inveterate traveler whom a Mexican journalist dubbed the "Yankee Gauguin" because of his affinity for the southern seas and tropical jungles. Hart described a mid-1920s trip to Mexico as a flight from modern civilization and congratulated himself when he did not see a single Ford during his first twenty-four hours there; the next day, however, he saw "the inevitable flivver following a train of burros" and decided to abandon his flight. Hart often selected Mexican landscapes or customs as the subjects of his work, which won praise for their color and composition, but there is no evidence that he was affected in any way by the work of Mexico's contemporary masters. He seems to have spent his time in rural Mexico, far from the artistic community.[104]

Marsden Hartley, already familiar with the work of Rivera and Orozco before he left for Mexico City in 1932, devoted himself to studying the Aztec and Maya cultures in the anthropological museum there. His Mexican paintings, however, though often based on real places, are replete with a private imagery and symbolism fostered by his reading of occult literature. Only in the flatness of his planes and in the use of intense but uniform color can there be seen suggestions of the work of Orozco, whom Hartley admired greatly.[105]

Andrew Dasburg, a longtime resident of New Mexico and collector of Indian artifacts, used his Guggenheim fellowship to spend three months in Mexico. He spent part of his time in Mexico City and the remainder in Taxco, where he occupied a house owned by John Evans, the son of Mabel Dodge Luhan. Dasburg met Diego Rivera, who may have inspired the full yet simplified forms of the work he did while in Mexico. One of the few outstanding pictures he painted there was *Taxco*.[106]

For these artists Mexico was but an interlude of temporary and limited significance. At the other extreme were a few artists whose Mexican experiences and exposure to Mexican art exerted a profound and permanent influence on their work, both formally and thematically. The primary example of this tendency was Paul O'Higgins, a native of Salt Lake City who was raised in California and studied art in San Diego. While on a visit to Mexico in 1924, he was invited to become an assistant to Rivera, with whom he worked on the frescoes at the Secretariat of Education and the Chapingo Agricultural College.

In May 1931 O'Higgins was the subject of the third and last exhibition of Frances Flynn Paine's series "A Cycle of Mexican Painters" at the John Levy Galleries. Included were paintings that reflected O'Higgins's proletarian outlook, such as *Brakeman, New York*, as well as others that were Mexican in theme. The *Art Digest* reported that his work was considered "so characteristically 'Mexican' that only his name betrays his nationality." Carlyle Burrows of the *Herald Tribune* echoed this opinion: "To all intents and purposes he is a dyed-in-the wool Mexican, in feeling as well as point of view and expression."[107] After a year in the Soviet Union, O'Higgins returned to Mexico, where he painted a mural, his first, in the Escuela Emiliano Zapata.

Another young painter who became thoroughly identified with the Mexican school was Maxine Albro, who had made two year-long visits to Mexico by 1931. The genre paintings and mural studies that she exhibited at the Delphic Studios in 1931 were said to be more indigenous than the products of native Mexicans by the critic of the *New York Times*, who observed: "In the case of a presumably sophisticated American artist, the crude color and drawing and the distinctly peasant humor have scarcely the virtue of spontaneity."[108] Albro assisted Rivera on his San Francisco murals and later did a fresco of her own in the Coit Tower in that city. This work, a cheerful and optimistic work titled *California Agriculture* (1934), clearly shows Rivera's influence.

Everett Gee Jackson, unlike many of his contemporaries, was not especially attracted by the work of the muralists at the time of his first visit to Mexico in 1923, when he traveled in the company of Lowell Houser, who had been a fellow student at the Chicago Institute of Art. At that time, Jackson was more interested in the shapes and colors around him than in the work of other artists.[109] He was also influenced by the preconquest sculpture he saw in Mexican museums. Jackson returned again and again to Mexico, which inspired much of his painting throughout his career. Yet his paintings were not perceived to be produced in accordance with a Mexican formula. "His is a more restrained idiom, possessing a quite individual clarity and strength."[110]

Many other American artists fell between these extremes: Henrietta Shore, George Biddle, Emil Bistram, Howard Cook, and Marion Greenwood, to name but a few. They traveled to Mexico and subsequently produced work that attested to their experiences there, either because of its form or its theme, yet Mexico did not absorb them as it did O'Higgins or Albro. Their exposure to Mexican culture and art, however, helped these artists to create work that was deemed to be at least as good as anything they had done earlier. Henrietta Shore, a close friend of Edward Weston, returned in 1928 from a five-month visit to Mexico with several new works, one of which, a drawing of an Indian mother and child, Weston considered "the finest thing she has ever done in any medium."[111] In 1930 her lithograph *Women of Oaxaca* was awarded the Graphic Arts prize of the San Francisco Art Association. Reviewing an exhibition of Biddle's work in 1929, Ruth Green Harris concluded that his visit to Mexico in 1928 had been more productive than his earlier travels. "Mexico seems to have done something to him emotionally. He is no longer limited to the business of making amusing decorations."[112] According to Howard Cook, the eighteen months he spent in Mexico after winning a Guggenheim fellowship "gave my work tremendous stimulus, allowing me freedom to develop new techniques, including my first fresco, as well as to attempt to realize a portrait of the serenity and beauty of the lives of the common Mexican people."[113] Cook's newfound interest in ordinary people led him to the American South after his fellowship was renewed. In 1933 one of his lithographs, *Mexican Interior*, won the first print prize to be awarded by the Philadelphia Art Alliance.

But the bond linking most of these artists was their experimentation with murals, either in Mexico or in the United States. During the 1930s the Mexican example was a major factor in the increased production of murals in the United States. The efforts of those such as Boardman Robinson and Thomas Hart Benton, who had long sought to stimulate American interest in murals as an art form, were now bolstered by the work of Orozco and Rivera, and Benton was promoted as a native counterpart to the latter. Above all, American muralists emulated the

Mexicans' devotion to native themes and their technical innovations, especially their use of fresco. According to Francis O'Connor, the Mexican influence can be seen most clearly in San Francisco's Coit Memorial Tower (1934), which contains twenty murals painted in the style and spirit of Rivera. Besides Albro's fresco on agriculture, the building contains murals on California themes by Victor Arnautoff, Ray Boynton, and others who had worked with Rivera in Mexico or the United States.[114] In addition, advocates of government sponsorship of murals in public buildings looked to the Mexican experience as a model. George Biddle cited the example of Mexico in appealing to Franklin and Eleanor Roosevelt for support in encouraging muralism in the United States:

> Rivera . . . told me personally that . . . he went directly to President Obregon and asked that the younger modern artists be given an opportunity, at workmen's wages, to carry out in murals the ideals of Mexican nationalism.
>
> There are many of our younger mural modern artists today who are conscious of the economic and social revolution through which America is going and who would be eager on the same conditions to express in permanent art forms the ideals for which the present administration is fighting.[115]

Exhortations such as these bore fruit in federal support for murals through the Treasury Department's Section of Painting and Sculpture, the Works Progress Administration/Federal Arts Project, and other programs in the 1930s. These programs employed numerous artists who had observed the work of Mexican muralists either in Mexico or in the United States. A few American artists also did murals in Mexico and other Latin American countries.

Marion Greenwood, who went to Mexico in December 1932 and rented the house of Moisés Sáenz in Taxco, did a fresco for the Hotel Taxqueño in that town. She later became the first woman to be engaged as a muralist by the Mexican government and worked on two other projects there: an eighty-six-foot-long mural on Tarascan Indians at the University of San Hidalgo in Morelia and a section of the Abelardo Rodríguez market in Mexico City on which her sister Grace also worked. Howard Cook also contributed a fresco to the Hotel Taxqueño.

Both Greenwood and Cook went on to do murals in public buildings in the United States. Greenwood painted murals in housing projects in Camden, New Jersey, and Brooklyn. Cook's fresco, *The Steel Industry*, for the federal courthouse in Pittsburgh earned him a Gold Medal for Mural Painting from the Architectural League of New York in 1936.[116] Emil Bistram, who was awarded a Guggenheim in 1931 to study fresco in Mexico, later painted murals in the county courthouse in Taos, New Mexico, and in the federal courthouse in Roswell, New Mexico.[117] Henrietta Shore painted six movable murals on California subjects which were later installed in public buildings in Santa Cruz and Monterey.[118] In the mid-1930s George Biddle painted five fresco panels in the Justice Department Building in Washington. He later did murals for the National Library in Rio de Janeiro and the Supreme Court in Mexico City.[119] In 1936–38 Lowell Houser, who had spent three years as a staff artist at Chichén Itzá, painted a mural in the post office in Ames, Iowa, that reflected his exposure to Mayan art and culture. Known as the *Ames Corn Mural*, it celebrates maize cultivation by depicting an ancient Maya farmer and a contemporary American farmer bending toward a massive ear of corn.[120] Ben Shahn did not visit Mexico himself, but he worked with Rivera at Rockefeller Center and at the New Worker's School. Between 1937 and 1942 he painted several murals for government agencies which give evidence of the lessons he had learned from Rivera regarding the use of fresco and the organization of pictorial elements on a wall.[121]

Despite the example of Rivera and Orozco, most American muralists eschewed the social protest so often evident in the work of these Mexican artists, preferring instead to create scenes that affirmed American traditions and values or the promise of the New Deal. This approach reflected the artists' own beliefs as well as the pressures of federal and local officials. In 1934 local criticism of leftist references in several panels in the Coit Tower resulted in the removal of a hammer and sickle from one of the murals. The episode made the Treasury Department, which had funded the murals, eager to avoid similar controversies in the future.[122]

If the Mexican example encouraged muralism and nationally oriented art among American artists, there is little evidence of American influence on Mexican art during the 1920s or early 1930s. While in New York, Orozco painted fourteen canvases of urban scenes that may have been influenced by the Precisionism of Charles Sheeler and Charles Demuth. By contrast, Tamayo gained familiarity with international art movements during his early years in New York but apparently little else. "New York was a very important art center," he recalled later, "but American painting was terrible."[123]

When American artists traveled to Mexico, they usually formed ties with the Mexican art world and had opportunities to exhibit their work. Before George Biddle went to Mexico in 1928, Orozco gave him letters of introduction to Dr. Atl and Jorge Enciso. During his visit, his work was exhibited at Frederick Davis's shop.[124] While living in Mexico City from 1926 to 1937 Caroline Durieux developed her skills as a lithographer with the printer Darío Mejía and held her first show there. Rivera painted her portrait and praised "the fine plastic quality of her work, its delightful color, and acute drawing."[125] The relations between the American and Mexican artistic communities led to the first major showing of modern French and American art in Mexico. Held in July 1929 at the Escuela de Bellas Artes, the exhibition was organized by Biddle and the Weyhe Gallery. More than three hundred works were shown, representing fifty-three French and forty-nine American artists, including Cezanne, Matisse, and Picasso among the former and Biddle, Yasuo Kuniyoshi, Edward Hopper, and Marsden Hartley among the latter.[126]

Edward Weston attracted more attention in Mexico than any American painter. Not only was his work exhibited on several occasions during his Mexican sojourn, but his photographs were also reproduced in avant-garde magazines. According to Charlot, Weston's way of handling substance, weight, and tactile substances helped remove the bias against representational art held by muralists like himself trained in current European styles. Rivera expressed his admiration for the photographer in *Mexican Folkways*: "Few are the modern plastic expressions that have given me purer and more intense joy than the master-pieces that are frequently produced in the work of Edward Weston, and I confess that I prefer the productions of this great artist to the majority of contemporary significant paintings."[127] Rivera also paid tribute to Weston by modeling his self-portrait in the education building on a photograph of him by Weston. Among those who saw Weston's photographs exhibited in Mexico City was the fledgling photographer Manuel Alvarez Bravo. After he met Tina Modotti in 1927, she sent some of his prints to Weston, who was favorably impressed.[128]

In general, however, artistic influence flowed from Mexico to the United States in the 1920s and 1930s. American interest in Mexican art remained high during the second half of the 1930s. The work of individual artists continued to be shown in major galleries, and exhibitions of Mexican art were held in several cities. Even Rivera was asked to paint a series of movable frescoes during the Golden Gate International Exposition in San Francisco in 1940. Fittingly, the decade ended with a major exhibition titled "Twenty Centuries of Mexican Art" at the Museum of Modern Art in New York. Running from May to October 1940, the exhibit was sponsored by the Mexican government and by the museum, part of which was converted into a Mexican market. At the invitation of the museum, Orozco painted a large movable fresco, *Dive Bomber*, a somber reminder of the global conflict then under way.[129]

After World War II the muralists and Mexican art in general fell from favor in the United States. Hurlburt believes that the ascendancy of abstract expressionism and the anticommunist fervor associated with the Cold War created an artistic environment hostile to the collectivist, didactic, and nationalist concerns at the root of Mexican muralism. In a 1974 volume, for example, Emily Genauer observed that while Tamayo's star had risen, the reputation of the muralists, except for Orozco, had declined. "They are seen today as greatly gifted but bombastic, illustrative, rhetorical painters, more energetic than truly creative." Four years later the critic John Canaday found it difficult to conceive "how vigorous [Rivera's] sterile interbreeding of Giottesque and pre-Columbian forms once seemed." Even Orozco was beginning to look like "a bombastic journalist," except for his murals at the Hospicio Cabañas in Guadalajara. By the mid-1980s there was some evidence of a renewal of interest in the Mexican muralists, such as a major retrospective at the Detroit Institute of Arts to commemorate the centenary of Rivera's birth in 1986 and the restoration of Orozco's New School murals as well as Siqueiros's *Tropical America*, which had been painted over at the request of the building's owner. In 1990 a major exhibition of Mexican art from preconquest times to the mid-twentieth century opened at New York's Metropolitan Museum nearly sixty years to the day after the show assembled by Harnoncourt. Mexico's president, Carlos Salinas de Gortari, hoped that the exhibit, together with related programs of Mexican music, dance, and literature, would serve as "a model for future cultural exchange" with the United States.[130] It seemed unlikely, however, that Mexican art of any era would ever again arouse the interest it had kindled from 1920 to 1940.

During these years Mexican art in its various manifestations—preconquest art, folk art, and contemporary muralism—stirred extraordinary enthusiasm in the United States and contributed immensely to the Mexican vogue of the era. Mexican art spoke eloquently to the many Americans who were questioning European dominance in the arts and expressing the desire for an auchthonous art based on national culture and traditions. Preconquest architecture and design were unquestionably American and might be suitable as models for contemporary structures in the United States. Folk art, the product of humble hands and not of machines, reflected the heritage and genius of an artistically gifted people. Mexico's modern masters, whether painting walls or canvases, drew on preconquest and traditional sources to create works that proclaimed their Mexicanness with an immediacy and authenticity that excited critics and viewers alike.

CHAPTER 5

Cultural Exchange in Literature, Music, and the Performing Arts

While the vogue of things Mexican was gaining momentum, Americans had many opportunities to be exposed to Mexico and its culture. As shown in earlier chapters, they might travel to Mexico, read works of nonfiction about the country, or visit exhibitions of Mexican art in the United States. Mexico was portrayed in other ways, too: in the theater, in motion pictures, in literature, and even in music. Many of these portrayals were superficial and perpetuated traditional stereotypes. Others, however, attempted a deeper analysis and, like many of the works of nonfiction, occasionally identified aspects of Mexican culture worthy of respect if not emulation by Americans. In literature, moreover, the years 1920–35 saw the first appearance in English of works by Mexican writers, who offered a more authentic literary view of Mexico. During this same period there was a corresponding dissemination of American cultural products in Mexico, and for the first time the films, music, and literature of the United States found audiences and readers there in significant numbers.

During the 1920s the Broadway theater regularly presented plays of varying degrees of quality and seriousness that were set in Mexico or on the border. Three plays of this type were shown early in the 1920 season, leading critic Alexander Woollcott to speculate that they reflected a postwar tendency to look elsewhere than Europe for inspiration.[1]

Most plays with Mexican settings featured treacherous Mexican bandits or other unsavory male characters and tempestuous half-caste women enamored of heroic Americans. An early example was *The Broken Wing* (1920), which ran for 248 performances. Among the characters was an American aviator who crashes in Mexico. He is discovered by a Mexican girl with whom he falls in love. She in turn is loved by a Mexican bandit, who holds the aviator for ransom. A somewhat similar play was *The Dove* (1925), which had a run of 207 performances. Set in the Purple Pigeon Cafe in Mexicana, Mexico, the play was peopled by characters who, as one critic said, "exist in no world outside the footlights at the Empire [Theatre]": a Mexican millionaire smitten with a cabaret dancer "of hot Mex temperament and broken English," who is in love with an American gangster.[2] A very successful musical in this vein was *Rio Rita* (1927), which ran for 494 performances. The characters included a Texas Ranger who pursues a Mexican bandit called Kinkajou. Both are in love with Rio Rita. The show, a lavish Ziegfeld production, was lent a degree of authenticity by the presence in the cast of dancer Pedro Rubín and by the inclusion of caricaturist Matías Santoyo among the costume designers.

The traditional Mexican bandit appeared in the guise of a general in a short-lived melodrama called *Spread Eagle* (1927), which ran for eighty performances. The play produced controversy, however, because of its openly antiwar message. Opening ten years to the day after the American declaration of war against Germany, the play dealt with the efforts of the American owner of a mine in Mexico to provoke intervention. He pays the general to start a revolution and employs the son of the American president in the hope that he will be killed. The play's depiction of the buildup of war fever as a result of the mine owner's machinations drew a protest from the Veterans of Foreign Wars, which called the play "positively un-American and unwholesome for American youth."[3]

Within this genre of conventional play there was only one innovation, which would be duplicated in motion pictures: the emergence of the picaresque Mexican bandit, no more realistic but different from the vengeful, cowardly "greaser" of tradition. He first appeared as Pancho López, the title character of *The Bad Man* (1920), which ran for 320 performances. Written by Porter Emerson Brown, the play was in essence a conventional melodrama set on a ranch near the Mexican border. López, well played by Holbrook Blinn, is in many respects the hero of the play. He saves the ranch for its young American owner, sees to it that the latter is united with the woman he loves, and disposes of the villain, a cowardly American millionaire. In addition, he gives the play a satiric edge by his penetrating observations about American life. For example, he proclaims the United States to be the least free of countries, for everyone is a slave: "slave to law, slave to custom, slave to everysing." In Mexico, by contrast, there is real freedom. "Ze soul she is free! You can do what you please, where you please, when you please—zat is, onless someone shoot you."[4]

Only two dramas presented on Broadway during this period dealt with strictly Mexican themes and characters. The first of these was *Juárez and Maximilian* by the Austrian writer Franz Werfel, which was presented by the Theatre Guild in 1926. The scenery was designed by Lee Simonson, who was to visit Mexico the following summer and become a proponent of Mexican art in the United States. Despite the title, the character of Juárez did not appear in the play, which revolved around Maximilian, who was played by Alfred Lunt, and Porfirio Díaz, portrayed by Edward G. Robinson. Although the critic of the *New York Sun* called *Juárez and Maxmilian* "a great play," the reviewer of the *Herald Tribune* found the production to be "a stately and dormant panorama."[5] It ran for only forty-two performances.

Fiesta (1929), the second drama with a Mexican theme, was a production of the Provincetown Playhouse and was written by Michael Gold, who had lived in Mexico ten years earlier and was now editor of the *New Masses*. Reminiscent of a short story Gold had published in the *Liberator* in 1920, the plot focused on a reform-minded hacendado and his unsuccessful efforts to regenerate his peons. The moral was that change depended on the enlightenment and receptiveness of the beneficiaries. Despite the insertion of Mexican dances in the production, the play failed to find an audience in New York and closed after only thirty-nine performances.[6]

During these years audiences in New York and other cities had other opportunities to sample Mexican music and dance. An early offering was the "Rancho Mexicano" segment of the Garrick Gaieties in 1925. The music for the number was the suite "Afternoon in Mexico" by the composer Ignacio Fernández Esperón, who also staged a performance of the *jarabe tapatió* dance for the segment.[7] In addition, Mexican music could be heard in concert halls and vaudeville theaters. Starting in 1926, for example, the soprano Clarita Sánchez gave concerts in New York to mixed, though generally favorable, reviews.[8] The programs usually included Mexican songs for which she wore native dress. In 1928 veteran musician Miguel Lerdo de Tejada took his Orquesta Típica to the United States for a ten-month tour of major cities, which was described as a gesture of reciprocity for Lindbergh's flight to Mexico. The orchestra, consisting of about thirty-five musicians and singers, was well received in New York, where it played at the Palace Theatre. One reviewer remarked: "It is doubtful if more charming melody from stringed instruments than that of the Típica group can be heard anywhere else in the world."[9] In a ceremony at City Hall Park the orchestra was awarded a gold medal on behalf of the Mexican Chamber of Commerce by Acting Mayor Joseph V. McKee, who donned Mexican garb for the occasion. A second "Típica" orchestra, led by Juan N. Torreblanca, undertook a twenty-week national tour in 1930–31, including performances at children's matinees. This group was also made up of about thirty-five members, including singers, a dance team, and a marimba band. According to the head of the agency that sponsored the tour, it had "brought out the friendly interest and inclinations of the American audiences for Mexican art."[10]

American audiences also had occasional opportunities to hear art music with Mexican elements. The Spanish guitarist Andrés Segovia sometimes included pieces by Manuel M. Ponce on the programs of his New York recitals, and contralto Sophie Braslau sang his "Estrellita" in a 1930 recital in Carnegie Hall. In 1934 the Philadelphia Orchestra under Leopold Stokowski presented the American premiere of Ponce's *Chapultepec* symphonic suite.[11]

The compositions of Carlos Chávez with their popular and indigenous allusions overshadowed Ponce's more traditional pieces, which drew on Mexico's musical legacy from Spain, and were warmly praised by musical nationalists such as Henry Cowell, who declared Chávez "worthy to be considered with the best, even as a leader." To be sure, the 1926 performance of Chávez's "Dance of Men and Machines" (from the ballet-symphony *H.P.*) at an International Composers' Guild concert led Olin Downes of the *New York Times* to express discomfiture over the "confounding mixture" of Mexican folk tunes and sounds that suggested noises made by machines. The critic of *Musical America*, however, found "humor in the combination, and eerie fancy as well."[12] In 1928 Chávez himself played his *Sonata for Piano* at the first of the Copland-

Sessions concerts of contemporary music, during which his *Three Sonatinas* were also performed. Although Olin Downes was again unimpressed, the reviewer for *Musical America* asserted: "The heavy rhythm together with the Mexican Indian themes employed by Mr. Chávez made his works the most interesting of the evening." Elsewhere *Musical America* called Chávez's *Sonata* "the only composition presented by the young writers which struck a really personal, and at the same time racial note."[13] When *H.P.* received its world premiere in 1932, critics found the choreography uninspired but expressed greater enthusiasm about Chávez's music, in which folk elements were present. Paul Rosenfeld had reservations about *H.P.* but declared its best sections to be "joyous and brilliant and energetic" and "like bursts of life and air and light" to those weary of European music.[14]

American motion pictures usually portrayed Mexican characters much as they were depicted in theatrical productions, the Mexican "greaser" being a popular villain among early scenario writers. Because these offensive portrayals provoked a strong reaction from the Mexican government in the early 1920s, American filmmakers shunned Mexican characters and settings in the mid- and late 1920s. In the early 1930s, however, Mexican characters began to return to motion picture screens.[15]

From the earliest days of the American motion picture industry the Mexican male was generally portrayed as cowardly, thievish, vengeful, and given to violence. Mexican women were depicted in a more positive manner and as legitimately capable of stirring romantic feelings on the part of American heroes. By contrast, a Mexican who tried to marry an American woman in *Desert Gold* (1919), based on the Zane Grey novel of the same name, was thrown off a cliff at the end of the movie.

In the early 1920s Mexican officials began to take action against films they considered to be derogatory to Mexico. This new stance can be attributed in part to the cultural nationalism of the era. Another factor was that more American films than ever before were shown in Mexico after World War I, when they displaced European productions, which had predominated before the war. The United States exported only 9,916 linear feet of film to Mexico in 1913, or about 2 percent of the amount exported to Cuba in the same year. By 1930 exports to Mexico totaled nearly 10 million linear feet, almost twice that exported to Cuba.[16]

In February 1922 the consul-general in New York announced that the

Mexican government not only would ban films derogatory to Mexico but also would forbid the entry of all other pictures made or distributed by the offending company. A Mexican official was quoted as saying: "The usual portrayal of the Mexican in moving pictures is as a bandit or a sneak, and naturally the Mexican government wishes this stopped."[17] In Mexico City *Excelsior* applauded the new policy, asserting that the Mexican movie character was never seen to perform a noble or courageous act; he was always base and cowardly, in short, the hateful "greaser."[18]

Mexico's action came at a critical moment for the American motion picture industry. Amid public complaints that motion pictures glorified crime and sexual license, it had recently established the Motion Picture Producers and Distributors of America (MPPDA) in an effort to prevent official censorship. In addition, the industry, on the verge of unprecedented expansion abroad, was eager to develop and protect foreign markets, including those in Latin America.

When Will H. Hays became head of the MPPDA in March 1922, one of the "emergencies" that demanded his attention was the Mexican ban. On April 13 the MPPDA board of directors unanimously approved a resolution condemning "the occasional and thoughtless practice of representing Mexican characters . . . as dictators, bandits, and in other offensive manner."[19] As Hays suspected, the resolution failed to placate the Mexican government, which proceeded to ban the entry of Famous Player–Lasky and Metro pictures. Accordingly, in September, the MPPDA sent a special emissary to Mexico to discuss the embargo with officials there, as well as the widespread showing of stolen or illegally copied prints of film. The result of these discussions was an agreement made on November 6, 1922, by which the MPPDA pledged that it would avoid the production of films that might be offensive to Mexico and would subject existing films to "strict censorship" to excise all references to Mexico.[20] In return, the government lifted bans on the pictures of Famous Players, Metro, and other companies affiliated with the MPPDA.

At the time of the negotiations, a list of fourteen films objectionable to Mexico was prepared. Among them were *Moran of the Lady Letty* (1922), which presumably was offensive because of scenes showing "cutthroat Mexicans," and *I Can Explain* (1922), a comedy-melodrama that featured an outlaw called "El Pavor." Tina Modotti played the role of one Carmencita Gardez in the latter film, which is ironic in view of her attachment to Mexico. Indeed, in 1920 she had told an interviewer from Los Angeles's *Heraldo de México* that she tried to avoid giving offense in her movie scenes about Mexico.[21]

Despite the 1922 agreement, problems continued during the next few years as the Mexican government imposed occasional bans on MPPDA films because of derogatory portrayals of Mexico and its people. Among the motion pictures deemed objectionable during this period was *The Broken Wing* (1923), which was based on the Broadway play of the same name. For their part, spokesmen for the American industry complained of confusing and arbitrary actions by Mexican officials. In a letter to the State Department on January 28, 1925, Hays stated: "The situation has reached the point in this country where a number of producing companies have given orders to their studios that under no circumstances are they to mention the word 'Mexican' or to show Mexican atmosphere or Mexican types in any picture they turn out."[22]

As Hays's comment indicates, motion picture producers increasingly dealt with the problem of Mexican bans by trying to avoid all references to Mexico. A survey of titles in the American Film Institute catalog of feature films shows a decline in the number of films with Mexican characters and settings. Whereas eighty such films are listed for 1921–25, only fifty-five are listed for the years 1926–30 (see Table 2).

In some instances producers simply transferred plots set in Mexico to other locales. Novelist Joseph Hergesheimer visited Mexico in 1925 to gather material for a movie about silver mining, but the Mexican government raised so many objections that the resulting film, *Flowers of*

Table 2. Films with Mexican Subjects, 1921–1930

1921: 13	1926: 10
1922: 17	1927: 13
1923: 13	1928: 6
1924: 21	1929: 9
1925: 16	1930: 17
Total: 80	Total: 55

Source: American Film Institute Catalog: Feature Films, 1921–1930, 2 vols. (New York: Bowker, 1971), subject index, under the headings Mexican border, Mexico, and others related to Mexico.

Night (1925), was set in California instead.[23] When a film version of the play *The Dove* was made in 1928, the locale was shifted from Mexico to an imaginary Mediterranean country called Costa Roja. Ironically, the Mexican actor Gilbert Roland played the role of the American hero in the movie.

By 1928, however, the practice of imposing official bans on offensive films and the companies that produced them had fallen into abeyance, though individuals publicly objected on occasion. In 1928 both *Excelsior* and *El Universal* carried articles condemning as insulting to Mexico a film called *The Showdown* (renamed *Lujuria* in Spanish), which was set in the oil fields of Tampico and which the critics erroneously believed was based on Hergesheimer's 1926 novel *Tampico*.[24] A film version of Hergesheimer's novel was produced in 1933 with the name *The Women I Stole*, but the setting was prudently moved to North Africa. The motion picture industry's continued sensitivity to the issue is evident in the comprehensive Production Code of 1930. The code affirmed that "the just rights, history, and feelings of any nation are entitled to consideration and respectful treatment" and that "the history, institutions, prominent people, and citizenry of other nations shall be represented fairly."[25]

Other issues of contention also arose. The advent of sound led to alarm in Mexico that the exhibition of films spoken in English would adversely affect the national language and culture. These concerns in turn aroused fears among American companies that the Mexican government would impede the showing of English-language films, but on July 29, 1929, Ambassador Manuel C. Téllez assured the MPPDA that the government had no such plans.[26] The American industry responded to the new situation by making approximately 125 Spanish-language films between the late 1920s and 1940. In addition, United Artists Corporation, which did not make Spanish "talkies," financed and distributed movies made in Latin America, such as *Almas Encontradas* (1934), directed by Rafael J. Sevilla and filmed in Mexico.[27]

As Table 2 indicates, by 1930 American moviemakers, presumably less fearful of bans, were more willing to make films with Mexican characters and settings. In some cases, they merely produced sound remakes of older films, such as *The Girl of the Rio* (1932), a talking version of *The Dove*. It differed from the earlier version in being set on the border and starring Dolores del Río as the cabaret dancer, "a fiery daughter of her own romantic Mexico—where blood runs hot and flashing eyes

Dolores del Río in *The Girl of the Rio* (1932). (Film Stills Archives, Museum of Modern Art)

beckon to bold adventures." Leo Carrillo, a Mexican-American, played the villain, whom he made "a man of moods and interesting humors."[28] Carrillo also played the villain in a sound remake of *The Broken Wing* (1932), in which Lupe Vélez portrayed the "fractious but charming" Mexican heroine. According to *Variety*'s review, Carrillo made so likable a villain that audiences would wish that he, instead of the American hero, got the girl.[29]

These comments suggest that the despicable "greaser" of the early days of film was being replaced by the picaresque type, who had first made an appearance in *The Bad Man*. Film versions of the play were made in 1923 and 1930. In the first of these, Holbrook Blinn repeated his highly praised stage performance; in the 1930 talkie Walter Huston played the title character, who was described as "the Robin Hood and Sherlock Holmes of Mexico." A Spanish-language version was also made in 1930. Starring Antonio Moreno in the title role, the film was a great success in Mexico City.[30]

This new filmic bad man became institutionalized in the figure of the Cisco Kid, played by Warner Baxter, who was the co-star of *In Old Arizona* (1929), the first sound picture to be filmed outdoors. The movie was based on a story by O. Henry, "The Caballero's Way," in which the Cisco Kid was a cruel and vengeful desperado but not a Mexican. In the 1929 film, the Kid is "a jolly romantic" Mexican who avenges himself on a faithless sweetheart but outwits the American lawman who tries to capture him. Baxter returned as the Cisco Kid in a film of the same name (1931). Publicity for this picture described the Kid as "a chivalrous bandit" who plagues the rich and helps the poor.[31]

The bad man with redeeming qualities was also evident in the conception of Francisco Villa in *Viva Villa!* (1934), which starred Wallace Beery in the title role. A farrago of fact and fiction based on a biography by Edgcumb Pinchon, the movie was filmed in Mexico with the cooperation of the government, which approved the scenario. Numerous Mexicans were employed as technical advisers and extras, and Villa's daughter was engaged to help promote the movie. Despite these precautions,

Wallace Beery, left, in *Viva Villa!* (1934). (Film Stills Archives, Museum of Modern Art)

the picture was dogged by controversy. The actor Lee Tracy, who was cast in a featured role, made insulting remarks about Mexico in public while drunk and was fired by Metro-Goldwyn-Mayer. In addition, the young writer Nellie Campobello led a campaign against the film on the grounds that it defamed Mexico.[32]

The controversy over *Viva Villa!* was minor compared to the storm that had greeted another motion picture with a Mexican theme the year before. *Que Viva México!*, the film that Sergei Eisenstein had planned to make in Mexico, was left uncompleted because of differences between him and his American financial backers, headed by the socialist novelist Upton Sinclair. After Eisenstein had returned to the Soviet Union, his film footage was edited in the United States and released in 1933 as *Thunder over Mexico*. Demonstrations and a torrent of denunciations, especially from communists, greeted the silent movie, for which Eisenstein had used mainly nonprofessional actors. Sinclair and his associates were attacked both in Mexico and the United States for having permitted the "mutilation" of Eisenstein's film. In addition, it was charged that the editing gave a false impression of contemporary Mexico. As one statement asserted, the Hollywood editors "completely distorted Eisenstein's original conception of a film that was intended to satirize rather than glorify the present reactionary Mexican regime."[33]

Neither Eisenstein nor Hollywood moviemakers were able or willing to make pictures that provided an authentic or sophisticated view of Mexico. *Thunder over Mexico* was visually arresting yet gave a simplistic interpretation of the origins of the revolution. American film producers and dramatists could barely conceive of a male Mexican character other than the bad man. It may be argued, nonetheless, that his transformation from the villainous "greaser" of silent films to the likable, clever, and heroic Cisco Kid represented an advance in the image of the Mexican male.

The perception of contemporaries that Mexico was enjoying "a general popular interest" in the United States by 1931 and that books on Mexico were pouring from the presses is borne out by the listings in the *Book Review Digest* for fiction as well as nonfiction in the years 1920–35. A count of works of fiction dealing with Mexico that were reviewed during these years shows that there were fourteen such titles for the years 1920–27. The number increased to thirty-one for the years 1928–35 (see Table 3).

The works of fiction listed in the *Book Review Digest* were, with a hand-

Table 3.　Works of Fiction about Mexico, 1920–1935

1920:	2	1928:	4
1921:	1	1929:	4
1922:	2	1930:	2
1923:	3	1931:	4
1924:	1	1932:	3
1925:	2	1933:	3
1926:	3	1934:	4
1927:	0	1935:	7
Total:	14	Total:	31

Source: Cumulative indexes, *Book Review Digest.* A count was made of works of fiction relating to Mexico under the subcategories Historical Novels and Novels of Locality. The years are those in which reviews appeared, not necessarily those in which the books were published.

ful of exceptions, written by Americans and fall into three general categories. Most were historical novels or tales of adventure set in Mexico or along the border but showing little evidence of experience of Mexico and its people by the author. A second category consists of works of fiction by persons who had firsthand knowledge of Mexico but chose not to emphasize Mexican characters; their plots deal mainly with foreigners in Mexico. The third and smallest category consists of works in which Mexican themes and characters predominate. None of these works attained great popular success, though several won critical approval and continue to be read for their literary value.

Several of the novels in the second category were written by persons whose Mexican experiences have been described elsewhere in this study. Gregory Mason, the archaeologist-journalist, published *Green Gold of Yucatan* (1926), an improbable narrative involving, among others, an American henequen tycoon, an American archaeologist, and a socialistic governor of Yucatán. Some episodes take place in Chichén Itzá, but there is no sign of Edward Thompson or of the Carnegie Institution. The American tycoon is not an admirable figure in this novel or in two others in this genre, Hergesheimer's *Tampico* (1926) and Carleton Beals's *Black River* (1934), both of which deal with the machinations of the American oil industry in Mexico.

Hergesheimer was at the height of his fame when *Tampico* was published, but the novel was not well received. As a modern commentator has observed, "Mexico served mostly as a rather exotic dash of local color, a fit place for casual killings and pleasure."[34] Beals's *Black River* is also set in Tampico and seeks to show that oil corrupts all who are involved in the industry, both Americans and Mexicans. One of the few admirable characters, an elderly Mexican lawyer, declares that because of oil a stench hovers over Tampico: "not merely oil-stench, the stench of brute power, greed, ruthlessness."[35]

In B. Traven's *Treasure of the Sierra Madre*, published in English translation in 1935, gold rather than oil is the corrupting force. Three American prospectors dominate the plot while Mexicans again play secondary roles, often depicted as simple-minded, superstitious, and cruel. The Indians' behavior, however, is asserted to be the result of three hundred years of oppression by Spaniards, mestizos, and above all the Catholic church. Moreover, they live a "natural" life, in contrast to the American characters, though these in turn can be considered victims of their own money-driven culture.[36]

This category also includes several less melodramatic works dealing with foreign reactions to Mexico, among them D. H. Lawrence's *Plumed Serpent*. Despite Lawrence's reputation, the novel did not impress Americans who were familiar with Mexico. Edward Weston believed that it reflected Lawrence's fear of Mexico and gave an inaccurate impression of the country.[37] In a review in *Mexican Folkways*, Frances Toor also suggested that Lawrence had been frightened by Mexico. She found the book "exceedingly tedious," giving "only a negative, one-sided view" of Mexico.[38] Katherine Anne Porter asserted that Lawrence's interpretation of Mexico was dominated by his own anxieties and that his "Indians are merely what the Indians might be if they were all D. H. Lawrences."[39]

Susan Smith, author of *Made in Mexico*, also wrote *The Glories of Venus* (1931), which was illustrated by José Clemente Orozco. The novel is peopled almost entirely by American expatriates, most of whom have vaguely intellectual or artistic reasons for being in Mexico. These expatriates look down on other Americans in Mexico, such as four young men whose "faces are like big pink masks, one-dimensional, expressionless." Although there are no major Mexican characters, the Mexicans' way of life is depicted in a positive fashion. Thus one character observes: "There is no one here so poor or so ragged that he can't take pleasure whenever it offers, and with perfect unconsciousness of his rags." Another character agrees: "You don't get any sense of defeat from these people, in spite of all their poverty."[40] One reviewer described the novel as "satiric entertainment" at the expense of the expatriates, for whom Mexico was "the newest expedient," a change from New York or Paris, and who talked of painting or writing but did little of either.[41]

Foreigners are also prominent in Katherine Anne Porter's long story *Hacienda*, which was published alone in 1934 and in a 1935 edition of her collection *Flowering Judas*. It is a roman à clef based on her experiences at the hacienda of Tetlapayac in the state of Hidalgo, where she observed Eisenstein at work. Although there are allusions to the shortcomings of the revolution, most of the leading characters are foreigners who seem like intruders in an alien environment. One of the least attractive is the American Kennerly, who is based on Hunter Kimbrough, brother-in-law of Upton Sinclair and Sinclair's representative in overseeing the production of Eisenstein's film. Kennerly despises Mexico and is perpetually angry because of the difficulty of dealing with Mexican officials and Russian filmmakers. The centerpiece of the essentially plotless story is the accidental shooting of a young woman by her brother, an actor in the film who is subsequently captured by another member of the cast. A similar incident had taken place during the filming of *Que Viva México!*

Only four of the works of fiction published during the years 1920–34 focused mainly on Mexican characters and themes. One of these was *Sad Indian* (1932) by Thames Williamson, a sociologist who had written other novels about inarticulate "primitive" people. The title character is a peasant who goes to the city to sell corn and suffers great humiliation there at the hands of mestizos, whom he despises. He even rejects Jesus Christ because He is the god of the mestizos. One reviewer called the book superficial and noted the incongruity between the title and the author's suggestion that the Indian would ultimately triumph over the mestizo.[42]

Two novels that dealt exclusively with Mexican characters and themes were by Mariano Azuela, one of only two Mexican novelists whose works were translated into English during this period. The first of his novels to be published in the United States was *Los de abajo*, which appeared in 1929 as *The Underdogs* in a translation by Enrique Munguía, a lawyer at the Mexican embassy in Washington; the introduction was by Carleton Beals. Although *Los de abajo* was first printed in an El Paso newspaper in 1916, it had fallen into obscurity in Mexico until the mid-1920s.[43] Therefore, the publication of the English version followed hard upon the rediscovery of the novel in Mexico itself. Waldo Frank and Anita Brenner both interested themselves in the translation of Azuela's works, and Frank wrote an enthusiastic review of *The Underdogs* in which he called Azuela "a great artist." The book sold only three thousand copies in the first three months after its publication, a figure that disappointed Munguía, though he considered the edition an artistic triumph.[44] Azuela's *Mala Yerba*, originally published in 1909, was translated by Brenner and appeared in 1932 as *Marcela*. Frank wrote a foreword in which he described the novel as a love story, a "class-conscious melodrama," and "a portrait—accurate, racy, true—of Mexican life." The book was well received by critics, one of whom observed that by showing Mexico from within it offered "a good balance against the many books of that long suffering land as seen by outsiders."[45]

Another Mexican work to be translated into English at this time was Martín Luis Guzmán's *El aguila y la serpiente*. Translated as *The Eagle and the Serpent* by Harriet de Onís, the book is a narrative of personal experience rather than a work of fiction yet contains novelistic features. It, too, was favorably reviewed, though some critics were taken aback by Guzmán's depiction of what one reviewer called "the macabre spectacle of the revolution."[46]

After 1920 short stories about Mexico were also published from time to time in American magazines and collections, though the precise number is difficult to determine. A few of the authors were respected literary figures such as D. H. Lawrence and Katherine Anne Porter, who published, in addition to *Hacienda*, five stories with a Mexican setting between 1922 and 1934. Nearly all the stories were written by non-Mexicans; the dearth of translations is perhaps not surprising because Mexicans produced few outstanding works in the genre during this period.

Although some of the stories, such as Edna Ferber's "They Brought Their Women" (1932) and Porter's "That Tree" (1934), are based on the experiences of foreigners in Mexico, a sizable number deal largely or exclusively with Mexican characters, especially Indians. In these stories the Indians are portrayed as mysterious beings of another culture whose actions are frequently cruel and violent though they may reflect a primitive logic. In Porter's "María Concepción," the title character murders the woman who has run away with her husband; the villagers protect her from the police, and she adopts the dead woman's child. In Oliver LaFarge's "A Family Matter," an Indian fleeing from the authorities impassively murders his wife and infant daughter because they cannot keep up with him and his four-year-old son. An aura of mystery also pervades "John of God, the Water Carrier" by María Cristina Chambers, a Mexican woman who wrote in English.[47] The title character is in love with a girl whom he has rescued from an earthquake, yet he gives her up to his younger brother.

In Wallace Smith's *The Little Tigress: Tales Out of the Dust of Mexico* (1923), "Butcher Fierro," one of Villa's lieutenants, is the personification of casual cruelty. In an essay in the same collection, however, Smith, an American veteran of the revolution, also indicts the cruelty of Americans toward Mexicans. "Mexican Atrocity," a story by Denton Limbaugh, which appeared in *Laughing Horse* (August 1925), belies its title. During a discussion of Mexican atrocities, an American recalls his experience while he lay seriously ill with fever in a Mexican border town. He was taken away by some unknown Mexicans and expected to be burned alive but instead was given a sweat bath, which saved his life.

The increasing interest in Mexico also generated numerous works of fiction for children, usually stories about contemporary rural people or the preconquest Maya. Idella Purnell and her husband, John M. Weatherwax, published seven fairy tales about ancient Yucatán in *Good Housekeeping* starting in September 1930. These were stories of long ago told to Little Boy Tilim by his grandmother. Purnell and Weatherwax published a related book for children, *The Talking Bird*, the same year. It was one of at least five children's books on Mexico appearing that year. Another was *Dark Side of Itza: The Story of a Pagan Princess* by Alida Sims Malkus. Designed for girls aged twelve to fifteen, it related the adventures of the daughter of a Maya priest in preconquest Yucatán.

The children's book that received the most attention in 1930 was Elizabeth Cutter Morrow's *The Painted Pig*, colorfully illustrated by René d'Harnoncourt, which described the efforts of eight-year-old Pedro to obtain a painted pig like his sister's. In the *Saturday Review of Literature*, Mary Austin called the story "credible and amusing, full of mysterious dark people . . . and animals busy with an equally mysterious and busy life of their own."[48] This heavily promoted book was the occasion for a tea party at a Brooklyn department store attended by five hundred children and the Mexican consul-general; Mexican dances were performed, and each youngster received a painted pig from Mexico to take home. According to Elizabeth Morrow, the book had had "a wonderful success"; she had been telling friends who wanted pigs that they might be ordered from Fred Davis, and she hoped that he had not been overwhelmed.[49] Other children's books with Mexican themes published in 1930 were *Tranquilina's Paradise* by Thomas Handforth and Susan Smith and *Pancho and His Burro* by Zhenya and Jan Gay.

The influx of Americans to Mexico after 1920 also resulted in the publication of numerous poems inspired or suggested by their Mexican experiences. Among the Americans who published such poetry after 1920 were Carleton Beals, Elizabeth Cutter Morrow, Idella Purnell, and Witter Bynner. The poems were usually short lyrics that took as their theme an aspect of the rural landscape, though individuals and preconquest culture also served as subjects. The poems were first published in magazines ranging from the obscure to those of larger circulation. Langston Hughes, for example, who made two youthful visits to Mexico in 1919 and 1920, wrote only one poem on a Mexican theme, "Mexican Market Woman," which was published in the *Crisis* in 1922. In 1930 Elizabeth Morrow published a tribute called "The Maguey" in *Harper's Magazine*. In the December 1932 issue of *Poetry*, Katherine Garrison Chapin, wife of Francis Biddle, described a Maya sculpture, which she equated with strength and austerity.

The largest number of poems on Mexican themes was produced by Witter Bynner. They first appeared in a wide variety of periodicals, including the *Ladies Home Journal*, the *New Republic*, and *Poetry*. Forty-nine of them were collected in *Indian Earth* (1929) as "Chapala Poems" and were uniformly praised by reviewers when the book was published. Modeled on the eight-line Chinese *shih*, the poems delicately evoke the people, wildlife, and landscape of the area near the lake, where "even the bats are beautiful." Only Carleton Beals, reviewing the volume in *Mexican Folkways*, had reservations because he did not think the poems fully captured Mexico. "[Bynner's] verse grows and expands with each reading, but do not look for the fierce despairing tenacity of the Mexican, his consistent cruel recklessness." Many years later, Richard Wilbur called the Chapala poems "a remarkably successful experiment" characterized by the "happy communion" evident between the poet and the culture he describes.[50]

Hart Crane never wrote the poem on the conquest of Mexico that he envisioned at the time of his arrival there in 1931. The principal work yielded by his Mexican sojourn was "The Broken Tower," which was published in the *New Republic* in June 1932, shortly after his suicide. According to Lesley Byrd Simpson, the poem was inspired by an incident in Taxco the previous January.[51] Crane and Simpson were admitted to the bell tower of a church there, and Crane was allowed to help ring the bells for a fiesta that day. The clamor of the bells as the sun rose over the mountains produced a state of feverish excitement in the poet, who immediately began to work on the poem. Although "The Broken Tower" is considered one of Crane's finest lyrics, it is an expression of personal concerns with no obviously Mexican references. At the time of his death, however, Crane left behind several unfinished poems with Mexican themes. One unpublished fragment was a tribute to the innate wisdom of the Indians, who "scan more news / On the hind end of their flocks each day / Than all the tourists bring their way." By contrast, "The Sad Indian," which Waldo Frank included in a 1933 edition of Crane's poems, acknowledges that the native is still a victim of "the lash, lost vantage, and the prison / His fathers took for granted ages since—."[52]

A long poem of the era with a Mexican setting is Archibald MacLeish's *Conquistador*, published in 1932 and a winner of the Pulitzer Prize. A first-person narrative, the poem describes the conquest of Mexico by Hernán Cortés in 1519–21 and is based loosely on the account of Bernal Díaz del Castillo. MacLeish went to Mexico in 1929 and retraced the Spaniards' route from Veracruz to Mexico City by car, mule, and donkey. Critics praised the literary qualities of the poem, yet some thought it overly reflective of the pessimism of the era. The reviewer of the *New Masses* was the most deprecatory, seeing in the poem nothing more than "the yearning of decadent bourgeois sophisticates for a simpler life, more direct, primitive, heroic."[53]

Although American periodicals were dotted with verse reflecting the Mexican experiences of Americans, only a few examples of Mexican poetry were translated and published in the United States. This neglect stands in contrast to American interest in Mexican art and even to the prompt translation of *Los de abajo* soon after its rediscovery in Mexico. Besides the barrier posed by language, there may be other explanations for American neglect of Mexican poetry. The revolution was not as direct and potent a stimulus to poetry as it was to art and fiction. The national elements so prominent in the latter were muted in poetry, and many younger poets continued to look abroad for contemporary models. Nor was there any dominant poetical movement comparable to muralism to become the focal point of foreign interest. The result was confusion. Carleton Beals was familiar with Mexican culture and was sufficiently interested in the work of Amado Nervo to translate some of his poems and to seek their publication in the United States. His 1929 analysis of the Estridentista movement is inaccurate, however, for he called it a national literature that had shaken off European influence and included Azuela among its adherents.[54]

The lack of interest in Mexican poetry is reflected in the contents of *Palms*, the little magazine published by Idella Purnell in Guadalajara from 1923 to 1926. Agustín Basave, an architect and writer and the only Mexican on the editorial staff, contributed articles on South American and Jalisco poets, but the magazine rarely carried any Mexican verse either in Spanish or in English translation. It is also significant that despite their long sojourns in Mexico and many contacts with Mexican intellectuals and artists, neither Crane nor Bynner developed close relationships with Mexican poets. Crane was introduced to some Mexican poets soon after his arrival but was not greatly impressed by them. "What makes me rather indifferent to all of them," he wrote, "is the fact that not one of them is really interested one iota in expressing anything indigenous; rather they are busy aping (as though it could be done in Spanish!) Paul Valéry, Eliot,—or more intensely, the Parnassians of 35 years ago." When Harriet Monroe, the editor of *Poetry*, visited Mexico in 1933, she met Edmundo O'Gorman and other poets she considered interesting through H. L. Davis. Typically, however, her greatest enthusiasm was reserved for preconquest ruins and the murals of Rivera, whom she compared to Dante in his ability to capture his era in his work.[55]

Some Mexican poetry was published in the United States in English translation, usually in obscure periodicals and anthologies. Among the most prolific translators was Alice Stone Blackwell, better known as a feminist and reformer, whose interest in oppressed peoples led her to translate poems from Russian, Yiddish, and Armenian as well as Spanish. By 1920 she had translated about ninety Mexican poems by twenty-four different authors. The authors whose works were chosen for translation were often of an earlier era. Blackwell's translations of poems by Manuel Gutiérrez Nájera appeared in *Poet Lore* (1919) and Isaac Goldberg's *Anthology of Mexican Poetry* (1925). Katherine Anne Porter published a translation of Sor Juana Inés de la Cruz's sonnet "To Her Portrait" in the *Survey* (1924). A translation of the same sonnet by Muna Lee appeared in the *American Mercury* (1925) and the *Bulletin of the Pan American Union* (1926).[56]

Twentieth-century poets were not completely ignored. Translations of several poems by Ezequiel Martínez were published. His well-known "Wring the Neck of the Swan" was translated by Muna Lee in 1925 in an issue of *Poetry* devoted to Spanish-American poetry. Three other Mexican poets—Luis G. Urbina, Luis Rosado Vega, and Salvador Díaz Mirón—were also represented in that number in translations by Lee. During his 1926 visit to Mexico, John Dos Passos met Manuel Maples Arce, the founder of Estridentismo, who was then living in Jalapa. The American novelist was impressed by Maples Arce's second volume of poetry, *Urbe* (1924), and translated it into English as *Metropolis* in 1929. The first book of poetry by a Mexican to be translated into English, *Urbe* attempts to portray the turbulence of contemporary Mexico City and relate it to the country's labor strife.[57] Contemporary poets also predominated in an anthology of Mexican poetry published in 1932 with translations by Edna Worthley Underwood.

Since it is generally agreed that Mexican drama was in a state of decadence during the 1920s, it is not surprising that this genre was virtually unrepresented in the United States, either on stage or in print. In keeping with current American interest in the indigenous culture of Mexico, *Poet Lore* published an article in 1926 on efforts to establish popular theater companies in several states; it also printed a short play created by one of these groups. Similarly, *Theatre Arts Monthly* published a colorful piece by Carleton Beals about the tent shows along the Alameda in Mexico City that appealed to the lower classes with their marionettes, music, and skits satirizing politicians and foreigners.[58]

During the 1920s Mexicans were exposed to American cultural products to a greater degree than ever before, a phenomenon that reflected the increasing recognition accorded American arts both at home and abroad after World War I. Motion pictures and popular music were the most widely disseminated and found an enthusiastic reception despite the concerns of nationalists and other critics. American art music and literature were purveyed on a much more limited scale and sometimes raised controversy.

Mexican intellectuals continued to regard American culture with ambivalence. Some still adhered to the traditional belief that Americans were totally materialistic and practical, as did a writer in *Contemporáneos* who found it difficult to conceive of an American who was anything more than an instrument of labor and production. In a similar vein, a reviewer of a book by André Siegfried agreed with Siegfried's contention that, despite its economic progress, the United States lagged behind Europe in culture and refinement. "That is why the United States until now has not produced a national art," said the reviewer, paraphrasing Siegfried. "They don't even feel the need to produce it."[59]

Statements by José Juan Tablada illustrate the ambivalence felt by Mexicans toward the cultural life of the United States. The stereotypical image of Americans as philistines, he said, was as false as the one that held all Mexicans to be trigger-happy bandits. Nevertheless, he also believed that in the United States art and literature had to struggle against the coarseness and indifference of a people who idolized boxers but ignored Poe.[60] Tablada, like other Mexicans who had firsthand knowledge of the United States, admired the libraries, museums, and fine orchestras to be found there. Indeed, Mexican writers sometimes proclaimed New York to be the musical capital of the world because of the quantity, quality, and variety of its offerings, which ranged from opera to vaudeville.[61] Such cultural activity would seem to belie the idea that Americans were indifferent to the arts, but it might merely reflect the power of the dollar to purchase from Europe what they could not create for themselves.

A few Mexicans, perhaps taking a cue from European fashion, found an exciting dynamism in some American arts, especially popular music, that accorded with their conception of what was appropriate for artistic renewal in the industrial age. Accordingly, jazz was sometimes seen as a musical representation of the energy, however disconcerting, of modern life. In a 1924 article Manuel Maples Arce asserted that jazz, like the poetry of the Estridentista movement he had founded, was based on elemental sounds reflective of urban industrial society.[62] In addition, American popular music was attractive to some Mexican intellectuals because of its association with blacks, a people whom they regarded with special interest. During her stay in New York in 1929–30 Antonieta

Rivas Mercado visited a night club that had black performers and was thrilled by the music and the dancing. Blacks, she believed, possessed a "religious sense of rhythm."[63]

By contrast, the inroads made by American popular music produced alarm among Mexican musicians and intellectuals, who considered it the product of an expansive American culture. In 1924 the philosopher Antonio Caso described a foxtrot band he had seen in New York. Caso viewed the band leader as a symbol of American rhythm, "that simple and formidable accelerated rhythm that is preparing to conquer the world." Composer Manuel M. Ponce was more critical, lamenting the invasion of Mexico by what he called the savage and cacophonous foxtrot. Ponce was especially distressed to see the youth of Mexico embrace the foxtrot but failing to see the threatening figure of Uncle Sam behind the music.[64]

The performance of American art music in Mexico during this period was mainly the result of the influence of Carlos Chávez. As director of the Symphony Orchestra of Mexico, he stirred controversy by scheduling a performance of John Alden Carpenter's dissonant *Skyscraper Suite* on October 7, 1928. As the piece ended, some in the audience hissed or shouted *Vivas!* to Beethoven. According to *Excelsior*, however, they were drowned out by the immense majority in the audience who applauded the work.[65] Manuel Barajas, the music critic of *El Universal*, launched a journalistic debate on the piece by calling it overly cerebral and expressing fear that Mexicans were Americanizing themselves to such an extent that their identity was in jeopardy. He also wondered why American whites like Carpenter borrowed so freely from the music of blacks, whom they despised.

Others chimed in, both to agree and to disagree with Barajas. One of those who dissented asserted that listening to the work of American composers did not mean Americanization. Another conceded that the *Skyscraper Suite* was disconcerting, but this did not mean that it was not good music. Still another pointed out that in using unconventional rhythms Carpenter was following the example of Stravinsky and Ravel. This writer also observed that the African melodies that had inspired Carpenter belonged to all humanity.[66]

Aaron Copland experienced similar responses to his music during his four-month stay in Mexico in 1932. After the all-Copland concert at the National Conservatory on September 2, *Excelsior* reported that the atonal *Variations for Piano* had been received coolly but that the choral piece *An Immortality* had brought the audience to its feet. Copland later recalled that his *Symphonic Ode* met with approval when it was performed by the Symphony Orchestra in November. When he played his *Piano Concerto* on another occasion, however, there was so much hissing that he wondered whether he should stop the performance. At a sign from Chávez, he went on. When he had finished, there was more applause than hisses, and he decided to take a bow.[67]

Besides popular music, the motion picture was the dominant form of American culture to penetrate Mexico after 1920. Not only were American motion pictures imported into Mexico in increasing quantities after World War I, but they also represented the overwhelming majority of the films shown there. According to contemporary estimates, by the mid-1920s over 95 percent of the offerings of Mexico's theaters were American films.[68] The dominance of American films was the result of the disruption of European production by the war, negligible production in Mexico, Hollywood's massive output of five hundred to seven hundred features a year by the early 1920s, and its aggressive marketing around the world. The major production companies all opened distribution offices in Mexico City during the 1920s. John Dewey identified motion pictures, along with the Ford automobile, as the key element in the Americanization of Mexico.[69]

Mexican audiences seem to have accepted American films wholeheartedly, though this may have been a result of American dominance. According to a Commerce Department report of 1930, the American films that were popular in Mexico were similar to the ones that were popular in the United States. "In the larger cities, such as the capital, dramas depicting the life of the wealthy class are in great demand, and comedies are very popular. In the smaller towns action pictures have great appeal."[70] It also appears likely that the controversies over the portrayal of Mexicans reflected the concerns of government officials and intellectuals rather than ordinary moviegoers.

Besides attacking American films for their depiction of Mexico and its people, Mexican intellectuals found the same defects in them that American critics did. José Vasconcelos, for example, railed against the silly, standardized productions of the Hollywood studios in which a happy ending was guaranteed. During a stay in New Haven in 1935–36 the poet Xavier Villaurrutia declared that American movies were becoming better technically but also more vacuous. Even so, he admitted that there were exceptions such as *The Petrified Forest* and *Mr. Deeds Goes to Town*, both of which he greatly enjoyed.[71]

The years after 1920 brought to Mexico increasing information about American fiction and poetry. The assertion of Arnold Chapman that Mexico "read some Mark Twain in the 'twenties but otherwise remained indifferent to the northern influence" in literature is an exaggeration. Mexicans might read American novels in the original if they knew English or in Spanish translation; at the least they would find them discussed in Mexican literary journals. Among contemporary novelists Dos Passos and Sinclair Lewis were probably the best known, the latter in part because of his criticism of American society. One critic considered the American people fortunate to possess a writer such as Lewis, who could help them understand themselves better.[72]

The diffusion of American poetry was more extensive than that of fiction, however. Literary magazines frequently printed articles about American poetry and translations of poems. Interest in American poetry was most frequently expressed by Salvador Novo, Xavier Villaurrutia, and other young writers associated with the magazines *Falange* (1922–23), *Ulises* (1927–28), and *Contemporáneos* (1928–31), the last of which was often attacked by literary nationalists for being overly cosmopolitan.[73] The reasons for the appeal of American poetry are not completely clear. The works of Poe, Whitman, and other nineteenth-century poets had won Mexican readers by the turn of the century. Mexican interest in later poets may have reflected a desire to throw off traditional influences both at home and from France. Novo suggested that the interest of French intellectuals in American poets spurred Latin Americans to follow their example.[74]

Novo is the poet most closely associated with the diffusion of American poetry. Born in 1904 and raised in the "barbarous north" of Mexico, he learned English as a child and became familiar with American poetry at an early age.[75] A 1925 collection of his essays contains a review of Vachel Lindsay's *Going-to-the-Sun* (1923) and translations of several poems. Novo was especially enthusiastic about the musicality of Lindsay's verse.[76] In *Return Ticket* (1928), his account of his first trip to the United States, during which he attended an educational conference in Honolulu, he wrote of purchasing books of poetry by Emily Dickinson and Edgar Lee Masters in a San Francisco bookstore and discussing the works of James Branch Cabell with a reporter in Hawaii. During a trip in 1933 that took him to New York and South America, he worked on his *Seamen Rhymes*, which are written partly in English and partly in Spanish.

Articles printed about American poetry in Mexico often asserted that it was undergoing a period of great vitality. Soon after returning to Mexico from Paris, Rafael Lozano published in the October 1923 number of *Falange* a short article in which he discussed what he called the revival of American poetry after a period of aridity.[77] He credited Edwin Arlington Robinson's *Children of Night* (1897) with initiating the revival and mentioned Edgar Lee Masters, Robert Frost, and Carl Sandburg as among the major American poets of the day. The same issue of *Falange* contained translations of poems by Masters, Sandburg, and others. The title of a 1925 article in another journal reprinted from a Spanish magazine also said poetry flourished in the United States.[78] The author mentioned the profusion of little magazines that published poetry and indicated that the United States had met Whitman's prescription for great poetry: the existence of a great audience. The resurgence of American poetry was again noted by Villaurrutia in *Contemporáneos* in 1928. Ezra Pound, whom Lozano had included among the minor poets of the United States, was singled out, along with Masters, Sandburg, and T. S. Eliot. Villaurrutia criticized a recent anthology of American poetry in French translation edited by Eugen Jolas on the grounds that it was undiscriminating and included only one or two poems by each poet represented.[79] A subsequent issue of *Contemporáneos* (July–August 1930) included a prose translation of Eliot's *Wasteland*.

The editors of *Contemporáneos* also revealed interest in American blacks. An early issue (October 1928) contained "Motivos negros," five short poems on black themes by Bernardo Ortiz de Montellano, including "Blues," "Jazz," and "Josephine Baker." Novo discussed poetry by American blacks in a brief article. The dilemma that confronted them, he said, was whether to ignore their color and write in standard English or to write in dialect, thereby accepting their subordinate status in American society. Among outstanding black poets he mentioned Langston Hughes, with whose Mexican sojourns he was familiar. The same issue contained translations of four of Hughes's poems by Villaurrutia. When Hughes returned to Mexico in 1934 for a stay of several months, he was feted by Mexican intellectuals, who hailed him as a great poet.[80]

Novo and Villaurrutia also played leading roles in introducing plays by Eugene O'Neill to the Mexican stage. In 1927, dissatisfied with the state of the commercial theater in Mexico, they founded the experimental Teatro Ulises with the assistance of Antonieta Rivas Mercado.[81] In January 1928 they presented a performance of O'Neill's *Welded*, translated by Novo, in Rivas Mercado's salon; the performance was repeated in March in a commercial theater but had little popular success. The following year Celestino Gorostiza wrote an appreciation of O'Neill's work in *Contemporáneos*, pointing out his increasing ability to penetrate the human mind and heart as he progressed from *The Hairy Ape* to *Desire Under the Elms*.[82]

In subsequent years productions of plays by O'Neill in Mexico City included *Anna Christie* (1932); *Where the Cross Is Made* (1932), directed by Gorostiza; *Lazarus Laughed* (1933, 1934); and *Diff'rent* (1934) in a translation by Novo. Except for these works by O'Neill, few other plays by Americans were presented in Mexico City, although *Street Scene* by Elmer Rice, whom Villaurrutia considered a major playwright comparable to O'Neill, was produced in 1931. A critic in the *Revista de Revistas* praised Rice's play, noting that it combined classical tragedy with the portrayal of modern life in "monstrous" New York, "a melting pot where the future human type is being created."[83]

The same writer disparaged Mexican prejudice against American drama and literature in general, which he believed was partly owing to the effect of dime novels and bad movies. On the contrary, he declared, American theatrical production was not merely first-rate; it was outstanding. Certainly Villaurrutia admired several American productions which he saw during his year in the United States. Although he gained little from the drama classes he attended at Yale University, he proclaimed Lillian Hellman's *Children's Hour* to be a "magnificent work on a daring theme" and enjoyed *Winterset* by Maxwell Anderson, whom he called the most vital American dramatist of the day.[84]

In contrast to the many American representations of Mexico in plays, motion pictures, and literature after 1920, there were few portrayals of the United States by Mexicans in these genres. Mexicans often discussed the character and behavior of Americans in nonfiction writing, but they rarely produced poetry, fiction, or drama in which these topics were prominent. John Rutherford found no important American characters in his study of the Mexican Revolution as seen through novels, though the few that appeared in minor roles were not depicted in a flattering light.[85] *Panchito Chapopote* (1928), a surrealist novel by Xavier Icaza, satirizes Americans who come to a small town looking for oil and spreading the "Saxon gospel": "Business, business and business. Time is money."[86] Icaza depicts the oilmen as exploiters of Mexico but characterizes Mexican officials the same way.

Several episodes of Martín Luis Guzmán's *Aguila y el serpiente* are set in the United States, but he presents only one American character of significance, a beautiful young woman who is believed to be a spy for Huerta. Salvador Novo also created an American woman character in a humorous playlet that first appeared in *El Universal Ilustrado* in 1924.[87] Mrs. Gutenberg, an American divorcee with a doctorate, marries a Mexican who has been studying at the University of Texas. They soon divorce to marry others, and she writes a book called *Truth about Mexico*. In his "Poemas proletarios" (1934) Novo poked fun at American cultural pilgrims to Mexico, calling them "great blond thinkers," defeated by the machine and deafened by the clamor of industry, who proclaim that comfort is harmony between man and his environment and that therefore the barefoot Indian at the door of his hut is more comfortable than Calvin Coolidge sipping Coca Cola at the Waldorf-Astoria.[88]

Most stereotypes about the United States that reached Mexicans in literary or dramatic form were likely to be generated by Americans themselves. This situation contrasted with the depiction of Mexicans in the United States, where plays and motion pictures often presented distorted and offensive portrayals. After 1920 the translation of Mexican literary works and the presentation of other forms of Mexican culture made possible an alternate and more authentic view of Mexico and its people. Meanwhile, the dissemination of American films, music, and literature in Mexico gave readers and audiences in that country a multifaceted image of American culture.

Conclusion

From 1920 to 1935 cultural relations between Mexico and the United States unfolded against a background of favorable cultural, political, and social conditions in the two countries. Prominent in this background was the global economic leadership of the United States, which had been newly confirmed by World War I. The war also left many Americans with a conviction that Europe was spiritually and intellectually bankrupt and reinforced the cultural nationalism that existed before 1914 as well as an interest in Latin America dating from the turn of the century. Cultural nationalists in the United States admired the murals of Diego Rivera, José Clemente Orozco, and other artists for their reliance on native themes and their revival of the indigenous fresco technique. They similarly hailed Carlos Chávez for incorporating native elements into his music. Associated with cultural nationalism was the sentiment that the United States was part of an American continent that had a certain unity of history and culture. Accordingly, many artists and intellectuals in the United States reassessed the culture of Native Americans and found linkages between them and the great preconquest civilizations to the south, about which more was constantly being learned. The artist Lowell Houser believed that the Mayas were the "fountain head" of all the other Native American cultures just as the Greeks had been the source of European cultures. "The other Indians were to the Mayas much as the out-of-the-way provinces of Rome were to the Greeks."[1] Thus a loosely conceived Mayan style could be promoted as an appropriately American model for contemporary architecture and design in the United States.

Many Mexican artists and intellectuals also shared a commitment to cultural nationalism during the 1920s, rejecting the European models that had dominated during the Porfiriato. For many, cultural nationalism meant immersion in purely Mexican traditions, but it did not necessarily exclude an American component. Mexicans might resent the economic hegemony of the United States and its history of military and diplomatic intervention, but the concept of American unity had a long tradition in Latin America and could be expanded to embrace North America as well as the Spanish-speaking regions of the continent. Orozco, for example, juxtaposed Anglo-Saxon and Hispanic American panels in his Dartmouth College frescoes, which were designed to represent "an American idea developed into American forms, American feeling, and as a consequence, into American style."[2]

Several more specific circumstances also encouraged the development of cultural relations during this period. During the early 1920s the revolution acted as a powerful lure to Americans of the liberal left who applauded the reform programs of the Obregón and Calles administrations and defended them against the assaults of critics in the United States. The Mexican government, eager to improve its image in the United States, pursued this goal in several ways: it welcomed American journalists and other sympathetic visitors such as the members of Hubert Herring's seminars, established the Summer School at the National University, and subsidized *Mexican Folkways*. The presence of Manuel Gamio and Moisés Sáenz in high office facilitated cultural exchange, for these graduates of American universities were familiar with the values and methodologies of American intellectuals. On the state level, too, a few Mexican officials sought to promote cultural relations. In Yucatán Governor Carrillo Puerto cooperated with Sylvanus Morley and others interested in Mayan antiquities. In 1926 the governor of Jalisco, José Zuno, purchased six prints of photographs by Edward Weston for the state museum. The same year he gave a $100 contribution for the support of *Palms* and in 1927 offered to assist its editor, Idella Purnell, with a projected lecture tour on Mexico in the United States. Such a tour would be especially timely, he wrote, at a moment when "the true Mexican intellectual and political values are so little known and despised" in the United States.[3]

By the time revolutionary momentum had ebbed in the late 1920s, Mexican culture, always an attraction, became the chief magnet for Americans. The cultural pilgrims who flocked to Mexico during these years often shared the romantic primitivism of the era and sought a simpler, more harmonious culture than the machine-driven society they knew at home, which, as the Great Depression showed, seemed incapable even of providing material security. Dwight Morrow, who hoped to use culture to defuse diplomatic and commercial tensions, and his wife encouraged this trend in a variety of ways, including their support of Mexican art. The Mexican government continued earlier programs geared to foreigners and by 1930 was also committed to the expansion of tourism. Meanwhile, the enthusiasm about Mexico generated by the books and articles published by American pilgrims helped to assure a friendly reception in literary and artistic circles for Mexico's cultural émigrés, whose accomplishments also whetted interest in the country.

Cultural exchange was advanced by the support of private institutions, which were in a position to finance programs that accorded with their internationalist orientation. Without their activities, the record of cultural relations with Mexico would have been considerably slimmer. In archaeology, important work was undertaken by the Carnegie Institution of Washington, Tulane University, and the American Museum of Natural History. While they existed, the Guggenheim fellowships for Latin America enabled numerous American writers, artists, and scholars to go to Mexico and afforded Mexican scientists the opportunity to do research in the United States. The financial aid of the General Education Board and the Carnegie Corporation facilitated the exhibition of Mexican art in the United States. The Social Science Research Council subsidized Robert Redfield's pioneering study of Tepoztlán and helped to finance the completion of Manuel Gamio's study of Mexican emigration to the United States.

Although the Redfield and Gamio studies were undertaken in response to what was perceived as a growing problem for the United States—the increase in Mexican emigration between 1910 and 1930—this issue remained peripheral as cultural relations warmed. In California the conferences and exchange programs arranged by Pomona College helped to acquaint teachers and social workers with the culture of an increasing number of the people they served. Elsewhere, the issue, even during the period of repatriation of recent immigrants, received scant attention from Americans interested in Mexico and from Mexican cultural figures in the United States. While in Mexico, the members of Herring's 1930 seminar took part in a symposium on Mexican immigration led by Paul Kellogg, editor of the *Survey*; the following year this magazine devoted its May 1, 1931, issue to Mexicans in the United States. Rivera's aid to Mexicans in Detroit has already been mentioned. Clearly, Mexican immigration to the United States provided the impetus for the production of several scholarly works and encounters among teachers and intellectuals from the two countries but otherwise had little impact on the development of cultural relations. David Alfaro Siqueiros's controversial mural *Tropical America* (1932) symbolized the situation. Intended as an attack on American imperialism in Latin America, it contained no obvious allusions to the current circumstances of Mexicans in the United States despite its location in the heart of the Mexican district of Los Angeles.

The development of cultural relations between the United States and Mexico inevitably raises the question of cultural imperialism because of the relative economic and military preponderance of the former. During the period in question, motion pictures and popular music were the most important cultural exports of the United States, though its literature was also becoming more widely known among educated Mexicans. That Mexican officials and intellectuals realized the importance of motion pictures as carriers of values and culture is shown by the government's attacks on the portrayal of Mexicans in American movies and the alarm generated by the arrival of films with English-language dialogue.

Discussions of cultural imperialism are usually confined to the cultural exports of the dominant power. It may be argued, however, that Americans engaged in a form of cultural imperialism when they claimed preconquest cultures as part of their own heritage. Imperialism based on the appropriation of another's culture was also at work when wealthy Americans purchased the paintings of contemporary Mexican artists or commissioned them to do murals in the United States. Although the Mexican government took steps to protect the country's preconquest and colonial cultural patrimony, it was not likely to prevent living artists from crossing the border or selling their work to American visitors. Such a position would have run counter to the open nature of the regime and its desire for harmonious relations with the United States. Contemporaries also justified the export of art by pointing to Mexico's inability to provide adequate economic rewards to its artists. Moreover, after decades of neglect or denigration, Mexicans generally approved of the success that their compatriots enjoyed in the United States. This very success, however, may have encouraged Mexican artists to become increasingly dependent on foreign validation as a prerequisite for gaining recognition and prestige at home.

Mexicans as well as Americans such as Beals and Chase realized that the American market for Mexican art and folklore might distort or trivialize the production of painters and craftsmen alike, leading them to fashion their works in accordance with the expectations of foreign art dealers and tourists. Orozco condemned the intrusion of folklore in Mexico's modern art and accused Rivera of encouraging this trend. Rivera indicated his own reservations in a 1936 fresco panel, *Touristic and Folkloric Mexico*. It shows a supercilious blonde tourist astride a donkey with Mexicans in folkloric costumes dancing around her. As early as 1924, Nemesio García Naranjo found it degrading that because of the current emphasis on folklore, Mexico was becoming known as a country for the amusement of curious tourists. Moreover, as Samuel Ramos pointed out, the picturesque characters and scenes that delighted tourists constituted "a Mexico for export . . . just as false as the romantic Spain of the tambourine."[4]

The development of cultural relations generated many works in which American artists and intellectuals expressed their reactions to Mexico. Waldo Frank summarized the phenomenon in 1931: "For intelligent North Americans to visit Mexico is getting to be a custom. . . . And since intelligent persons in our business world are very likely to write and to paint, the list grows of records—literary, sociological, plastic—of these journeys. The intelligent American, of course, is dissatisfied. Mexico vaguely seems to offer from afar something which he lacks and craves. And still more vaguely and deeply, Mexico seems to be his."[5]

Not only did American visitors to Mexico produce an increasing number of "records" about the country, but the perceptions and ideas they articulated differed substantially from those of earlier travelers. According to anthropologist Edward Bruner, ethnographies are shaped "by an implicit narrative structure, by a story we tell about the people we study."[6] If we may liken American records of Mexico produced after

1920 to ethnographies, we can see that they told a story that was not completely new but that modified or eliminated important features of the older story. Literary travelers to Mexico during the Porfiriato, though often enjoying Mexico's quaintness and leisurely pace, had generally expressed dismay at the country's technological backwardness and had applauded signs of change, such as the construction of railroads and incipient industrialization. Criticism of the political system was almost totally absent, the best-known exception being John Kenneth Turner's *Barbarous Mexico* (1910), and it was often asserted that Mexicans were incapable of, or at least unready for, political democracy.

After 1920, despite an occasional work that was highly critical, Mexico was portrayed more positively than ever before and from a perspective that was less ethnocentric. Those on the liberal-left end of the political spectrum, such as Frank Tannenbaum and Carleton Beals, created an interpretation of the Mexican Revolution that depicted it as a justified and beneficent, if necessarily violent, movement that deserved American support. Even the acknowledgment of shortcomings in the realization of the revolution's goals and Beals's frank admission that it had stalled by 1930 did not entail a rejection of the revolutionary process itself.

Even more pervasive in the new story was the way in which the culture of Mexico's peasant and indigenous peoples was presented. It was now shown to possess many admirable traits. The individual in such cultures, though subject to ills of poverty and ignorance that the revolution was trying to correct, lived a life free of modern anxieties in which work, play, and religion formed an integrated whole. Moreover, Mexican peasants were gifted with an innate aesthetic sensibility that enabled them to create beautiful objects for everyday use and to surround themselves with color and design. In the new Mexican story even the previously ubiquitous "greaser" no longer had a place, having been banished from the American stage and screen, to be replaced by a new kind of bad man, often brave and good-hearted.

A major element in the new American story about Mexico was that it was a place of great sensory power, or as Carleton Beals put it, "Mexico, for most casual visitors, is a land to be seen, smelled, tasted."[7] He said that his own bond with Mexico had progressed beyond sensory experience, but nearly all travelers who recorded their impressions made reference to the subject.

Americans generally responded enthusiastically to the sounds, smells, and tastes of Mexico. They often took note of the ringing of church bells or the sound of music and a wide range of smells, especially the fragrance of flowers. Of the flowers in her garden, Katherine Anne Porter declared to a friend: "The sweet smells around here would send you off your head." Sometimes smells blended in combinations unfamiliar to Americans. A passage in Susan Smith's novel *The Glories of Venus* describes such a mélange of odors in the market in Iguala: "There was a smell of rope and spices and leather and of *chile* cooking in grease and *frijoles* simmering in earthen pots and fruit going just a little bad in the sun—the pervasive, adventurous smells of markets in the 'hot country'." Many visitors also made reference to Mexico's savory food, and Edward Weston stated in his journal shortly after his arrival in 1923: "I have yet to eat a poorly cooked dish in Mexico." Years after the event Everett Gee Jackson described in his memoirs an unforgettable lunch in a hamlet near Chapala; he speculated that the qualities that caused the Indians of the area to make their homes and utensils charming and artistic also made their simple food delicious.[8]

Despite the many references to Mexico's sounds and smells and to the taste of its food, the country's impact was overwhelmingly visual, or as Dos Passos put it, "Everything's so Goddamned pictorial it takes my breath away." The Mexican scene perceived by travelers was marked by vivid color and brilliant sunlight. Everett Gee Jackson, for example, recalled the "bright and sparkling sunlight" in Guanajuato that turned even garbage-strewn alleyways into "visual magic." William Spratling emphasized color in his description of rural "Mexicanitos" who came to Taxco on market days: "They come . . . in pink undershirts and freshly starched white *calzones*. Sometimes the pink is more lavender, with pleated full white waists and a broad silk scarf, pink or magenta, around a neck that is golden brown."[9]

The American's story of Mexico often details a mixture of sensory effects. During her first visit in 1929, Ione Robinson described Mexico City to her mother: "there is a great deal of filth in the streets, but one gets the impression in spite of that that there is a certain cleanliness because the air is so fresh and clear, the sunlight sparkles like a diamond, and the sky is filled with transparent white clouds." In his autobiography Ernest Gruening also evoked Mexico's multifaceted sensory impact in recalling the scene that greeted him when he arrived in 1922:

There was color everywhere on the storefronts, painted with intriguing figures and legends. Flowers were in abundance: bloodred poinsettia, crimson hibiscus, orange *flamboyans*, roses, tulips, lillies, and draped over age-tinted walls, bougainvillea with magenta, red, pink, orange and yellow blossoms. The air was filled with their fragrance and with such earthy odors as frying cornmeal. The sounds were equally fascinating: the pat-a-pat as the *tortillera* shaped the cornmeal . . . and floating even from the humblest hut, the songs and music of the people.[10]

Only rarely did an American visitor fail to mention the Mexican landscape or its sounds and smells, and it was even more unusual for a visitor to express an aversion to them. One of the latter was Marsden Hartley, for whom Mexico's picturesqueness eventually became tiresome. For most American visitors, Mexico's sensory stimulation left a positive impression, as Beals affirmed in a 1927 memoir of his first visit: "Mexico taught me my first true lessons in aesthetics; it stimulated and awakened in me as never before the keen pleasurable life of the senses: form, colour, rhythm—things omnipresent in Mexico."[11]

Why Mexico made such a strong impression on travelers' senses is not completely clear. Psychologists and others agree that an individual's perception of an environment depends not only on its material reality but also on variables such as his or her expectations, imagination, training, and receptivity. According to Claude Levy-Leboyer, "In preceiving the environment, the perceiver constructs it, and the result of the perceptual elaboration is individual to each person."[12] On one hand, we can speculate that the United States was drab and uniform in contrast to Mexico. This was the belief of Edward Weston, for example, who found that even American grocery stores paled when compared with Mexican markets, each of which had "a new note in display, besides peculiarities of costume and variety in food." California seemed "curiously flat" to Elizabeth Prall Anderson when she visited after living in Taxco. "People took buses to work all at the same time. . . . Sidewalks were uninteresting after cobblestones. No wild, clamorous bells assailed the senses."[13]

American visitors to Mexico undoubtedly anticipated great sensory and especially visual stimulation because of conventional affirmations of the country's picturesqueness and the artistry of its people. Mexico's visual power was so frequently asserted that it can be classified as a *topos*, "a commonly held notion about someone or something which is accepted as true virtually without question and carries rhetorical weight because of this special status accorded it by a particular audience."[14] Thus prospective tourists who consulted the 1930 edition of *Terry's Guide* would learn that Mexico was "a winsome, sunlit land; artistic, intellectual, extraordinarily picturesque."[15] Moreover, the art training and aesthetic sensibility that characterized many cultural pilgrims presumably made them even more likely than the average tourist to discern pictorial qualities in the Mexican landscape.

Mexicans agreed that the United States was insipid and homogeneous in comparison to their homeland. Their story about the United States was that the latter, though made up of people of different cultures, was fundamentally uniform in its way of life. Only blacks were recognized as constituting a possible exception to this generalization. In a 1923 article written in New York Rafael de Zayas Enríquez explained that uniformity was basic to the American character. Everything was modeled in accordance with a single standard, which was not unchanging but was rigidly observed until a new one was decreed.[16] Moisés Sáenz made a similar point in addressing the members of Herring's seminar in 1930. Whereas Mexico was characterized by heterogeneity, the United States was homogeneous. During a recent trip to the United States, he had traveled in standard trains that ran on standard time with standard equipment. The food and newspapers and motion pictures were the same everywhere, and everyone listened to "Amos 'n' Andy." Upon arriving in California in 1930 to paint the Prometheus fresco at Pomona College, Orozco declared that the blossom-covered orange trees smelled "divinely," but he was soon complaining that the orange groves smelled of fertilizer and were so uniform that they seemed more like a factory than an orchard. In general, he said, the area was pretty but too orderly and too highly urbanized.[17]

On occasion, it must be admitted, Mexican visitors expressed admiration for some aspect of the American landscape. While en route to California after his year at Yale, Villaurrutia marveled at the sky in Albuquerque and, once arrived, he pronounced Point Lobos in Carmel to be "a veritable paradise." José Vasconcelos admired the solidity and beauty of the University of Chicago, which formed an island of calm within the great, agitated city.[18]

In contrast to many of his contemporaries, Diego Rivera found beauty in American industry. Long enamored of the mechanical, he was fascinated by the industrial technology of the United States and during his

California stay urged Americans: "Become aware of the splendid beauty of your factories, admit the charm of your native houses, the lustre of your metals, the clarity of your glass." His murals at the Detroit Institute of Arts can therefore be interpreted as an expression of his aesthetic admiration for American science and technology, though they also suggest the danger of dehumanization that they posed to the worker. By contrast, the section on the modern machine age in Orozco's Dartmouth murals, described by Lewis Mumford as a "cold metallic hell," is an abstraction that cannot be associated with any specific place despite the American theme of the mural.[19]

If Mexican travelers differed in their visual response to the United States, they uniformly found fault with what Orozco called the "detestable" food. Villaurrutia singled out the *"hot choco"* [sic] he drank in New Haven, which had only the vaguest resemblance in color and taste to the real article. Vasconcelos found American soda fountains to be the embodiment of Yankee efficiency, but the soft drinks and ice cream they dispensed were insipid. Harvey Levenstein has shown that the American diet became more bland and homogeneous after 1920. It is therefore not surprising that Martín Luis Guzmán's positive comments about American food recall an earlier period. Describing an American home in San Antonio where he boarded with Vasconcelos and Alberto J. Pani, the narrator of *El aguila y la serpiente* recalls the aromas of coffee, flour, and vanilla that presaged the "sober, succulent" breakfasts of "fine aesthetic quality." He also gives a sensuous account of breakfast in the sumptuous dining room of the Hotel McAlpin in New York.[20]

The abundance of records in which Americans articulated their reactions to Mexico bears witness to the powerful imprint the country left on a wide variety of political and cultural pilgrims. Because of their writings and creative endeavors and those of Mexicans in the United States, the American public in general had greater access to more numerous and more authentic representations of Mexican culture than ever before. It is impossible to ascertain what effect, if any, these representations had on attitudes toward Mexico. There is, however, considerable evidence that the Mexican vogue reached beyond the relatively small number of artists and intellectuals who created it. Major exhibitions of Mexican art, such as the Metropolitan show of 1930 and Rivera's exhibit at the Museum of Modern Art, drew record crowds. Moreover, much Mexican art was exhibited outside of New York; the Metropolitan show, for example, traveled to thirteen other cities, a number larger than originally intended. The presence of Chase's *Mexico: A Study of Two Americas* on *Publishers Weekly*'s best-seller list for six months also testifies to current interest in Mexico, as does the increase in the number of novels and works of non-fiction dealing with that country published in the early 1930s. The rise in tourism and the continuing success of the Summer School and Herring's seminars are further evidence of contemporary interest.

In Mexico, meanwhile, American literature and art circulated within small but influential groups, such as the *Contemporáneos* circle. Popular music and motion pictures reached much larger audiences, the success of the latter being demonstrated by the growth of film exports from the United States. At the same time the residence in the United States of cultural émigrés such as Orozco and Chávez meant that influential artists and intellectuals were receiving direct exposure to American culture.

More problematic is the task of determining the extent to which the dissemination of Mexican culture in the United States, and vice versa, affected relations between the two governments. Contemporaries assumed that cultural exchange would result in greater mutual understanding, which in turn would yield improved economic and diplomatic relations beneficial to both countries. As shown in Chapter 1, a few were convinced that cultural relations could be manipulated to advance one country's policies or interests at the expense of the other. Ambassador Sheffield, who viewed the Summer School and Herring's seminars as instruments of Mexican propaganda, was a representative of the latter school. Ambassador Morrow was an exponent of the former attitude. During his years in Mexico City, his promotion of Mexican culture, ably seconded by his wife, went hand in hand with his efforts to ease diplomatic tensions. Both campaigns were on the whole successful, but that diplomatic rapprochement was required for the flowering of cultural relations is as likely as the reverse.

Cultural relations between the United States and Mexico did not come to a halt in 1935. On the contrary, they continued and even expanded during the following decade. But the excitement and sense of discovery that characterized American attitudes toward Mexico in the 1920s had abated by the late 1930s. Moreover, changes within the two countries and in the international arena created new interests and concerns.

In Mexico the revolution experienced its "last great reforming phase" under Lázaro Cárdenas, who began a six-year term as president on December 1, 1934.[21] After successfully asserting his authority over Calles, he launched a divisive program of agrarian reform and institutional change that was more nationalist and statist than those of any of his predecessors. Cárdenas also encouraged popular mobilization more systematically than did Obregón or Calles. The climax of Cardenismo came with the nationalization of the foreign-owned petroleum industry in 1938. Afterward the president responded to mounting economic difficulties and class polarization by following a more conciliatory course and designated General Manuel Avila Camacho, a moderate, as his successor.

Amid the domestic ferment, international affairs also assumed great importance for Mexico as Cárdenas pursued a resolutely antifascist policy abroad, especially in relation to the Spanish Civil War. The Mexican government supported the Loyalist cause both morally and materially and accepted approximately thirty thousand refugees between 1937 and 1945, including numerous philosophers, historians, and other intellectuals. Finding a haven in the government-financed Casa de España (1938) and its successor, El Colegio de México (1940), these refugees were to exert great influence on Mexican education, scholarship, and intellectual life in general.[22] In contrast to the 1920s, Mexican relations with the United States remained relatively cordial despite the president's nationalization of the oil industry, partly because of growing American desire for solidarity in the Western Hemisphere in the face of deteriorating conditions in Europe and Asia.

During the Cárdenas years cultural nationalism remained a powerful force in art and literature. Muralism continued to dominate Mexican art, though the visit of André Breton in 1938 "implanted the seed of a luxuriant Surrealist influence."[23] Fiction assumed a more overtly nationalistic orientation with the appearance of Indigenist novels such as *El indio* (1935) by Gregorio López y Fuentes and *Resplandor* (1937) by Mauricio Magdaleno, both of which were translated into English by Anita Brenner. The 1930s also produced a series of proletarian novels by José Mancisidor, Enrique Othón Díaz, and others.[24] In general Mexican cultural production after 1935 exhibited few innovations likely to arouse excitement in the United States comparable to that of the period 1920–35.

The United States in some ways followed a course similar to Mexico's in the mid- and late 1930s as the New Deal promoted economic recovery and reform and both the administration and the public became increasingly preoccupied with international affairs. American artists and intellectuals of a liberal-left orientation were either absorbed by events in Europe and Asia or turned inward to focus on native issues and themes as cultural nationalism reached its apogee. The cultural criticism of earlier years yielded to affirmation, even complacency. In a 1938 collection of essays Harold E. Stearns, who had despaired of American civilization in the 1920s, expressed satisfaction over the stability of the United States in comparison with Europe, which he attributed partly to the relative economic abundance of the former. Another contributor to this collection proclaimed American art to be not only distinctively national but also "sufficiently endowed with plastic vitality or formal creativeness to stand with the major civilized cultures in other lands."[25] In this altered context Americans continued to admire Mexican art and the achievements of the revolution, but they were less likely than before to use Mexican culture as an example to point up deficiencies in American life.

The United States government directly entered the sphere of cultural relations for the first time in the late 1930s, partly in response to the need felt by State Department officials to counter the activities of fascist governments and the Soviet Union. But Latin America as a whole, rather than Mexico, became a focal point of government attention. Thus at the Inter-American Conference for the Maintenance of Peace in 1936 the United States approved treaties providing for the exchange of publications, students, and professors among all the American republics and for promotion of exhibitions of American art. In 1940 the government established the Office of the Coordinator of Inter-American Affairs. Under the energetic leadership of Nelson Rockefeller, the office exhibited an activist, somewhat anti-European orientation that reflected a "near-craze for Pan-Americanism."[26]

With the end of the war, official interest in cultural relations with Mexico and Latin America did not disappear, but the region now became one of several that were targets of American efforts, which were more extensive than ever before. Universities, philanthropic foundations, and other private institutions also remained active in Mexico. The Carnegie Institution continued the Yucatán project until the late 1950s, when a new director ended all research that was not in the natural sciences. Starting in 1942, the Rockefeller Foundation provided funds for El Colegio de México that supported studies in philology and history and helped make possible the publication of Daniel Cosío Villegas's monumental *Historia moderna de México*. In general, however, Mexico was relegated to a relatively minor role in the global network of public and private cultural relations.

Despite the altered bases of cultural exchange between Mexico and the United States after 1935, many individuals who had forged linkages in the 1920s maintained them for the rest of their lives. Rufino Tamayo, who was less associated with the cultural nationalism of the immediate postrevolutionary period than were the muralists, continued to burnish his reputation in the United States, where he lived for extended periods starting in the 1930s. Carlos Chávez, whose compositions began to move away from nationalism in the 1930s, also preserved his ties with the American musical community.

Mexican performing artists who had distinguished themselves in the United States had a varied experience after 1935. José Mojica underwent a religious awakening and in 1941 entered a Franciscan monastery in Lima, where he remained for the rest of his life. Dolores del Río made her first Mexican film in 1943 and soon became a major figure in Mexico's growing motion picture industry. From 1939 to 1943 Lupez Vélez made a series of films based on the character of the Mexican Spitfire, but she committed suicide in 1944. As the performers of the 1920s and 1930s died or retired, they were not usually replaced, and Anthony Quinn was the only major motion picture star of a later generation who was recognizably Mexican. By 1960, moreover, a variant of the "greaser" had returned to the screen as American movies increasingly depicted Mexicans and Latin Americans in general almost exclusively as violence-prone criminals and revolutionaries.[27] Later these stereotypes were supplemented by that of the Latin American drug trafficker.

Of the Americans active in the promotion of cultural relations from 1920 to 1935, only a few lost their personal and professional association with Mexico. Ernest Gruening, named governor of Alaska in 1939, became increasingly involved in local and national politics, serving as senator from the newly created state from the mid-1950s until 1969. René d'Harnoncourt joined the staff of the Museum of Modern Art in 1944 and became its director in 1949, a position he held for nearly twenty years.

Others broadened their Mexican interests to encompass all of Latin America. Carleton Beals remained active as a journalist until the 1970s, producing many articles and books on Latin America. His *Coming Struggle for Latin America* (1938), which warned of fascist penetration of the region, went through six printings, and *Dawn over the Amazon* (1943), an adventure novel about a German-Japanese invasion of South America, became a selection of the Literary Guild. In the late 1940s and 1950s, however, he found it difficult to place his work because of diminishing interest in Latin America and the decline of leftist outlets.[28]

Frank Tannenbaum joined the history department of Columbia University in 1935. He continued to write extensively about Latin America, producing an important book on slavery in the New World as well as another book about Mexico, the controversial *Mexico: The Struggle for Peace and Bread* (1950), in which he expressed doubts about contemporary conditions there, especially the headlong rush to industrialize at the expense of agriculture and the continuing personalism in politics. The historian Lesley Byrd Simpson called the book "heart-breaking" and surmised that writing it must have cost Tannenbaum considerable pain.[29]

Hubert C. Herring and the Committee on Cultural Relations with Latin America not only continued the annual summer seminars in Mexico until 1941 but also held institutes on inter-American affairs in Lima and in Brazil and Argentina. In 1944 Herring was named professor of Latin American civilization at Pomona College; later he wrote *A History of Latin America* (1955), which was for many years a standard text in the field.

Many others kept their ties with Mexico. In 1940 Witter Bynner bought a house in Chapala, to which he returned regularly for the rest of his life. Despite change, he still found the town attractive, as he explained to Idella Purnell in 1949: "The cosy [sic] village we loved has gone and the lake is going; but the air is full of sun and birds; and I work happily six or more hours a day."[30] He recreated his first trip to Mexico in 1923 in his memoir *Journey with Genius: Recollections and Reflections Concerning the D. H. Lawrences* (1951). Jean Charlot remained in the United States, eventually settling in Hawaii, but he maintained his interest in Mexican art, about which he wrote extensively. Having won a Guggenheim fellowship, he returned to Mexico in the mid-1940s to do research for his book on the mural renaissance. At the National Preparatory School he found his own mural intact, save for the additions in pencil and chalk of "unkind students."[31]

William Spratling lived in Taxco until his death in an automobile accident in 1967. During these years the crafts revival he had stimulated continued to flourish and the town retained its attraction for tourists and expatriates. Spratling also remained interested in Mexican art, bequeathing his collection to various museums at the time of his death. Frances Toor was never able to revive *Mexican Folkways*, but she published other works dealing with Mexico, including *Treasury of Mexican Folklore* (1947). After 1935 Anita Brenner also wrote frequently on Mexico, her best-known text being *The Wind That Swept Mexico* (1943), a summary of the revolution that was accompanied by an excellent selection of photographs. Starting in 1955 she also edited a magazine, *Mexico This Month*. Alma Reed moved to Mexico City after World War II and wrote a biography of Orozco (1955) that emphasized the years when she guided his career. She also served as the official historian of the Water Sports and Exploration Club of Mexico, which, after her death in 1966, arranged for the burial of her remains in Mérida.

Reed, like Brenner, Toor, Tannenbaum, and others, received the order of the Aztec Eagle from the Mexican government, the highest honor it can bestow on a foreigner. The honor was well deserved. They and other Americans of their generation not only explained Mexico to the United States but for the first time offered an interpretation of its people and culture that was not derogatory but affirmative. In this task they were aided by many Mexicans, such as Manuel Gamio, Moisés Sáenz, Diego Rivera, José Clemente Orozco, and Carlos Chávez, who helped to acquaint their compatriots with the art and culture of the United States. Their efforts succeeded because intellectual and artistic conditions in the two countries were propitious. After 1935 the environment was different, but the foundations laid in the years 1920–35 were the basis for permanent linkages between the United States and Mexico that became a routine though valuable part of the relations between the two countries.

Notes

Abbreviations

BPAU *Bulletin of the Pan American Union*
EX *Excelsior* (Mexico City)
IA Records of the Department of State Relating to Internal Affairs of Mexico, 1910–1929. Washington: National Archives, 1959. Microcopy M-274.
MF *Mexican Folkways*
NR *New Republic*
NYHT *New York Herald Tribune*
NYT *New York Times*
PR Records of the Department of State Relating to Political Relations Between the United States and Mexico. Washington: National Archives, 1960. Microcopy 314.
RR *Revista de Revistas* (Mexico City)
TN *The Nation*
TS *The Survey*

Preface

1. *NYHT*, April 21, 1929, sec. 6, p. 1, May 3, 1929, p. 19; *NYT*, May 3, 1929, p. 19.

2. For a discussion of the various meanings of *culture*, see Raymond Williams, *The Sociology of Culture* (New York: Schocken Books, 1982), pp. 10–13.

3. James Clifford, *The Predicament of Culture: Twentieth-Century Ethnography, Literature, and Art* (Cambridge, Mass.: Harvard University Press, 1988), p. 232.

4. Henry C. Schmidt, "The American Intellectual Discovery of Mexico in the 1920's," *South Atlantic Quarterly* 77 (Summer 1978): 335–51; John L. Brown, "The Exuberant Years: Mexican-American Literary and Artistic Relations, 1920–1930," *Mexican Forum* 2 (October 1982): 9–12; Fredrick B. Pike, "Latin America and the Inversion of United States Stereotypes in the 1920s and 1930s," *The Americas* 42 (October 1985): 131–62; John A. Britton, *Carleton Beals: A Radical Journalist in Latin America* (Albuquerque: University of New Mexico Press, 1987); Laurance P. Hurlburt, *The Mexican Muralists in the United States* (Albuquerque: University of New Mexico Press, 1989). Pike's *The United States and Latin America: Myths and Stereotypes of Civilization and Nature* (Austin: University of Texas Press, 1992) appeared too late to be consulted for this study.

5. *NYHT*, June 9, 1935, sec. 7, p. 5.

Introduction

1. *Tercer censo de población de los Estados Unidos de México*, 36 vols. (Mexico City: Departamento de Aprovisionamientos Generales, 1918), 2:156–65.

2. Linda B. Hall and Don M. Coerver, *Revolution on the Border: The United States and Mexico, 1910–1920* (Albuquerque: University of New Mexico Press, 1988), pp. 126–30.

3. Alan Knight, *The Mexican Revolution*, 2 vols. (Cambridge: Cambridge University Press, 1986), 1:78; John Mason Hart, *Revolutionary Mexico: The Coming and Process of the Mexican Revolution* (Berkeley: University of California Press, 1987); Ramón E. Ruiz, *The Great Rebellion: Mexico, 1905–1924* (New York: Norton, 1980).

4. Stuart F. Voss, "Nationalizing the Revolution: Culmination and Circumstance," in *Provinces of the Revolution: Essays on Regional Mexican History, 1910–1929*, ed. Thomas Benjamin and Mark Wasserman (Albuquerque: University of New Mexico Press, 1990), pp. 273–74.

5. John T. Reid, "The Rise and Decline of the Ariel-Caliban Antithesis in Spanish America," *The Americas* 34 (1977–78): 345–55. On the popularity of baseball, see William H. Beezley, "The Porfirian Persuasion: Sport and Recreation in Modern Mexico," in Beezley, *Judas at the Jockey Club and Other Episodes of Porfirian Mexico* (Lincoln: University of Nebraska Press, 1987), pp. 17–26.

6. Mary Kay Vaughan, *The State, Education, and Social Class in Mexico, 1880–1928* (DeKalb: Northern Illinois University Press, 1982), pp. 236–37.

7. Federico Gamboa, *Mi diario*, 3 vols. (Mexico City: Ediciones Bota, n.d.), 3:380.

8. *México Moderno* 1 (September 1, 1920): 121.

9. Justo Sierra, *En tierra yankee (Notas a todo vapor)* (Mexico City: Tipografía de la Oficina Impresora del Timbre, 1898), pp. 95, 195–96; Manuel Gamio, *Forjando patria*, 2d ed. (Mexico City: Editorial Porrúa, 1960), pp. 149–51.

10. See José Juan Tablada, *La feria de la vida (Memorias)* (Mexico City: Ediciones Bota, 1937), pp. 244–45. See also Luis Leal, "Native and Foreign Influences in Contemporary Mexican Fiction," in *Tradition and Renewal: Essays on Twentieth-Century Latin American Literature and Culture*, ed. Merlin H. Forster (Urbana: University of Illinois Press, 1975), pp. 102–8.

11. Gamboa, *Mi diario*, 3:326–37.

12. "Una bella traducción de Walt Whitman," *RR* 10 (May 4, 1919): 15; "Grandes poetas de Norte-América traducidos al español," ibid. (June 15, 1919): 19.

13. For translations, see John E. Englekirk, *Bibliografía de obras norteamericanas en traducción española* (Mexico City, 1944).

14. Charles M. Flandrau, *Viva Mexico!* (1908; rpt. New York: Appleton-Century, 1937), pp. 253–54. Early attitudes toward Mexicans are described in Raymund A. Paredes, "The Mexican Image in American Travel Literature, 1831–1869," *New Mexico Historical Review* 52 (January 1977): 5–29, and Garold L. Cole, "The Birth of Modern Mexico, 1867–1911: American Travelers' Perceptions," *North Dakota Quarterly*, Spring 1977, pp. 54–72.

15. José Mojica, *I, a Sinner: The Autobiography of Fray José Francisco de Guadalupe Mojica, O.F.M.* (Chicago: Franciscan Herald Press, 1963), p. 181.

16. *NYT*, May 30, 1920, sec. 2, p. 2.

17. Blaine P. Lamb, "The Convenient Villain: The Early Cinema Views the Mexican-American," *Journal of the West* 14 (October 1975): 75–81.

18. *NYT*, May 30, 1920, sec. 7, p. 16.

19. Sylvanus G. Morley Diary, 1923, pt. 7, August 26, 1923, American Philosophical Society, Philadelphia. On Davis's career in Mexico, see Erna Fergusson, *Mexico Revisited* (New York: Knopf, 1955), pp. 305–8.

20. D. H. Lawrence, *The Plumed Serpent* (New York: Knopf, 1952), p. 28; Jean Charlot to Ross Parmenter, March 9, 1974, Jean Charlot Collection, Thomas Hale Hamilton Library, University of Hawaii at Manoa. On the Casa de Alvarado, see Philip Ainsworth Means, "Zelia Nuttall: An Appraisal," *Hispanic American Historical Review* 13 (1933): 487–89.

21. "Roberto Montenegro," *Arts & Decoration* 11 (October 1919): 274.

22. *NYT*, March 28, 1916, p. 11.

23. Emily S. Rosenberg, *Spreading the American Dream: American Economic and Cultural Expansion, 1890–1945* (New York: Hill & Wang, 1982); Frank Costigliola, *Awkward Dominion: American Political, Economic, and Cultural Relations with Europe, 1919–1933* (Ithaca: Cornell University Press, 1984), p. 20.

24. Burton Benedict, ed., *The Anthropology of World's Fairs: San Francisco's Pan-*

ama Pacific Exposition of 1915 (London: Scolar Press, 1983); Robert W. Rydell, *All the World's a Fair: Visions of Empire at American International Expositions, 1876–1916* (Chicago: University of Chicago Press, 1984); Richard H. Collin, *Theodore Roosevelt, Culture, Diplomacy, and Expansion: A New View of American Imperialism* (Baton Rouge: Louisiana State University Press, 1985).

25. Frank A. Ninkovich, *The Diplomacy of Ideas: U.S. Foreign Policy and Cultural Relations, 1938–1950* (Cambridge: Cambridge University Press, 1981), pp. 8–23.

26. Henry Grattan Doyle, "Spanish Studies in the United States," *BPAU* 60 (March 1926): 223–34; "The First Annual Meeting," *Hispania* 1 (February 1918): 15; J. R. Spell, "Spanish Teaching in the United States," ibid. 10 (May 1927): 141–59.

27. Charles E. Chapman, "The Founding of the Review," *Hispanic American Historical Review* 1 (February 1918): 8–23; J. Franklin Jameson, "A New Historical Journal," ibid., pp. 2–7. The new journal suffered from inadequate financial support and suspended publication in 1922. It reappeared in 1926 under the sponsorship of Duke University Press.

28. Carlos E. Castañeda and Jack Autry Dabbs, *Guide to the Latin American Manuscripts in the University of Texas Library* (Cambridge, Mass.: Harvard University Press, 1939), p. vii; Library of Congress, *Hispanic Foundation*, Departmental and Divisional Manuals No. 12 (Washington, D.C.: N.p., 1950), pp. 3–4; *NYHT*, October 5, 1930, sec. 2, p. 5.

29. Lewis Hanke, ed., *Do the Americas Have a Common History: A Critique of the Bolton Theory* (New York: Knopf, 1964), p. 16. Bolton's essay "The Epic of Greater America" appears on pp. 67–100. See also Arthur P. Whitaker, *The Western Hemisphere Idea: Its Rise and Decline* (Ithaca: Cornell University Press, 1954), pp. 142–44.

30. *NYT*, April 20, 1921, p. 1.

31. See Arthur Frank Wertheim, *The New York Little Renaissance: Iconoclasm, Modernism, and Nationalism in American Culture, 1908–1917* (New York: New York University Press, 1976); Alan Howard Levy, *Musical Nationalism: American Composers' Search for Identity* (Westport, Conn.: Greenwood Press, 1983); and Charles C. Alexander, *Here the Country Lies: Nationalism in the Arts in Twentieth-Century America* (Bloomington: Indiana University Press, 1980), p. xii (quote); John K. Howat, Foreword, in Marshall B. Davidson and Elizabeth Stillinger, *The American Wing at the Metropolitan Museum of Art* (New York: Knopf, 1985), p. 6.

32. See T. J. Jackson Lears, *No Place of Grace: Antimodernism and the Transformation of American Culture, 1880–1920* (New York: Pantheon Books, 1981), and Miles Orvell, *The Real Thing: Imitation and Authenticity in American Culture, 1880–1940* (Chapel Hill: University of North Carolina Press, 1989).

33. File Jean Charlot, 1923: Notes on First Mural, Charlot Collection.

34. Daniel Cosío Villegas, *Memorias* (Mexico City: Editorial Joaquín Mortiz, 1976), pp. 91–92.

35. Moisés González Navarro, *El Porfiriato—Vida social*, vol. 4 of Daniel Cosío Villegas, ed., *Historia moderna de México*, 9 vols., 3d ed. (Mexico City: Editorial Hermes, 1973), pp. 640, 703–4.

36. Jean Charlot, *Mexican Art and the Academy of San Carlos, 1785–1915* (Austin: University of Texas Press, 1962), pp. 153–54.

37. Alberto J. Pani, *Apuntes autobiográficos*, 2 vols., 2d ed. (Mexico City: Librería de Manuel Porrúa, 1950), 1:310; *EX*, September 19, 1921, p. 4, September 26, 1921, sec. 2, p. 2, September 28, 1921, sec. 2, p. 3.

38. *EX*, Dec. 2, 1930, sec. 2, p. 1, December 23, 1930, sec. 2, p. 1, December 24, 1930, sec. 2, p. 1.

39. Vaughan, *The State, Education, and Social Class*, pp. 239–66.

40. Samuel Ramos, *Profile of Man and Culture in Mexico*, trans. Peter G. Earle (Austin: University of Texas Press, 1962), p. 106. For literary trends during the 1920s, see two articles by John S. Brushwood: "Literary Periods in Twentieth-Century Mexico: The Transformation of Reality," in *Contemporary Mexico*, ed. James W. Wilkie, Michael C. Meyer, and Edna Monzón de Wilkie (Los Angeles: UCLA Latin American Center, 1976), pp. 671–83, and "Innovation in Mexican Fiction and Politics (1910–1934)," *Mexican Studies* 5 (Winter 1989): 69–88.

41. Antonio Caso, "La opinión de América," *Repertorio Americano* 8 (March 24, 1924): 13; Henry C. Schmidt, *The Roots of "Lo Mexicano": Self and Society in Mexican Thought, 1900–1934* (College Station: Texas A & M University Press, 1978), p. 98.

42. Quoted in Hurlburt, *Mexican Muralists*, p. 196.

Chapter 1

1. Paul Hollander, *Political Pilgrims: Travels of Western Intellectuals to the Soviet Union, China, and Cuba, 1928–1978* (New York: Oxford University Press, 1981).

2. Estados Unidos Mexicanos, Departamento de Estadística Nacional, *Resumen del censo general de habitantes de 30 de noviembre de 1921* (Mexico City: Talleres Gráficos de la Nación, 1928), pt. 2, p. 67.

3. U.S. Department of Commerce, Bureau of Foreign Commerce, *Survey of International Travel* (Washington, D.C.: U.S. Government Printing Office, 1956), p. 7.

4. Ricardo Romo, *East Los Angeles: History of a Barrio* (Austin: University of Texas Press, 1983), p. 59. See also Lawrence A. Cardoso, *Mexican Emigration to the United States, 1897–1931* (Tucson: University of Arizona Press, 1980).

5. The three articles by Kenneth L. Roberts in volume 200 of the *Saturday Evening Post* were "Wet and Other Mexicans," February 4, 1928, p. 10; "Mexi-

cans or Ruin," February 18, 1928, p. 14; and "The Docile Mexican," March 10, 1928, p. 39.

6. *Pomona College Quarterly*, January–March 1923, pp. 106–9, and January 1926, pp. 71–77.

7. Romo, *East Los Angeles*, p. 8.

8. James Rockwell Sheffield to James W. Wadsworth, Jr., March 4, 1926, James Rockwell Sheffield Papers, Manuscripts and Archives, Yale University Library, New Haven. On Sheffield's mission, see two works by James J. Horn: "Diplomacy by Ultimatum: Ambassador Sheffield and Mexican-American Relations, 1924–1927" (Ph.D. dissertation, State University of New York at Buffalo, 1969), and "U.S. Diplomacy and 'The Specter of Bolshevism' in Mexico (1924–1927)," *The Americas* 32 (1975–76): 31–45.

9. William Harrison Richardson, *Mexico through Russian Eyes, 1806–1940* (Pittsburgh: University of Pittsburgh Press, 1988), p. 121.

10. W. F. Buckley to Seattle Chamber of Commerce, March 16, 1921, 711.12/322, PR; Claude I. Dawson, January 29, 1923, 711.12/493, PR.

11. *Escuela de verano: Cursos para estudiantes mexicanos y extranjeros* (Mexico City: N.p., 1926), pp. 33–36. See also "Informe sobre cursos de verano," in *El movimiento educativo en México* (Mexico City: Dirección de Talleres Gráficos, 1922), pp. 501–5, and Fannie E. Ratchford, "Summer School South of the Rio Grande," *TS* 50 (July 15, 1923): 450–51.

12. *Escuela de Verano*, p. 31; "Eleventh Session of Summer School of University of Mexico," *BPAU* 61 (April 1927): 370.

13. *NYT*, November 30, 1924, sec. 2, p. 6; Helen Bowyer, "Why Not Mexico This Summer?" *TN* 116 (May 23, 1923): 594.

14. Claude I. Dawson to Secretary of State, May 28, 1923, 812.42/77, IA.

15. Diana K. Christopulos traces the attitude of the American left to developments in Mexico in "American Radicals and the Mexican Revolution, 1900–1925" (Ph.D. dissertation, State University of New York at Binghamton, 1980).

16. Ibid., pp. 415–22.

17. Carleton Beals, *Glass Houses: Ten Years of Free-Lancing* (Philadelphia: J. B. Lippincott, 1938), p. 36; Manuel Gomez, "From Mexico to Moscow," *Survey*, no. 53 (October 1964): 33–47, and no. 55 (April 1965): 116–25.

18. O. Gaylord Marsh to Secretary of State, October 11, 1918, 812.00/22315, IA. On Haberman, see two works by Gregory A. Andrews: "American Labor and the Mexican Revolution, 1910–1924" (Ph.D. dissertation, Northern Illinois University, 1988), pp. 272–334, and "Robert Haberman, Socialist Ideology and the Politics of National Reconstruction in Mexico, 1920–1925," *Mexican Studies* 6 (Summer 1990): 189–211.

19. See John Kenneth Turner, "Is Mexico in Danger?" *Liberator* 2 (June

1919): 19–21, and Irwin Granich [Michael Gold], "Well, What about Mexico?" ibid. 3 (January 1920): 24–28. Turner's and Granich's rebuttals to each other appear ibid. (March 1920): 40–41, and Eastman's comment ibid. (May 1920): 6.

20. Gregory Mason, "A Communistic State in Old Mexico," *Travel* 41 (October 1923): 16–20.

21. O. Gaylord Marsh to Secretary of State, March 29, 1923, 812.4054/13, IA. The text of the divorce law appears in *TN* 116 (May 23, 1923): 608.

22. *EX*, April 3, 1921, p. 1, April 4, 1921, p. 1, May 17, 1921, p. 1, May 18, 1921, p. 1; Christopulos, "American Radicals and the Mexican Revolution," pp. 432–35.

23. Frank Seaman [Charles Phillips], "Freedom in Mexico," *Liberator* 4 (September 1921): 25.

24. On Leighton, see a memorandum from Claude I. Dawson to George T. Summerlin, forwarded by the latter to the secretary of state, March 17, 1923, 812.20211/10, IA.

25. Christopulos, "American Radicals and the Mexican Revolution," pp. 448–49.

26. Harvey A. Levenstein, *Labor Organizations in the United States and Mexico: A History of Their Relations* (Westport, Conn.: Greenwood, 1971), pp. 106–10; Andrews, "American Labor," pp. 258–60, 314.

27. *Liberator* 11 (October 1923): 7.

28. Peter G. Filene, *Americans and the Soviet Experiment, 1917–1933* (Cambridge, Mass.: Harvard University Press, 1967), p. 141.

29. On the Soviet reception of foreign intellectuals, see Sylvia R. Margulies, *The Pilgrimage to Russia: The Soviet Union and the Treatment of Foreigners, 1924–1937* (Madison: University of Wisconsin Press, 1968).

30. Harold E. Stearns, ed., *Civilization in the United States: An Inquiry by Thirty Americans* (New York: Harcourt, Brace, 1922), p. vii; Granich, "Well, What about Mexico?" p. 28.

31. John Dewey, *Impressions of Soviet Russia and the Revolutionary World: Mexico—China—Turkey* (New York: New Republic, 1929), p. 31.

32. Frederic W. Leighton to Carleton Beals, January 6, 1924, Box 165, Carleton Beals Collection, Department of Special Collections, Mugar Memorial Library, Boston University.

33. Gruening describes his early life in his autobiography, *Many Battles* (New York: Liveright, 1973). For his decision to go to Mexico see ibid, pp. 108–18.

34. Ibid., p. 110.

35. Morley Diary, 1923, pt. 5, June 20, 22.

36. Gruening, *Many Battles*, pp. 124–27.

37. Ernest Gruening, "The Man Who Brought Mexico Back," *Collier's* 72

(September 29, 1923): 7; "The New Era in Mexico," *Century* 109 (March 1925): 649–58; "Up in Arms Against Ignorance," *Collier's* 72 (December 1, 1923): 8; "Emerging Mexico," *TN* 120 (June 17, 1925): 683; "Felipe Carrillo," *TN* 118 (January 16, 1924): 61–62. See also two other articles by Gruening on Carrillo: "The Assassination of Mexico's Ablest Statesman," *Current History* 19 (February 1924): 736–40, and "A Maya Idyll," *Century* 107 (April 1924): 832–36.

38. Details of Tannenbaum's early life can be found in Helen Delpar, "Frank Tannenbaum: The Making of a Mexicanist, 1914–1933," *The Americas* 45 (October 1988): 153–71.

39. José F. Gutiérrez to Agrupaciones Obreras Confederadas del País, August 1, 1922, Box 3, and Frank Tannenbaum to Louis [Tannenbaum], July 29, 1922, Box 5, Frank Tannenbaum Papers, Rare Book and Manuscript Library, Columbia University, New York.

40. *TS* 52 (May 1, 1924): 186; Paul Kellogg to Tannenbaum, September 17, 1923, Box 3, Tannenbaum Papers.

41. Tannenbaum to Esther Abramson Tannenbaum, undated 1925 and November 8, 1925, Box 5, ibid. On Retinger, see John Pomian, ed., *Joseph Retinger: Memoirs of an Eminence Grise* (Sussex, Eng.: Sussex University Press, 1972).

42. Tannenbaum to Esther Tannenbaum, November 30, 1925, January 18, 1926, Box 5, Tannenbaum's diary, January 18, 1926, Box 57, Tannenbaum Papers.

43. Tannenbaum to Esther Tannenbaum, February 10, March 28, 1926, Box 5, ibid. On the luncheon see also Tannenbaum to Secretary of State Frank B. Kellogg, February 18, 1926, Box 3, ibid.; a report by Sheffield, February 16, 1926, 711.12/685, PR; and Horn, "Diplomacy by Ultimatum," pp. 91–94. On Caruana see Robert E. Quirk, *The Mexican Revolution and the Catholic Church, 1910–1929* (Bloomington: Indiana University Press, 1973), pp. 159–61.

44. Ezequiel Chávez to Tannenbaum, December 5, 1925, Box 2, and Enrique Jiménez D. to Tannenbaum, January 7, 1926, Box 3, Tannenbaum Papers; Frank Tannenbaum, "The Miracle School," *Century* 106 (August 1923): 499–506; *TS*, May 1, 1924, back cover; *EX*, December 16, 1927, p. 9.

45. Frank Tannenbaum, "The Stakes in Mexico," *TS* 51 (January 1, 1924): 318–20; Tannenbaum, "Mexico—A Promise," ibid., May 1, 1924, pp. 129–32.

46. Journal, p. 25, Box 40, Tannenbaum Papers. Another member of the expedition was a photographer, Traven Torsvan, supposedly of Norwegian nationality. He was in reality the German-born author known as B. Traven. See two works by Heidi Zogbaum: *B. Traven: A Vision of Mexico* (Wilmington, Del.: Scholarly Resources, 1992) and "Traven Meets Frank Tannenbaum," an unpublished paper.

47. Carleton Beals, *Brimstone and Chili: A Book of Personal Experiences in the Southwest and in Mexico* (New York: Knopf, 1927), p. 4. See also Britton, *Carleton Beals*, pp. 1–29.

48. Beals, *Glass Houses*, p. 175.

49. Beals to H. L. Mencken, October 1923, Box 165, Beals Collection.

50. Carleton Beals and Roberto Haberman, "The Mexican Revolution," *Liberator* 3 (July 1920): 5–11; Beals, "The Obregón Regime," *TS* 52 (May 1, 1924): 136–37.

51. Carleton Beals, "Mexico's Bloodless Victory," *TN* 124 (January 26, 1927): 85–86.

52. Carleton Beals, "The Mexican Church Goes on Strike," *TN* 123 (August 18, 1926): 145–47. See also the chapter on the church in *Mexico: An Interpretation* (New York: B. W. Huebsch, 1923).

53. Beals to Herbert Croly, June 23, 1927, Box 167, Beals Collection.

54. Robert Haberman to Beals, February 11, 1925, Carrie Chapman Catt to Beals, November 1, December 17, 1926, Henry Lane Wilson to James Brown Scott, copy, December 20, 1926, Box 166, Beals to Henry Lane Wilson, January 12, 1927, Box 167, ibid. See also Britton, *Carleton Beals*, pp. 521–55.

55. For Wolfe's early political activities and his stay in Mexico, see his *A Life in Two Centuries: An Autobiography* (New York: Stein & Day, 1981), pp. 136–359.

56. Bertram D. Wolfe, "A New Page in Mexico's History," *Liberator*, February 1924, pp. 21–23; Wolfe, "Take the Road to the Left," ibid., April 1924, pp. 21–24; Wolfe, "Gompers, agente del imperialismo yanqui," *El Machete*, no. 19 (October 30–November 6, 1924): 2.

57. *El Universal*, July 2, 1925, p. 1; *EX*, July 2, 1925, p. 1; Wolfe, *Life*, pp. 355–59.

58. Bertram D. Wolfe, "Art and Revolution in Mexico," *TN* 119 (August 27, 1924): 207–8.

59. Enrique Hank López, *Conversations with Katherine Anne Porter: Refugee from Indian Creek* (Boston: Little, Brown, 1981), pp. 17–18; Joan Givner, *Katherine Anne Porter: A Life* (New York: Simon & Schuster, 1982), p. 147.

60. Katherine Anne Porter, "Why I Write about Mexico," in *The Collected Essays and Occasional Writings of Katherine Anne Porter* (New York: Delacorte Press, 1970), pp. 355–56.

61. Katherine Anne Porter, *Outline of Mexican Arts and Crafts* (Los Angeles: Young & McCallister, 1922).

62. Katherine Anne Porter, "Where Presidents Have No Friends," in *Collected Essays*, p. 413, and "The Mexican Trinity," ibid., p. 399.

63. *El Universal*, September 21, 1922, p. 1, September 26, 1922, p. 3; *EX*, September 21, 1922, sec. 2, p. 1, October 22, 1922, p. 3. For a romanticized account of Reed's early life, see H. Allen Smith, *The Pig in the Barber Shop* (Boston: Little, Brown, 1958), pp. 92–104.

64. *Revista de Yucatán*, February 24, 1923, p. 4; February 26, 1923, p. 4.

65. "The Waiting Ghosts of the Maya," *NYT*, March 18, 1923, sec. 4, p. 3; Morley Diary, 1923, pt. 2, March 24.

66. Morley Diary, 1923, pt. 1, February 27, March 4.

67. *Revista de Yucatán*, July 5, 1923, p. 8, July 19, 1923, p. 3.

68. Morley Diary, 1923, pt. 7, August 15.

69. Frances Toor, *Mexican Popular Arts* (Mexico City: Frances Toor Studios, 1939), pp. 10–11.

70. Frances Toor, "Mexican Folkways," *MF* 7 (October–November 1932): 208. See also Engracia Loyo, "Lectura para el pueblo," *Historia Mexicana* 33 (January–March 1984): 318–20.

71. John Dos Passos, *The Fourteenth Chronicle: Letters and Diaries of John Dos Passos*, ed. Townsend Ludington (Boston: Gambit, 1973), p. 365. On Dos Passos's visit, see Townsend Ludington, *John Dos Passos: A Twentieth Century Odyssey* (New York: Dutton, 1980), pp. 250–53.

72. John Dos Passos, *The Best Times: An Informal Memoir* (New York: New American Library, 1966), p. 171.

73. John Dos Passos, "Paint the Revolution!" *New Masses* 2 (March 1927): 15; Dos Passos, "Zapata's Ghost Walks," ibid. 3 (September 1927): 11–12.

74. Bynner described his travels with the Lawrences in *Journey with Genius: Recollections and Reflections Concerning the D. H. Lawrences* (1951; rpt. New York: Octagon Books, 1974).

75. Willard (Spud) Johnson, "Novelizing with the Lawrences on the Mexican Riviera," typescript, p. 8, Willard Johnson Papers, Harry Ransom Humanities Research Center, University of Texas, Austin.

76. Witter Bynner, *Selected Letters*, ed. James Kraft (New York: Farrar, Straus, Giroux, 1981), p. 96.

77. Bynner, *Selected Letters*, p. 107.

78. Witter Bynner to Idella Purnell [Stone], June 26, August 26, September 2, 1925, Idella Purnell Stone Papers, Harry Ransom Humanities Research Center, University of Texas, Austin.

79. Witter Bynner, "While the Train Pauses at Torreon," *Laughing Horse*, no. 14 (Autumn 1927): 3–4.

80. Weston's years in Mexico are described in detail in Edward Weston, *The Daybooks of Edward Weston*, ed. Nancy Newhall, 2 vols. (Rochester, N.Y.: George Eastman House, 1961–66), vol. 1, and Amy Conger, *Edward Weston in Mexico, 1923–1926* (Albuquerque: University of New Mexico Press, 1983), esp. pp. 4–7; Mildred Constantine, *Tina Modotti: A Fragile Life* (New York: Paddington Press, 1975), pp. 39–58.

81. Weston, *Daybooks*, 1:27, 97.

82. Diego Rivera, "Edward Weston and Tina Modotti," *MF* 2 (April–May 1926): 16.

83. Weston, *Daybooks*, 1:14, 190. See also Conger, *Edward Weston in Mexico*, p. xiii.

84. Bebe Fenstermaker, "Conversation with Emily Edwards," *San Antonio Conservation Newsletter*, July–August 1980. See also Weston, *Daybooks*, 1:101; Britton, *Carleton Beals*, pp. 32–33.

85. Carleton Beals, "Carrying Civilization to Mexico," *American Mercury* 1 (February 1924): 227. See also Frank Tannenbaum, "The Yanqui Alien," *Pan-American Entente* 1 (July 1, 1925): 3–4.

86. Conger, *Edward Weston in Mexico*, pp. 48–51; Anita Brenner, "A Mexican Renascence," *Arts* 8 (September 1925): 127–50. Brenner's educational history appears in a Columbia University transcript enclosed with a letter to Franz Boas, October 2, 1931, Reel 33, Franz Boas Professional Correspondence, American Philosophical Society, Philadelphia. See also Richard D. Woods, "Anita Brenner: Cultural Mediator," *Studies in Latin American Popular Culture* 9 (1990): 209–22.

87. Lowell Houser to Idella Purnell [Stone], undated (probably 1925), Stone Papers; Everett Gee Jackson, *Burros and Paintbrushes: A Mexican Adventure* (College Station: Texas A & M University Press, 1985), p. 133.

88. Roque Armando, "'Tata Nacho' y la música popular mexicana," *RR* 15 (May 31, 1925): 20.

89. Armando C. Amador, "Vasconcelos y la Institución Harrison," *RR* 17 (September 12, 1926): 22.

90. Howard Thomas Young, "José Juan Tablada, Mexican Poet (1871–1945)" (Ph.D. dissertation, Columbia University, 1956), pp. 38–39.

91. Tablada to Genaro Estrada, March 10, 12, 1924, in *José Juan Tablada en la intimidad (con cartas y poemas inéditos)*, ed. Nina Cabrera de Tablada (Mexico City: Imprenta Universitaria, 1954), pp. 134–37; José Juan Tablada, "Orozco, the Mexican Goya," *International Studio* 78 (March 1924): 492–500.

92. "The Mexican Art Invasion," *Current Opinion* 76 (March 1924): 305–7.

93. *EX*, July 26, 1925, sec. 4, p. 6; Bernard F. Reilly, Jr., "Miguel Covarrubias: An Introduction to His Caricatures," in *Miguel Covarrubias Caricatures*, ed. Beverly J. Cox and Donna Jones Anderson (Washington, D.C.: Smithsonian Institution Press, 1985), pp. 23–29. According to Witter Bynner, he gave Covarrubias a letter of introduction to Van Vechten (*Journey with Genius*, pp. 28–29).

94. *NYT*, June 28, 1925, sec. 8, p. 1, November 24, 1925, p. 28, December 13, 1925; *NYHT*, November 24, 1925, p. 24; *World*, November 24, 1925, p. 13.

95. Guillermo Contreras, *Silvestre Revueltas: Genio atormentado* (Mexico City: Grabados de Gráfica Popular, 1954), pp. 66–73.

96. *NYHT*, March 14, 1926, p. 22; *World*, March 15, 1926, p. 9; *Sun*, March 15, 1926, p. 19. For a survey of the composer's life, see José Velasco Urda, *Julián Carrillo: Su vida y su obra* (Mexico City: Grupo 13 Metropolitano, 1945). On the American Symphony Orchestra, see *NYT*, January 17, 1915, p. 22, and María

Cristina Mena, "Julián Carillo: The Herald of a Musical Monroe Doctrine," *Century* 89 (March 1915): 753–59.

97. Velasco Urda, *Julián Carrillo*, pp. 337–39; H. T. Craven, "Stokowski Presents 'Thirteenth Sound'," *Musical America* 45 (March 12, 1927): 23. See also Oscar Thompson, "'The 13th Sound'—And the Music of the Future," ibid., November 6, 1926, p. 3; "Fractions of Tones Sponsored by Stokowski," ibid., March 19, 1927, p. 4; *NYHT*, March 9, 1927, p. 17; *World*, March 9, 1927, p. 13; *NYT*, March 9, 1927, p. 28; *Sun*, March 9, 1927, p. 17, March 12, 1927, p. 9.

98. On Chávez, see Roberto García Morillo, *Carlos Chávez: Vida y obra* (Mexico City: Fondo de Cultura Económica, 1960), and Robert L. Parker, *Carlos Chávez: Mexico's Modern-Day Orpheus* (Boston: Twayne, 1983).

99. *Musical Courier* 90 (February 12, 1925): 1. See also ibid. 84 (January 5, 1922): 5; "Agricultural World Lost Engineer When José Mojica Turned to Music," *Musical America* 45 (December 11, 1926): 32; and Mojica, *I, a Sinner*, pp. 37–259.

100. DeWitt Bodeen, "Ramón Novarro," *Films in Review* 18 (November 1967): 528–47.

101. DeWitt Bodeen, "Dolores del Río," ibid. (May 1967): 266–83; José Gómez-Sicre, "Dolores del Río," *Americas* 19 (November 1967): 8–17; Weston, *Daybooks*, 1:52; *NYT*, May 17, 1927, p. 7.

102. *Revista de Yucatán*, October 15, 1923, p. 3.

103. Rafael Fuentes, "El alma mexicana en Hollywood," *RR* 16 (February 14, 1926): 43.

104. "Toward a Better Pan American Understanding," *BPAU* 58 (August 1924): 772–83; José Vasconcelos, *El desastre*, in *Obras completas*, 3 vols. (Mexico City: Libreros Mexicanos Unidos, 1957–59), 1:1457–59.

105. Andrews, "American Labor," p. 257; Horn, "Diplomacy by Ultimatum," pp. 38–41; *NYT*, October 29, 1924, p. 23; *NYHT*, October 29, 1924, p. 5.

106. See Harry Edwin Rosser, "Beyond Revolution: The Social Concern of Moisés Sáenz, Mexican Educator (1888–1941)" (Ph.D. dissertation, American University, 1970). Sáenz was well connected politically. His younger brother Aarón was secretary of foreign relations (1924–27) and governor of Nuevo León (1927–30). His younger sister Elisa married a son of President Calles.

107. *Los Angeles Times*, December 3, 1925, sec. 2, p. 1, December 4, 1925, sec. 2, p. 1; Gabriella de Beer, *José Vasconcelos and His World* (New York: Las Americas Publishing Co., 1966), p. 112.

108. *NYT*, August 13, 1927, p. 5; *EX*, September 2, 1927, p. 1; Alfonso Taracena, *La verdadera revolución mexicana*, 18 vols. (Mexico City: Editorial Jus and Impresora Juan Pablos, 1960–65), 13:54–62.

109. Alva W. Taylor, "Why There Is Trouble in Mexico," *Christian Century* 43 (September 9, 1926): 1109. See also Taylor, "Mexico's Church War," ibid. (Sep-

tember 30, 1926): 1198–1200; *NYT*, July 29, 1926, p. 1, August 7, 1926, p. 2, August 11, 1926, p. 2.

110. Hubert C. Herring, "The Sun Shines in Mexico," *Congregationalist*, February 26, 1925, pp. 265–66.

111. "Traveling Conference Reports on Mexico," *Christian Century* 43 (June 3, 1926): 721. See also *NYT*, April 8, 1926, p. 8, April 25, 1926, p. 23; *EX*, April 10, 1926, p. 3.

112. Herbert A. Jump, "Some Adventures of an Amateur Propagandist," *Christian Century* 43 (November 18, 1926): 1420–22. See also John R. Scotford, "The Ambassador Meets Some Citizens," ibid. (May 20, 1926): 644–45.

113. Hubert C. Herring, "Feeling Mexico's Pulse," *Congregationalist*, May 27, 1926, p. 650. See also Herring, "Mexico's Spiritual Rebirth," *Christian Century* 43 (July 22, 1926): 916–17.

114. *NYT*, December 30, 1926, p. 12.

115. *NYT*, January 9, 1927, p. 1, January 10, 1927, p. 3, February 6, 1927, p. 18; *EX*, January 9, 1927, p. 1.

116. Hubert C. Herring, "The Issue, Mr. President, Is Chivalry," *Congregationalist*, February 24, 1927, p. 234; Herbert Croly, "Mexico and the United States," *NR* 50 (March 30, 1927): 164; Herring to Beals, January 31, 1927, Box 167, Beals Collection.

117. *NYT*, January 21, 1927, p. 14, January 22, 1927, p. 12; January 26, 1927, p. 18.

118. Rabbi Bernard Heller to President Coolidge, January 27, 1927, 711.12/936, PR; Report by James Rockwell Sheffield, January 10, 1927, 711.12/869, PR.

119. *Congressional Record*, 69th Cong., 2d sess. pt. 4, p. 4599.

120. *Chicago Tribune*, August 9, 1923, p. 1; Dawson to Summerlin, forwarded to Secretary of State, March 17, 1923, 812.20211/10, IA.

121. *Congressional Record*, 69th Cong., 2d sess., pt. 5, pp. 5750–54.

122. James Rockwell Sheffield to William Howard Taft, February 9, 1927, Sheffield Papers; Sheffield to Secretary of State, December 11, 1926, 812.20211/45, IA.

123. James Rockwell Sheffield to Secretary of State, February 19, 1926, 711.12 Forged Correspondence/8, PR. See other items in this group, especially Robert LaFollette to Secretary of State, March 12, 1926, 711.12 FC/22, and James Rockwell Sheffield to Secretary of State, March 20, 1926, 711.12 FC/40.

124. Gruening, *Many Battles*, pp. 131–34; *NYT*, December 16, 1927, p. 1, January 5, 1928, p. 1, January 8, 1928, p. 5, January 12, 1928, p. 9; "The Forgery as to *The Nation*," *TN* 125 (December 21, 1927): 699; "Who Is Hearst's Forger?" *TN* 126 (January 18, 1928): 59.

125. James Rockwell Sheffield to Frank Kellogg, July 1, 1926, and Sheffield to William Howard Taft, February 9, 1927, Sheffield Papers.

126. *EX*, May 30, 1927, p. 4.

127. James Rockwell Sheffield to Nicholas Murray Butler, February 11, 1927, and Sheffield to C. P. Anderson, March 7, 1927, Sheffield Papers.

Chapter 2

1. *NYT*, April 15, 1933, p. 12.

2. Quoted in Richard Anthony Melzer, "Dwight Morrow's Role in the Mexican Revolution: Good Neighbor or Meddling Yankee?" (Ph.D. dissertation, University of New Mexico, 1979), p. 514. On the attempt against Ortiz Rubio's life, see *EX*, February 6, 1930, p. 1.

3. *EX*, February 4, 1930, sec. 2, p. 2.

4. *EX*, April 3, 1930, p. 1, April 23, 1930, p. 1; *NYT*, June 17, 1928, sec. 3, p. 2, April 26, 1930, p. 6. On the promotion of tourism, see also Melzer, "Dwight Morrow's Role," pp. 309–17.

5. *EX*, June 4, 1929, p. 1, June 5, 1929, p. 1.

6. José Miguel Petersen, "Hands Across the Rio Grande," *American Mercury* 16 (January 1929): 99.

7. Katharine Dos Passos, "Just Over the Border," *Woman's Home Companion* 59 (September 1932): 12.

8. U.S. Department of Commerce, *International Travel*, p. 7.

9. *EX*, December 22, 1929, p. 1, January 2, 1930, pp. 1, 3, January 24, 1930, p. 1, February 9, 1930, sec. 2, p. 2, February 13, 1930, p. 3; *NYT*, January 24, 1930, p. 1, January 25, 1930, p. 1. On Modotti's difficulties with the Mexican government, see Constantine, *Tina Modotti*, pp. 127–68; Taracena, *Verdadera revolución*, 14:243, and ibid., 16:33. In 1929 Modotti had been accused of complicity in the murder of her lover, Juan Mella, a young Cuban communist living in Mexico City.

10. *NYT*, February 15, 1930, p. 6; Carleton Beals, *The Great Circle: Further Adventures in Free-Lancing* (Philadelphia: J. B. Lippincott, 1940), pp. 226–43; *NR* 62 (February 26, 1930): 29; Carleton Beals to State Department, February 18, 1930, Box 170, Beals Collection.

11. Juan de Torres, "The Mexican Reaction," *New Masses* 5 (September 1929): 13; Carleton Beals, "Has Mexico Betrayed Her Revolution?" *NR* 67 (July 22, 1930): 249. See also Carleton Beals, "The Balance Sheet of the Revolution," in *The Genius of Mexico*, ed. Hubert C. Herring and Katherine Terrill (New York: Committee for Cultural Relations with Latin America, 1931), pp. 313–26.

12. Ernest Gruening, *Mexico and Its Heritage* (New York: D. Appleton-Century, 1940), p. 664; *Saturday Review of Literature* 5 (November 3, 1928): 314.

13. Carleton Beals, "The Mexican Commonwealth," *TN* 127 (December 5, 1928): 632–34; Frank Tannenbaum, "Viva Mexico," *NR* 57 (December 12, 1928): 108–9; Carlos Pereyra, "Dos casos de masoquismo," *Antorcha* 1 (August 1931): 12–16.

14. Ernest Gruening, "Mexico at the Threshold of a New Future," *Current History* 30 (September 1929): 1046–51. See also Gruening, "The Recurring Rebellion in Mexico," *NR* 58 (March 27, 1929): 162–65.

15. Frank Tannenbaum to Colonel [J. J. Coss], December 3, 21, 1933, Box 7, Tannenbaum Papers.

16. Frank Tannenbaum, *Peace by Revolution: Mexico after 1910* (New York: Columbia University Press, 1968), pp. 206, 246. This reprint is identical with the 1933 edition except for the change in the subtitle.

17. *Saturday Review of Literature* 10 (January 6, 1934): 393.

18. Carleton Beals, "Place by Default," *TN* 138 (January 10, 1934): 50–51.

19. Britton, *Carleton Beals*, pp. 93–94; "Entre libros," *Antorcha* 1 (July 1931): 60; Carleton Beals to Bruce Bliven, August 31, 1930, Box 170, Beals Collection.

20. On Porter's stay in Mexico, see Givner, *Katherine Anne Porter*, pp. 224–42. Day described her Xochimilco house in "Spring Festival in Mexico," *Commonweal* 12 (July 16, 1930): 296. On Eisenstein's film project, see Harry M. Geduld and Ronald Gottesman, eds., *Sergei Eisenstein and Upton Sinclair: The Making and Unmaking of "Que Viva México!"* (Bloomington: Indiana University Press, 1970).

21. Bynner, *Selected Letters*, pp. 137–38; "Fragments from a Mexican Journal," typescript, p. 6, Johnson Papers.

22. Frances Toor, "Mexican Folkways," *MF* 7 (October–November 1932): 210–11; Frances Toor to Carleton Beals, February 24, 1930, Box 170, Beals Collection; *San Francisco Chronicle*, January 21, 1930, East Bay sec., p. 1; *EX*, April 1, 1930, p. 1.

23. Anita Brenner to Beals, August 23, 1928, Box 168, Beals Collection; Waldo Frank, "The Mexican Invasion," *NR* 60 (October 23, 1929): 276; Geduld and Gottesman, eds., *Eisenstein and Sinclair*, p. 5. The title of Brenner's dissertation is "The Influence of Technique on the Decorative Style in the Domestic Pottery of Culhuacán."

24. Stephen P. Duggan to Alfonso Pruneda, September 28, 1927, Box 1, Folder 1, Series X, Dwight W. Morrow Papers, Amherst College Archives, Amherst, Mass. For the background of Morrow's selection for the ambassadorship, see, Melzer, "Dwight Morrow's Role," pp. 165–74.

25. Dwight Morrow to Ernest Gruening, October 19, 1929, Dwight W. Morrow Papers; Ernest Gruening, "A New Era of Peaceful Relations with Mexico," *Current History* 29 (March 1929): 931–32.

26. Elizabeth Morrow, *The Mexican Years: Leaves from the Diary of Elizabeth Cutter Morrow* (New York: Spiral Press, 1953), p. 29.

27. Will Rogers, "More Letters from a Self-Made Diplomat to His President," *Saturday Evening Post* 200 (May 19, 1928): 109. See also Melzer, "Dwight Morrow's Role," pp. 206–9, and *EX*, December 2, 1927, p. 3.

28. Will Rogers, "More Letters from a Self-Made Diplomat to His President," *Saturday Evening Post* 200 (May 12, 1928): 4.

29. *EX*, December 14, 1927, p. 1, December 15, 1927, p. 1.

30. *EX*, December 16, 1927, pp. 1, 9; *NYT*, December 19, 1927, p. 1, December 21, 1927, p. 1; Melzer, "Dwight Morrow's Role," pp. 215–22; Charles W. Hackett, "Success of Lindbergh's Good-Will Mission to Mexico," *Current History* 27 (February 1928): 727–29; Anne Morrow Lindbergh, *Bring Me a Unicorn: Diaries and Letters of Anne Morrow Lindbergh, 1922–1928* (New York: Harcourt Brace Jovanovich, 1971), p. 89.

31. *NYT*, December 29, 1927, p. 2; Melzer, "Dwight Morrow's Role," p. 221.

32. *NYT*, June 14, 1928, p. 19; Melzer, "Dwight Morrow's Role," pp. 317–30; "Successful Flight of Mexico's Lone Eagle," *BPAU* 62 (July 1928): 703–6.

33. Notes for Smith College Alumnae Assembly Talk, June 1928, Box 61, Elizabeth Morrow Papers, Sophia Smith Collection, Smith College, Northampton, Mass.; Morrow, *Mexican Years*, p. 11.

34. Elizabeth Morrow, "Our Street in Cuernavaca," *American Mercury* 23 (August 1931): 411–18; Morrow, *Mexican Years*, pp. 32, 158; Elizabeth Morrow, *Casa Mañana* (Croton Falls, N.Y.: Spiral Press, 1932).

35. Morrow, *Mexican Years*, p. 143.

36. Unsigned letter to Rivera (carbon copy), December 5, 1929, Dwight W. Morrow Papers; Hayden Herrera, *Frida: A Biography of Frida Kahlo* (New York: Harper & Row, 1983), p. 104.

37. Morrow, *Mexican Years*, p. 359; Alfredo Nisser, "Ante los frescos del palacio de Cortés," *RR* 21 (February 8, 1931): 23, and 21 (February 15, 1931): 36–38.

38. On Harnoncourt's early life, see Biographical Material, Reel 3830, René d'Harnoncourt Papers, Archives of American Art, Smithsonian Institution, Washington, D.C.; and *René d'Harnoncourt, 1901–1968: A Tribute, October 8, 1968, Sculpture Garden, The Museum of Modern Art*.

39. Weston, *Daybooks*, 1:172.

40. René d'Harnoncourt, *Mexicana: A Book of Pictures* (New York: Knopf, 1931). See also René Harnoncourt [*sic*], *Domingos mexicanos*, of which three hundred copies were published by Frederick Davis.

41. *NYT*, October 26, 1930, sec. 4, p. 26.

42. Details of Spratling's early years can be found in his posthumously published *File on Spratling: An Autobiography* (Boston: Little, Brown, 1967). See also his two-part article "Some Impressions of Mexico" in *Architectural Forum* 47 (July 1927): 1–8, and (August 1927): 161–68.

43. Elizabeth Morrow, "In Taxco's Sun," *Forum* 92 (December 1934): 368.

44. William Spratling to Elizabeth Morrow, January 31, 1931, Correspondence about Mexico Interests, Elizabeth Morrow Papers. See also Spratling to Dwight Morrow, May 10 [1929?], and August 16, 1930, Dwight Morrow Papers.

45. Beals, *Great Circle*, p. 323; Bynner, *Selected Letters*, pp. 136–37; Witter Bynner to Idella Purnell [Stone], December 20, 1931, Stone Papers; Elizabeth Anderson and Gerald R. Kelly, *Miss Elizabeth: A Memoir* (Boston: Little, Brown, 1969), p. 224.

46. Richard H. Pells, *Radical Visions and American Dreams: Culture and Social Thought in the Depression Years* (New York: Harper & Row, 1973), pp. 98–103.

47. Frank's relations with Spain and Spanish America are discussed in Michael A. Ogorzaly, "Waldo Frank: Prophet of Hispanic Regeneration" (Ph.D. dissertation, University of Notre Dame, 1982); Irene Rostagno, "Waldo Frank's Crusade for Latin American Literature," *The Americas* 46 (July 1989): 41–69; and two articles by Arnold Chapman in *Hispania*: "Waldo Frank in the Hispanic World: The First Phase," 44 (December 1961): 626–34, and "Waldo Frank in Spanish America: Between Journeys, 1924–1929," 47 (September 1964): 510–21. For Tablada's comments on Frank, see *EX*, September 8, 1921, p. 3, and for Frank's statement to Azuela, see Beatrice Berler, ed., *Epistolario y archivo: Mariano Azuela* (Mexico City: Centro de Estudios Literarios, UNAM, 1969), p. 35. Frank's message to Mexican writers can be found in *Repertorio Americano* 8 (August 4, 1924): 305–6.

48. Waldo Frank, *Memoirs of Waldo Frank*, ed. Alan Trachtenberg (Amherst: University of Massachusetts Press, 1973), pp. 155–61; Ogorzaly, "Waldo Frank," p. 116; Taracena, *Verdadera revolución*, 15:190–91.

49. Waldo Frank, "The Problem of the Relations between the Two Americas," in "The Fourth Annual Session of the Seminar in Mexico, July 14–August 2, 1929," mimeographed, pp. 104–9.

50. Waldo Frank, "Pilgrimage to Mexico," *NR* 67 (July 1, 1931): 184.

51. Waldo Frank, "How I Came to Communism," *New Masses* 8 (September 1932): 7.

52. Stuart Chase, *Mexico: A Study of Two Americas* (New York: Macmillan, 1931), p. 205.

53. *TN* 133 (August 12, 1931): 165.

54. *New Masses* 7 (September 1931): 18.

55. Morrow's review is in *NYHT*, August 9, 1931, sec. 11, p. 1; Gruening's is in the *Saturday Review of Literature* 8 (August 8, 1931): 35–36; and Beals's is in *TN* 133 (August 26, 1931): 209–10.

56. Aldous Huxley, "Mexico: The Industrial and the Primitive," *Spectator* 152 (April 13, 1934): 569.

57. Carleton Beals, *Mexican Maze* (N.p.: Book League of America, 1931), pp. 117, 158.

58. Mary Austin, "Mexicans and New Mexico," *TS* 66 (May 1, 1931): 143; Mary Austin, *Earth Horizon: Autobiography* (Boston: Houghton Mifflin, 1932), p. 365.

59. Marsden Hartley to Rebecca Strand, November 27, 1931, Letters, 1928–43, Roll X3, Elizabeth McCausland Papers, Archives of American Art, Smithsonian Institution, Washington, D.C.

60. Spratling, *File on Spratling*, p. 58.

61. Edna Ferber, *They Brought Their Women: A Book of Short Stories* (1933; rpt. Freeport, N.Y.: Books for Libraries Press, 1970), p. 199; Weston, *Daybooks*, 2:244.

62. Joseph Freeman, "The Well-Paid Art of Lying," *New Masses* 7 (October 1931): 10–11.

63. *EX*, July 6, 1930, sec. 2, p. 1.

64. See Purnell's application for a Guggenheim fellowship, 1932, Stone Papers.

65. *Pomona College Quarterly Magazine*, January 1927, pp. 80–84; *Pomona College Magazine*, December 1928, pp. 91–92; *Mexico: Lectures before the Inter-America Institute* (Claremont, Calif., 1929); George S. Burgess to Frank Tannenbaum, July 24, 1928, and program for Conference on Mexico, February 9–11, 1928, Box 2, Tannenbaum Papers.

66. Hubert C. Herring, "Bridging the Rio Grande," *Religious Education* 24 (January 1929): 4–5; see enclosure with Hubert C. Herring to Frank Tannenbaum, October 27, 1928, Box 2, Tannenbaum Papers.

67. *EX*, July 9, 1923, sec. 2, p. 2.

68. Herring, "Bridging the Rio Grande," pp. 4–6; Committee on Cultural Relations with Latin America, Inc., "Report of the Executive Director for the Year 1931," Hubert C. Herring Folder, 1931–32, Series I, Business Affairs and Public Activities Files, 1900–31, Dwight W. Morrow Papers

69. "Report for 1931," pp. 8–9; Hubert C. Herring to Elizabeth Morrow, January 5, 1932, Elizabeth Morrow Papers.

70. John Simon Guggenheim Memorial Foundation, *Reports of the Secretary-Treasurer, 1929, 1930* (New York, n.d.), pp. 15–16. The Latin American Exchange Fellowships are briefly described in John Simon Guggenheim Memorial Foundation, *Reports of the President and the Treasurer, 1983* (New York, n.d.), pp. xvii–xxvi. The names and projects of recipients from 1930 through 1935 can be found in the secretary's reports for those years.

71. Anita Brenner to Franz Boas, January 18, 1931, Reel 32, Boas Professional Correspondence; *NYT*, July 2, 1938, p. 13.

72. *NYT*, March 20, 1932, sec. 8, p. 11. See also Don McDonagh, *Martha Graham: A Biography* (New York: Praeger, 1983), pp. 88–89.

73. Application for a Guggenheim Fellowship, 1932, Stone Papers.

74. Anita Brenner to Franz Boas, January 18, 1931; Prospero Mirador, "Anita Brenner pide sus albricias," *RR* 20 (January 25, 1931): 30–31; Prospero Mirador, "Carleton Beals, becado en México," *RR* 21 (April 19, 1931): 20–21. See also Carleton Beals to Ernestine Evans, May 3, 1931, Box 171, Beals Collection.

75. Ione Robinson, *A Wall to Paint On* (New York: Dutton, 1946), p. 117. This volume consists of Robinson's letters to her mother describing her experiences in Mexico and elsewhere.

76. Zohmah Charlot, "Mexican Memories [1931]," ed. Ronn Ronck, unpublished manuscript, pp. 2–38, Charlot Collection. See also Carleton Beals, *House in Mexico* (New York: Hastings House, 1958), p. 88.

77. Robinson, *Wall to Paint On*, p. 202.

78. Malcolm Cowley, *The Dream of the Golden Mountains: Remembering the 1930s* (New York: Penguin Books, 1981), pp. 53–55; Frank, *Memoirs*, p. 243; Hart Crane, *The Letters of Hart Crane, 1916–1932*, ed. Brom Weber (New York: Hermitage House, 1952), p. 372.

79. Crane, *Letters*, pp. 371–72; *EX*, April 18, 1931, sec. 2, p. 1.

80. Crane, *Letters*, pp. 384–87; Susan Jenkins Brown, *Letters and Memories of Hart Crane, 1923–1932* (Middletown, Conn.: Wesleyan University Press, 1968), pp. 163–64.

81. Crane, *Letters*, pp. 388, 394.

82. Ibid., pp. 382, 391.

83. Givner, *Katherine Anne Porter*, pp. 234–37; Samuel Loveman to Grace Hart Crane, n.d., Hart Crane Papers, Rare Book and Manuscript Library, Columbia University, New York.

84. Crane, *Letters*, pp. 404, 408.

85. Marsden Hartley to "Darling Adelaide," n.d., Reel X4, McCausland Papers.

86. Samuel Loveman to Grace Hart Crane, n.d., Crane Papers.

87. Crane, *Letters*, p. 405.

88. Marsden Hartley to Rebecca Strand, November 27, December 2, 1931, Reel X3, McCausland Papers.

89. Marsden Hartley to "Don old dear," March 21, 1933, ibid.; Crane, *Letters*, p. 404.

90. Journal, 1931–34, undated entry, H. L. Davis Papers, Harry Ransom Humanities Research Center, University of Texas, Austin. For a discussion of Davis's literary production, see Eli S. Jenkins, "H. L. Davis: A Critical Study" (Ph.D. dissertation, University of Southern California, 1960).

91. Journal, 1931–34, July 10 [1932], undated entry, Davis Papers.

92. Howard S. Phillips, "Exodus or Reconquest," *Mexican Life* 3 (November–December 1927): 34.

93. The fullest discussion of the repatriation drive appears in Abraham Hoffman, *Unwanted Mexican Americans in the Great Depression: Repatriation Pressures, 1929–1939* (Tucson: University of Arizona Press, 1974). See also Cardoso, *Mexican Emigration*, pp. 139–48, and Mercedes Carrera de Velasco, *Los mexicanos que devolvió la crisis, 1929–1932* (Tlatelolco: Secretaría de Relaciones Exteriores, 1974).

94. Francisco E. Balderrama, *In Defense of La Raza: The Los Angeles Mexican Consulate and the Mexican Community, 1929–1936* (Tucson: University of Arizona Press, 1982), pp. 40–41.

95. Dennis Nodin Valdés, "Mexican Revolutionary Nationalism and Repatriation during the Great Depression," *Mexican Studies* 4 (Winter 1988): 1–23.

96. *New Orleans Times-Picayune*, June 15, 1929, p. 1. See also *EX*, June 18, 1929, p. 1.

97. El Caballero des Grieux, "El espíritu latino en la patria de Lindbergh," *RR* 19 (March 25, 1928): 20; "Mexicanos que triunfan: José Mojica," ibid. (May 27, 1928): 31; Alfonso Pinto, "When Hollywood Spoke Spanish," *Americas* 32 (October 1980): 8; Pressbook, *One Mad Kiss*, New York Public Library of the Performing Arts.

98. Carl J. Mora, *Mexican Cinema: Reflections of a Society, 1896–1980* (Berkeley: University of California Press, 1982), pp. 34–35.

99. Emily Genauer, *Rufino Tamayo* (New York: Harry N. Abrams, 1974), pp. 36–37; *Sun*, October 23, 1926, p. 5; José Clemente Orozco, *Cartas a Margarita, 1921–1949*, ed. Tatiana Herrera Orozco (Mexico City: Ediciones Era, 1987), p. 115. Orozco's letters to his wife during their periods of separation give a detailed account of his activities and feelings. He resided in the United States until mid-1934, making a trip to Mexico in the summer of 1929 and traveling to Europe for the first time in the summer of 1932. During this time Orozco's wife and three children spent approximately two years with him in the United States.

100. Jean Charlot, "Orozco's Stylistic Evolution," in *An Artist on Art: Collected Essays of Jean Charlot*, 2 vols. (Honolulu: University of Hawaii Press, 1972), 2:285–86. See also Anita Brenner to Charlot, January 16, 1947, Charlot Collection.

101. Orozco, *Cartas a Margarita*, p. 137. See also Reed's *Orozco* (New York: Oxford University Press, 1956), though its accuracy in some respects has been called into question by Hurlburt (*Mexican Muralists*, pp. 32, 56, 59).

102. José Clemente Orozco, *The Artist in New York: Letters to Jean Charlot and Unpublished Writings, 1925–1929*, trans. Ruth L. C. Simms (Austin: University of Texas Press, 1974), pp. 76, 81.

103. Selden Rodman, *Mexican Journal: The Conquerors Conquered* (New York: Devin-Adair, 1958), p. 167; Orozco, *Cartas a Margarita*, p. 102.

104. Orozco, *Artist in New York*, pp. 37–38.

105. Reed, *Orozco*, pp. 52–53.

106. Orozco, *Artist in New York*, p. 82.

107. Antonieta Rivas Mercado, *Cartas a Manuel Rodríguez Lozano (1927–1930)*, ed. Isaac Rojas Rosillo (Mexico City: Sep/Setentas, 1975), p. 108. She appears prominently as Valeria in the fourth volume of Vasconcelos's autobiography, *El proconsulado*, in *Obras completas*, 2:120–503. See also Jean Franco, *Plotting Women: Gender and Representation in Mexico* (New York: Columbia University Press, 1989), pp. 112–28.

108. Rivas Mercado, *Cartas a Rodríguez Lozano*, pp. 110, 114, 121, 133.

109. Ibid., pp. 104, 109–10.

110. Orozco, *Artist in New York*, pp. 45, 65, 70, 71, 83–84; Orozco, *Cartas a Margarita*, p. 150; Reed, *Orozco*, pp. 90–96; *Time*, October 13, 1930, p. 30.

111. Genauer, *Rufino Tamayo*, pp. 36–37; Parker, *Carlos Chávez*, pp. 5–6.

112. *NYT*, November 29, 1926, p. 16; *Musical America* 45 (December 4, 1926): 7.

113. *NYHT*, April 23, 1928, p. 13; *NYT*, April 23, 1928, p. 28; *Musical America* 48 (May 12, 1928): 20.

114. Frances Flynn Paine to Elizabeth Morrow, September 14, 1928, Box 61, Elizabeth Morrow Papers.

115. Orozco, *Cartas a Margarita*, pp. 99, 222; Jaime Torres Bodet, *Tiempo de arena*, in *Obras escogidas* (Mexico City: Fondo de Cultura Económica, 1961), p. 325; Xavier Villaurrutia, *Cartas de Villaurrutia a Novo (1935–1936)* (Mexico City: Instituto de Bellas Artes, Departamento de Literatura, 1966), p. 32; José Vasconcelos, "Gigantasia," in *Obras completas*, 1:169; Salvador Novo, "Continente vacío," in *Toda la prosa* (Mexico City: Empresa Editoriales, 1964), p. 234.

116. Aaron Copland, "Carlos Chávez—Mexican Composer," *NR* 54 (May 2, 1928): 322–23.

117. Oliver Daniel, *Stokowski: A Counterpoint of View* (New York: Dodd, Mead, 1982), pp. 277–78; *EX*, January 20, 1931, p. 1, January 23, 1931, sec. 2, p. 1, January 26, 1931, p. 4, January 29, 1931, p. 3; *NYT*, April 5, 1931, sec. 8, p. 8. See also Brunhouse, *Morley*, pp. 216–17.

118. Daniel, *Stokowski*, pp. 282–83; *NYT*, February 3, 1932, p. 19; Harry L. Hewes, "The Mexican Ballet-Symphony 'H.P.,'" *BPAU* 66 (June 1932): 421–24.

119. Michael E. Hoffman, ed., *Paul Strand: Sixty Years of Photographs* (Millerton, N.Y.: Aperture, 1976), p. 155.

120. Ibid.; *EX*, February 2, 1933, p. 1.

121. Hoffman, ed., *Paul Strand*, pp. 25–26.

122. Ibid., pp. 156–57; *NYT*, April 21, 1937, p. 18; *NR* 90 (May 5, 1937): 387; *TN* 144 (May 8, 1937): 545; *Commonweal* 26 (May 21, 1937): 104.

123. Aaron Copland and Vivian Perlis, *Copland: 1900 through 1942* (New York: St. Martin's/Marek, 1984), pp. 212–13; *EX*, September 1, 1932, sec. 2, p. 4.

124. Copland and Perlis, *Copland*, pp. 213–16, 245.

125. Ibid., p. 216.

Chapter 3

1. Ramón Beteta, *Pensamiento y dinámica de la revolución mexicana: Antología de documentos politicosociales*, 2d ed. (Mexico City: Editorial México Nuevo, 1951), pp. 72–74. On *indigenismo*, see Alan Knight, "Racism, Revolution and *Indigenismo*: Mexico, 1910–1940," in *The Idea of Race in Latin America, 1870–1910*, ed. Richard Graham (Austin: University of Texas Press, 1990), pp. 71–113.

2. *Resumen del censo general de . . . 1921*, pt. 2, p. 62. The census classified 8,504,561 persons, or 59.88 percent of the population, as being of mixed racial ancestry.

3. Robert Fay Schrader, *The Indian Arts and Crafts Board: An Aspect of New Deal Indian Policy* (Albuquerque: University of New Mexico Press, 1983), p. 12.

4. John Collier, "The Red Atlantis," *TS* 49 (October 1, 1922): 16–17.

5. Gruening, *Mexico and Its Heritage*, p. 70.

6. *NYT*, November 1, 1925, sec. 9, p. 5.

7. Witter Bynner, "While the Train Pauses," *Laughing Horse*, no. 14 (Autumn 1927): 2.

8. Editor's Foreword, *MF* 1 (June–July 1925): 3.

9. Randolph C. Downes, "A Crusade for Indian Reform, 1922–1934," *Mississippi Valley Historical Review* 32 (December 1945): 331–54.

10. Juan Ortega y Medina, "Monroismo arqueológico: Un intento de compensación de americanidad insuficiente," in Ortego y Medina, *Ensayos, tareas y estudios históricos* (Xalapa: Universidad Veracruzana, 1962), pp. 37–86.

11. A biographical sketch of Tozzer appears in Gordon Randolph Willey, *Portraits in American Archaeology: Remembrances of Some Distinguished Americanists* (Albuquerque: University of New Mexico Press, 1988), pp. 267–90. See also J. O. Brew, ed., *One Hundred Years of Anthropology* (Cambridge, Mass.: Harvard University Press, 1968).

12. Ignacio Bernal, *A History of Mexican Archaeology* (London: Thames & Hudson, 1980), p. 140.

13. Lewis Morgan, "Montezuma's Dinner," *North American Review* 122 (April 1876): 265–308. See also Bernal, *History of Mexican Archaeology*, pp. 144–45, and Benjamin Keen, *The Aztec Image in Western Thought* (New Brunswick, N.J.: Rutgers University Press, 1971), pp. 387–99.

14. Keen, *Aztec Image*, pp. 409, 493.

15. Robert L. Brunhouse devotes a chapter to Brasseur in his *In Search of the Maya: The First Archaeologists* (Albuquerque: University of New Mexico Press, 1973), pp. 113–35.

16. *NYT*, March 2, 1930, p. 3; *EX*, March 3, 1930, p. 2.

17. On Le Plongeon, see Brunhouse, *In Search of the Maya*, pp. 136–65, and Willis Fletcher Johnson, "Pioneers of Maya Research," *Outlook* 134 (July 25, 1923): 474–76.

18. Material on Thompson can be found in Brunhouse, *In Search of the Maya*, pp. 166–95; Edward H. Thompson, *People of the Serpent: Life and Adventure among the Mayas* (Boston: Houghton Mifflin, 1932); and T. A. Willard, *The City of the Sacred Well* (New York: Century, 1926).

19. *NYT*, December 28, 1924, sec. 2, p. 14, June 4, 1937, p. 23; *EX*, October 7, 1926, sec. 2, p. 2.

20. Morley Diary, 1923, pt. 5, June 19, 24; Weston, *Daybooks*, 1:59; Porter, "The Charmed Life," in Porter, *Collected Essays*, p. 427.

21. Zelia Nuttall, "The Island of Sacrificios," *American Anthropologist* n.s., 12 (June 1910): 257–95; Alfred M. Tozzer, "Zelia Nuttall," ibid. 35 (1933): 476–77; Ross Parmenter, "Glimpses of a Friendship," in *Pioneers of American Anthropology*, ed. June Helm (Seattle: University of Washington Press, 1966), pp. 83–103.

22. Parmenter, "Glimpses of a Friendship," p. 112; David Strug, "Manuel Gamio, la Escuela Internacional y el origen de las excavaciones en las Américas," *América Indígena* 31 (October 1971): 833–34; Zelia Nuttall to Franz Boas, September 27, 1909, Boas to Nicholas Murray Butler, June 26, 1910, Reel 10, Boas to Genaro García, May 14, 1910, and to J. Walter Fewkes, May 27, 1910, Reel 11, Boas Professional Correspondence.

23. Ricardo Godoy, "Franz Boas and His Plans for an International School of American Archaeology and Ethnology in Mexico," *Journal of the History of the Behavioral Sciences* 13 (July 1977): 230–33.

24. Ibid., pp. 233–34; George Grant McCurdy, "Seventeenth International Congress of Americanists: Second Session—City of Mexico," *American Anthropologist* n.s. 12 (October–December 1910): 600–605.

25. Strug, "Manuel Gamio," pp. 838–42; Godoy, "Franz Boas," pp. 233–35; "Summary of the Work of the International School of American Archaeology and Ethnology in Mexico, 1910–1914," *American Anthropologist* n.s., 17 (1915): 384–95.

26. *NYT*, May 13, 1912, p. 8; Godoy, "Franz Boas," pp. 235–36; Harvey A. Levenstein, "Franz Boas as a Political Activist," *Kroeber Anthropological Society Papers* 29 (Fall 1963): 20–21.

27. *TN* 109 (December 20, 1919): 797; Gamio to Boas, September 8, 1919, Boas to Gamio, December 19, 1919, Reel 20, Boas Professional Correspondence.

28. Nuttall to Boas, October 11, 1928, Reel 29, Boas Professional Correspondence; Parmenter, "Glimpses of a Friendship," pp. 135–41.

29. Manuel Gamio, *La población del valle de Teotihuacán*, 5 vols. (1922; rpt.

Mexico City: Instituto Nacional Indigenista, 1979), 1:x–xi. See also Juan Comas, "Estudio preliminar," in Manuel Gamio, *Antología* (Mexico City: Universidad Nacional Autónoma Mexicana, 1975), p. xix.

30. Gregory Mason, "Rediscovering America," *Saturday Evening Post* 202 (October 5, 1929): 120. See also another article by Mason, "America's Buried Past," ibid. 201 (January 19, 1929): 37–43.

31. *Revista de Yucatán*, July 17, 1923, p. 1.

32. Morley Diary, 1923, pt. 5, June 21; Robert L. Brunhouse, *Sylvanus G. Morley and the World of the Ancient Maya* (Norman: University of Oklahoma Press, 1971), pp. 191–92.

33. See Brunhouse, *Morley*, for the archaeologist's early life.

34. *Revista de Yucatán*, May 26, 1921, p. 5.

35. Ibid., February 16, 1923, p. 4.

36. Morley Diary, 1923, pt. 1, February 9, 19.

37. Ibid., March 1.

38. "Waiting Ghosts of the Maya," *NYT*, March 18, 1923, sec. 4, p. 3.

39. "Great Maya Find of Relics Revealed," *NYT*, March 2, 1923, p. 3; "The Well of the Mayas' Human Sacrifice," *NYT*, April 8, 1923, sec. 4, p. 9.

40. Morley Diary, 1923, pt. 2, March 17; Brunhouse, *Morley*, pp. 190–91.

41. Morley Diary, 1923, pt. 4, June 5.

42. Ibid., pt. 5, June 16, 30.

43. Ibid., pt. 6, July 6. The text of the contract appears in the *Revista de Yucatán*, July 15, 1923, p. 1.

44. *NYT*, August 14, 1923, p. 16.

45. Morley Diary, 1923, pt. 6, July 16, 18, 20, 27, ibid., 1924, pt. 2, May 24, June 3.

46. Carnegie Institution of Washington, *Year Book No. 23* (Washington, D.C., 1924), pp. 209–21. The progress of work at Chichén Itzá can be traced in subsequent yearbooks of the CIW, and additional information appears in J. Eric S. Thompson, *Maya Archaeologist* (London: Robert Hale, 1963), pp. 15–39, and M. Robert Ewing, "A History of the Archaeological Activity at Chichen-Itza, Yucatan, Mexico" (Ph.D. dissertation, Kent State University, 1972).

47. Jean Charlot, unpublished manuscript pages (505–6) of *The Mexican Mural Renaissance, 1920–1925* (New Haven: Yale University Press, 1963), Charlot Collection.

48. A discussion of the new orientation can be found in Carnegie Institution of Washington, *Year Book No. 29* (Washington, D.C., 1930), pp. 91–119; Alfred V. Kidder, "A Program for Maya Research," *Hispanic American Historical Review* 17 (May 1937): 160–69; and Brunhouse, *Morley*, pp. 276–77.

49. J. Eric S. Thompson, "Sylvanus G. Morley, 1883–1940," *American Anthropologist* 51 (April–June 1949): 296; Carnegie Institution of Washington, *Year*

Book No. 23, p. 209; Carnegie Institution of Washington, *Year Book No. 26* (Washington, D.C.: 1927), p. 259. Eric Thompson refers to Morley's "atrocious" Spanish (*Maya Archaeologist*, p. 21).

50. Carnegie Institution of Washington, *Year Book No. 24* (Washington, D.C., 1925), p. 251.

51. *Diario de Yucatán*, March 11, 1928, p. 1; Carnegie Institution of Washington, *Year Book No. 33* (Washington, D.C., 1934), p. 82.

52. Morley Diary, 1923, pt. 7, August 30, 1923; Brunhouse, *Morley*, pp. 210–11.

53. Morley Diary, 1924, pt. 2, July 5; Carnegie Institution of Washington, *Year Book No. 27* (Washington, D.C. 1928), pp. 288, 293; *Diario de Yucatán*, March 8, 1928, p. 1.

54. On the Mexican government's action against Thompson, see *EX*, July 8, 1926, p. 1, July 9, 1926, p. 1; *Revista de Yucatán*, August 28, 1926, p. 3, November 3, 1926, p. 4; *NYT*, September 6, 1926, p. 2; Alexander W. Weddell to Secretary of State, June 29, 1926, 812.927/12, IA; Brunhouse, *In Search of the Maya*, p. 191.

55. Maler's articles can be found in the *Revista de Yucatán*, July 16–August 10, 1926. An essay on Maler appears in Robert L. Brunhouse, *Pursuit of the Ancient Maya: Some Archaeologists of Yesterday* (Albuquerque: University of New Mexico Press, 1975), pp. 5–28.

56. *EX*, July 9, 1926, p. 5; Thompson, *People of the Serpent*, pp. 299–300. See also Edward H. Thompson to Assistant Secretary of State, July 22, 1926, 812.927/13, IA.

57. Brunhouse, *In Search of the Maya*, p. 192; Brunhouse, *Morley*, p. 210. In 1959 and 1974 the Peabody Museum turned over to the Mexican government more than three hundred gold, copper, and jade objects from the cenote in exchange for study collections of preconquest ceramics and colonial materials. See Clemency Chase Coggins and Orrin C. Shane III, eds., *Cenote of Sacrifice: Maya Treasures from the Sacred Well at Chichen Itza* (Austin: University of Texas Press, 1984), p. 25.

58. On Blom's life, see Robert L. Brunhouse, *Frans Blom, Maya Explorer* (Albuquerque: University of New Mexico Press, 1963).

59. The official account of the expedition is [Frans Blom and Oliver LaFarge], *Tribes and Temples: A Record of the Expedition to Middle America Conducted by the Tulane University of Louisiana*, 2 vols. in 1 (New Orleans: Tulane University, 1926). On LaFarge, see D'Arcy McNickle, *Indian Man: A Life of Oliver LaFarge* (Bloomington: Indiana University Press, 1971).

60. Diary of Frans Blom on First Tulane Expedition to Middle America, pp. 61, 88, 112, 149, Latin American Library, Tulane University, New Orleans.

61. [Blom and LaFarge], *Tribes and Temples*, 1:82–90; Jacques Soustelle, *The*

Olmecs: The Oldest Civilization in Mexico, trans. Helen R. Lane (Garden City: Doubleday, 1984), pp. 9–15.

62. [Blom and LaFarge], *Tribes and Temples*, 1:336.

63. McNickle, *Indian Man*, p. 42.

64. [Blom and LaFarge], *Tribes and Temples*, 2:449.

65. On this expedition, see Brunhouse, *Blom*, pp. 88–113.

66. Gregory Mason, "The Riddles of Our Own Egypt," *Century* 107 (November 1923): 43–59.

67. The *New York Times* carried numerous articles about the expedition between January 4, 1926, p. 3, and May 30, 1926, sec. 8, p. 9. See especially January 17, 1926, sec. 9, p. 1, May 9, 1926, sec. 9, p. 3, and May 16, 1926, sec. 9, p. 4. An essay on Spinden appears in Brunhouse, *Pursuit of the Ancient Maya*, pp. 92–128.

68. *NYHT*, February 20, 1928, p. 13, March 1, 1928, p. 1, March 2, 1928, p. 1; *New Orleans Times-Picayune*, February 7, 1928, p. 12; *Diario de Yucatán*, February 14, 1928, p. 1; Mason, "America's Buried Past," pp. 37–40.

69. *NYHT*, March 1, 1928, p. 1.

70. *NYT*, August 18, 1929, sec. 9, p. 11. The *Times* carried several articles on the flight, from October 5, 1929, p. 12, through October 13, 1929, p. 23.

71. Brunhouse, *Blom*, p. 126; Gregory Mason, *South of Yesterday* (New York: Henry Holt, 1940), p. 55. See also *NYT*, December 16, 1930, p. 12, December 14, 1930, p. 9.

72. Parmenter, "Glimpses of a Friendship," pp. 145–46; *EX*, May 18, 1928, p. 4; Morrow, *Mexican Years*, p. 65. See also *EX*, May 19, 1931, sec. 2, p. 1.

73. Byron Cummings, "Cuicuilco and the Archaic Culture of Mexico," *Scientific Monthly* 23 (October 1926): 289–304; Cummings, "Cuicuilco and the Archaic Culture of Mexico," *University of Arizona Bulletin* 4 (November 15, 1933). This was Cummings's only fieldwork outside the United States (Willey, *Portraits in American Archaeology*, p. 6).

74. Bernal, *History of Mexican Archaeology*, pp. 167–68; Willey, *Portraits in American Archaeology*, p. 179; Theodora Kroeber, *Alfred Kroeber: A Personal Configuration* (Berkeley: University of California Press, 1970), pp. 147–48.

75. Willey, *Portraits in American Archaeology*, p. 99. See also George H. Sherwood to J. M. Puig Casauranc, June 7, 1928, along with Program of Dr. G. C. Vaillant's Studies in Mexico, Moisés Sáenz to Sherwood, July 4, 1928, Sherwood to Ezequiel Padilla, June 1, 1929, and Vaillant to Sherwood, November 27, 1931, Reel 1217, Archives, Department of Library Services, American Museum of Natural History, New York.

76. George C. Vaillant, "Shadow and Substance in Cultural Relations," *Scientific Monthly* 60 (May 1945): 373.

77. John F. Coggswell, "The Mystery of the Jewel-Covered Warriors," *Popular*

Mechanics 57 (April 1932): 530. On Caso, see *Homenaje al Doctor Alfonso Caso* (Mexico City: Imprenta Nuevo Mundo, 1951). See also Bernal, *History of Mexican Archaeology*, p. 178; *NYT*, January 18, 1932, p. 1; Beatrice Newhall, "The Treasure of Monte Albán," *BPAU* 66 (June 1932): 405–18; Alfonso Caso, "Monte Albán, Richest Archaeological Find in America," *National Geographic Magazine* 62 (October 1932): 512. On the Nuttall controversy see Parmenter, "Glimpses of a Friendship," p. 146.

78. "The Treasure of Monte Albán," *BPAU* 67 (December 1933): 899–903; *NYT*, June 16, 1933, p. 19, October 1, 1933, sec. 9, p. 5; "American Jewels," *American Magazine of Art* 26 (October 1933): 467–72.

79. Brunhouse, *Blom*, pp. 114–18; *New Orleans Times-Picayune*, January 4, 1930, p. 19; *School Arts* 33 (October 1933): 100–101, 114–15.

80. For a discussion of the "Apollonian ethnography" of the 1920s, see George W. Stocking, Jr., "The Ethnographical Sensibility of the 1920s and the Dualism of the Anthropological Tradition," in *Romantic Motives: Essays on Anthropological Sensibility*, ed. Stocking (Madison: University of Wisconsin Press, 1989), pp. 208–76. The Sapir quotation appears on pp. 216–17. For the early history of anthropology, see Charles Frantz, "Relevance: American Ethnology and the Wider Society, 1900–1940," in *Social Contexts of American Ethnology, 1840–1984*, ed. June Helm (Washington, D.C.: American Ethnological Society, 1985), pp. 83–96.

81. *EX*, June 6, 1925, p. 1, June 7, 1925, p. 1, June 8, 1925, p. 1; Comas, "Estudio preliminar," pp. xxxvii–xl.

82. Manuel Gamio, *Mexican Immigration to the United States: A Study of Human Migration and Adjustment* (Chicago: University of Chicago Press, 1930); "Why the Social Science Research Council Favored the Study of Mexican Immigration to the United States and Commended It to Dr. Manuel Gamio," attachment to Roland B. Dixon to Manuel Gamio, October 25, 1928, Box 1, Folder 54, Series X, Ambassador to Mexico, 1927–30, Dwight W. Morrow Papers; Cardoso, *Mexican Emigration to the United States*, pp. 103–4.

83. Ricardo Godoy gives a detailed account of the origins of Redfield's study in "The Background and Context of Redfield's *Tepoztlán*," *Journal of the Steward Archaeological Society* 10 (Fall 1978): 47–79. See also Robert V. Kemper, "From Nationalism to Internationalism: The Development of Mexican Anthropology, 1934–1946," in *Social Contexts of American Ethnology*, ed. Helm, p. 140.

84. Robert Redfield, "Among the Middle Americans," *University of Chicago Magazine* 20 (March 1928): 244.

85. *American Anthropologist* 33 (April–June 1931): 236–38. See also a review by Robert S. Lynd in the *American Journal of Sociology* 36 (March 1931): 823–24.

86. *NR* 64 (September 24, 1930): 160.

87. *International Journal of Ethics* 42 (April 1932): 354.

88. Asael T. Hansen, interview with Lawrence C. Kelly, April 10–11, 1979,

typescript, pp. 25–26. The Yucatán project's history can be traced in the annual reports of the CIW, starting with *Year Book No. 29*, pp. 111–12.

89. On Villa Rojas, see the book he coauthored with Redfield, *Chan Kom: A Maya Village* (Washington, D.C.: Carnegie Institution of Washington, 1934), pp. vii–viii, and his essay "Fieldwork in the Mayan Region of Mexico," in *Long-Term Field Research in Social Anthropology*, ed. George Foster et al. (New York: Academic Press, 1979), pp. 45–64, as well as Paul Sullivan, *Unfinished Conversations: Mayas and Foreigners Between Two Wars* (New York: Knopf, 1989). Hansen described his relations with Rubio Mañé in an interview with the author on April 16, 1987.

90. Milton Singer, "Robert Redfield's Development of a Social Anthropology of Civilizations," in *American Anthropology: The Early Years*, ed. John V. Murra (Minneapolis: West, 1976), p. 247. See also Charles Leslie, "The Hedgehog and the Fox in Robert Redfield's Career," ibid., p. 157.

91. Grant D. Jones, Introduction, in *Anthropology and History in Yucatán* (Austin: University of Texas Press, 1977), p. xii. See also Arnold Strickon, "Hacienda and Plantation in Yucatán: An Historical and Ecological Consideration of the Folk-Culture Continuum in Yucatán," *America Indígena* 25 (January 1965): 35–63. On Roys and Scholes, see J. Eric S. Thompson, "Ralph Loveland Roys, 1879–1965," *American Antiquity* 32 (January 1967): 95–99, and Richard E. Greenleaf, "France Vinton Scholes (1897–1979): A Memoir," *Hispanic American Historical Review* 60 (February 1980): 90–94.

92. Paul S. Taylor, *A Spanish-Mexican Peasant Community: Arandas in Jalisco, Mexico* (Berkeley: University of California Press, 1933).

93. Parsons's personal and professional lives are traced in Peter H. Hare, *A Woman's Quest for Science: Portrait of Anthropologist Elsie Clews Parsons* (Buffalo: Prometheus Books, 1985).

94. Elsie Clews Parsons to Franz Boas, February 5, 1931, Reel 32, Boas Professional Correspondence.

95. Elsie Clews Parsons, *Mitla, Town of the Souls* (Chicago: University of Chicago Press, 1936), pp. 13, 536.

96. Hare, *Woman's Quest for Science*, p. 156.

97. Ralph L. Beals, "Fifty Years in Anthropology," *Annual Review of Anthropology* 11 (1982): 7–8.

98. Ibid., p. 9; Hare, *Woman's Quest for Science*, pp. 158–61; Elsie Clews Parsons to Franz Boas, December 21, 1932, Reel 34, Boas Professional Correspondence.

99. Ralph Beals to Carleton Beals, December 25, 1932, Beals Collection; Cynthia Hewitt de Alcántara, *Anthropological Perspectives on Rural Mexico* (London: Routledge & Kegan Paul, 1984), pp. 29–32.

100. David M. Fawcett and Teri McLuhan, "Ruth Leah Bunzel," in *Women Anthropologists: A Biographical Dictionary*, ed. Ute Gacs, Aisha Khan, et al., (West-

port, Conn.: Greenwood Press, 1988), p. 32; Ruth Bunzel to Franz Boas, December 20, 1930, Reel 32, January 31, 1932, Reel 34, Boas Professional Correspondence.

101. See the following articles in *Progressive Education* 9 (February 1932): W. Carson Ryan, Jr., and Rose K. Brandt, "Indian Education Today," pp. 81–86; Oliver LaFarge, "An Experimental School for Indians," pp. 87–94; Moisés Sáenz, "The School and Culture," pp. 99–111.

102. *EX*, November 16, 1933, p. 1.

103. John Collier, *From Every Zenith: A Memoir* (Denver: Sage Books, 1963), pp. 115, 126. See also Kenneth R. Philp, *John Collier's Crusade for Indian Reform, 1920–1954* (Tucson: University of Arizona Press, 1977), pp. 3, 46–47.

104. Collier, *From Every Zenith*, pp. 355–56.

105. John Collier to Lewis Meriam, September 1, 1931, Reel 3, John Collier Papers, Manuscripts and Archives, Yale University Library, New Haven.

106. Ibid.; Collier to A. A. Grorud, October 7, 1931, carbon, Box 2, Tannenbaum Papers; John Collier, "Mexico: A Challenge," *Progressive Education* 9 (February 1932): 95–98.

107. Vera Connolly, "The End of a Long, Long Trail," *Good Housekeeping* 98 (April 1934): 252.

108. John Collier, "A Lift for the Forgotten Red Man," *NYT*, May 6, 1934, sec. 6, p. 10.

109. Schrader, *Indian Arts and Crafts Board*, pp. 129–32.

110. Philp, *Collier's Crusade*, pp. 329–40.

111. Collier to Mary Louis Doherty, January 12, 1934, Reel 12, to Miss [Anne M.] Mumford, April 19, 1938, Reel 14, Collier Papers. See also John Collier, *The Indians of the Americas* (New York: Norton, 1947), pp. 161–62.

112. Rosser, "Beyond Revolution," p. 357; Collier, *Indians of the Americas*, p. 292.

113. Collier, *Indians of the Americas*, pp. 293–95; Kenneth R. Philp, "John Collier and the Indians of the Americas: The Dream and the Reality," *Prologue* 11 (Spring 1979): 10–11.

114. Lewis outlines his differences with Redfield in his *Life in a Mexican Village: Tepoztlán Restudied* (Urbana: University of Illinois Press, 1951), pp. 428–40. See also Susan M. Rigdon, *The Culture Facade: Art, Science and Politics in the Work of Oscar Lewis* (Urbana: University of Illinois Press, 1988), pp. 28–36.

115. Rigdon, *Culture Facade*, p. 205.

Chapter 4

1. Anita Brenner, *Idols behind Altars* (New York: Harcourt, Brace, 1929), p. 32.

2. *Boston Evening Transcript*, November 29, 1930, pt. 5, p. 1.

3. *Art News* 15 (October 14, 1916): 3; *NYT*, October 8, 1916, sec. 5, p. 17, April 27, 1918, p. 14.

4. *NYT*, October 9, 1915, p. 8. On Zayas, see "Marius de Zayas, a Master of Ironical Caricature," *Current Literature* 44 (March 1908): 281–83; Marius de Zayas, "How, When, and Why Modern Art Came to New York," *Arts Magazine* 54 (April 1980): 96–126; William Innes Homer, *Alfred Stieglitz and the American Avant-Garde* (Boston: New York Graphic Society, 1977), pp. 52–55, 194–96; Sue Davidson Lowe, *Stieglitz: A Memoir/Biography* (New York: Farrar, Straus, Giroux, 1983), pp. 198–203.

5. *Arts & Decoration* 11 (May 1919): 2; *NYT*, April 20, 1919, sec. 3, p. 4.

6. *Art News* 18 (December 6, 1919): 2; *NYT*, December 4, 1919, p. 16.

7. Frederick P. Keppel and R. L. Duffus, *The Arts in American Life* (New York: McGraw-Hill, 1933), pp. 19–20, 39, 66.

8. José Juan Tablada, "Recent Activities in Mexican Art," *Parnassus* 2 (April 1930): 16.

9. Francis O'Connor, "The Influence of Diego Rivera on the Art of the United States during the 1930s and After," in *Diego Rivera: A Retrospective* (New York: Founders Society, Detroit Institute of the Arts with Norton, 1986), p. 159.

10. See Barbara Rose, *American Art since 1900*, rev. ed. (New York: Praeger, 1975), pp. 91–92, and George H. Roeder, Jr., *Forum of Uncertainty: Confrontations with Modern Painting in Twentieth-Century American Thought* (Ann Arbor: UMI Research Press, 1980), quotation on p. 83.

11. Brenner, "Mexican Renascence," p. 137.

12. H. Wayne Morgan, *New Muses: Art in American Culture, 1865–1920* (Norman: University of Oklahoma Press, 1978), pp. 50–56.

13. Thomas Hart Benton, *An American in Art: A Professional and Technical Autobiography* (Lawrence: University Press of Kansas, 1969), pp. 61–62.

14. Morgan, *New Muses*, pp. 164–66; Roeder, *Forum of Uncertainty*, pp. 99–100.

15. Zayas, "How, When, and Why Modern Art Came to New York," p. 109; Homer, *Stieglitz*, pp. 198–99.

16. Edgar L. Hewett, "The Art of the Earliest Americans," *American Magazine of Art* 13 (September 1922): 290; John Sloan, "The Indian as Artist," *TS* 67 (December 1, 1931): 243. See also J. J. Brody, *Indian Painters and White Patrons* (Albuquerque: University of New Mexico Press, 1971), and Van Deren Coke, *Taos and Santa Fe: The Artist's Environment, 1882–1942* (Albuquerque: University of New Mexico Press, 1963).

17. Walter Pach, "The Art of the American Indian," *Dial* 68 (January 1920): 62, and "The Greatest American Artists," *Harper's Magazine* 148 (January 1924): 18.

18. *NYT*, December 20, 1914, sec. 5, p. 11; Lowe, *Stieglitz*, p. 162.

19. *Art News*, October 14, 1916, p. 3.

20. D. Cartuel, "The Aztec Studio, San Francisco," *Art and Archaeology* 12 (July 1921): 40; "Mexican Art Exhibit Held in California," *Mexican Review* 4 (July 1921): 40; *NYT*, December 2, 1928, sec. 10, p. 12.

21. *San Francisco Chronicle*, May 1, 1921, p. 6; Don McDonagh, *Martha Graham: A Biography* (New York: Praeger, 1973), pp. 26–27.

22. Marjorie Ingle, *Mayan Revival Style: Art Deco Mayan Fantasy* (1984; rpt. Albuquerque: University of New Mexico Press, 1989), pp. 10, 13–19. See also E. Bradford Burns, "The Maya Imprint on Los Angeles," *Americas* 33 (November–December 1981): 41–48.

23. Ingle, *Mayan Revival Style*, pp. 24–28; *EX*, April 16, 1930, p. 1.

24. Ingle, *Mayan Revival Style*, pp. 44–51; Brunhouse, *Morley*, p. 318; Donald E. Marquis, "Archaeological Aspects of the Mayan Theatre of Los Angeles, California," *Art and Archaeology* 29 (March 1930): 98–111.

25. *NYT*, October 4, 1925, sec. 13, p. 22. See also Ingle, *Mayan Revival Style*, pp. 51–56, and two works by Bossom: "New Styles in American Architecture," *World's Work* 56 (June 1928): 189–95, and *Building to the Skies: The Romance of the Skyscraper* (London: Studio, 1934). Bossom also found models for American architecture in Mexico's colonial buildings. See his *An Architectural Pilgrimage in Old Mexico* (New York: Charles Scribner's Sons, 1924).

26. *Diario de Yucatán*, March 1, 1928, p. 1.

27. *International Studio* 57 (December 1915): 66; Ingle, *Mayan Revival Style*, pp. 41–44; Alfred C. Bossom, "Furnishing the Modern Apartment with Distinction," *Arts & Decoration* 20 (February 1924): 24–25; Edgar Lloyd Hampton, "Rebirth of Prehistoric American Art," *Current History* 25 (February 1927): 634.

28. Thomas Craven, "The Independent Exhibition," *NR* 34 (March 14, 1923): 71; Alma M. Reed, *The Mexican Muralists* (New York: Crown, 1960), p. 35; Claude Bragdon, "An Alphabet of Form," *Architectural Record* 61 (February 1927): 97–104. See also *NYHT*, November 28, 1926, sec. 6, p. 3, and Ruth Harwood, "Designs from the Seven Primitive Motifs," *Design* 29 (July–August 1927): 52–56; Diego Rivera, "Children's Drawing in Mexico," *School Arts* 31 (February 1932): 379.

29. Holger Cahill, Introduction to *American Folk Art: The Art of the Common Man in America, 1750–1900* (New York: Museum of Modern Art, 1932), pp. 3–6. See also *Arts* 5 (March 1924): 61, and Beatrix T. Rumford, "Uncommon Art of the Common People," in *Perspectives on American Folk Art*, ed. Ian M. G. Quimby and Scott T. Swank (Winterthur, Del.: Henry Francis duPont Winterthur Museum, 1980), pp. 14–32.

30. Dr. Atl [Gerardo Murillo], *Los artes populares en México* (Mexico City: Li-

brería Cultura, 1921), p. 7. See also Justino Fernández, *Roberto Montenegro* (Mexico City: Universidad Nacional Autónoma Mexicana, 1962), pp. 13–19, and "The Davis Collection," *Mexico This Month*, September 1957, p. 23.

31. Crane, *Letters*, p. 388.

32. Francis Toor, "Arts in Mexico," *School Arts* 31 (February 1932): 323; Susan Smith, *Made in Mexico* (New York: Knopf, 1930), p. 3; Chase, *Mexico*, pp. 170–71.

33. Beals, *Mexican Maze*, p. 356; Chase, *Mexico*, pp. 187–88.

34. Porter, *Outline of Mexican Arts and Crafts*. Givner is wrong in implying (*Katherine Anne Porter*, p. 167) that the exhibit was never shown in the United States because of the opposition of the American government. For a survey of exhibitions of Mexican folk art, including two in nineteenth-century London, see James Oles's unpublished paper "From 'Modern Mexico' to Mexico's Modernism: Mexican Folk Art on Public Display, 1823–1940" (1990).

35. *Los Angeles Times*, November 12, 1922, sec. 3, p. 20.

36. Ibid., sec. 2, p. 3; November 23, 1922, sec. 2, p. 9. See also ibid., November 19, 1922, sec. 2, p. 1.

37. Alon Bement to Charles R. Richards, September 21, 1927, Folder 3342, Box 321, General Education Board Archives, Rockefeller Archive Center, North Tarrytown, New York.

38. W. W. Brierley to Alon Bement, October 20, 1927, and Bement to Charles R. Richards, September 24, 1928, ibid.; Frances Flynn Paine to Alon Bement, May 18, 1928, copy, Box 61, Elizabeth Morrow Papers.

39. Bement to Brierley, April 4, July 13, 1933, Folder 3342, Box 321, General Education Board Archives; Charles R. Richards to Thomas B. Appleget, May 23, 1928, Folder 961, Box 107, Cultural Interests Series, Record Group 2, Rockefeller Family Archives, Rockefeller Archive Center; Robert De Forest to Dwight Morrow, December 2, 1927, Box 1, Folder 42, Series X, Ambassador to Mexico, 1927–30, Dwight W. Morrow Papers.

40. Frances Flynn Paine to Charles R. Richards, May 19, 1928, copy, folder entitled "Paine Mexican Arts Association," Box 11, Abby Aldrich Rockefeller Papers, Record Group 2, Rockefeller Family Archives.

41. Thomas B. Appleget, memorandum, June 5, 1928, Appleget to Paine, June 12, October 18, 1929, Folder 961, Box 107, Cultural Interests Series, Record Group 2, Rockefeller Family Archives; Paine to Elizabeth Cutter Morrow, September 14, November 20, 1928, Box 61, Elizabeth Morrow Papers; Frances Flynn Paine, "Mexico and Her Decorative Arts," *Design* 32 (November 1930): 129; Orozco, *Artist in New York*, pp. 56–57.

42. E. S. Booth to Charles R. Richards, June 26, 1929, copy, Box 61, Elizabeth Morrow Papers. See also Elizabeth Morrow to Frances Flynn Paine, February 27, 1929, ibid.

43. Elizabeth Morrow to Mrs. John D. Rockefeller, July 16, 1929, ibid.

44. *NYT*, December 10, 1930, p. 28. See also the association's certificate of incorporation as well as minutes of the first two meetings of the board of directors in Folder 961, Box 107, Cultural Interests Series, Record Group 2, Rockefeller Family Archives.

45. Abby Aldrich Rockefeller to Winthrop W. Aldrich, February 17, 1931, Winthrop W. Aldrich to Abby Aldrich Rockefeller, February 27, 1931, Frances Flynn Paine to Abby Aldrich Rockefeller, September 14, 1931, A. W. P[ackard], memorandum, December 3, 1931, all in Folder 961, Box 107, Cultural Interests Series, Record Group 2, Rockefeller Family Archives; Marion Oettinger, Jr., *Folk Treasures of Mexico* (New York: Harry Abrams, 1990), pp. 48–51.

46. Diego Rivera (as told to Katherine Anne Porter), "The Guild Spirit in Mexican Art," *TS* 42 (May 1, 1924): 178.

47. Brenner, *Idols behind Altars*, p. 60.

48. Mexican muralism of the 1920s is discussed in numerous works, among them Charlot, *Mexican Mural Renaissance*; Reed, *Mexican Muralists*; and Emily Edwards, *Painted Walls of Mexico: From Prehistoric Times Until Today* (Austin: University of Texas Press, 1966).

49. This paragraph and the two that follow are based largely on an unpublished chapter, "The United States and the Renaissance," of Charlot's *Mexican Mural Renaissance* (ms. pp. 544–60), Charlot Collection.

50. *Art News* 21 (March 3, 1923): 2; *NR*, March 14, 1923, p. 70.

51. On the controversy over the murals, see also Charlot, *Mural Renaissance*, pp. 280–93; *EX*, June 26, 1924, sec. 2, p. 1; *El Universal*, July 11, 1924, p. 12, July 12, 1924, p. 12. For the foreigners' protest, see Charlot, *Mexican Mural Renaissance*, p. 286.

52. *Los Angeles Times*, December 1, 1925, sec. 2, p. 12, December 6, 1925, sec. 3, p. 43; Baltasar Fernández Cue, "El triunfo de la pintura mexicana," *RR* 16 (January 31, 1926): 24–25; "Hispano-American Art and Artists," *BPAU* 60 (April 1926): 359–67.

53. Carlos Mérida to Carleton Beals, December 27, 1925, Box 166, Beals Collection. See Anita Brenner, "An Artist from the Maya Country," *International Studio* 83 (April 1926): 85–87; Carleton Beals, "The Art of a Guatemalan Painter," *Arts & Decoration* 26 (February 1927): 63; *NYT*, April 4, 1926, sec. 8, p. 14.

54. *Sun*, October 23, 1926, p. 5; *NYT*, November 13, 1927, sec. 9, p. 12; *NYHT*, November 13, 1927, sec. 6, p. 11; Makedonio Garza, "Los mexicanos en Nueva York," *RR* 18 (February 13, 1927): 7; Genauer, *Rufino Tamayo*, pp. 37–38.

55. *NYT*, January 22, 1928, sec. 9, p. 12; *Art Digest* 2 (Mid-January 1928): 1; *NYHT*, January 29, 1928, sec. 7, p. 11.

56. René d'Harnoncourt to Ezequiel Padilla, December 20, 1929, Reel 3830,

Harnoncourt Papers. See also *Mexican Arts: Catalogue of an Exhibition Organized for and Circulated by the American Federation of Arts, 1930–1931*, pp. ix–x.

57. "Carnegie Corporation Project: René d'Harnoncourt," no. 633 (transcript), Oral History Research Office, Columbia University, p. 3.

58. *Mexican Arts*, pp. 3–4; 42–43.

59. Guillermo Rivas, "Notes of the Carnegie Exhibit," *Mexican Life* (August 1930): 23–25. See also *El Universal*, June 29, 1930, p. 1.

60. *Bulletin of the Metropolitan Museum of Art* 25 (October 1930): 224–25.

61. "Carnegie Corporation Project," pp. 10–11; L.M., "The Mexican Exhibition," *American Magazine of Art* 22 (January 1931): 3–4; Florence T. Griswold to Dwight Morrow, August 17, 1931, Mexican Art Exhibits Folder, 1931–32, Series I, Business Affairs and Public Activities Files, 1900–31, Dwight W. Morrow Papers; Keppel and Duffus, *Arts in American Life*, p. 82.

62. *Sun*, October 14, 1930, p. 14; Virgil Barker, "October Exhibitions," *Arts* 8 (October 1930): 17–18; *NYHT*, October 12, 1930, sec. 8, p. 10; *Boston Evening Transcript*, November 29, 1930, pt. 5, p. 1.

63. May Durlin to René d'Harnoncourt, June 11, 1932, Correspondence, Reel 3830, Harnoncourt Papers; Dorothea Fricke, undated statement, ibid.; *NYT*, October 15, 1930, p. 22.

64. *Sun*, April 29, 1929, p. 9; *International Studio* 93 (May 1929): 80; Reed, *Orozco*, pp. 97–100, 107–11; *NYHT*, April 21, 1929, sec. 7, p. 10. See also *EX*, April 25, 1929, p. 10.

65. *NYT*, February 9, 1930, sec. 8, p. 13; *Arts* 16 (February 1930): 423; Reed, *Orozco*, pp. 132–37, 166–68; *New York Evening Post*, February 8, 1930, sec. 3, p. 12; *Parnassus* 2 (February 1930): 6; Orozco, *Cartas a Margarita*, pp. 25–26, 170, 190.

66. Hurlburt, *Mexican Muralists*, pp. 26–41. My account of the three artists' American murals relies heavily on Hurlburt's detailed and comprehensive study. See also David W. Scott, "Orozco's Prometheus," *College Art Journal* 17 (Fall 1957): 2–18.

67. Reed, *Orozco*, p. 191; Robinson, *Wall to Paint On*, p. 151.

68. Hurlburt, *Mexican Muralists*, pp. 42–87. See also Orozco, *Cartas a Margarita*, p. 235.

69. *NYT*, January 25, 1931, sec. 8, p. 12, February 1, 1931, sec. 8, p. 13; Hurlburt, *Mexican Muralists*, p. 267, n. 105.

70. *Art Digest* 8 (September 1, 1934): 1–2; ibid. 9 (October 15, 1934): 8–10.

71. Lewis Mumford, "Orozco in New England," *NR* 80 (October 10, 1934): 231–35; *NYT*, February 25, 1934, sec. 9, p. 12.

72. Frederic W. Leighton, "Rivera's Mural Paintings," *International Studio* 78 (February 1924): 380; José Juan Tablada, "Diego Rivera—Mexican Painter," *Arts* 4 (October 1923): 221–33.

73. Harry W. Laidler, "Rivera, Socialist Painter of Mexico," *Mentor* 14 (April 1926): 17.

74. Ernestine Evans, "If I Should Go Back to Mexico," *Century* 111 (February 1926): 459–60.

75. Orozco, *Artist in New York*, p. 73. See also Lee Simonson to Carleton Beals, May 15, 1928, Box 168, Beals Collection.

76. Katherine Field Caldwell, "An American Patron," *Magazine of Art* 31 (August 1938): 448–49.

77. *American Architect* 135 (May 20, 1929): 672.

78. *San Francisco Chronicle*, January 5, 1930, sec. 5, p. 5, January 12, 1930, sec. 5, p. 5.

79. Hurlburt, *Mexican Muralists*, pp. 98–109, 113–22.

80. *San Francisco Chronicle*, November 16, 1930, p. 4D, November 23, 1930, p. 4D, February 22, 1931, p. 5D, March 1, 1931, p. 5D.

81. *Creative Art* 8 (May 1931): 323.

82. *NYT*, July 19, 1931, p. 21.

83. Frances Flynn Paine to Abby Aldrich Rockefeller, August 1, 1931, and receipt signed by Rivera, in folder entitled "Paine Mexican Arts Association," Box 11, Abby Aldrich Rockefeller Papers, Record Group 2, Rockefeller Family Archives; Frances Flynn Paine to Abby Aldrich Rockefeller, September 14, 1931, Folder 961, Box 107, Cultural Interests Series, ibid.

84. Hurlburt, *Mexican Muralists*, pp. 123–27; *Diego Rivera* (New York: Museum of Modern Art, 1931); *Art Digest* 6 (January 3, 1932): 3; ibid. (January 15, 1932): 5.

85. *NYT*, December 22, 1931, p. 28.

86. *New York Evening Post*, December 26, 1931, sec. 3, p. 3.

87. Harrison Kerr, "Matisse and Rivera," *Trend* 1 (March–May 1931): 16–19.

88. Frank C. Hanighen, "A Mexican Painter," *Commonweal* 15 (November 25, 1932): 98–99; Frances Flynn Paine to Abby Aldrich Rockefeller, August 13, 1930, Folder 961, Box 107, Cultural Interests Series, Record Group 2, Rockefeller Family Archives; *Diego Rivera*, p. 35.

89. "Diego Rivera and the John Reed Club," *New Masses* 7 (February 1932): 31, 22–25. See also Edmund Wilson, "Detroit Paradoxes," *NR* 75 (July 12, 1933): 230–33.

90. Hurlburt, *Mexican Muralists*, pp. 127–58. See also Dorothy McMeekin, *Diego Rivera: Science and Creativity in the Detroit Murals* (East Lansing: Michigan State University Press, 1985), pp. 58–63; *Art Digest* 7 (April 1, 1933): 4–6; ibid. (April 15, 1933): 6.

91. Hurlburt, *Mexican Muralists*, pp. 159–93; Diego Rivera, *Portrait of America*, with explanatory text by Bertram D. Wolfe (New York: Covici-Friede, 1934), pp. 82–232. The panels were eventually donated to the International Ladies Gar-

ment Workers Union, and most were exhibited at Unity House, the union's summer resort, until they were destroyed by fire in 1969.

92. *Art Digest*, April 1, 1933, p. 30; Thomas Craven, "Art and Propaganda," *Scribner's Magazine* 95 (March 1934): 189–94.

93. *Art Digest* 7 (June 1, 1933): 7; *NYT*, June 10, 1933, p. 15; Ione Robinson, "Fresco Painting in Mexico," *California Arts and Architecture* 41 (June 1932): 36.

94. *Art Digest* 7 (July 1, 1933): 12.

95. See "Vanity Fair's Own Miniature Eden Musee," *Vanity Fair* 29 (November 1927): 70; "The World in Wax," ibid. 31 (September 1928): 68; "Six Little Directors in a Terrible Wax," ibid. 32 (May 1929): 78; *NYT*, November 24, 1929, sec. 10, p. 13; *Art Digest* 4 (December 1, 1929): 14. The Mexican press also reported on Hidalgo's successes in New York. See, for example, Don Folias, "Luis Hidalgo se va," *RR* 16 (May 30, 1926): 21; "Las caricaturas de Luis Hidalgo," ibid. 19 (July 7, 1929): 23; *EX*, February 1, 1931, p. 2.

96. *NYT*, March 30, 1930, sec. 8, p. 12; *Art News* 28 (March 29, 1930): 15. See also Anita Brenner, "Carlos Mérida," *Creative Art* 6 (April 1930): supp. 93.

97. *Art News* 29 (May 2, 1931): 10; *NYT*, May 3, 1931, sec. 8, p. 10; *Creative Art* 8 (June 1931): 450; *International Studio* 99 (June 1931): 66. Clausell received little attention from these critics.

98. *Parnassus* 3 (April 1931): 5. See also *NYT*, April 1, 1931, p. 36; *Art News* 29 (April 4, 1931): 10; *Creative Art* 8 (May 1931): 375.

99. *Arts* 17 (May 1931): 581–82.

100. *International Studio* 99 (June 1931): 62. See also *NYT*, May 8, 1931, p. 30; Lincoln Kirstein, "Jean Charlot," *Creative Art* 9 (October 1931): 306–11.

101. *NYHT*, October 5, 1930, sec. 8, p. 10, December 7, 1930, sec. 8, p. 10, December 14, 1930, sec. 8, p. 10; *NYT*, December 7, 1930, sec. 9, p. 12, May 9, 1931, p. 13.

102. George Raphael Small, *Ramos Martínez: His Life and Art* (Westlake Village, Calif.: F. & J. Publishing Corp., 1975), pp. 99–103.

103. Hurlburt, *Mexican Muralists*, pp. 195–245.

104. *George O. "Pop" Hart: Twenty-Four Selections from His Work* (New York: Downtown Gallery, 1928); *George Overbury "Pop" Hart: Catalog of an Exhibition of Oils, Water Colors, Drawings and Prints* (Newark, N.J.: Newark Museum, 1935); *Art News* 24 (January 2, 1926): 5; ibid. (May 8, 1926): 5; Guillermo Rivas, "George 'Pop' Hart, a Yankee Gauguin," *Mexican Life* 4 (June 1928): 25–27.

105. Elizabeth McCausland, *Marsden Hartley* (Minneapolis: University of Minnesota Press, 1952), p. 45; Barbara Haskell, *Marsden Hartley* (New York: Whitney Museum of American Art, 1980), pp. 93–94.

106. Van Deren Coke, *Andrew Dasburg* (Albuquerque: University of New Mexico Press, 1979), p. 90.

107. *Art Digest* 5 (May 15, 1931): 10; *NYHT*, May 24, 1931, sec. 8, p. 7. On O'Higgins's background, see Reed, *Mexican Muralists*, pp. 113–14.

108. *NYT*, December 8, 1931, p. 34. See also *San Francisco Chronicle*, March 8, 1931, p. 5D; *Art Digest* 6 (January 1, 1932): 19; Charlotte Streifer Rubinstein, *American Women Artists from Early Indian Times to the Present* (Boston: G. K. Hall, 1982), pp. 261–64.

109. Everett Gee Jackson to the author, May 3, 1986; Jackson, *Burros and Paintbrushes*, p. 40.

110. Reginald Harkness Poland, "Some Far Western Artists Worth Knowing Better," *Parnassus* 9 (April 1937): 7. See also *California Arts and Architecture* 35 (March 1929): 52.

111. Weston, *Daybooks*, 2:50. See also *Art Digest* 4 (May 1, 1930): 9, and Roger Aikin, "Henrietta Shore: A Retrospective—1900–1963," in *Henrietta Shore: A Retrospective Exhibition* (Monterey Peninsula Museum of Art, 1986), pp. 8–34.

112. *NYT*, November 3, 1929, sec. 9, p. 13. See also George Biddle, *An American Artist's Story* (Boston: Little, Brown, 1939), p. 263.

113. Howard Cook, "The Road from Prints to Frescoes," *Magazine of Art* 35 (April 1942): 4. See also *Art Digest* 8 (January 1, 1934): 21.

114. Greta Berman, *The Lost Years: Mural Painting in New York City under the WPA Federal Art Project, 1935–1943* (New York: Garland, 1978), pp. 37, 59–60; Matthew Baigell, *Thomas Hart Benton* (New York: Harry N. Abrams, n.d.), p. 111; O'Connor, "Influence of Diego Rivera," pp. 161, 171–73. See also reprint of the catalog of a 1932 exhibition at the Museum of Modern Art called "Murals by American Painters and Photographers," in *American Art of the 20's and 30's* (New York: Arno Press for the Museum of Modern Art, 1969).

115. George Biddle to Eleanor Roosevelt, June 28, 1933, Reel P17, George Biddle Papers, Archives of American Art, Smithsonian Institution, Washington, D.C. See also Biddle, *American Artist's Story*, p. 268.

116. Henry Saltpeter, "Marion Greenwood," *American Artist* 12 (January 1948): 14; Rubinstein, *American Women Artists*, pp. 217–18; Francis O'Connor, ed., *Art for the Millions* (Greenwich, Conn.: New York Graphic Society, 1973), p. 279; Cook, "Road from Prints to Frescoes," p. 4; Coke, *Taos and Santa Fe*, p. 126.

117. Coke, *Taos and Santa Fe*, p. 129.

118. Richard Lorenz, "Henrietta Shore: The Mural Paintings," in *Henrietta Shore*, pp. 39–43.

119. George Biddle, "Notes on Fresco Painting," *Magazine of Art* 31 (July 1938): 406–9; *NYT*, November 8, 1973, p. 50.

120. See two articles by Mary L. Meixner in *Palimpsest* 66 (January–February 1985): "Lowell Houser and the Genesis of a Mural," pp. 2–13, and "The Ames Corn Mural," pp. 14–29.

121. O'Connor, "Influence of Diego Rivera," pp. 166–70. See also "Ben Shahn," no. 1168 (transcript), Oral History Research Office, Columbia University.

122. Karal Ann Marling, *Wall-to-Wall America: A Cultural History of Post Office Murals in the Great Depression* (Minneapolis: University of Minnesota Press, 1982), pp. 45–48; Belisario R. Contreras, *Tradition and Innovation in New Deal Art* (Lewisburg, Pa.: Bucknell University Press, 1983), pp. 44–46, 184; Steven M. Gelbert, "Working to Prosperity: California's New Deal Murals," *California History* 58 (Summer 1979): 98–127.

123. Annick Sanjurio Casciero, "The Poet of Mexican Realism," *Americas* 42, no. 4 (1990): 46; Dore Ashton, "Mexican Art of the Twentieth Century," in *Mexico: Splendors of Thirty Centuries* (New York: Metropolitan Museum of Art, 1990), p. 596.

124. José Clemente Orozco to George Biddle, April 25, 1928, Reel P17, Biddle Papers; *EX*, August 16, 1928, sec. 2, p. 7.

125. Quoted in Carl Zigrosser, *The Artist in America: Twenty-Four Close-Ups of Contemporary Printmakers* (New York: Knopf, 1942), p. 127. See also [Richard Cox] *Caroline Durieux: Lithographs of the Thirties and Forties* (Baton Rouge: Louisiana State University Press, 1977), pp. 6–10.

126. *Contemporáneos* 5 (August 1929): 60–67; *EX*, April 5, 1929, sec. 2, p. 1, July 14, 1929, sec. 3, p. 2, July 16, 1929, sec. 2, p. 1.

127. Charlot, "The United States and the Renaissance"; Diego Rivera, "Edward Weston and Tina Modotti," *MF* 2 (April–May 1926): 16.

128. Constantine, *Tina Modotti*, pp. 112–14.

129. Bertram Wolfe, *The Fabulous Life of Diego Rivera* (New York: Stein & Day, 1963), pp. 363–66; *Twenty Centuries of Mexican Art* (New York and Mexico City: Museum of Modern Art and Instituto de Antropología e Historia de México, 1940); *Art Digest* 14 (August 1, 1940): 7.

130. Genauer, *Rufino Tamayo*, p. 16; "John Canaday on Art," *NR* 178 (January 7, 1978): 26–27; *NYT*, national ed., October 11, 1988, p. 7, March 20, 1990, p. A8, September 11, 1990, p. B1.

Chapter 5

1. *NYT*, December 5, 1920, sec. 7, p. 1.

2. *NYT*, February 22, 1925, sec. 7, p. 1; *Variety*, February 18, 1925, p. 22. Data regarding plays, including plot summaries and number of performances given, can be found in Samuel L. Leiter, *The Encyclopedia of the New York Stage, 1920–1930*, 2 vols. (Westport, Conn.: Greenwood Press, 1985).

3. *NYT*, April 21, 1927, p. 14. For reviews see *NYT*, April 5, 1927, p. 30; *NR* 50 (April 20, 1927): 248–50; *TN* 124 (April 20, 1927): 460–61.

4. Burns Mantle, *The Best Plays of 1920–1921* (New York: Dodd, Mead, 1921), pp. 278–79. For reviews see *NYT*, August 31, 1920, p. 7; *World*, August 31, 1920, p. 9; *Variety*, September 3, 1920, p. 16.

5. *Sun*, October 12, 1926, p. 20; *NYHT*, October 12, 1926, p. 16.

6. *NYT*, September 18, 1929, p. 35; *Theatre Arts* 13 (November 1929): 805–6, 808. See Irwin Granich, "Two Mexicos—A Story," *Liberator* 3 (May 1920): 29–34.

7. *Sun*, June 12, 1925, p. 18.

8. Reports on her recitals can be found in *Musical America* 45 (November 13, 1926): 11; *NYT*, February 20, 1928, p. 14; M. Chejade B., "Nuestros compatriotas en los grandes teatros neoyorquinos," *RR* 19 (March 18, 1928): 32.

9. *NYHT*, March 13, 1928, p. 20. See also *NYT*, March 13, 1928, p. 23, March 21, 1928, p. 30, and Mario Talavera, *Miguel Lerdo de Tejada: Su vida pintoresca y anecdótica* (Mexico City: Editorial "Compás," n.d.), pp. 166–68.

10. Howard W. Fisk, "Mexico's Ambassador of Music Completes Good Will Tours," *Modern Mexico* 2 (April 1931): 22–23. See also "Colorful Music Will Mark Típica Tour," *Musical America* 50 (January 10, 1930): 10, and *San Francisco Chronicle*, January 31, 1931, p. 8.

11. See *Musical America* 50 (January 25, 1930): 107; ibid., February 10, 1930, p. 25; ibid. 51 (February 25, 1931): 39; ibid. 54 (November 25, 1934): 14.

12. Ibid. 45 (December 4, 1926): 7; *NYT*, November 29, 1926, p. 16; Henry Cowell, "Carlos Chávez," *Pro Musica Quarterly* 7 (June 1928): 19.

13. *Musical America* 48 (May 12, 1928): 20; Barthold Fles, "Chávez Lights New Music with Old Fires," ibid. (September 15, 1928): 5; *NYT*, April 23, 1928, p. 20.

14. Paul Rosenfeld, "American Premieres," *NR* 70 (April 20, 1932): 273–74. The unusual costumes and decorations that Rivera designed for *H.P.* drew more comment than the music or the dancing.

15. For portrayals of Mexicans in American films, see the article by Blaine P. Lamb and George H. Roeder, Jr., "Mexicans in the Movies: The Image of Mexicans in American Films, 1894–1947," unpublished paper, 1971. A detailed account of Mexican efforts to end offensive portrayals can be found in Helen Delpar, "Goodbye to the 'Greaser': Mexico, the MPPDA, and Derogatory Films, 1922–1926," *Journal of Popular Film and Television* 12 (Spring 1984): 34–41.

16. U.S. Department of Commerce, Bureau of Foreign and Domestic Commerce, *Motion Pictures in Mexico, Central America, and the Greater Antilles* (Washington, D.C.: U.S. Government Printing Office, 1931), p. 1.

17. *NYT*, February 11, 1922, p. 15.

18. *EX*, May 22, 1922, p. 1.

19. Will H. Hays, *Memoirs* (Garden City, N.Y.: Doubleday, 1955), pp. 329, 333; Will H. Hays to Secretary of State Charles Evans Hughes, October 9, 1924, 812.4061/44, IA.

20. Claude I. Dawson to Secretary of State, November 13, 1922, 812.4061/ 34, IA.

21. *El Heraldo de México*, May 16, 1920, p. 7. Production data and brief plot summaries of 1920s films can be found in the *American Film Institute Catalog: Feature Films, 1921–1930*, 2 vols. (New York: Bowker, 1971).

22. Will H. Hays to Joseph C. Grew, January 28, 1925, 812.4061/51, IA.

23. Joseph Hergesheimer, "Shapes in Light," *Saturday Evening Post* 198 (March 20, 1925): 119.

24. *EX*, October 4, 1928, sec. 2, p. 11; *El Universal*, October 4, 1928, sec. 2, p. 1, October 6, 1928, p. 9.

25. The code appears in Martin Quigley, *Decency in Motion Pictures* (New York: Macmillan, 1937), pp. 52–70. See also *EX*, April 3, 1930, p. 5.

26. C. C. Margon to Dwight Morrow, June 20, 1929, 812.4061/107, IA; Manuel C. Tellez to F. L. Herron, July 29, 1929, 812.4061/111, ibid.

27. Emilio García Riera, *Historia documental del cine mexicano: Epoca sonora* (Mexico City: Ediciones Era, 1969), 1, statistical appendix; Gaizka S. de Usabel, *The High Noon of American Films in Latin America* (Ann Arbor: UMI Research Press, 1982), pp. 105–6.

28. Pressbook, *Girl of the Rio*, New York Public Library of the Performing Arts; *NYT*, January 9, 1932, p. 21, May 9, 1932, p. 19.

29. *NYT*, March 26, 1932, p. 17; *Variety*, March 29, 1932, p. 24.

30. *NYT*, October 9, 1923, p. 17, September 27, 1930, p. 21; *Variety*, October 8, 1930; Usabel, *High Noon of American Films*, p. 91.

31. *NYT*, January 21, 1929, p. 18, October 24, 1931, p. 20; Pressbook, *The Cisco Kid*, New York Public Library of the Performing Arts. "The Caballero's Way" appeared in O. Henry's collection *Heart of the West* (New York: McClure, 1907).

32. *NYT*, November 21, 1933, p. 22, November 22, 1933, p. 23, November 23, 1933, p. 21, April 15, 1934, sec. 10, p. 4; *EX*, November 21, 1933, p. 1, November 22, 1933, sec. 2, p. 1, November 23, 1933, sec. 2, p. 1, November 26, 1933, p. 1; Allen L. Woll, *The Latin Image in American Film*, rev. ed. (Los Angeles: UCLA Latin American Center Publications, 1980), pp. 45–49; Pressbook, *Viva Villa!*, New York Public Library of the Performing Arts.

33. Geduld and Gottesman, eds., *Eisenstein and Sinclair*, pp. 407–20; *NYT*, September 25, 1923, p. 18.

34. Drewey Wayne Gunn, *American and British Writers in Mexico* (Austin: University of Texas Press, 1974), p. 90.

35. Carleton Beals, *Black River* (Philadelphia: J. B. Lippincott, 1934), p. 128.

36. See *Saturday Review of Literature* 12 (June 22, 1935): 14; *NR* 83 (July 31, 1935): 342.

37. Weston, *Daybooks*, 1:181.

38. *MF* 2 (August–September 1926): 45–46.

39. "Quetzalcoatl," in Porter, *Collected Essays*, pp. 421–25.

40. Susan Smith, *The Glories of Venus: A Novel of Modern Mexico* (New York: Harper & Bros., 1931), pp. 14–15, 145–46.

41. *NYT*, September 27, 1931, sec. 4, p. 16.

42. *Saturday Review of Literature* 9 (November 5, 1932): 223. See also *NYT*, September 11, 1932, sec. 5, p. 7.

43. John E. Englekirk, "The 'Discovery' of *Los de Abajo*," *Hispania* 18 (1935): 53–62.

44. Beatrice N. Berler, ed., *Epistolario y archivo: Mariano Azuela* (Mexico City: Centro de Estudios Literarios, UNAM, 1969), p. 16.

45. *NYT*, September 25, 1932, sec. 5, p. 7.

46. *NYT*, November 9, 1930, sec. 5, p. 7.

47. Chambers's story, which originally appeared in the *New Criterion*, was selected for Edward J. O'Brien, ed., *The Best Short Stories of 1928* (New York: Dodd, Mead, 1928).

48. *Saturday Review of Literature* 7 (November 15, 1930): 326.

49. "The Painted Pig Party," *Modern Mexico* 2 (March 1931): 22; Elizabeth Cutter Morrow to Frederick Davis, December 15, 1930, Box 61, Elizabeth Morrow Papers.

50. *MF* 5 (July–September 1929): 159; Richard Wilbur, Critical Introduction, in Witter Bynner, *Selected Poems*, ed. James Kraft (New York: Farrar, Straus, Giroux, 1978), pp. cvi–cvii.

51. *New English Weekly* 1 (September 15, 1932): 531.

52. Hart Crane, *The Collected Poems of Hart Crane*, ed. Waldo Frank (New York: Liveright, 1933), p. 145; R. W. B. Leavis, *The Poetry of Hart Crane* (Princeton: Princeton University Press, 1967), pp. 406–7.

53. Archibald MacLeish, *Letters of Archibald MacLeish, 1907–1982*, ed. R. H. Winnick (Boston: Houghton Mifflin, 1983), pp. 225–26; *New Masses* 8 (July 1932): 26.

54. Carleton Beals, "The 'Estridentistas' and Other Writers of Revolutionary Mexico," *Bookman* 69 (May 1929): 280–85. See also Kenneth Charles Monahan, "Manuel Maples Arce and *Estridentismo*" (Ph.D. dissertation, Northwestern University, 1975), pp. 181–82.

55. Crane, *Letters*, p. 372; Harriet Monroe, "Mexico," *Poetry* 42 (May 1933): 92–101.

56. "A Notable Translator," *Mexican Review* 3 (January 1920): 24; For English translations of the works of Mexican poets, see two articles by Remigio Ugo Pane in volume 18 (1945–46) of the *Bulletin of Bibliography*: "Amado Nervo, Mexico, 1870–1919: A Bibliography of His Poems in English Translation," pp. 126–28, and "Three Mexican Poets . . . A Bibliography of Their Poems in English Translation," pp. 233–34.

57. Monahan, "Manuel Maples Arce and *Estridentismo,*" pp. 174–75; Luis Mario Schneider, *El Estridentismo o una literatura de la estrategia* (Mexico City: Instituto Nacional de Bellas Artes, Departamento de Literatura, 1970), pp. 99–100.

58. "La Chinita," *Poet Lore* 37 (Spring 1926): 107–19; Lilian Saunders, "The Regional Theatre of San Juan Teotihuacán," ibid. (Autumn 1926): 468–73. A contemporary play by Julio Jiménez appeared in English translation as "The Unforeseen," ibid. 35 (Spring 1924): 1–42. See also Carleton Beals, "Las Carpas," *Theatre Arts Monthly* 12 (February 1928): 99–108.

59. Alfonso Casal, "Norteamérica, paradigma continental," *Contemporáneos* 10 (April 1931): 86; Mario Santa Cruz, "La civilización norteamericana," *RR* 17 (August 28, 1927): 8. Siegfried's book was translated into English by H. H. Hemming and Doris Hemming as *America Comes of Age* (New York: Harcourt, Brace, 1927).

60. José Juan Tablada, Introduction to *Método de dibujo: Tradición, resurgimiento y evolución del arte mexicano,* by Adolfo Best Maugard (Mexico City: Departamento Editorial de la Secretaría de Educación, 1923), p. xxii. See also three articles by Tablada reprinted in the Costa Rican journal *Repertorio Americano*: "Norte América rudamente juzgada," 3 (September 5, 1921): 9–10; "Porqué nos ignoran los norteamericanos?" 6 (September 17, 1923): 372; and "Dempsey, el hombre más bruto del mundo," 7 (October 29, 1923): 86.

61. See, for example, Luis Lara Pardo, "La música mexicana en Nueva York," *RR* 10 (November 12, 1919): 24–25; *EX,* February 13, 1930, p. 2.

62. Schneider, *Estridentismo,* pp. 94–95.

63. Rivas Mercado, *Cartas a Manuel Rodríguez Lozano,* pp. 98–99.

64. Antonio Caso, "La sonrisa de Mr. Godwin," *RR* 14 (March 2, 1924): 4; Manuel M. Ponce, "S. M. El Fox," *México Moderno* 9 (May 1, 1921): 180–81.

65. *EX,* October 9, 1928, p. 4.

66. *El Universal,* October 8, 1928, p. 5, October 12, 1928, p. 7, October 13, 1928, p. 7, October 17, 1928, p. 10.

67. *EX,* September 3, 1932, sec. 2, p. 6; Copland and Perlis, *Copland,* p. 216.

68. *Film Daily Year Book 1925,* p. 657.

69. John Dewey, *Impressions of Soviet Russia and the Revolutionary World: Mexico—China—Turkey* (New York: New Republic, 1929), p. 177.

70. U.S. Department of Commerce, *Motion Pictures in Mexico,* p. 2.

71. José Vasconcelos, "Temas de Chicago," in *Obras completas,* 1:180; Villaurrutia, *Cartas,* pp. 37, 50, 68.

72. Arnold Chapman, *The Spanish American Reception of United States Fiction, 1920–1940* (Berkeley: University of California Press, 1966), p. 5; Alberto Nin Frias, "El alma norteamericana a través de Sinclair Lewis," *RR* 21 (February 22, 1931): 19–21. This article was probably reprinted from an Argentine periodical.

According to Englekirk, *Bibliografía*, Dos Passos's *Manhattan Transfer* and three novels by Lewis—*Babbitt, Arrowsmith,* and *Elmer Gantry*—were published in Spanish in Madrid between 1929 and 1935.

73. John Brushwood, "'Contemporáneos' and the Limits of Art," *Romance Notes* 5 (Spring 1964): 128–32; Edward John Mullen, Jr., "A Study of *Contemporáneos: Revista Moderna de Cultura* (1928–1931)" (Ph.D. dissertation, Northwestern University, 1968), pp. 50–53.

74. Salvador Novo, "Mis poetas favoritos norteamericanos," in Antonio Magaña-Esquivel, *Salvador Novo* (Mexico City: Empresas Editoriales, 1971), p. 215.

75. Michele Muncy, *Salvador Novo y su teatro (Estudio crítico)* (Madrid: Ediciones Atlas, 1971), p. 12.

76. "El buen te y la poesía de Vachel Lindsay," in Novo, *Toda la prosa*, pp. 60–67.

77. Rafael Lozano, "Los nuevos poetas de los Estados Unidos," *Falange*, October 1923, pp. 375–80.

78. Enrique Diez Canedo, "El país donde florece la poesía: U.S.A.," *Antorcha* 1 (May 16, 1925): 22–23.

79. Xavier Villaurrutia, "Guía de poetas norteamericanos," *Contemporáneos* 2 (September 1928): 91–97. This article is reprinted in Xavier Villaurrutia, *Obras* (Mexico City: Fondo de Cultura Económica, 1953), pp. 687–92.

80. Salvador Novo, "Notas sobre la poesía de los negros en los Estados Unidos," *Contemporáneos* 10 (September–October 1931): 197–200; Arnold Rampersad, *The Life of Langston Hughes*, 2 vols. (New York: Oxford University Press, 1986), 1:301–6; Langston Hughes, *I Wonder as I Wander* (New York: Rinehart, 1956), pp. 285–300.

81. *Ulises* 1 (February 1928): 38; Muncy, *Salvador Novo*, pp. 43–45.

82. Celestino Gorostiza, *Contemporáneos* 5 (November 1929): 329–31. Plays performed in Mexico City are listed in Enrique de Olavarria y Ferrari, *Reseña histórica del teatro en México, 1538–1911*, 5 vols. (Mexico City: Editorial Porrúa, 1961), vol. 5.

83. Villaurrutia, "Elmer Rice en México," in *Obras*, pp. 729–32; Vixe, "Frente al escenario," *RR* 21 (September 13, 1931): 4.

84. Villaurrutia, *Cartas*, pp. 41, 53.

85. John Rutherford, *Mexican Society during the Revolution: A Literary Approach* (Oxford: Clarendon Press, 1971), p. 272. Merle Simmons's study of *corridos* (popular ballads) dating from 1910 to 1950 reveals that a number of them characterized Americans as greedy, arrogant, and cowardly. The United States was described as a good place to work and earn money. See Merle E. Simmons, *The Mexican Corrido as a Source for Interpretive Study of Modern Mexico (1870–1950)* (Bloomington: Indiana University Press, 1957), pp. 419–61.

86. Xavier Icaza, *Panchito Chapopote* (Mexico City: Editorial Cultura, 1928), p. 29.

87. Salvador Novo, "Divorcio: Drama ibseniano en cinco actos," in Novo, *Toda la prosa*, pp. 43–50.

88. Salvador Novo, "Poemas proletarios," in Magaña-Esquivel, *Salvador Novo*, pp. 140–44.

Conclusion

1. Lowell Houser to Mickey, September 7, 1930 (copy made available by Mary L. Meixner).

2. Quoted in Hurlburt, *Mexican Muralists*, p. 61.

3. José G. Zuno to Idella Purnell [Stone], April 1, 1927, Stone Papers. See also Idella Purnell to Zuno, January 8, 1926, ibid., and Weston, *Daybooks*, 1:127.

4. *El Universal*, August 11, 1924, p. 3; Samuel Ramos, *Profile of Man and Culture in Mexico*, trans. Peter G. Earls (Austin: University of Texas Press, 1962), p. 103. On the exploitation of Mexican art and culture, see also *EX*, May 24, 1931, p. 5, and Reed, *Orozco*, pp. 85–86.

5. *NR* 67 (July 1, 1931): 183–84.

6. Edward M. Bruner, "Ethnography and Narrative," in *The Anthropology of Experience*, ed. Victor W. Turner and Edward M. Bruner (Urbana: University of Illinois, 1986), p. 139.

7. Beals, *Glass Houses*, p. 206.

8. Givner, *Katherine Anne Porter*, p. 233; Smith, *Glories of Venus*, p. 21; Weston, *Daybooks*, 1:18; Jackson, *Burros and Paintbrushes*, pp. 30–31.

9. John Dos Passos, *The Fourteenth Chronicle: Letters and Diaries of John Dos Passos*, ed. Townington Ludington (Boston: Gambit, 1973), p. 365; Jackson, *Burros and Paintbrushes*, p. 44; William Spratling, *A Small Mexican World* (Boston: Little, Brown, 1964), p. 17. This volume is a new edition of Spratling's *Little Mexico* (1932).

10. Robinson, *Wall to Paint On*, p. 88; Gruening, *Many Battles*, p. 110.

11. Beals, *Brimstone and Chili*, p. 318.

12. Claude Levy-Leboyer, *Psychology and Environment*, trans. David Canter and Ian Griffiths (Beverly Hills: Sage, 1982), p. 50. See also John A. Jakle, *The Visual Elements of Landscape* (Amherst: University of Massachusetts Press, 1987), pp. 140–41. For Mexico's visual impact on an American traveler of a later generation, see Ross Parmenter, *The Awakened Eye* (Middletown, Conn.: Wesleyan University Press, 1968).

13. Weston, *Daybooks*, 1:181; Anderson and Kelly, *Miss Elizabeth*, p. 225.

14. Susan Moakes, "The Rhetoric of Travel: The French Romantic Myth of Naples," *Ethnography* 33 (1986): 141.

15. T. Philip Terry, *Terry's Guide to Mexico*, rev. ed. (Boston: Houghton Mifflin, 1930), p. iii.

16. *Revista de Yucatán*, April 19, 1923, p. 3.

17. Moisés Sáenz, "The Genius of Mexican Life," in *The Genius of Mexico*, ed. Herbert C. Herring and Katherine Terrill (New York: Committee for Cultural Relations with Latin America, 1931), pp. 3–5; Orozco, *Cartas a Margarita*, p. 208.

18. Villaurrutia, *Cartas a Novo*, pp. 73, 77; Vasconcelos, "Temas de Chicago," in *Obras completas*, 1:176.

19. Quoted in Hurlburt, *Mexican Muralists*, pp. 71, 122.

20. Xavier Villaurrutia, *Cartas de Villaurrutia a Novo (1935–36)* (Mexico City: Instituto de Bellas Artes, Departmento de Literatura, 1966), p. 68; Vasconcelos, "Los refrescos," in *Obras completas*, 1:134–37; Harvey A. Levenstein, *Revolution at the Table: The Transformation of the American Diet* (New York: Oxford University Press, 1988), pp. 161–93; Martín Luis Guzmán, *El aguila y la serpiente* (Mexico City: Editorial Anahuac, 1941), pp. 37–38, 171–72.

21. Allen Knight, "Mexico, c. 1930–1946," in *Cambridge History of Latin America*, ed. Leslie Bethell, vol. 7 (New York: Cambridge University Press, 1990), p. 7. See also Stuart F. Voss, "Nationalizing the Revolution: Culmination and Circumstance," in *Provinces of the Revolution: Essays on Regional Mexican History, 1910–1929*, ed. Thomas Benjamin and Mark Wasserman (Albuquerque: University of New Mexico Press, 1990), pp. 287–306, and Albert R. Michaels, "The Crisis of Cardenismo," *Journal of Latin American Studies* 2 (1970): 51–79.

22. T. G. Powell, *Mexico and the Spanish Civil War* (Albuquerque: University of New Mexico Press, 1981); Patrica W. Fagen, *Exiles and Citizens: Spanish Republicans in Mexico* (Austin: University of Texas Press, 1973).

23. Dore Ashton, "Mexican Art of the Twentieth Century," in *Mexico: Splendors of Thirty Centuries* (New York: Metropolitan Musueum of Art, 1990), p. 558.

24. Carlos Monsiváis, "La cultura mexicana en el siglo XX," in Wilkie et al., pp. 653–54; Adalbert Dessau, *La novela de la revolución mexicana* (Mexico City: Fondo de Cultura Económica, 1972), pp. 298–335.

25. Harold E. Stearns, ed., *America Now: An Inquiry into the Civilization of the United States* (New York: Literary Guild of America, 1938), pp. 87, 380–81.

26. Ninkovich, *Diplomacy of Ideas*, pp. 35–49.

27. Woll, *Latin Image in American Film*, pp. 106–18.

28. Britton, *Carleton Beals*, pp. 204–9.

29. *Hispanic American Historical Review* 30 (August 1950): 346.

30. Witter Bynner to Idella Purnell Stone, May 21, 1949, Stone Papers.

31. Jean Charlot, unpublished manuscript pages of *Mexican Mural Renaissance*, p. 509, Charlot Collection.

Selected Bibliography

Unpublished Sources

Archives

American Museum of Natural History, New York, New York
　　Department of Library Services, Archives
American Philosophical Society, Philadelphia, Pennsylvania
　　Franz Boas, Professional Correspondence (microfilm)
　　Sylvanus G. Morley, Diary
Amherst College, Archives, Amherst, Massachusetts
　　Dwight W. Morrow Papers
Archives of American Art, Smithsonian Institution, Washington, D.C.
　　George Biddle Papers
　　René d'Harnoncourt Papers (microfilm reels 3830, 3831)
　　Elizabeth McCausland Papers (Marsden Hartley)
Boston University, Mugar Memorial Library, Department of Special Collections
　　Carleton Beals Collection
Columbia University, Rare Book and Manuscript Library, New York, New York
　　Hart Crane Papers (microfilm)
　　Frank Tannenbaum Papers
Rockefeller Archive Center, North Tarrytown, New York
　　General Education Board Archives

Rockefeller Family Archives
  Cultural Interest Series, Record Group 2
  Abby Aldrich Rockefeller Papers, Record Group 2
Smith College, Sophia Smith Collection, Northampton, Massachusetts
  Elizabeth Cutter Morrow Papers
Tulane University, Latin American Library, New Orleans, Louisiana
  Frans Blom, Diary of First Tulane Expedition to Middle America
University of Hawaii at Manoa, Thomas Hale Hamilton Library, Honolulu, Hawaii
  Jean Charlot Collection
University of Texas, Harry Ransom Humanities Research Center, Austin, Texas
  Witter Bynner Papers
  H. L. Davis Papers
  Willard Johnson Papers
  Idella Purnell Stone Papers
Yale University, Library, Manuscripts and Archives, New Haven, Connecticut
  John Collier Papers (microfilm)
  James Rockwell Sheffield Papers

Dissertations

Andrews, Gregory Alan. "American Labor and the Mexican Revolution, 1910–1924." Ph.D. dissertation, Northern Illinois University, 1988.

Christopulos, Diana K. "American Radicals and the Mexican Revolution, 1900–1925." Ph.D. dissertation, State University of New York at Binghamton, 1980.

Ewing, M. Robert. "A History of the Archaeological Activity at Chichen-Itza, Yucatan, Mexico." Ph.D. dissertation, Kent State University, 1972.

Horn, James John. "Diplomacy by Ultimatum: Ambassador Sheffield and Mexican-American Relations, 1924–1927." Ph.D. dissertation, State University of New York at Buffalo, 1969.

Melzer, Richard Anthony. "Dwight Morrow's Role in the Mexican Revolution: Good Neighbor or Meddling Yankee?" Ph.D. dissertation, University of New Mexico, 1979.

Monahan, Kenneth Charles. "Manuel Maples Arce and *Estridentismo*." Ph.D. dissertation, Northwestern University, 1975.

Mullen, Edward John, Jr. "A Study of *Contemporáneos: Revista Mexicana de Cultura* (1928–1931)." Ph.D. dissertation, Northwestern University, 1968.

Ogorzaly, Michael A. "Waldo Frank: Prophet of Hispanic Regeneration." Ph.D. dissertation, University of Notre Dame, 1982.

Rosser, Harry Edwin. "Beyond Revolution: The Social Concern of Moisés Sáenz, Mexican Educator (1888–1941)." Ph.D. dissertation, American University, 1970.

Young, Howard Thomas. "José Juan Tablada, Mexican Poet (1871–1945)." Ph.D. dissertation, Columbia University, 1956.

Zelman, Donald Lewis. "American Intellectual Attitudes toward Mexico, 1908–1940." Ph.D. dissertation, Ohio State University, 1969.

Other Unpublished Materials

Hansen, Asael T., interview with author, April 16, 1987.

Herring, Helen B., letter to author, May 26, 1983.

Jackson, Everett Gee, letter to author, May 3, 1986.

Oles, James. "From 'Modern Mexico' to Mexico's Modernism: Mexican Folk Art on Public Display, 1823–1940." Unpublished paper, 1990.

Records of the Department of State Relating to Internal Affairs of Mexico, 1910–29, National Archives, Washington, D.C., 1959 (Microcopy M-274).

Records of the Department of State Relating to Political Relations between the United States and Mexico, 1910–29, National Archives, Washington, D.C., 1960 (Microcopy 314).

Roeder, George H., Jr. "Mexicans in the Movies: The Image of Mexicans in American Films, 1894–1947." Unpublished paper, 1971.

Transcripts, Oral History Research Office, Columbia University
    "Thomas Hart Benton"
    "Daniel Cosío Villegas"
    "Carnegie Corporation Project: René d'Harnoncourt"
    "Ben Shahn"

Zogbaum, Heidi. "Traven Meets Frank Tannenbaum." Unpublished paper, 1991.

Published Sources

Bibliographies and Reference Works

American Film Institute Catalog: Feature Films, 1921–1930. 2 vols. New York: Bowker, 1971.

Englekirk, John E. *Bibliografía de obras norteamericanas en traducción española.* Supplement to *Revista Iberoamericana.* Mexico City: N.p., 1944.

Forster, Merlin H. *An Index to Mexican Literary Periodicals.* New York: Scarecrow Press, 1966.

Foster, David W. *Mexican Literature: A Bibliography of Secondary Sources*. Metuchen, N.J.: Scarecrow Press, 1981.

Gunn, Drewey Wayne. *Mexico in American and British Letters: A Bibliography of Fiction and Travel Books Citing Original Editions*. Metuchen, N.J.: Scarecrow Press, 1974.

Kemper, Robert V., and John F. S. Phinney. *The History of Anthropology: A Research Bibliography*. New York: Garland, 1977.

Leiter, Samuel L. *The Encyclopedia of the New York Stage, 1920–1930*. 2 vols. Westport, Conn.: Greenwood Press, 1985.

The New York Times Film Reviews, 1913–1968. 6 vols. New York: New York Times and Arno Press, 1970.

Pane, Remigio Ugo. "Amado Nervo, Mexico, 1870–1919: A Bibliography of His Poems in English Translation." *Bulletin of Bibliography* 18 (1945–46): 126–28.

————. "Three Mexican Poets . . . A Bibliography of Their Poems in English Translation." *Bulletin of Bibliography* 18 (1945–46): 233–34.

Rubinstein, Charlotte Streifer. *American Women Artists from Early Indian Times to the Present*. Boston: G. K. Hall, 1982.

Woods, Richard Donovon. *Mexican Autobiography: An Annotated Bibliography*. Westport, Conn.: Greenwood Press, 1988.

Books and Pamphlets

Aguirre Beltrán, Gonzalo, ed. *Antología de Moisés Sáenz*. Mexico City: Ediciones Oases, 1970.

Alexander, Charles C. *Here the Country Lies: Nationalism and the Arts in Twentieth-Century America*. Bloomington: Indiana University Press, 1980.

Anderson, Elizabeth, and Gerald R. Kelly. *Miss Elizabeth: A Memoir*. Boston: Little, Brown, 1969.

Atl, Dr. [Gerardo Murillo]. *Las artes populares en Mexico*. Mexico City: Librería "Cultura," 1921.

Balderrama, Francisco E. *In Defense of La Raza: The Los Angeles Mexican Consulate and the Mexican Community, 1929–1936*. Tucson: University of Arizona Press, 1982.

Beals, Carleton. *Black River*. Philadelphia: J. B. Lippincott, 1934.

————. *Brimstone and Chili: A Book of Personal Experiences in the Southwest and in Mexico*. New York: Knopf, 1927.

————. *Glass Houses: Ten Years of Free-Lancing*. Philadelphia: J. B. Lippincott, 1938.

————. *The Great Circle: Further Adventures in Free-Lancing*. Philadelphia: J. B. Lippincott, 1940.

————. *House in Coyoacán*. New York: Hastings House, 1958.

————. *Mexican Maze*. N.p.: Book League of America, 1931.

————. *Mexico: An Interpretation*. New York: B. W. Huebsch, 1923.

Bernal, Ignacio. *A History of Mexican Archaeology*. London: Thames & Hudson, 1980.

[Blom, Frans, and Oliver LaFarge.] *Tribes and Temples: A Record of the Expedition to Middle America Conducted by the Tulane University of Louisiana*. 2 vols. in 1. New Orleans: Tulane University, 1926.

Blumenthal, Henry. *American and French Culture, 1800–1900*. Baton Rouge: Louisiana State University Press, 1975.

Brenner, Anita. *Idols behind Altars*. New York: Harcourt, Brace, 1929.

Britton, John A. *Carleton Beals: A Radical Journalist in Latin America*. Albuquerque: University of New Mexico Press, 1987.

Brunhouse, Robert L. *Frans Blom, Maya Explorer*. Albuquerque: University of New Mexico Press, 1976.

————. *In Search of the Maya: The First Archaeologists*. Albuquerque: University of New Mexico Press, 1973.

————. *Pursuit of the Ancient Maya: Some Archaeologists of Yesterday*. Albuquerque: University of New Mexico Press, 1975.

————. *Sylvanus G. Morley and the World of the Ancient Maya*. Norman: University of Oklahoma Press, 1971.

Bynner, Witter. *Indian Earth*. New York: Knopf, 1929.

————. *Selected Letters*. Edited by James Kraft. New York: Farrar, Straus, Giroux, 1981.

————. *Selected Poems*. Edited by James Kraft. New York: Farrar, Straus, Giroux, 1978.

Cardoso, Lawrence A. *Mexican Emigration to the United States, 1897–1931*. Tucson: University of Arizona Press, 1980.

Cartas de Villaurrutia a Novo (1935–1936). Mexico City: Instituto de Bellas Artes, Departamento de Literatura, 1966.

Carter, Paul J. *Waldo Frank*. New York: Twayne, 1967.

Chapman, Arnold. *The Spanish American Reception of United States Fiction, 1920–1940*. Berkeley: University of California Press, 1966.

Charlot, Jean. *The Mexican Mural Renaissance, 1920–1925*. New Haven: Yale University Press, 1963.

Chase, Stuart. *Mexico: A Study of Two Americas*. New York: Macmillan, 1931.

Collier, John. *From Every Zenith: A Memoir*. Denver: Sage Books, 1963.

Conger, Amy. *Edward Weston in Mexico, 1923–1926*. Albuquerque: University of New Mexico Press, 1983.

Constantine, Mildred. *Tina Modotti: A Fragile Life.* New York: Paddington Press, 1975.

Copland, Aaron, and Vivian Perlis. *Copland: 1900 through 1942.* New York: St. Martin's/Marek, 1984.

Cosío Villegas, Daniel. *Memorias.* Mexico City: Editorial Joaquín Mortiz, 1976.

Crane, Hart. *The Letters of Hart Crane, 1916–1932.* Edited by Brom Weber. New York: Hermitage House, 1952.

Diego Rivera: A Retrospective. New York: Founders Society, Detroit Institute of Arts with Norton, 1986.

Dos Passos, John. *The Best Times: An Informal Memoir.* New York: New American Library, 1966.

Frank, Waldo. *Memoirs of Waldo Frank.* Edited by Alan Trachtenberg. Amherst: University of Massachusetts Press, 1973.

Gamio, Manuel. *Forjando patria.* 2d ed. Mexico City: Editorial Porrúa, 1960.

———. *Mexican Immigration to the United States: A Study of Human Migration and Adjustment.* Chicago: University of Chicago Press, 1930.

Geduld, Harry M., and Ronald Gottesman, eds. *Sergei Eisenstein and Upton Sinclair: The Making & Unmaking of "Que Viva México!"* Bloomington: Indiana University Press, 1970.

Genauer, Emily. *Rufino Tamayo.* New York: Harry N. Abrams, 1974.

Givner, Joan. *Katherine Anne Porter: A Life.* New York: Simon & Schuster, 1982.

Gruening, Ernest. *Many Battles.* New York: Liveright, 1973.

———. *Mexico and Its Heritage.* New York: D. Appleton-Century, 1940.

Gunn, Drewey Wayne. *American and British Writers in Mexico.* Austin: University of Texas Press, 1974.

Helm, June, ed. *Pioneers of American Anthropology.* Seattle: University of Washington Press, 1966.

———. *Social Contexts of American Ethnology, 1840–1984.* Washington, D.C.: American Ethnological Society, 1985.

Hoffman, Abraham. *Unwanted Mexican Americans in the Great Depression: Repatriation Pressures, 1929–1939.* Tucson: University of Arizona Press, 1974.

Hoffman, Michael E., ed. *Paul Strand: Sixty Years of Photographs.* Millerton, N.Y.: Aperture, 1976.

Hollander, Paul. *Political Pilgrims: Travels of Western Intellectuals to the Soviet Union, China, and Cuba, 1928–1978.* New York: Oxford University Press, 1981.

Homenaje al Doctor Alfonso Caso. Mexico City: Imprenta Nuevo Mundo, 1951.

Hurlburt, Laurance P. *The Mexican Muralists in the United States.* Albuquerque: University of New Mexico Press, 1989.

Ingle, Marjorie. *Mayan Revival Style: Art Deco Fantasy.* 1984. Reprint. Albuquerque: University of New Mexico Press, 1989.

Jackson, Everett Gee. *Burros and Paintbrushes: A Mexican Adventure.* College Station: Texas A & M University Press, 1985.

Keen, Benjamin. *The Aztec Image in Western Thought.* New Brunswick, N.J.: Rutgers University Press, 1971.

McNickle, D'Arcy. *Indian Man: A Life of Oliver LaFarge.* Bloomington: Indiana University Press, 1971.

Maples Arce, Manuel. *Soberana juventud.* Madrid: Editorial Plenitud, 1967.

Mason, Gregory. *Green Gold of Yucatan.* New York: Duffield, 1926.

——. *South of Yesterday.* New York: Henry Holt, 1940.

Meyer, Eugenia. *Conciencia histórica norteamericana sobre la Revolución de 1910.* Mexico City: Instituto Nacional de Antropología e Historia, 1970.

Mojica, José. *I, a Sinner: The Autobiography of Fray José Francisco de Guadalupe Mojica, O.F.M.* Chicago: Franciscan Herald Press, 1963.

Mora, Carl J. *Mexican Cinema: Reflections of a Society, 1896–1980.* Berkeley: University of California Press, 1982.

Morrow, Elizabeth. *Casa Mañana.* Croton Falls, N.Y.: Spiral Press, 1932.

——. *The Mexican Years: Leaves from the Diary of Elizabeth Cutter Morrow.* New York: Spiral Press, 1953.

——. *The Painted Pig.* New York: Knopf, 1930.

Muncy, Michele. *Salvador Novo y su teatro (Estudio crítico).* Madrid: Ediciones Atlas, 1971.

Murra, John V., ed. *American Anthropology: The Early Years.* Minneapolis: West, 1976.

Ninkovich, Frank A. *The Diplomacy of Ideas: U.S. Foreign Policy and Cultural Relations, 1938–1950.* Cambridge: Cambridge University Press, 1981.

Novo, Salvador. *Antología, 1925–1965.* Mexico City: Editorial Porrúa, 1966.

——. *Toda la prosa.* Mexico City: Empresas Editoriales, 1964.

Orozco, José Clemente. *The Artist in New York: Letters to Jean Charlot and Unpublished Writings, 1925–1929.* Translated by Ruth L. C. Simms. Austin: University of Texas Press, 1974.

——. *An Autobiography.* Translated by John Palmer Leeper. Austin: University of Texas Press, 1962.

——. *Cartas a Margarita, 1921–1949.* Edited by Tatiana Herrera Orozco. Mexico City: Ediciones Era, 1987.

Ortega y Medina, Juan. *Ensayos, tareas y estudios históricos.* Xalapa: Universidad Veracruzana, 1962.

Parker, Robert L. *Carlos Chávez: Mexico's Modern-Day Orpheus.* Boston: Twayne, 1983.

Parsons, Elsie Clews. *Mitla, Town of the Souls.* Chicago: University of Chicago Press, 1936.

Pells, Richard H. *Radical Visions and American Dreams: Culture and Social Thought in the Depression Years.* New York: Harper & Row, 1973.

Philp, Kenneth R. *John Collier's Crusade for Indian Reform, 1920–1954*. Tucson: University of Arizona Press, 1977.

Porter, Katherine Anne. *The Collected Essays and Occasional Writings of Katherine Anne Porter*. New York: Delacorte Press, 1970.

———. *Outline of Mexican Arts and Crafts*. Los Angeles: Young & McCallister, 1922.

Redfield, Robert. *Tepoztlán, a Mexican Village: A Study of Folk Life*. Chicago: University of Chicago Press, 1930.

Reed, Alma M. *The Mexican Muralists*. New York: Crown, 1960.

———. *Orozco*. New York: Oxford University Press, 1956.

Richardson, William Harrison. *Mexico through Russian Eyes, 1806–1940*. Pittsburgh: University of Pittsburgh Press, 1988.

Rivas Mercado, Antonieta. *Cartas a Manuel Rodríguez Lozano (1927–1930)*. Edited by Isaac Rojas Rosillo. Mexico City: Sep/Setentas, 1975.

Robinson, Cecil. *Mexico and the Hispanic Southwest in American Literature*. Tucson: University of Arizona Press, 1977.

Robinson, Ione. *A Wall to Paint On*. New York: Dutton, 1946.

Roeder, George H., Jr. *Forum of Uncertainty: Confrontations with Modern Painting in Twentieth-Century American Thought*. Ann Arbor: UMI Research Press, 1980.

Romo, Ricardo. *East Los Angeles: History of a Barrio*. Austin: University of Texas Press, 1983.

Rosenberg, Emily S. *Spreading the American Dream: American Economic and Cultural Expansion, 1890–1945*. New York: Hill & Wang, 1982.

Schmidt, Henry C. *The Roots of "Lo Mexicano": Self and Society in Mexican Thought, 1900–1934*. College Station: Texas A & M University Press, 1978.

Schneider, Luis Mario. *El Estridentismo o una literatura de estrategia*. Mexico City: Instituto Nacional de Bellas Artes, Departamento de Literatura, 1970.

Smith, Robert F. *The United States and Revolutionary Nationalism in Mexico, 1916–1932*. Chicago: University of Chicago Press, 1972.

Smith, Susan. *The Glories of Venus: A Novel of Modern Mexico*. New York: Harper & Bros., 1931.

———. *Made in Mexico*. New York: Knopf, 1930.

Smith, Wallace. *Tales Out of the Dust of Mexico*. New York: G. P. Putnam's Sons, 1923.

Spratling, William. *File on Spratling: An Autobiography*. Boston: Little, Brown, 1967.

———. *A Small Mexican World*. Boston: Little, Brown, 1964.

Tablada, Nina Cabrera de. *José Juan Tablada en la intimidad (con cartas y poemas inéditos)*. Mexico City: Imprenta Universitaria, 1954.

Talavera, Mario. *Miguel Lerdo de Tejada: Su vida pintoresca y anecdótica*. Mexico City: Editorial "Compas," n.d.

Tannenbaum, Frank. *Peace by Revolution: Mexico after 1910* (New York: Columbia University Press, 1968).

Taracena, Alfonso. *La verdadera revolución mexicana*. 18 vols. Mexico City: Editorial Jus and Impresora Juan Pablos, 1960–65.

Terry, T. Phillip. *Terry's Guide to Mexico*. Rev. ed. Boston: Houghton Mifflin, 1930.

Thompson, Edward H. *People of the Serpent: Life and Adventure among the Mayas*. Boston: Houghton Mifflin, 1932.

Vasconcelos, José. *Obras completas*. 3 vols. Mexico City: Libreros Mexicanos Unidos, 1957–59.

Vasconcelos, José, and Manuel Gamio. *Aspects of Mexican Civilization*. Chicago: University of Chicago Press, 1926.

Vaughan, Mary Kay. *The State, Education, and Social Class in Mexico, 1880–1928*. DeKalb: Northern Illinois University Press, 1982.

Velasco Urda, José. *Julián Carrillo: Su vida y su obra*. Mexico City: Grupo 13 Metropolitano, 1945.

Villaurrutia, Xavier. *Obras*. Mexico City: Fondo de Cultura Económica, 1953.

Weston, Edward. *The Daybooks of Edward Weston*. Edited by Nancy Newhall. 2 vols. Rochester, N.Y.: George Eastman House, 1961–66.

Willey, Gordon Randolph. *Portraits in American Archaeology: Remembrances of Some Distinguished Americanists*. Albuquerque: University of New Mexico Press, 1988.

Williams, Raymond. *The Sociology of Culture*. New York: Schocken Books, 1982.

Wolfe, Bertram D. *The Fabulous Life of Diego Rivera*. New York: Stein & Day, 1963.

———. *A Life in Two Centuries: An Autobiography*. New York: Stein & Day, 1981.

Woll, Allen L. *The Latin Image in American Film*. Rev. ed. Los Angeles: UCLA Latin American Center Publications, 1980.

Articles and Book Chapters

Bailey, David C. "Revisionism and the Recent Historiography of the Mexican Revolution." *Hispanic American Historical Review* 58 (February 1978): 62–79.

Beals, Carleton. "Las carpas." *Theatre Arts Monthly* 12 (February 1928): 99–108.

Beals, Ralph L. "Fifty Years in Anthropology." *Annual Review of Bibliography* 11 (1982): 1–23.

Biddle, George. "Mural Painting in America." *American Magazine of Art* 27 (July 1934): 361–71.

Bodeen, DeWitt. "Dolores del Río." *Films in Review* 18 (May 1967): 266–83.

———. "Ramón Novarro." *Films in Review* 18 (November 1967): 528–47.

Brenner, Anita. "A Mexican Rebel." *Arts* 12 (October 1927): 201–9.

———. "A Mexican Renascence." *Arts* 8 (September 1925): 127–50.

Britton, John A. "In Defense of Revolution: American Journalists in Mexico, 1910–1929." *Journalism History* 5 (Winter 1978–79): 124–36.

———. "Moisés Sáenz: Nacionalista mexicano." *Historia mexicana* 22 (July–September 1972): 77–97.

Brown, John L. "The Exuberant Years: Mexican-American Literary and Artistic Relations, 1920–1930." *Mexican Forum* 2 (October 1982): 9–12.

Burns, E. Bradford. "The Maya Imprint on Los Angeles." *Americas* 33 (November–December 1981): 41–48.

Cline, Howard. "Mexican Community Studies." *Hispanic American Historical Review* 32 (May 1952): 212–42.

Cole, Garold L. "The Birth of Modern Mexico, 1867–1911: American Travelers' Perceptions." *North Dakota Quarterly*, Spring 1977, pp. 54–72.

Cook, Howard. "The Road from Prints to Frescoes." *American Magazine of Art* 35 (January 1942): 4–10.

Delpar, Helen. "Frank Tannenbaum: The Making of a Mexicanist, 1914–1933." *The Americas* 45 (October 1988): 153–71.

———. "Goodbye to the 'Greaser': Mexico, the MPPDA, and Derogatory Films, 1922–1926." *Journal of Popular Film and Television* 12 (Spring 1984): 34–41.

Doyle, Henry Grattan. "Spanish Studies in the United States." *Bulletin of the Pan American Union* 60 (March 1926): 223–34.

Godoy, Ricardo. "The Background and Context of Redfield's *Tepoztlán.*" *Journal of the Steward Anthropological Society* 10 (Fall 1978): 47–79.

———. "Franz Boas and His Plans for an International School of American Archaeology and Ethnology in Mexico." *Journal of the History of the Behavioral Sciences* 13 (July 1977): 228–42.

Goldman, Shifra M. "Siqueiros and Three Early Murals in Los Angeles." *Art Journal* 33 (Summer 1974): 321–27.

Gruening, Ernest. "The Mexican Renaissance." *Century* 85 (February 1924): 520–35.

Gutiérrez, José. "La inolvidable *Peregrina.*" *Selecciones del Reader's Digest*, November 1968, pp. 57–64.

Kidder, Alfred V. "A Program for Maya Research." *Hispanic American Historical Review* 17 (May 1937): 160–69.

Knight, Alan. "Racism, Revolution, and *Indigenismo*: Mexico, 1910–1940." In *The Idea of Race in Latin America, 1870–1940*, edited by Richard Graham, pp. 71–113. Austin: University of Texas Press, 1990.

Lamb, Blaine P. "The Convenient Villain: The Early Cinema Views the Mexican-American." *Journal of the West* 14 (October 1975): 75–81.

Leal, Luis. "Native and Foreign Influences in Contemporary Mexican Fiction." In *Tradition and Renewal: Essays on Twentieth-Century Latin American Literature and Culture*, edited by Merlin H. Forster, pp. 102–28. Urbana: University of Illinois Press, 1975.

Levenstein, Harvey A. "Franz Boas as a Political Activist." *Kroeber Anthropological Society Papers* 29 (Fall 1963): 15–24.

Meixner, Mary L. "The Ames Corn Mural." *Palimpsest* 66 (January–February 1985): 14–29.

———. "Lowell Houser and the Genesis of a Mural." *Palimpsest* 66 (January–February 1985): 2–13.

"The Mexican Art Invasion." *Current Opinion* 76 (March 1924): 305–7.

Pach, Walter. "The Art of the American Indian." *Dial* 68 (January 1920): 57–65.

———. "Impresiones sobre el arte actual de México." *México Moderno* 2 (October 1922): 131–38.

———. "The Popular Arts of Mexico." *Freeman* 6 (January 31, 1923): 496–97.

Paredes, Raymund A. "The Mexican Image in American Travel Literature, 1831–1869." *New Mexico Historical Review* 52 (January 1977): 5–29.

Philp, Kenneth R. "John Collier and the Indians of the Americas: The Dream and the Reality." *Prologue* 11 (Spring 1979): 5–21.

Pike, Fredrick B. "Latin America and the Inversion of United States Stereotypes in the 1920s and 1930s." *The Americas* 42 (October 1985): 131–62.

Pinto, Alfonso. "When Hollywood Spoke Spanish." *Americas* 32 (October 1980): 3–8.

Reid, John T. "The Rise and Decline of the Ariel-Caliban Antithesis in Spanish America." *The Americas* 34 (1977–78): 345–55.

Salpeter, Henry. "Marion Greenwood: An American Artist of Originality and Power." *American Artist* 12 (January 1948): 14–19.

Schmidt, Henry C. "The American Intellectual Discovery of Mexico in the 1920's." *South Atlantic Quarterly* 77 (Summer 1978): 335–51.

Spratling, William. "Figures in a Mexican Renaissance." *Scribner's Magazine* 85 (January 1929): 14–21.

———. "Some Impressions of Mexico." *Architectural Forum* 47 (July 1927): 1–8, (August 1927): 161–68.

Strug, David. "Manuel Gamio, la Escuela Internacional y el origen de las excavaciones en las Américas." *América Indígena* 31 (October 1971): 825–44.

Tablada, José Juan. "Diego Rivera—Mexican Painter." *Arts* 4 (October 1923): 221–33.

———. "Mexican Painting of Today." *International Studio* 76 (January 1923): 267–76.

Tozzer, Alfred M. "Zelia Nuttall." *American Anthropologist* n.s., 35 (1933): 475–82.

Woods, Richard D. "Anita Brenner: Cultural Mediator of Mexico." *Studies in Latin American Popular Culture* 9 (1990): 209–22.

Zayas, Marius de. "How, When, and Why Modern Art Came to New York." *Arts Magazine* 54 (April 1980): 96–126.

Index

About the Author

Helen Delpar is Associate Professor of History at The University of Alabama. She received her bachelor's degree from Douglass College, her master's degree from New York University, and her doctorate from Columbia University. Her other publications include *Red Against Blue: The Liberal Party in Colombian Politics, 1863–1899* (1981), *The Discoverers: An Encyclopedia of Explorers & Exploration* (1979), and *Encyclopedia of Latin America* (1974).